HUMAN SEXUALITY
a social psychological
approach

PRENTICE-HALL, INC., ENGLEWOOD CLIFFS, NEW JERSEY 07632

JEFFREY S. VICTOR
State University of New York

HUMAN SEXUALITY
a social psychological approach

Library of Congress Cataloging in Publication Data

Victor, Jeffrey S
   Human sexuality

   Bibliography: p.
   Includes index.
   1. Sex instruction. 2. Sex.
3. Sex (Psychology) 4. Social psychology.
I. Title.
HQ35.2.V5   301.41   79-25733
ISBN 0-13-447474-0 pbk.

HQ35
.2
.V5

Photo credits

Laura Hoeting: pages 81, 98, 107, 137, 163, 291

Jim Harrison: page 43

Irene Springer: pages 171, 234, 341, 282, 296

Stan Wakefield: pages 2, 12, 36, 70, 84, 90, 112, 125, 132, 150, 156, 178, 193, 200, 209, 211, 218, 222, 244, 257, 264, 272, 324

Printed in the United States of America

10 9 8 7 6 5 4 3 2 1

**Editorial/production supervision and interior design by Marina Harrison
Cover design by A Good Thing, Inc.
Manufacturing buyer: Ray Keating**

PRENTICE-HALL INTERNATIONAL, INC., *London*
PRENTICE-HALL OF AUSTRALIA PTY. LIMITED, *Sydney*
PRENTICE-HALL OF CANADA, LTD., *Toronto*
PRENTICE-HALL OF INDIA PRIVATE LIMITED, *New Delhi*
PRENTICE-HALL OF JAPAN, INC., *Tokyo*
PRENTICE-HALL OF SOUTHEAST ASIA PTE. LTD., *Singapore*
WHITEHALL BOOKS LIMITED, *Wellington, New Zealand*

This book is dedicated to the memory
of my maternal grandparents

ADOLF HRUSKA

born 1881 in Ruzomberok, Czechoslovakia
died 1967 in the United States

SAROLTA SALZER HRUSKA

born 1887 in Budapest, Hungary
died 1965 in the United States

contents

preface

When I first started writing this book, there were few human sexuality textbooks available. These pioneering textbooks were admirable books, but they lacked many qualities that might have enabled them to be more interesting, relevant, and useful. While writing this book, I have tried to keep in mind several goals necessary to meet better the learning needs of students and instructional needs of teachers.

ABOUT THIS BOOK: FOR STUDENTS

A preface in a textbook is rarely addressed to those people who must invest more time and energy into reading it than do professors. Nevertheless, I feel that it is useful for me as an author to offer a brief statement about this book for students.

1) I have tried to create a textbook which is interesting as it is possible for textbooks to be. I have tried to make it free of unnecessary technical jargon and easy to understand by a reader who has had no previous college training in biology, psychology, or sociology.

2) I have also tried to offer a useful examination of those sexual matters that are of greatest concern to people in the course of their everyday life. In my judgement, these sexual matters are ones in which a reader feels new information may help him or her to change or enhance his or her life. More specifically, these matters involve sexual aspects of personality (e.g. self-concept, sexual responses, sexual fantasies) and sexual aspects of interpersonal relations (e.g. sexual expectations of others, sexual activities with others, sexual conflicts with others).

3) Finally, I have tried to offer a presentation and explanation of information drawn from recently published research. I believe that such writing must not only be worded clearly, but must also avoid intrusive moralizing (whether a traditional or newer unconventional persuasion).

Attempts to offer useful ideas to other people very easily tempt a writer into preaching about how people "should" behave. In order to avoid this temptation, I have carefully tried to avoid offering moral guidance or advice about how the reader "should" behave sexually. In this spirit, I have avoided any declarations about what is (or isn't) normal and healthy in sexual behavior. In my view, these terms are merely modern code words for moral judgement and have doubtful place in a science of human behavior. I hope, however, that the reader understands that the spirit of scientific neutrality does not conceal a covert approval (or disapproval) of any behavior. Moreover, as a teacher, I hope that this peculiar neutrality provokes the reader to be more sensitively aware and reflective of his or her own personal morality.

In order to accomplish these goals, I have worked closely with my own students. Students in my human sexuality classes and my student assistants have read manuscript chapters and offered me many useful suggestions for developing my book into an effective learning tool. If the product of these many labors falls short of its potential, that is only because I may have chosen to neglect student advice, which I should have thought about more carefully.

Finally, I have kept in mind a student readership ranging from ages eighteen to eighty. An increasing proportion of college students are in their 20s, 30s, and 40s. Therefore, I have tried to include a broad range of topics relevant to the varied concerns of readers at different stages of the life cycle. Hopefully, this book will be equally useful to unmarried people, as well as their parents.

ABOUT THIS BOOK: FOR TEACHERS

College professors usually use textbooks as a teaching aid to supplement their classroom instruction. Teachers use textbooks as a means of communicating to students an understanding of the complexities, subtleties, and broad range of issues on a topic. They do not have sufficient time to do so in a classroom. Keeping this function in mind, my writing has been guided by several goals.

1) I have tried to create a coherent picture of the sex research findings of psychologists, sociologists and anthropologists. In order to do so, I have collected copies of thousands of research articles published in behavioral science journals. Many of the findings reported here have been neglected in other human sexuality textbooks. I have tried to weave many separate bits of information into a well-integrated fabric, following major paths of scientific inquiry. Unfortunately, I had to omit consideration of some important topics due to problems of length. Yet, the topics included range from biochemical matters to historical concerns.

2) I have tried to offer a presentation of human sexuality consistent with the main lines of theory in contemporary behavioral science. Toward this end, I have used cognitive social learning theory from psychology and symbolic interactionist theory from sociology to organize a point-of-view upon human sexuality, which I hope is truly interdisciplinary. My academic training has been quite interdisciplinary across the various behavioral sciences, including graduate degrees in psychology and sociology, plus culture in personality research in a foreign society (France). I feel comfortable conversing in psychological or sociological language and thought. Whether I am equally fluent in both languages is a matter for the reader to judge.

3) Finally, I wanted to paint a picture of human sexual behavior which could be seen within the larger setting of human existence. Too often, human sexual behavior is artificially presented as a series of sex acts disassociated from any connection with more mundane facets of human existence. I believe that students need and want to know much more about sexuality than copulation and masturbation. They want to understand the connection between human sexuality, love, conflict, play and work.

ACKNOWLEDGEMENTS

A great many people have helped me develop this textbook during the five years from its conception to its publication. Publishing convention allows me to record a few personal words of gratitude for some of them, so that I may reciprocate, in a simple way, their favors.

My greatest debt of gratitude, one which I will never be able to refund, is owed to my wife: Michele Honoré Victor. I thank her for her careful reading of my preliminary manuscripts, and her invaluable gift of thoughtful criticism and advice about sexual matters from a woman's perspective. She corrected some misunderstandings I had and enabled me to feel more confident in writing about both male and female sexuality, in the face of possible accusations of sexist ignorance. Yet, while giving me this help she suffered as a "book widow", knowing that the possible success of this book could not compensate her for years of loneliness.

Many of my colleagues read certain manuscript chapters and offered me suggestions relative to their areas of specialization. In particular, I would like to thank Harry Bridges for his help. As my Chairman, he also offered me valuable support, when certain influentials regarded my textbook project as an unnecessary distraction from more important labors.

I would also like to thank Lynne Flagg for her exceptionally careful typing work. Her patience in the face of erratic deadlines was admirable.

At Prentice-Hall, I would like to note my appreciation of Jim Morlock, who suggested the idea for this book, presenting me with an entirely unexpected career opportunity. Also, I owe a debt to Ed Stanford, who was willing to offer a contract to this previously inexperienced writer and patiently shepherded him through the development of the manuscript. My appreciation is also due to my production editor, Marina Harrison, who strove to make the final product consistent with this author's vision of a textbook, as well as differing corporate requirements.

I would like to thank the following scholars, who reviewed the developing manuscript, for their careful criticism and suggestions: Carole Kirkpatrick, James D. Hansen, Emily S. Davidson, Lee K. Frank, David A. Schulz, Peter S. Friedman, James E. Cherry, James L. Hawkins, Cole V. Smith, David A. Edwards, Neil Smelser, and Diane I. Levande.

Finally, I wish to acknowledge a debt of gratitude to the librarians of the James Prendegast Library and the New York State Interlibrary Loan System. Without the information distribution system designed to facilitate research and scholarship, it would not have been possible to research the information for this book sufficiently to this author's satisfaction.

Jeffrey S. Victor
Jamestown, New York

HUMAN SEXUALITY
a social psychological
approach

The word *sex* seems to have a multitude of meanings. It is used in a great variety of contexts. The word *sex* is used, for example, in reference to reproduction, pleasure, and differences in anatomy and personality. To avoid confusion, it is useful to make some distinctions in the meanings of human sexuality. Three fundamental aspects of human sexuality are: (1) reproduction; (2) eroticism; and (3) gender. These are the three basic phenomena upon which scientists focus their research in their study of human sexuality.

reproductive sexuality

One central focus of sex research involves biological conception and procreation. Of primary concern are the aspects of anatomy and physiology which enable conception. A secondary research concern may be people's attitudes toward the body, particularly toward genitals and reproductive processes, such as menstruation and pregnancy. Another secondary research concern in reproductive sexuality involves "fertility behavior," such as the use of contraceptives, deliberate family planning, and abortion. Sex education in public schools is almost entirely about reproductive sexuality.

erotic sexuality

Another primary focus of sex research involves feelings of bodily pleasure arising from the genitals. Some specific matters of research attention include the in-

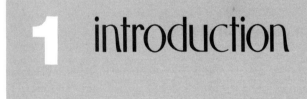

1 introduction

terpersonal behavior, the personal attitudes, and the physiological processes which enhance or interfere with erotic pleasure. A particularly important research concern involves the content and processes of learning which affect sensations of erotic pleasure. This textbook is primarily concerned with erotic sexuality.

Reproduction and eroticism are clearly distinct. Men and women may both have sexual intercourse and yet not experience any erotic pleasure. On the other hand, erotic pleasure may occur without presenting any possibility for reproduction. Nonreproductive erotic pleasure may result from such activities as masturbation, homosexual contact, and sexual intercourse with effective contraception. In addition, many reproductive processes such as menstruation, pregnancy, and childbirth, are not directly related to erotic pleasure.

gender sexuality

Sex research also focuses on the social categories of male and female. The primary research concern involves the social expectations, patterns of behavior, and personal attitudes which distinguish males and females. Male-female relationships, other than reproductive or erotic, are central matters in the scientific study of gender sexuality.

Gender is very often not directly related to either reproduction or eroticism. Examples are numerous: differences in male and female clothing styles; differences in occupations once considered either masculine or feminine; differences in toys considered appropriate for boys and for girls; differences in the household division of activities between husbands and wives in such activities as washing dishes and washing the family car. Almost all aspects of gender sexuality are undergoing rapid change in American society today.

THE SCIENTIFIC INVESTIGATION OF HUMAN SEXUALITY

Scientific research involves the use of careful, systematic methods to investigate the nature of human existence. The scientific eye has turned more and more to aspects of human existence which were once known and understood only through the wisdom of tradition. New ways of "seeing" the nature of human existence emerged as the authority of tradition gradually gave way to direct, empirical methods of research. The germ theory of disease, the theory of biological evolution, and the atomic theory of matter have reshaped our understanding of the world in which we live. It was inevitable that the scientific eye would turn to a rational exploration of human sexuality. When that exploration began in the late days of Victorianism, it caused quite a bit of controversy. The shock waves are still being felt.

the humanistic values of science

Some persons are under the impression that science embodies no values—moral, ethical, or otherwise. Yet, this is simply not true. Even when scientists are at work as professional researchers, certain values guide their behavior (Barber, 1952). Curiosity and knowledge are esteemed over blind acceptance and superstition. To the scientist, knowledge is always better than ignorance. In contrast, persons of another mind might believe that "some stones are better left unturned," that curiosity and exploration are sometimes dangerous. Still others prefer to have their world shrouded in a veil of mystery, finding the mysteriousness poetic and enjoyable.

Beyond curiosity and a search for new knowledge, scientists are also expected to esteem a certain kind of *skepticism*. Unquestioning belief is suspect, not only when in the form of prevailing popular opinion, but also in science itself. Scientists are expected to be able to doubt and to challenge accepted thought and practice. Consequently, science never contains a body of finished principles. Science is continuously in the process of development. Indeed, it is best to think of science as a process, rather than as a body of knowledge or a group of authority figures.

The process of science evolves through the research (hypothesis testing) of scientists, working as individuals or teams. It also evolves through the conflict of contradictory hypotheses between scientists. Scientists promote the hypotheses which emerge after careful examination of alternatives. Scientists of a particular viewpoint are challenged by others to publish research evidence adequate enough to persuade the community of skeptics. Thus, *science evolves through a process of argument and counterargument*. Sometimes radical shifts develop in the interpretations held by the community of scientists. Rarely does the path of development follow a direct line of reasoning (Kuhn, 1970). This is why frontier research is often confusing to laymen.

Once it is understood that science encourages the values of curiosity, skepticism, and public argumentation, it becomes clear why the guardians of Victorian tradition were so disturbed about the intrusion of scientific research into the realm of sexual matters. Previously, sexuality had been the subject of concern only for theologians and moralists and an occasional literary intellectual. The penetrating light of science into matters of sex made Victorian hypocrisy and romantic idealism difficult to maintain.

FIELDS OF SEX RESEARCH

The study of human sexuality is touched by many fields of scientific specialization. Sex research is not a special focus of any one field of scientific research. It is an interdisciplinary concern. This is what makes the study of human sexuality so fascinating and so complicated. Few other subjects of investigation are relevant to so many specialized areas of knowledge. To understand human sexual behavior, one must have an adequate knowledge of body chemistry, human physiology, the processes of learning, and the effects of social forces upon interpersonal relationships. In addition, full understanding of human sexuality is aided by knowledge of the following: the history of sexual customs, laws governing sexual behavior, religious beliefs about human sexuality, and artistic and literary explorations of human sexuality. Obviously, there is too much specialized knowledge for any one person to know in a lifetime. So, sex research must depend upon specialists who at times may neglect important considerations which lie outside their specialized area of competence.

Within the fields of sex research, there are two basic approaches: (1) medical research; and (2) behavioral science research. This is a somewhat artificial and convenient division. However, it is one which helps to understand two major perspectives of the nature of human sexuality. These contrasting perspectives are partly a consequence of differing professional goals. Medical researchers are primarily concerned with obtaining practical knowledge which is directly useful in helping patients with sexual problems. Behavioral science researchers are primarily concerned with obtaining knowledge of sexual behavior which contributes toward a better understanding of the basic principles of human behavior. Neither of these approaches are better than the other. Both contribute knowledge useful for understanding human sexuality.

medical research

Toward the end of the nineteenth century, the first people to carry out serious sex research were physicians. They sought to understand certain kinds of personal problems of the patients who came to them for help. Many of their patients expressed feelings of discomfort, pain, and fatigue without having any known disease or physical damage.

These doctors started from a concern about illness and focused their attention upon bodily functioning. The method of research involved doing case studies of the patient's life experience. Sometimes, physicians also made case studies of other people, such as sex criminals, who could be easily identified by their bizarre behavior. The basic goal of these doctors was to find therapy techniques which could help cure the "sickness" they saw in their patients.

Freud. Among these physicians was *Sigmund Freud,* whose theories were to become most influential. His work represents a major shift in Western civilization's understanding of human sexuality. Freud was a billiant theorist and prodigious researcher, writer, and publicist. He shocked the Victorian mind by differing from conventional medical interpretations of sexuality and by developing a broad theory of personality which gave a crucial role to sexual desire (Freud, 1905). Freud believed that many psychological disturbances were a result of the social and personal repression of sexual desire, rather than an outcome of excessive lust. An even greater offense to Victorian prudery was Freud's belief that adult psychological problems stemmed from a perversion of childhood sexuality caused by deeply disturbing childhood experiences. The Victorians viewed "normal" children as basically lacking any sexual feelings. Freud's theory of psychological development was counter to this belief and even proposed that childhood sexual feelings had a determining impact upon personality development. Whether or not all of Freud's theories were accurate, one must admire his courage in assaulting the polite conspiracy of silence which dominated Victorian sexual life.

Freud's theories of sexuality and personality were derived from the method he developed of investigating the experiences of his patients. He asked them probing questions, encouraged them to let their thoughts wander and to talk about anything that flashed into their minds. Then he listened very carefully to their sometimes long, rambling monologues. This free-association technique of psychological analysis differed greatly from the kind of treatment that patients with personal problems previously received from their doctors—Freud seriously listened to them.

Freud's theories of sexual behavior are not being used in this book. Nevertheless, we must recognize Freud's lasting contribution to the scientific study of human sexuality. Most important, he helped to make sex research respectable. Freud cut a path into uncharted territory which many later scientists could follow. In addition, Freudian theories (and popular distortions of them) had great historical influence in reducing Victorian repressiveness and hypocrisy. His theories were used to spearhead attacks upon Victorian morality, especially by literary intellectuals.

Psychoanalysts, psychiatrists, and psychologists.   The difference between psychoanalysts, psychiatrists, and psychologists is usually a matter of confusion for students. Psychoanalysts and psychiatrists are essentially members of the helping professions, while psychologists are trained to be behavioral science researchers.

Psychoanalysts are counselors for people's personal problems who follow one variation or another of the personality theory and therapy technique developed by Freud. They do not necessarily have to have an M.D. degree. However, in actuality, most of them are medical doctors.

Psychiatry is a legally recognized medical specialization, like surgery or gynecology, and requires an M.D. degree. Most psychiatrists have been biology majors as undergraduates before going to medical school. After receiving an M.D. degree, they specialize in psychiatry, which is considered the study of mental disorders. Only people with M.D. degrees can prescribe drugs. Psychiatrists take a few courses in psychological research and theory (Kiesler, 1977), however, most of their specialized training is in the helping techniques of psychotherapy. In the past, their training was heavily oriented toward psychoanalytic theory and therapy. This is no longer as true as it was in the past. Psychiatry students are now being introduced to many different approaches to psychotherapy, such as existential analysis, gestalt therapy, and behavior modification therapy. The training of psychiatrists is still essentially in practical helping services, rather than in basic behavioral science research. Only a few psychiatrists engage in basic behavioral science research, or have the training to do so (Kiesler, 1977). Psychiatrists are particularly competent to help people with problems which have their origin in bodily malfunctions.

Psychologists are trained to be behavioral science researchers, and receive a Ph.D. Psychology is a vast field covering many specialized research subdivisions, including: physiological, developmental, educational, social, and clinical psychology. Clinical psychologists are those who receive specialized training for research into personal problems. Clinical psychologists also have training in therapy techniques and can work as counselors for personal problems just as psychiatrists do. However, psychologists cannot prescribe drugs and are usually subordinate to psychiatrists when working with them in organizations. Very few clinical psychologists use psychoanalytic personality theory or therapy which, in university departments of psychology (unlike in medical schools), is now generally regarded as being no longer scientifically useful for psychological research. Most psychologists (other than clinical psychologists) function as researchers and teachers, rather than as counselors.

Masters and Johnson. A recent example of medical research which has had great historical impact is the work of William Masters and Virginia Johnson (1966). Their research investigated physiological responses during sexual activity. Their research also falls within the medical approach because the emphasis is biological and their ultimate goal was therapy for patients with personal problems. Their research is important because it provided major new information about bodily sexual functioning and corrected many popular misconceptions of that functioning. The first substantial publication of their research findings took place in 1966, and unlike the work of Freud, it was generally greeted with praise. Freud's death occurred in 1939, and a generation later, public attitudes toward sex research had changed immensely. Yet, one thing is historically surprising. It took until the space age 1960s for basic research on sexual response to be conducted. Before the work of Masters and Johnson, basic scientific knowledge to help people who had problems in sexual functioning was simply not available to medical doctors.

Masters and Johnson relied upon laboratory research methods to obtain their findings. They investigated the physiological responses of hundreds of men and women during acts of sexual intercourse and masturbation. To do this, they employed clinical interviews, direct observation, motion picture recordings, and physiological measuring instruments. They even used a minature camera, built into an artificial penis, for recording responses within the vagina, it provided very useful findings. One of Masters and Johnson's findings of major historical significance was that male and female sexual responses are not as different as had been believed for centuries.

behavioral science research

Kinsey. The behavioral science sex research of Alfred Kinsey has had great historical impact on our understanding of human sexuality. Kinsey collected huge amounts of data about the sexual practices of American men and women. Beginning in the late 1930s and continuing through the 1940s, Kinsey and a research team gathered detailed information about the sexual lives of more than 16,000 people. Their method employed intensive, probing interviews with volunteers who were selected to be reasonably representative of the American population. The massive amount of data was then statistically analyzed in terms of differences in sex, age, marital status, religion, geography, education, and occupation. Kinsey's goal was to obtain basic information about the diversity of human sexual behavior.

When Kinsey's research was finally published in 1948 and 1953, it was met with a sensational public reaction. Filled with statistics as they were, these research documents made rather dull reading (Kinsey et al., 1948; Kinsey et al., 1953). Yet, they very quickly became best sellers. Why? One major reason was that the Kinsey research was yet another assault upon the lingering Victorian conspiracy of silence in sexual matters. The Kinsey research provided evidence of the very widespread occurrence of tabooed sexual practices, such as premarital and extramarital sex, masturbation, and oral-genital contact. It demonstrated the existence of a wide gap between publicly professed standards of sexual behavior and actual practice. The reliability of the Kinsey research was much criticized. Yet, it has essentially withstood the test of time. The findings have been confirmed by numerous other research projects. The Kinsey research provided something peculiar and new in history. It offered a method for checking the sexual practices in a society against the ideals being preached.

It is ironic that this pioneering behavioral science sex research project was inspired and organized by a biologist rather than a behavioral scientist. (Kinsey was a respected specialist in the study of insects!) Perhaps that is the reason why his analysis of American sexual behavior was not closely interrelated with behavior science research and theory about human behavior. However, Kinsey did make sex research respectable for behavioral scientists. He provided the stimulus needed to encourage a few behavioral scientists to apply their research skills to the investigation of sexual behavior. The work Kinsey began carries on at the Institute of Sex Research at Indiana University which he established and at other universities throughout the country. Today, the behavioral science understanding of human sexuality has moved far beyond the tabulation of sexual practices (as this book demonstrates). The study of human sexual behavior has become integrated into the study of human behavior.

Sociology.   The research methods and goals of Kinsey are most similar to those of sociologists. Sociologists are particularly interested in the behavior of groups in the population of society as a whole. They seek knowledge about the social forces which influence the ways in which people behave toward each other in relationships.

Sociologists, for example, have conducted a great many questionnaire and interview studies of premarital and marital sexual behavior as part of their concern with mate-selection and marital relations. Much of that research has focused upon college students because of the ease of using college students as research volunteers. More recently, many sociologists have moved out from the universities into "the field" to study the sexual behavior of special groups. They have carried out field studies of homosexuals, mate-swappers, and prostitutes. This research is particularly important because it does not rely upon clinical patients. These studies are part of a subfield called the sociology of deviant behavior which studies behavior which is contrary to the dominant rules of society. Sociologists have also recently been very active in research on male-female gender roles and the effects of sexual discrimination in American society.

Anthropology.   *Anthropologists* study the behavior and cultures of people in nonindustrial societies. Anthropological research provides a comparative perspective for the study of human behavior. It offers an understanding of the great diversity in sexual and other customs in different societies throughout the world. Most anthropologists have gathered information about sexual practices as part of their investigation of family systems in the nonindustrial world. However, few anthropologists have investigated sexual behavior, in particular.

Anthropologists have shown how differences in people's culture bring about great variations in the behavior expected of males and females. They also have shown how differences in sexual behavior are a result of differences in people's beliefs about the meaning of existence. Their research demonstrates that some societies are very repressive regarding sexual behavior, while other societies are permissive of most forms of sexual expression.

Psychology.   Psychologists are interested primarily in studying the behavior, thinking, and emotional responses of individuals—or what may be called patterns of personality. They are also interested in studying the behavior of people toward each other in relationships.

Much of the research of psychologists takes place in laboratories where carefully controlled experiments are conducted in order to make precise observations of the subjects under study. Psychologists have used laboratory experiments, for example, to investigate people's attitudes and emotional reactions to erotic stimulation in the form of sexually explicit slides, movies, and tape recordings. They have used these methods, also, to investigate feelings of sex guilt as well as the psychological causes of sexual dysfunctions. They have even used laboratory experiments to investigate the kinds of communication which result in mutual attraction and self-disclosure between subjects. These studies are part of pioneering psychological investigations of love and intimate relations.

Psychologists have also used techniques such as questionnaires and interviews to investigate such matters as the development of sexual attitudes in children and adolescents. In a related concern, psychologists have done a great many studies of male-female differences in personality and gender identity among children and adolescents.

Perhaps the most important psychological research concerns the nature of human learning processes. An application of findings about the processes of learning enables us to better understand how people learn their personal sex attitudes and patterns of sexual behavior.

HUMAN SEXUALITY: A SOCIAL PSYCHOLOGICAL APPROACH

social psychology

Social psychology is a special branch of both psychology and sociology. It also overlaps the study of personality in culture within the field of anthropology. Consequently, social psychology offers a very useful interdisciplinary perspective on human behavior. It brings together the resources of many different specialists.

The research focus of social psychologists centers upon interpersonal behavior (or what may also be called *interaction,* or *social relationships*). They are also particularly concerned with personality in society—the connections between the personal world of the individual and impersonal social forces beyond the control of the individual. In their research, they must remain sensitive to the effects upon human behavior of both personal meanings and shared cultural meanings. The meanings attributed to behavior differ between children and adults, between men and women, and between people from different cultural backgrounds.

Increasingly, social psychologists from both psychology and sociology are working closely with each other. Consequently, the theories which they use in their research are increasingly similar, even if they are given different names.

the social psychology of sexual behavior

The social psychological interpretation of human behavior offers a particular point of view of human sexual behavior. Sexual behavior is seen as a product of: (1) the biological capacity for sexual arousal; (2) personal goals; and (3) sociocultural expectations for behavior. According to social psychologists, human sexual behavior is not a manifestation of any powerful biological "drive" or instinct. Sexual behavior is rather easily inhibited or facilitated by the brain's symbolic functioning. It is shaped by a person's painful and pleasurable experience. A person's sexual behavior may express rather diverse emotions, such as affection, hostility, curiosity, or desires for power and achievement.

Most important, for social psychologists, sexual behavior forms a social bond between human beings. Sexual behavior between individuals may be cooperatively guided by mutually shared expectations; or it may result in interpersonal conflict when persons hold incompatible expectations for each other's behavior. In addition, sexual behavior between individuals is strongly influenced by social forces in society, such as technology, religion, politics, and economics. Therefore, the sexual relationships people experience with pleasure and pain differ between societies and over historical time. Sexual relationships may be more commonly cooperative in one society and may be more commonly conflict-ridden in another society. Sexual relationships may be a common source of pleasure, affection, and recreation; or they may be an arena for the expression of hostility, achievement, and dominance.

For the social psychologist, human sexuality is not a mere "thing of the flesh," but a continuously changing expression of human aspirations. Sexual behavior is not merely a matter of anatomy in action, but a bridge between separate subjective worlds of experience.

part one

SEXUAL FUNCTIONING

THE PHYSIOLOGY OF SEXUAL RESPONSE

Knowledge of human sexual anatomy and physiology is very helpful in setting aside unnecessary worries caused by superstition and misinformation. However, sometimes when such information is presented with much unfamiliar clinical terminology, it merely adds to the confusion and apprehension. Therefore, the following section will present a brief summary of essential information about human sexual anatomy and physiology. *Anatomy* is the study of the structure of body parts, while *physiology* focuses upon the functioning of those parts. This information is especially useful in understanding the biological aspects of sexual contact and sexual pleasure. A discussion of sexual reproduction will be presented in Chapter 3, and a discussion of sexual dysfunctions will be presented in Chapter 4.

THE MALE AND FEMALE GENITALS

female genital anatomy

The detailed configuration of the genital area in women is much less obvious to the view than it is in men. Some women can be almost as unfamiliar as are many men with the appearance of the female genital parts. Only with the assistance of a mirror can women easily see the details of their genital anatomy.

The most visibly obvious feature of women's genital anatomy is the pubic

2 sexual anatomy and physiology

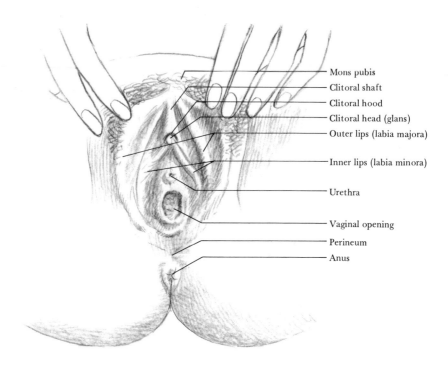

Mons pubis
Clitoral shaft
Clitoral hood
Clitoral head (glans)
Outer lips (labia majora)

Inner lips (labia minora)

Urethra

Vaginal opening
Perineum
Anus

External female genitalia. (David A. Schulz, *Human Sexuality*, © 1979, page 63.)

hair which covers the pubic mound (mons veneris) and outer labial lips (labia majora). In some women, pubic hair may be even more extensive, growing up toward the navel. The pubic mound is composed of fatty tissue lying beneath the skin over the pubic bone. The term *vulva* is used to refer to all the exterior parts of genital tissue, including the outer and inner labial lips (labia majora and labia minora), the clitoris and its hood, and the vestibule.

The *labia majora* are rounded folds of skin over fatty tissue. Inside these folds are the *labia minora,* which are much thinner folds of hairless tissue. Their vertical length greatly varies between individuals. Usually these inner labial lips are closed over the vestibule. However, in response to sexual arousal they expand and separate, providing access to the vagina. They are rich in nerve endings and very sensitive to tactile contact during sexual arousal. At the top of the inner labial lips, where they join together, is the clitoris. Only the head (glans) of the clitoris may be visible, with the remainder below skin surface. The *clitoris* is a small bump-shaped organ composed of erectile tissue. It is the most sensitive spot in the female genitals and plays a crucial role in the triggering of orgasm. During sexual arousal, it expands slightly in length and diameter, although this may not be easily visible. Like the penis, it expands under sexual arousal by becoming filled with blood. When not in a state of sexual arousal, the clitoris is covered by a fold of skin, known as the *hood* or *prepuce,* which extends from the labia minora. Therefore, it is often not easily visible. The *vestibule* is the cleft between the inner labial lips. It contains the vaginal entrance and urinary opening (vaginal and urinary orifices). The urinary opening appears as a tiny slit and is also not easily visible.

In most women who have not experienced sexual intercourse, the *hymen,* a thin membrane rings the entrance to the vagina. The hymen has no particular bodily function. It appears in a great variety of shapes and may be very flexible or very rigid. A traditional myth suggests that all women have hymens until their first experience of sexual intercourse, and that the occasion is normally painful and bloody for a woman. Actually, in some women, the hymen may be absent or broken in youthful accidents. In others, it may be so small and flexible as to be unnoticeable during intercourse. Women who have unusually thick and rigid hymens can save some unnecessary pain by visiting a gynecologist to have it surgically modified, although this is generally unnecessary.

If not washed frequently, the female genital area can easily become malodorous, although the odor is no more unusual than that which can develop in any other body crevice, such as under the arms or between the toes. The odor simply results from the accumulation of perspiration and smegma and can be eliminated by washing. *Smegma,* similar to that which occurs under the foreskin of the penis, is a product of bodily secretions binding together old, sloughed off skin cells. When not removed over a long period, it can cause painful adhesions between the clitoris and its covering hood. Some "feminine hygiene" deodorants are available, but these are considered harmful by some physicians because they may cause irritation to sensitive tissues or may destroy the body's natural balance of necessary bacteria. Washing carefully with soap and water is more effective and less potentially harmful to the sensitive skin.

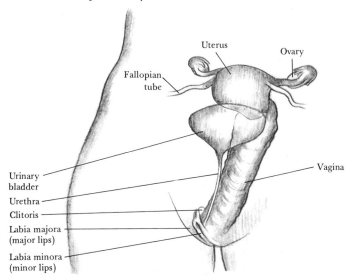

Internal view of female genital area. (David A. Schulz, *Human Sexuality,* page 66.)

The *vagina* is an elastic canal between the exterior vulva and the interior cervix. The average length of the vagina is between 3 and 4 inches. The diameter of the vagina is so flexible that it can expand to receive a penis of any width. Considering that a newborn baby can normally pass down this elastic tube, a sexually inexperienced woman need have no worry about being able to accommodate an object the size of a penis. (Rare cases of undeveloped vaginas can be corrected by surgery.) The lower third of the vagina is somewhat sensitive to touch, as well as heat and pain. However, the upper two thirds contain few nerve endings, causing it to be rather insensitive to stimulation (Masters and Johnson, 1966). In response to sexual excitation, the walls of the vagina secrete a thick fluid which lubricates the vaginal canal. Without such lubrication, penetration of the penis is extremely difficult, causing harsh friction and pain to a woman. (This if often the case in forced sexual intercourse.)

The vaginal muscles which run along the length of the vagina ordinarily contract automatically during sexual arousal and orgasm. However, women can learn to exert voluntary control over these muscles, so that they can deliberately contract and release them during sexual intercourse. Such an ability, acquired through exercise, can enhance both partners' pleasure. After the birth of several children, the vaginal muscles have a tendency to become distended and relaxed, enlarging the vaginal canal. Consequently, the vagina may offer a less firm hold during sexual intercourse and this may be felt as less pleasurable by the sexual partners. However, vaginal exercises can also remedy this difficulty.

male genital anatomy

The male genital organs are more external and visible than are the female genital organs. Consequently, men are more easily and rapidly aware of their own sexual responsiveness than are women. The shaft of the *penis* is filled with sponge like erectile tissue which expands when filled with blood, enlarging the size of the penis. The average size of the penis, in both flaccid and erect states, varies greatly between men. In a flaccid state, the size of the penis is usually between 3 and 4 inches long, while in the erect state it is usually about 6 inches long and 1½ inches in diameter. The expansion in small penises is usually greater than it is in larger ones, so that there is much less variation in length during erection. Penis size is unrelated to a man's height or body build. Size is also unrelated to a man's ability to provide a woman with sexual pleasure, contrary to the traditional myth amongst men which encourages such an erroneous belief. On a psychological level, it is rare to find women who are especially responsive to a penis of exceptionally large size. However, homosexuals are known to be particularly concerned about penis size as an erotic symbol. Probably, they respond more to male mythology than do most women. A great many young men (and some not so young) exhibit the same sort of anxiety about penis size that some adolescent girls exhibit about the size of their breasts. These needless worries reflect the general confusion of quantity with quality which plagues many aspects of American social life.

At birth, the head or glans of the penis is covered by a fold of skin known as the *foreskin*. In a majority of American men, however, the foreskin is absent. It is usually removed shortly after birth while an infant is still at a hospital. This operation is known as *circumcision*. It is medically regarded as a preventive health measure. In young infants with foreskins, the penis must be carefully cleaned almost daily to remove the accumulation of smegma. Without such cleaning, smegma can build up and cause painful adhesions between the foreskin and glans, and also sometimes infections. This is also true of adult males having penis foreskin. However, frequent cleaning of the genitals of all men is necessary to eliminate a source of ill odor.

The *glans* at the tip of the penis varies in size and shape, but its configuration is usually much like that of a bell. At its top is a small slit which is the urinary opening, or more technically, the orifice of the urethra, which runs the length of the penis up to the bladder. The lower edges of the glans, the *corona*, are particularly sensitive during sexual arousal. So is the *frenum*, a small spot of skin just below the front of the glans. The skin along the shaft of the penis is loosely attached, enabling expansion during erection. Just below the skin, large veins are frequently visible, especially during erection.

The *scrotum* is the sac which holds the testicles. Unlike the penis, the scrotum is covered with pubic hair, as is the pubic area above the penis. The skin of the scrotum is very loose and flexible, allowing it to expand and contract with body temperature. When exposed to cool temperatures, it contracts, bringing the testicles closer to the body's warmth. When exposed to high temperatures, the scrotum expands, allowing the testicles to move away from the body.

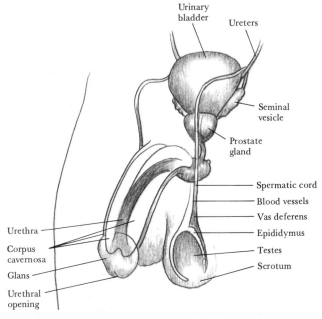

Internal view of male genital area. (David A. Schulz, *Human Sexuality*, page 60.)

This response to temperature is related to the need for proper temperature conditions for the production of sperm in the testicles. The *testicles* (also called *testes*) are two oval-shaped organs within the scrotum. They are very sensitive to pain, so that even a mild blow against them usually causes extreme pain. The appearance of the scrotum is rarely symmetrical. One side is usually lower than the other.

The fluid which is ejaculated from the penis is called *semen*. It contains the sperm cells necessary for reproduction, as well as various other substances such as proteins, cholesterol, and enzymes. The texture of semen varies from time to time and between individuals. Sometimes it is very thick, like mucus, while other times it is thin and watery. Its color is milky white to transparent. Chemically, semen is highly alkaline, like soap. The alkalinity, in contrast to acidity, favors the survival of sperm cells. It enables semen to neutralize body acids (such as uric acid) which might be found in the urethra and vagina and could damage the sperm cells.

An important interpersonal consideration relevant to the foregoing description concerns aesthetics more than anatomy. Our past tradition leads us to see the genital regions as a particularly unattractive, if not an ugly, part of the human body. This is certainly an excellent example of the proposition that ugliness is in the eye of the beholder. There exists no intrinsic reason in form or texture for the female or male genitals to be seen as unattractive, or more so than any other part of the body.

THE MALE AND FEMALE SEXUAL RESPONSE CYCLES

The information in this section is a brief summary of some of the research findings of William Masters and Virginia Johnson as published in their book, *Human Sexual Response* (1966). Their work was a major step forward in our understanding of ourselves as human beings. One of their most important discoveries was that human sexual responses follow a basic sequence from initial sexual arousal to relaxation. This sequence, or cycle, can be divided into four phases. Masters and Johnson have termed these phases: (1) excitement; (2) plateau; (3) orgasm; and (4) resolution. The *excitement* phase is the stage of initial sexual arousal and build-up of bodily tension. The *plateau* phase is a short platform of intense anticipatory tension, from which the peak of orgasmic release is launched. The *resolution* phase involves a gradual relaxation and diffusion of bodily tension. In each of these phases, there are distinct physical reactions. An identification of these physiological responses was one of the main products of Masters' and Johnson's research efforts. Another important contribution of this research was the insight that sexual responses in men and women are more similar than they are different. This contrasts with traditional beliefs which emphasize differences between male and female sexual response. Therefore, this section will follow the sexual response cycle of both sexes at each phase. Important differences will also be noted particularly as they relate to interpersonal consequences.

Knowledge of the sexual response cycle is useful in understanding subjective feelings and bodily responses. The interpersonal implications of sexual response will be emphasized in this section as well as in the next. Knowledge of physiological responses in sexual arousal has been found to be extremely useful for therapists and counselors seeking to help clients with personal sex problems.

the excitement phase

The length of the initial phase of sexual arousal varies considerable. It can last as briefly as two or three minutes or as long as several hours. The length of time necessary to build up to a plateau phase of energy depends upon such factors as psychological attitude, mood, environmental conditions, level of bodily fatigue, and effectiveness of stimulation. Therefore, average lengths of time are somewhat meaningless. One important consideration relative to the build-up of sexual tension during the excitement phase is that there is usually a time differential between men and women. Men generally move toward a plateau level of tension more abruptly and rapidly, causing them to be ready for orgasm before their partners. However, this is not due to physiological factors (Masters and Johnson, 1966). Instead, it is a consequence of social psychological forces which are a product of learning. It usually takes longer for psychological disinhibition and anticipation to take effect in the sexual arousal of women in our society. Generally, men find it easier to move spontaneously with their feelings of sexual arousal within an interpersonal relationship. Yet, given an appropriate interpersonal context and effective stimulation, women move toward orgasm as rapidly as do men. Movement toward orgasm need not become a race toward a finish line. Many couples prefer to control and extend their movement toward orgasm in order to savor feelings of sensual pleasure. The length of the excitement phase also has a relationship to the resolution phase. Generally, the more the excitement phase is extended, the longer the time necessary to diffuse sexual tensions will be.

A great many physiological changes take place during the excitement phase. Some are obvious, while others are very subtle. Initial physiological response to sexual arousal in both sexes include increased heartbeat, muscular tension (myotonia), and congestion of the genital tissues with blood (vasocongestion). In the man, this rapidly produces *erection* of the penis. In men under the age of 40, this response usually takes only 3 to 8 seconds. In older men the response is less abrupt and more gradual. Penile erection may be lost and regained several times when the excitement phase is deliberately prolonged. Initial responses in the female body are not as easily recognized as "sexual" by adolescent women without sexual experience. Instead, they often perceive themselves to be merely excited or nervous. However, genital congestion commences *vaginal lubrication*. When such lubrication is copious, it offers a more ob-

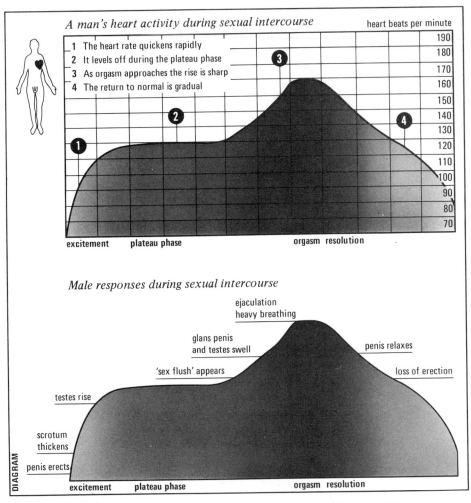

A man's heart activity during sexual intercourse — heart beats per minute

1 The heart rate quickens rapidly
2 It levels off during the plateau phase
3 As orgasm approaches the rise is sharp
4 The return to normal is gradual

190 180 170 160 150 140 130 120 110 100 90 80 70

excitement   plateau phase   orgasm resolution

Male responses during sexual intercourse

ejaculation
heavy breathing

glans penis
and testes swell   penis relaxes

'sex flush' appears   loss of erection

testes rise

scrotum
thickens

penis erects

excitement   plateau phase   orgasm resolution

DIAGRAM

(Edwin J. Haeberle, *The Sex Atlas,* © 1978. Reprinted by permission of Seabury Press.)

vious sign of sexual arousal. Vaginal lubrication generally commences 10 to 30 seconds after sexual arousal.

Several other less obvious changes take place in a women's genitals early in the excitement phase. The labia begin to swell as they become congested with blood. In women who have not given birth to children, the outer labial lips will gradually flare outward from the vaginal entrance. In women who have had children, they will separate slightly and hang downward. The inner labial lips undergo even more marked enlargement, and gradually separate as lubrication takes effect. Changes also take place in the clitoris. Early in the excitement phase, the clitoris begins to swell and enlarges slightly as it fills with blood. Expansion of the clitoris may move its head (glans) out from under the hood so that it becomes visible. However, such visibility may not be present in a great many

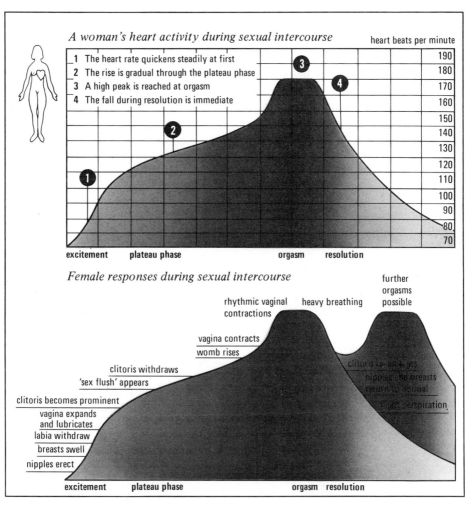

A woman's heart activity during sexual intercourse — heart beats per minute

1 The heart rate quickens steadily at first
2 The rise is gradual through the plateau phase
3 A high peak is reached at orgasm
4 The fall during resolution is immediate

190
180
170
160
150
140
130
120
110
100
90
80
70

excitement   plateau phase   orgasm   resolution

Female responses during sexual intercourse

further orgasms possible

rhythmic vaginal contractions   heavy breathing

vagina contracts
womb rises

clitoris withdraws
'sex flush' appears

clitoris re-emerges
nipples and breasts return to normal
slight perspiration

clitoris becomes prominent
vagina expands and lubricates
labia withdraw
breasts swell
nipples erect

excitement   plateau phase   orgasm   resolution

(Edwin J. Haeberle, *The Sex Atlas,* © 1978. Reprinted by permission of Seabury Press.)

women, when most of the expansion takes place under the skin. Direct stimulation of the clitoris with sufficient lubrication will generally cause more rapid and greater expansion than indirect stimulation, as during sexual intercourse. (However, that is sometimes more irritating than pleasurable.) An important change also takes place in the vagina. The walls in the upper two-thirds of the vagina balloon or expand outward from the vaginal canal, as it is pulled upward by the uterus. In this way, the vaginal canal is lengthened by about 25 percent. When this increased length is added to the enlarged labia, enough room becomes available for almost any size penis, without much possibility of harsh blows against a woman's interior organs. (Although this possibility is influenced by the position of intercourse.)

There are several other physical changes in women during the excitement phase of sexual response. The nipples and areolae (the dark area surrounding the nipples) of the breasts become erect in almost all women, usually even before the start of vaginal lubrication. The breasts themselves also gradually begin to swell and enlarge. (Nipple erection in women may also be a response to conditions other than sexual arousal, such as exposure to chilly air or cold water.)

Erection of the nipples caused by sexual arousal, but without breast enlargement, also occurs in about 30 percent of men (Masters and Johnson, 1966). Another physical change occurs in all men, although it is rarely recognized. The scrotum thickens and tightens as the testicles are pulled up toward the body. However, this firmness and immobility of the scrotum remains for no longer than five to ten minutes, after which the scrotal sac again softens and becomes pendulous. The elevation of the scrotum and testicles occurs again and lasts during the plateau and orgasmic phases of sexual response.

Sexual excitement in both men and women is also characterized by increased muscular tension. Various body muscles involuntarily tense and contract. This may be felt in the muscles of the legs, arms, hands, neck, lower abdomen, and pelvic region. The muscular tension causes restless, rapid body movement, as the feeling of nervous excitability becomes increasingly obvious. Occasionally, muscular spasms in the pelvic region may become disconcerting, especially for an adolescent woman with little sexual experience for whom disinhibition is not yet easy and spontaneous. If she deliberately tries to tighten her pelvic muscles, it is likely to restrain her orgasmic responsiveness later because she is unable to relax.

The *subjective effects* of these physiological changes vary between people. Generally a woman feels a throbbing, congested sensation in the genital area, combined with a sensation of "emptiness" in the lower abdomen and bodily nervousness. Again, in adolescent women with little or no sexual experience, these subjective feelings may be very difficult to discern and identify with erotic meaning. In men, a subjective feeling of throbbing is centered in the erect penis. This is another reason why men can more easily perceive their own sexual arousal. Consequently, in an interpersonal encounter men often become more quickly and self-consciously aware of their own sexual excitement than women. This is especially true when the men and women are adolescents engaged in light petting. He is apt to mistake her affectionate playfulness for the enjoyment of sensual pleasure, and she may regard her own feelings as being joyfulness and excitement without sexual arousal.

the plateau phase

The transition between excitement and plateau phases of sexual response is not marked by an abrupt physical change. Instead, many of the physiological responses which occurred during the excitement phase became extended and intensified. Essentially, the plateau phase involves a high level of physical tension which anticipates the peak of orgasmic response. Muscular tension and nervous energy reach a high pitch. The respiration rate increases as breathing becomes rapid and heavy, pumping oxygen into the body. Genital congestion and engorgement is marked, and the penis becomes very rigid. Subjective sensations of pleasurable, genital throbbing become intense in both men and women. The genital areas also become highly sensitive to tactile contact.

Certain subtle physical changes do occur during the plateau phase. Many of these are not easily observed. However, one that may be seen is the sex flush. It is a reddish-pink rash which spreads over portions of the body. It appears on occasion in about 75 percent of women, and usually begins during the latter part of the excitement phase. Later, it becomes much more pronounced in these women during the plateau phase. It may spread over the face, throat, shoulders, chest, breasts, and abdomen. Its presence, and the extent and intensity of coloration, vary from occasion to occasion. Its presence terminates abruptly with orgasm. A more limited sex flush appears in about 25 percent of men, usually during the plateau phase immediately before orgasm. When the sex flush appears in men, it tends to be limited to the upper chest, throat, and face.

Additional skin color changes occur in the genital tissue during the plateau phase. The inner labial lips (labia minora) of women very commonly show a dramatic deepening of color. In women who have had no children, the labia minora change color from pink to crimson red as orgasm approaches, while in women who have had children the labia minora turn a deep wine-red color. In some men, a skin color change occasionally appears in the penis, as the ridges of the corona turn deep, purplish-red. In some men, also, there occurs a further enlargement of the glans of the penis. Much more commonly observed is a pre-ejaculatory secretion which appears out of the urinary opening at the tip of the penis. It is secreted by the Cowper's gland and is not semen. However, sperm may get into this fluid, making it capable of impregnation. This secretion is an occasional source of pregnancy in cases where ejaculation in the vagina has been deliberately avoided using the very fallible method of contraception known as withdrawal (coitus interruptus).

Still other changes occur in a woman's breasts and genitals. In the breasts, the areolae become increasingly swollen around the nipples, making it appear as if the nipples have relaxed and lost their erection. This reaction is more pronounced in women who have not breast fed an infant. In a woman's genitals, the clitoris shrinks in size and withdraws beneath its surrounding hood. The upper two-thirds of the vagina undergoes further enlargement as it is pulled up by the uterus. Meanwhile, the lower third of the vagina contracts, so that during sexual intercourse it involuntarily tightens around the penis.

During sexual intercourse, the initial slow pelvic thrusting forward and back is deliberate and voluntarily controlled. However, once thrusting becomes rapid and forceful, it is very difficult to retain deliberate control. Body movements, then, become more like involuntary responses. This is particularly true in men as they approach imminent orgasm. Consequently, when mutual orgasm is desired, a woman should feel orgasm coming before a couple start rapid and forceful thrusting movements. It is obvious that adequate communication is essential for such coordinated pacing to occur.

the orgasmic phase

Orgasm is the shortest phase of sexual response, lasting only a matter of seconds. The intense muscular tension, which has previously been cultivated deliberately, is now released by involuntary muscle spasms which generate waves of pleasurable feeling.

The general nature of orgasm in both men and women is remarkably similar. In women, muscular spasms start in the lower portion of the vagina which had become constricted during the plateau phase. This is followed by rhythmical waves of contractions in the uterus, which descend from its top to the cervix. (These waves of contractions in the uterus are somewhat similar to those which occur during the delivery of an infant, but are much milder.) In men, spasmodic contractions start in the urethral tube at the point of connection with the prostate gland. The internal receptacles holding sperm and secretions contract and release them into the urethra. Along the urethra, powerful waves of contractions create pressure which expels semen in the response of ejaculation. It is interesting to note that the timing of the initial orgasmic spasms in both men and women is the same. The intervals between these contractions are about eight-tenths of a second during the first three or four spasms. Afterward, the intervals between contractions become weaker. The physiological intensity of orgasm is a product of the number of contractions experienced. A mild orgasm may involve three to five contractions, while one that is experienced as more intense may involve eight to ten contractions, or more. Generally, women have a capacity for a greater number of orgasmic spasms than do men, extending their orgasm over a longer time (Masters and Johnson, 1966). Yet, the intensity of orgasm itself depends upon other factors, such as the amount and type of stimulation, level of fatigue, psychological receptivity to erotic stimulation, and the interpersonal relationship.

The orgasmic phase is characterized by muscular tension (myotonia) beyond that of the plateau phase. The intense, involuntary muscular strain may cause bodily soreness the following day. This is, of course, particularly true in men and women who do not get much other exercise daily. An intense orgasm may leave similar muscular soreness to that which is experienced by the occasional tennis player, after a period of exhaustive tennis activity. Muscular tension and spasms very frequently occur in the hands and feet, in the long muscles of the legs, arms, and neck; and in the muscles of the lower back and buttocks. Muscles in the face may also be distorted with strain. These responses usually are not noticed at the time. Orgasm is ultimately a response of the whole body and not simply the genitals.

Orgasm is also accompanied by other bodily changes. Usually, the respiration rate increases. When orgasm is particularly intense, breathing may be twice as fast as normal. The rate of heart beat and the level of blood pressure also increases, sometimes to one-third higher than normal. If a sex flush is exhibited, skin coloration will briefly deepen. The muscles of the rectum may also contract spasmodically. In some women, the urinary opening occasionally becomes stretched, evoking the subjective feeling of an urge to urinate. (Involuntary loss of urine may actually occur in women having full bladders during orgasm. It is a potential embarrassment that causes occasional worry.)

If orgasm is not achieved after the plateau phase, it may take quite a long time for the genital sensitivity and bodily nervousness to subside. By implication, then, reaching the plateau phase of sexual response without going on to orgasm can be quite frustrating. The consequences are often sleeplessness and irritability, even though no bodily damage occurs. Such a plight happens to many teenagers after an extended session of foreplay (petting). But, it also occurs to many women, whose partners are too quick to reach orgasm and afterward provide no further stimulation. After months, or years, of such frustration, women may no longer desire sexual contact with their partners.

The subjective feelings of orgasm. It is very difficult to describe the subjective feelings of orgasm. It has been the subject of frequent attempts and much debate. Masters and Johnson (1966) conducted interviews with several hundred persons immediately after they had orgasmic experiences, in order to obtain a consensual description of their subjective feelings. The following descriptions are derived from that source. First, it should be noted that there is considerable variation in feeling, not only between individuals, but in the same person on different occasions.

Among women, the onset of orgasm is experienced as a sudden stop of physical tensions. This is followed by a wave of sensual pleasure, which radiates from the clitoris throughout the lower abdomen (the pelvic area). Simultaneously, there occurs a feeling of "blacking-out"; a loss of awareness of the surrounding environment, as if any possible distraction is irrelevant. (Some women actually do faint on occasion.) In addition, many women experience an overwhelming awareness of their genital region as the total focus of experience. This may be combined with a great urge to push the inner organs downward. Momentarily later, a wave of warmth sweeps over the whole body radiating from the pelvic region. Finally, this is followed by feelings of muscular spasms and throbbing in the pelvic area. The experience of these feelings varies with the intensity of orgasm. This variation also exists in the orgasmic feelings of men.

Among men, the instant prior to orgasm is experienced as one of intense anticipation. This is often expressed as feeling like "orgasm is about to come," or feeling like "one is about to explode." Immediately after, at the onset of orgasm, there is a feeling of sudden release from tension and loss of all voluntary control. This is followed by a reduced awareness of the surrounding environment and an intense awareness of what seems to be large quantities of fluid being forced from the penis, as if under great pressure. In men, the initial contractions are felt as most intense and the succeeding contractions as weaker. Contrastingly, most women experience each succeeding contraction as more intense (Masters and Johnson, 1966).

In another respect, the orgasmic responses of women and men differ. During orgasm, most men prefer to thrust one or two times into the vagina, and then push deeply, holding motionless onto their partner (Masters and Johnson, 1966). In contrast, during orgasm, many women prefer continued genital movement, or even increasingly rapid thrusting of the penis. Such thrusting provides gentle friction to the clitoris, by moving it against its hood. These response tendencies are obviously incompatible (Masters and Johnson, 1966). Increased movement can mute a man's orgasm through overstimulation. Yet, lack of such movement can weaken a woman's orgasm, by not providing sufficient stimulation. This is another difficulty encountered when a couple constantly seek simultaneous orgasms. Many sex therapists suggest that the expectation of consistently experiencing simultaneous orgasms during sexual relations is impractical (Heiman et al., 1976).

In other ways, however, it can be seen that the subjective experience of orgasm is surprisingly similar in men and women. One recent study attempted to find out if the subjective feelings of orgasm in men and women could be distinguished from written descriptions of the experience (Vance and Wagner, 1976). A sample of 48 descriptions were obtained from male and female college students. Any references to male or female anatomy were removed. The descriptions were then given to a panel of judges composed of male and female psychologists, medical students, and gynecologists, who were asked to identify the male and female orgasmic experiences among the 48 descriptions. The judges' attempts to do so were no better than chance. They could not distinguish between male and female written descriptions of subjective orgasmic experience. Therefore, the researchers suggested that the subjective experience of orgasm in men and women is essentially the same.

A curious finding in the research of Masters and Johnson was that most women reported experiencing more intense orgasms during masturbation than during sexual intercourse. (Nevertheless, most of the women still found orgasm during sexual intercourse to be more satisfying.) Women can continue to stimulate their clitoris during masturbation, while during intercourse such friction often ceases before a woman has received sufficient clitoral stimulation. Men can provide similarly intense orgasms by offering gentle clitoral friction using manual or oral caresses.

One continuing debate centers around the question of whether or not women subjectively experience different types of orgasm. Freud made a distinction between clitoral and vaginal orgasms in women. However, the research of Masters and Johnson (1966) could find no physiological differences in the nature of female orgasm. During a short period of time thereafter, it seemed as if the debate had been laid to rest.

Recently, the debate has stirred up anew. The research of Fisher (1973),

Hite (1976), and others has found that a great many, if not most, women are able to make subjective distinctions between the types of orgasms they experience, from purely clitoral stimulation and from penile penetration. One hypothesis distinguishes between three types of female orgasms: (1) clitoral-vulval, (2) vaginal-uterine, and (3) a combination of the previous two (Singer and Singer, 1972). These distinctions are made on the basis of physiological responses to the main sources of stimulation. Some recent research seems to support the contention that the different subjective orgasmic experiences of women are linked to distinctly different patterns of physiological response (Fox, 1976). The research found evidence that orgasms subjectively experienced as being vaginal-uterine were more likely to be associated with a woman's sudden holding of her breath, and with a sudden drop of pressure in a woman's uterus. The researcher concluded that vaginal-uterine orgasms are more likely to terminate sexual tension. The researcher also suggested that clitoral-vulval orgasms are more likely to result in the desire for further release of sexual tension through multiple successive orgasms. Descriptions of the subjective feelings associated with these orgasms vary. One researcher summarized the descriptions of a large sample of women in terms of the following adjectives: (1) Clitoral-vulval orgasms were described as "warm," "ticklish," "electrical," and "sharp"; (2) vaginal-uterine orgasms were described as "throbbing," "deep," "soothing," and "comfortable" (Fisher, 1973).

Multiple orgasms.   One important difference between male and female orgasmic responses was confirmed by the Masters and Johnson research. This difference is the capacity for multiple orgasms in women. Women, unlike most men, are capable of repeating orgasms successively, one after another to a point of exhaustion. As one orgasmic peak is attained, another can follow. In addition, each successive orgasm is not felt as weaker, but rather more intense. Most women who are aware of this possibility can easily experience three to six successive orgasms during a period of several minutes—providing, of course, that they are erotically receptive and not overly fatigued after a long day's work.

It can be a bit of a problem for a man to provide his partner with multiple orgasms through sexual intercourse. To do so, he must exert considerable control, preventing his own movement toward orgasm while under intense stimulation. Some men are able to do so, but others find that it makes sexual activity more work than play. The easiest means by which a man can provide his partner with multiple orgasms is through manual or oral-genital caresses. However, a woman's multiorgasmic potential need not be a source of constant sexual worry. Many women have an occasional desire for multiple orgasms, but probably few women desire the experience on a regular basis.

Whether or not men are capable of multiple successive orgasms is still a matter of dispute. Kinsey's (1948) research found that about 15 percent of teenage men and about 77 percent of men at age 30 claimed to experience multiple orgasms. Recently, a team of researchers tested the claims of a sample of fourteen men in a physiology laboratory (Robbins and Jensen, 1977). They found that, indeed, the men's bodies responded with three to ten successive orgasm-like reactions without ejaculation, until they experienced a final orgasm with ejaculation. This research may indicate that many men can learn to voluntarily stop their ejaculation, while experiencing orgasm (Robbins and Jensen, 1977). The technique of doing so, appears to involve learning a response of relaxation (rather than increasing tension) to the sensations of impending orgasm (Travis, 1976). If the male multiple orgasm requires special learning and practice, than it differs in nature from the female multiple orgasm, which does not seem to require any special effort. Whether or not the effort adds anything to personal and mutual sexual satisfaction is a question of values. Neither men nor women have any reason to feel inadequate for not experiencing multiple orgasms.

the resolution phase

After orgasm is experienced, the body returns to the functional state which existed previous to sexual arousal. The resolution phase, then, essentially involves bodily changes which reverse those which occurred during the plateau and excitement phases of sexual response. Usually, this reversal of a sexually stimulated state occurs more rapidly in men than in women, particularly in relation to genital decongestion. Erection is lost much more rapidly than is congestion of the clitoris and vagina. However, in both men and women, muscular tension is normally dissipated in less than five minutes.

The major difference between the physiological responses of men and women occurring during the resolution phase is the existence of a *refractory period* in men. The refractory period is a period of time after orgasm when men are insensitive to sexual stimulation. During the refractory period, genital stimulation will not cause sexual arousal, and it may even be physically irritating. It is a period of necessary relaxation, before orgasm can again take place. The length of the refractory period differs between men and in the same man on different occasions. Yet, it largely depends upon age. In young men, the refractory period may only be several minutes until a second orgasm can occur, while in older men many hours may be necessary until a second orgasm can be experienced. The existence of a refractory period in the sexual response of men contrasts sharply with the capacity of women for multiple orgasms. It makes extremely unlikely any possibility for multiple orgasms to be experienced by a couple simultaneously during intercourse.

After orgasm, most women and many men in an intimate relationship prefer to remain in continued embrace for a while and enjoy some gentle caressing. They often appreciate some tender expressions of affection after enjoying sensual pleasure together. Unfortunately, some people ignore this satisfying psychological epilogue and abruptly change to another activity. Some persons simply turn over and go to sleep immediately after experiencing orgasm. Some persons jump out of bed to wash their genital organs. Such abrupt change can leave the other partner, who may desire some continued expression, feeling like the music was interrupted before its final notes. Being able to relax and enjoy the afterglow of sensual pleasure is an important psychological satisfaction for couples sharing an intimate relationship.

SEX AND DRUGS

Throughout the ages, persons in many societies have sought substances to enhance sexual desire and sexual arousal. Substances which are attributed the power to increase sexual desire are called *aphrodisiacs*. Popular mythology in various societies have attributed aphrodisiac power to many foods, such as bull's testicles and oysters. The belief in the Orient that powdered rhinoceros horn is an aphrodisiac has contributed to the near extinction of the animal. In Europe, an ancient substance made from a certain beetle, popularly called "Spanish fly," has been used in attempts to enhance sexual desire. Actually, the substance is an extreme irritant to the mucous membranes of the urogenital tract, and is even poisonous when taken in large doses. In American society today, a wide variety of synthetic and natural substances are attributed aphrodisiac qualities. The most commonly used of these substances are alcohol and marijuana. Therefore, these substances will be the focus of attention in this section.

alcohol

Even though there is a great deal of speculation, there is surprisingly little concrete research on the effects of alcohol upon sexual desire and sexual arousal. It is widely believed that drinking a moderate amount of alcohol will release a person's sexual inhibitions, and thereby increase sexual desire. Yet, evidence from clinical studies indicates that the chronic consumption of large quantities of alcohol often results in male impotence, which is very difficult to reverse even after years of sobriety (Lemere and Smith, 1973).

Only recently have the effects of alcohol upon sexual arousal been investigated through experimental laboratory techniques. A series of research projects gave various amounts of alcohol to samples of men and women; then the subjects were shown sexually explicit films in a private room while their physiological level of sexual arousal was being monitored electronically (Brinddell and Wilson, 1976; Wilson and Lawson, 1978). The level of male sexual arousal was monitored by a guage attached to the penis that measured penile tumescence. The level of female sexual arousal was monitored by a device inserted in the vagina that measured vaginal blood pressure. The research found that after initial heightened sexual arousal in both men and women, increasing amounts of alcohol were directly correlated with signs of progressively decreasing levels of sexual arousal. In other words, the research indicates that alcohol consumption in progressively higher amounts decreases the body's ability to respond with sexual arousal to erotic stimulation. Consumption of high doses of alcohol may make a male temporarily incapable of erection, and a female temporarily incapable of orgasm. Chronically high consumption can make such unresponsiveness lasting, through the process of conditioning.

Yet, the question remains whether or not consumption of a small amount of alcohol actually relaxes and disinhibits a person, enabling the person to be more responsive to sexual stimulation. The authors of the previous research directed a clever and careful laboratory experiment designed to test this question (Wilson and Lawson, 1976). A sample of 40 male college students were divided into four separate testing groups. All four groups of men were given something to drink, either alcohol or a placebo, and then shown a sexually explicit film while their level of sexual arousal was being monitored. Group 1 was given alcohol (vodka) to drink and told that it was alcohol. Group 2 was given only tonic to drink, but they were told that it was alcohol. Group 3 was given tonic to drink and told that it was only tonic. Finally, Group 4 was given alcohol to drink, but told that it was tonic. All doses of alcohol were moderate rather than strong. The results of the experiment were fascinating. The two groups of men who believed that they drank alcohol responded to the erotic film with greater penile tumescence than the two groups of men who believed that they drank tonic. The group of men who showed the least physiological sexual arousal was the group that drank alcohol, believing it to be tonic. This experiment demonstrates that alcohol itself does not increase sexual arousal, nor does it appear to release sexual inhibitions (Wilson, 1977). The researchers offered the conclusion that it is the belief or expectation that alcohol enhances sexual arousal which causes sexual arousal to be heightened, not the alcohol itself. Even more important, this experiment demonstrates the crucial effects of learned factors, especially anticipation, in heightening sexual arousal. (See Chapter 6 for a more detailed discussion of sexual arousal.)

marijuana

There is an unfortunate lack of adequate experimental research on the effects marijuana has upon sexual arousal. This is largely because of the moral and political controversy surrounding use of the drug. Sometimes the political conflict even affects scientific research. In 1976, for example, the House of Representatives voted to cut off funding for a proposed government supported research experiment designed to investigate the effects of marijuana smoking upon sexual arousal (similar to the studies done with alcohol). News of the research had stirred up angry protests in the area near the university where the research had been planned.

The precise extent to which marijuana is used in conjunction with sexual activity is unknown, although indirect evidence indicates that the practice is now rather common. In 1975, *Redbook Magazine* published a survey of 100,000 women who responded to a questionnaire in the magazine about their sexual behavior (Levin and Levin, 1975). The findings are, of course, not representative of all American women. However, they do indicate the behavior of

readers of a conventional women's magazine. The findings about marijuana use were surprising. About one-third of the women acknowledged that they often or occasionally engaged in sexual activity after smoking marijuana. More important, the practice was particularly common among younger women in their twenties. Use of marijuana before sexual activity ranged from 63 percent of women under the age of twenty, to only 5 percent of women over the age of forty.

Several surveys of the perceived effects of marijuana have found that over half of users report that it usually or occasionally enhances their sexual pleasure (Tart, 1970; Halikas et al., 1971; Goode, 1974; Koff, 1974). A minority of users, however, report that it has no effect upon their sexual pleasure. Therefore, it is quite unclear if the sexual effects of marijuana are caused by expectancy, as with alcohol, or whether they are caused by the psychophysiological effects of the drug itself (Goode, 1974). Field and laboratory research have both demonstrated that the expectancy effect is crucial in an individual's psychological reactions to the bodily changes caused by the drug (Becker, 1953; Weil et al., 1968).

One survey obtained data about the perceived sexual effects of marijuana from 345 students at eight universities (Koff, 1974). Curiously, more women (about 60 percent) than men (about 40 percent) reported that it increased their sexual desire. Yet, when the question concerned feelings of sexual pleasure, more men (about 60 percent) than women (about 40 percent) reported that marijuana increased their enjoyment of sexual activity. As a possible explanation of this reversal, the researcher suggested that women were more likely than men to need a symbolic excuse for pursuing their sexual desires. On the other hand, he suggested that the psychophysiological effects of marijuana itself are more likely to increase men's rather than women's enjoyment of sexual activity. Marijuana may heighten direct physical sensations, but confuse the cognitive appraisal of ongoing activity. Thus, marijuana smoking may intensify the sensations of skin contact and orgasm, but confuse the perception of verbal and nonverbal communication. The research also found, importantly, that increasingly high doses of marijuana were associated with decreased reports of sexual desire and sexual pleasure (Koff, 1974).

Much more research into the effects of marijuana smoking on sexual arousal is needed. The question of whether marijuana increases sexual pleasure by intensifying a person's sensate focus or by the expectancy effect must be regarded as unsettled.

A wide variety of other drugs are less commonly used by Americans in conjunction with sexual activity, including cocaine, amphetamines, LSD, and amyl nitrite (Jarvik and Brecher, 1977). There has been been even less adequate research into the effects of these drugs upon sexual arousal.

SEXUALLY TRANSMITTED DISEASES

Sexually transmitted diseases, or venereal diseases, as they were formerly called, are diseases which are transmitted through the contact of mucous tissue during sexual activity. Such activity may include genital intercourse, oral-genital sex, anal intercourse, and even kissing. Normally, the disease microorganisms cannot live outside of the body, so that they are dependent upon direct contact for transmission. There are a wide variety of sexually transmitted diseases, but only the most commonly occurring of them will be covered here.

After decades of declining incidence, these diseases have again become prevalent. Some have reached what may be considered epidemic proportions. According to United States government estimates in 1977, there were 100,000 to 150,000 new cases of syphilis and 2 to 2.5 million new cases of gonorrhea in the United States (Jerrick, 1978). The incidence of these diseases have been increasing sharply since the mid-1960s in most industrial societies (Morton, 1977). The reasons for the increase are probably a result of: (1) the increasing sexual activity of unmarried young people;   (2) the declining use of the condom as a form of contraception; and   (3) the evolution of penicillin-resistant strains of gonorrhea.

gonorrhea

Gonorrhea is the most frequently reported communicable disease in the United States today, other than the common cold. It is caused by a form of bacteria which thrives in the warmth and moisture of the mucous membranes. This tissue is found in the mouth and throat, the vagina and cervix, the urethra and the anal canal. Gonorrhea is transmitted through sexual contact with an infected person.

However, sometimes repeated contact with an infected person is necessary for the disease to be transmitted. Newborn babies can also contract gonorrhea from an infected mother during childbirth.

Symptoms.   In men, the early symptoms of gonorrhea begin to appear in 2 to 7 days after infection in about 80 percent of cases (Hart, 1977). The urethral canal becomes inflamed, causing a burning pain during urination. There is also an oozing discharge of pus from the penis. At first, this discharge is watery, but it rapidly becomes thicker and yellowish in color. Without medical treatment, these symptoms usually subside in about eight weeks (Hart, 1977). However, the disease is usually still present and remains contagious. With the progression of infection, serious complications may result including constriction of the urethra, painful swelling of the testes, and sterility. These symptoms are often accompanied by fever, fatigue, sore throat, arthritic pains, and sores on the skin.

In women, gonorrhea is much more likely to lack obvious symptoms during the early stages of infection. It is estimated that only about 20 percent to 30 percent of women experience serious early symptoms of gonorrhea (Morton, 1977). Therefore, women are usually unaware of their infection and don't seek medical treatment. Women may not become aware of their infection until their male partner develops obvious symptoms. Serious complications during advanced stages of gonorrhea are more common in women than in men because of the absence of obvious early indicators.

When early symptoms of gonorrhea are present in women, they may include a painful inflammation of the vulva, and sometimes a slight pus-like discharge from the cervix. The infection may also spread to the urethra, causing a painful burning sensation during urination. In some cases, the infection spreads to the anal canal, causing a painful inflammation there. Serious complications occur later, when the infection progresses through a woman's internal organs. It may spread to the Fallopian tubes and ovaries. If the disease remains untreated, the Fallopian tubes may become blocked and permanently damaged. Hormone production in the ovaries may also be disrupted. The result can lead to an impaired ability to conceive or even sterility (Hart, 1977). Internal gonorrhea infection is indicated by dull to severe abdominal pain. In some cases, a woman may also experience painful and irregular menstruation.

Prevention and treatment.   Certain precautions can reduce, but not eliminate, the chances of contracting gonorrhea from an infected person. These include a thorough washing of the genitals with soap and water before and after sexual intercourse, and the use of an antiseptic douche by a woman. This must be done, in addition to the use of a condom by the man (Hart, 1977). However, gonorrhea may also be spread by oral-genital contact and kissing, so that in many cases, precautions are rendered inadequate.

Gonorrhea is usually treated effectively with injections of penicillin. However, other antibiotic drugs may have to be used in cases where a person is allergic to penicillin or where the strain of gonorrhea is resistant to the effects of penicillin. If a person is treated in the early stages of the disease, there is not likely to be any permanent physical damage.

syphilis

The use of penicillin has dramatically reduced the past devastating consequences of syphilis. Although no newly resistant strains of syphilis have evolved, the disease is on the increase again. It is caused by a spiral-shaped form of bacteria. This microorganism thrives in the same warm and moist tissue as does gonorrhea, but it enters the body directly through the skin. After entering the body, the disease goes through several stages of development.

Symptoms.   The beginning or primary stage of syphilis is usually easy to identify in 90 percent of men by the presence of a crusty sore at the place where the microorganism entered the skin (Rome et al., 1976). This sore, called a *chancre* (pronounced "shanker"), may appear from 9 days to 3 months after the initial infection (Hart, 1977). The chancre is usually a painless sore. But, when the crust is broken, it may ooze fluids which contain millions of the disease organisms. The chancre is usually located on the external genitals, but can appear anywhere else that the organism may have entered the body, such as on the lips, in the mouth, or around the anus. In women, the chancre commonly forms on the inner labia, in the vagina, or on the surface of the cervix. Consequently, only about 10 percent of women who contract syphilis notice the appearance of a chancre (Rome et al., 1976). Therefore, women may suffer the advanced stages of the disease, as with gonorrhea, without having been alerted to their initial infection. The chancre usually disappears within 4 weeks as the infection spreads elsewhere in the body (Hart, 1977).

The secondary stage of syphilis usually begins within 2 to 4 months after the initial infection and lasts for several weeks (Hart, 1977). Its symptoms include a non-itching, reddish rash over the skin on parts of the body. The rash has a tendency to appear and fade, only to return again (Morton, 1977). This symptom may be accompanied by a wide variety of other indicators, such as sores in the mouth, loss of hair, low fever, headache, sore throat, and general fatigue. Unfortunately, these symptoms can easily be confused with indicators of other diseases, even by competent medical doctors. So, there is much possibility for syphilis to advance further.

Next, syphilis enters a latent stage when all outward symptoms subside. This stage may last 5 to 50 years, or as long as the infected person's life (Morton, 1977). During this stage, the disease is not contagious. Nevertheless, the disease in a pregnant woman may still be transmitted to her unborn child, often resulting in a miscarriage or stillborn infant (Rome et al., 1976). In some cases, when the disease is transmitted to an unborn child, there may be no obvious symptoms at birth; but when the child reaches 15 to 30 years of age, the symptoms begin to appear (Morton, 1977).

The most severe effects of syphilis occur after the long latency stage. This late stage of syphilis affects one in four cases of persons not treated for the disease (Morton, 1977). The disease organisms may attack and damage any of several vital body organs, including the heart and brain. Consequently, a victim of this stage of the disease may suffer paralysis, blindness, syphilitic insanity, or death.

Prevention and treatment.   The precautions a person may take to prevent contraction of syphilis are similar to those for gonorrhea with similar shortcomings. Syphilis is very effectively treated with injections of penicillin. Other antibiotic drugs may be used for patients who are allergic to penicillin. If the disease is treated before the late stage, there is usually no permanent physical damage.

genital herpes

Genital herpes is caused by a virus (herpes simplex, type 2), which is very similar to the one that causes cold sores. There are some reports that the incidence of genital herpes has increased greatly in recent years, although there are no reliable health surveys about it (Jerrick, 1978). This disease has also come to public attention because of some research indicating its frequent association with later cancer of the cervix (Reyner, 1975).

Symptoms.   The symptoms of a genital herpes infection usually are small painful sores, which look much like blisters (or cold sores). In women, these sores may be in the vagina, or on the external genitals, thighs, or the anus. In men, they usually appear on the penis. If the blisters are broken, any contact with them can be very painful. Other symptoms may include: fever, headache, swollen and tender lymph nodes, lack of appetite, and general fatigue. These symptoms very much resemble those of a low grade flu infection. After about 2 or 3 weeks, the sores heal, and the other symptoms subside. However, the disease is often not eliminated, and the symptoms may continually reappear from time to time. New outbreaks occur, especially when the body has been weakened by other diseases or emotional distress.

The disease may be transmitted by an infected pregnant mother to her unborn child. In such cases, about one-half of the children are stillborn or suffer severe brain damage (Hart, 1977).

Prevention and treatment.   Transmission of genital herpes *may* be prevented by male use of a condom, however, this is not certain (Hart, 1977). Unfortunately, there is no known cure for the disease once a person is infected. Current medical care consists of attempts to alleviate some of the distressful symptoms with analgesics (pain-killing drugs). Routine Pap smears for women are necessary, to check for possible early signs of cervical cancer.

Entire books are written on the topics of pregnancy, childbirth, contraception, and abortion. It is not possible within the scope of this book to present very detailed information about these important matters. Instead, this chapter aims to present only an overview of those matters which are of greatest concern to young people. More detailed information can be found in the works cited in the bibliography. Several particularly useful books include those by Guttmacher (1973), The Boston Women's Health Book Collective (1976), and Shapiro (1977).

CHILDBEARING

conception

Conception occurs when a sperm unites with an ovum (egg cell). Usually, several hundred million sperm cells are ejaculated by a male in approximately a teaspoonful of semen. Only several hundred manage to move from the vagina through the cervix and the uterus to the fallopian tube, where conception occurs. Movement of the sperm is facilitated by its tail, and by muscular contractions of the uterine wall. Ovulation, which is the release of an ovum from the ovary, normally occurs approximately once every month. After being released from the ovary an ovum moves down the fallopian tube. When conception occurs, the fertilized egg immediately undergoes a series of divisions, becoming a hollow ball of cells (known as a blastocyst). It takes about 6 or 7 days for the fertilized egg to

3 childbearing and contraception

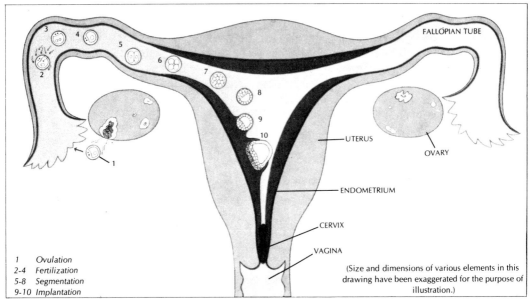

1   Ovulation
2-4   Fertilization
5-8   Segmentation
9-10 Implantation

(Size and dimensions of various elements in this drawing have been exaggerated for the purpose of illustration.)

From ovulation to implantation. (Edwin J. Haeberle, *The Sex Atlas,* © 1978. Reprinted by permission of Seabury Press.)

move down the fallopian tube and become implanted in the uterine wall. Pregnancy begins with implantation.

Signs of pregnancy.   There are a number of physical changes which indicate that a woman is pregnant. Some of the usual signs of pregnancy, however, are also symptoms of various physical disorders. Therefore, self-diagnosis may lead to mistaken judgements, which are less likely to be made by a physician. The physical changes or signs of pregnancy can be categorized in terms of their reliability as presumptive, probable, and positive.

Presumptive signs indicate possible pregnancy, but they are also common indicators of other underlying bodily changes. The first evidence of pregnancy is the cessation of menstruation. However, this is a very uncertain indicator. On one hand, the temporary cessation of menstruation commonly occurs for reasons other than pregnancy; on the other hand vaginal bleeding sometimes occurs in pregnant women because of certain disorders. Another sign is nausea, or "morning sickness," which actually may be experienced anytime during the day. Many women, however, never experience morning sickness. When it does occur, it usually begins about 2 weeks after the first missed menstrual period and lasts no longer than 4 to 6 weeks. A frequent need to urinate is also a presumptive sign of pregnancy. This experience usually occurs between the twelfth and sixteenth weeks following a missed menstrual period. A number of changes in the breasts are also signs of pregnancy. The breasts become slightly enlarged and their veins become more prominent. The nipples and areolae also become enlarged, darker in color, and unusually sensitive to touch. Additional presumptive signs of pregnancy may be frequent fatigue, sudden dizziness, unusual food cravings, and abundant salivation.

Probable signs of pregnancy are much more reliable, but still do not provide conclusive evidence. These indicators usually must be identified by an obstetrician. They include changes in the size of the uterus, softening of the cervix, and the occurrence of uterine contractions. These changes occur between the eighth and twelfth week of pregnancy and can be detected by means of a pelvic examination.

Today, very reliable laboratory techniques are available for diagnosing pregnancy, beginning two weeks after a missed menstrual period. The new pregnancy test is about 95 percent reliable (Pincus et al., 1976). The test can be performed in a matter of a few minutes, so that a woman who is concerned about a possible pregnancy can obtain information the same day as the test. The test determines the presence of a pregnancy hormone called human chorionic gonadotropin (HCG), from a urine sample by means of a chemical reaction. The results of the test are usually double checked by a later physical examination. In addition, home test kits have been developed and are now available in pharmacies. Newer tests are now available which are able to detect pregnancy at an even earlier date. However, these tests rely upon expensive radioimmunoassay equipment and are not yet widely available (Pincus et al., 1976).

Positive signs of pregnancy are those which only occur during pregnancy. They include listening for the fetal heartbeat and detecting fetal movements. A physician, using a stethoscope, may be able to hear the fetal heartbeat by the fourth month of pregnancy. However, new ultrasonic equipment can confirm the presence of a fetus, and its heartbeat, previous to that time.

Bodily changes during pregnancy. A normal pregnancy usually lasts between 240 and 300 days, with the average length being about 266 days, or approximately 9 months. The development of pregnancy is often divided into 3 month periods called the first, second, and third trimesters.

The bodily changes of the first 3 months include those previously described as presumptive signs of pregnancy. During the second 3 months, the weight of a woman's uterus increases about 20 times and enlargement of a woman's abdomen begins to show. Also, during this stage a woman is usually able to feel movements of the fetus. Beginning in the middle of this stage, a yellow fluid called colostrum may flow occasionally out of the nipples. Several other discomforts may also be experienced including: increased sweating, muscle cramps in the legs, indigestion, constipation, nosebleeds, swelling of the body extremities, and high blood pressure. Facial and body pigment may also darken. Medical assistance, careful nutrition, and avoiding the heavy use of tobacco and alcohol is advised.

During the third trimester, a woman's abdomen becomes large and firm, and she may feel increasingly uncomfortable. Movements of the fetus, as it kicks or changes position, may often be seen and felt from the outside. There are also

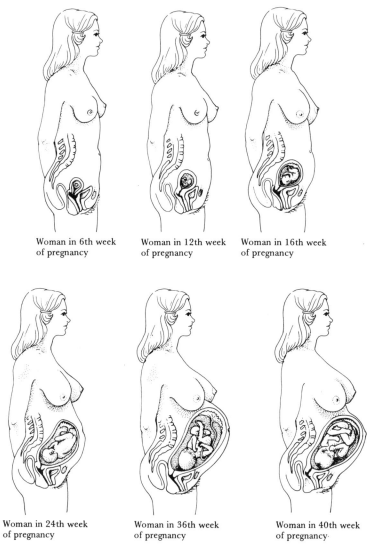

Woman in 6th week
of pregnancy

Woman in 12th week
of pregnancy

Woman in 16th week
of pregnancy

Woman in 24th week
of pregnancy

Woman in 36th week
of pregnancy

Woman in 40th week
of pregnancy·

Development of fetus, by weeks. (David A. Schulz, Stanley F. Rodgers, *Marriage, the Family, and Personal Fulfillment*, © 1975, p. 136.)

occasional painless contractions of the uterus. Several discomforts may be experienced caused by pressure of the enlarged uterus against internal organs. These may include: shortness of breath, a frequent urge to urinate, indigestion, and backaches. Ankle swelling is also a common discomfort. Between 4 to 2 weeks before childbirth, although sometimes earlier, the baby's head settles into a woman's pelvis. This relieves some of the internal pressure against her diaphragm and stomach.

childbirth: labor and delivery

The processes of labor can be divided into three stages: dilatation, expulsion, and placental.

The dilatation stage begins as strong uterine contractions start to occur at intervals of every 10 to 20 minutes. Each contraction lasts about 25 to 30 seconds and usually does not cause much discomfort. These muscular contractions force the cervix to enlarge in diameter in response to the pressure of contents of the uterus pushing against the opening. During this stage a mucous plug is expelled from the cervix, and the membrane of the amniotic sac surrounding the baby may rupture releasing amniotic fluid into the vagina. Often, however, the membrane is very strong and must be punctured artificially. As the dilatation stage progresses, the interval between contractions shortens and the contractions become more intense and often painful.

Just before the expulsion stage, the interval between contractions may be only 2 or 3 minutes. When the cervix has opened wide enough for the passage of the baby, the expulsion stage begins. The dilatation stage is the longest part of labor, and may take anywhere between 2 and 24 hours for completion.

The baby is born during the expulsion stage. It begins as part of the baby's body—usually the head—passes through the enlarged cervix and moves into the vagina. Uterine contractions now occur at 1 to 2 minute intervals and can be aided by the mother's active pushing if she is not anesthetized (Bell et al., 1976). Each contraction pushes the baby further out. The expulsion stage may last anywhere from a half hour or less to two hours or more.

Before the baby begins to emerge from the mother's vagina, most American doctors routinely perform an episiotomy. This is an incision, made by surgical scissors, in the tissue near the entrance to the vagina (the perineum). It is a precautionary measure, designed to prevent jagged tears in this tissue which

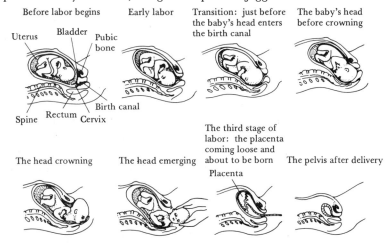

Stages of childbirth. (David A. Schulz, Stanley F. Rodgers, *Marriage, the Family, and Personal Fulfillment*, © 1975, p. 136.)

may be very difficult to repair. The incision is sewn closed immediately after delivery. In the past, many women suffered life-long medical problems caused by childbirth damage to their vaginal tissues. However, advocates of natural childbirth argue that this incision is usually unnecessary if a woman is properly relaxed and coordinated in her pushing movements. There is some good research evidence from other societies to support this argument (Newton, 1975).

The last stage of labor is the delivery of the placenta, which detaches from the wall of the uterus. It is through the placenta and umbilical cord that nutrients were circulated from the mother's body to the baby. This stage may last from only a few minutes to a half hour.

There are many individual variations in the process of labor, as well as certain complications which occasionally occur. It is wise to read about these matters to have more secure feelings about childbirth. Knowledge often reduces unnecessary anxieties and allows a greater appreciation of life.

In recent years, many books and articles have been written about new methods of childbirth. These methods are variously called *natural childbirth, childbirth without pain,* or the *Lamaze method.* Courses are now being offered around the country which train couples in useful skills to help prepare them for the experiences of labor. In one sense, these new methods represent a response to the depersonalization of childbirth brought on by modern hospital practices and are an attempt to return childbirth to the place of an important life event. The skills learned by women often help them to eliminate unnecessary anxieties which intensify pain and impede the normal processes of labor. In addition, the new interest in natural childbirth is partly a response to concerns about the detrimental effects of drugs, such as anesthetics, upon the baby during labor. A large scale government study has found evidence that these pain-killing drugs have long lasting harmful effects upon the linguistic and cognitive abilities of children (*Human Behavior,* 1978).

breastfeeding

In recent years, there has been a revival of a lost art: breastfeeding. One survey found that as of 1974, about 38 percent of American mothers started breast-feeding their babies in the hospital (*Pediatric News,* 1976). Breastfeeding previously had declined from the 1930s, when about 75 percent of mothers breastfed their infants, to the early 1960s when only about 30 percent of mothers used the practice (Hirschman and Sweet, 1974). There are indications that increasing numbers of college educated women have an interest in trying this age-old approach to infant care. Some see it as an expression of new feminism, others as a concern for infant health, and still others as an emotionally rewarding affirmation of the mother-infant relationship.

A careful comparison of the chemistry of human milk with manufactured baby formula finds that there is indeed strong evidence that human milk is usually better for the infant's health (*Consumer Reports,* 1977). Human milk provides many beneficial ingredients which are not available in baby formula. It

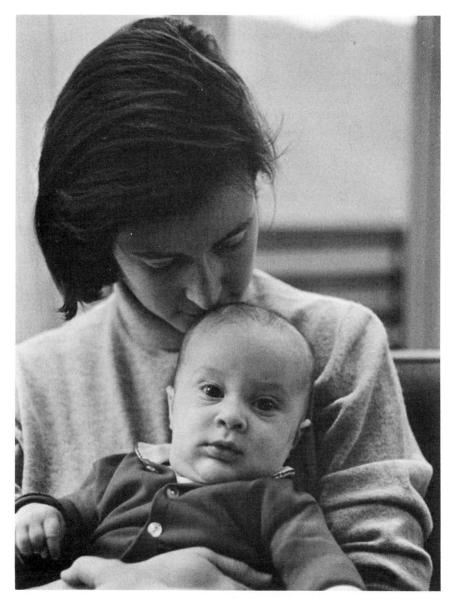

provides several biochemicals which protect the infant against a variety of respiratory and gastrointestinal infections for a period of several months. Some scientists also believe that human milk protects infants against allergies. In addition, breastfeeding does not have a tendency to promote unhealthy infant obesity, as does bottle feeding. The problem of infant obesity is increased when parents mix sugar into baby formula, leading to an early "sweet tooth." (Many scientists believe that infant obesity is a forerunner of adult health problems caused by being overweight.) Recent research also indicates that human milk is particularly suitable for the rapid growth of the infant's brain and nervous system (*Consumer Reports,* 1977).

There are also several benefits of breastfeeding for the mother. Breastfeeding stimulates hormones which cause the uterus and other internal organs to contract more rapidly to their former condition. Mothers can also find deep emotional satisfactions in breastfeeding. Many mothers find emotional pleasure in their ability to offer direct sustenance to the infant. There may even be a hormonal link between this pleasure and sensations of sensual arousal stimulated by breastfeeding (Newton, 1973). Finally, breastfeeding offers several practical advantages to bottle feeding. It is always easily available at the correct temperature and at a cheaper cost. More women are now breastfeeding outside the home than was the situation in the past, so this change may allow for greater mobility.

Breastfeeding, however, does not prevent the possibility of conception by suppressing ovulation, as was traditionally believed. Some women ovulate and do get pregnant again while breastfeeding (Shapiro, 1977). Therefore, if a couple wants to avoid another pregnancy, some form of contraception should be used. Relative to this, it should be noted that many doctors advise against use of the birth control pill while breastfeeding because it may decrease the mother's milk.

There are a variety of problems which can discourage a woman's decision to breastfeed. Many doctors are indifferent to the advantages of breastfeeding and some even jokingly discourage the practice (Brack, 1975). Breastfeeding disrupts the hospital routine. Most American hospitals have no provision for infant feeding on demand rather than on a time schedule. Women usually must make special arrangements with hospital authorities to breastfeed, and nurses may be annoyed by such special requests. In addition, many American women learn attitudes toward breastfeeding which provoke anxieties about the practice. Prudishness about body functions causes many women to regard the practice as "animalistic" or vulgar (Newton, 1973). They worry that they will be embarrassed by the reactions of friends and relatives. In addition, many women hold the false belief that breastfeeding will cause their breasts to sag.

Then, too, there are certain practical advantages of bottle feeding, especially for working women. Bottle feeding can be done by babysitters and husbands. It can also be done in any public place, without fear of embarrassment. (Some breastfeeding mothers gain flexibility by occasionally refrigerating their own milk in bottles for use by babysitters.)

Some women worry that they will be unable to breastfeed their babies. Actually, about 95 percent of women are physically capable of doing so. Anxiety and emotional disturbance inhibit a woman's milk "let down" reflex so a relaxed attitude during breastfeeding is a necessity (Newton, 1973). Detailed information about breastfeeding techniques, breast care, and maternal nutrition can be found in some recent maternity preparation books. Information can also be obtained from a local chapter of La Leche League, an organization whose goal is to encourage breastfeeding.

sexual interaction during pregnancy and after

Many couples have concerns about sexual intercourse during pregnancy. They worry about whether or not sexual activity may harm the fetus, or harm the wife's internal organs, or induce premature labor. In almost all cases, these worries are unnecessary. The available evidence indicates that there is no need to avoid sexual intercourse throughout the period of pregnancy, except in unusual circumstances (Clark and Hale, 1974; Woods, 1975).

There is a great variation in the advice offered by doctors. Some suggest that sexual activity is permissible throughout pregnancy while others suggest a period of abstinence during the last 3 to 6 weeks (Clark and Hale, 1974). Those doctors who recommend a period of abstinence usually cite possible infection, rupture of membranes, or premature labor as their reasons. Actually, such caution is necessary only in rare cases (Clark and Hale, 1974). Sexual abstinence may be appropriate in cases where women have had previous miscarriages, or in cases of uterine bleeding, or when the membranes have already been ruptured (Woods, 1975). Otherwise, there is no need to avoid sexual activity. Worries that orgasmic contractions can induce premature labor in women with normal pregnancies are unnecessary. Cases in which orgasm has set off labor have occurred shortly before the expected termination of pregnancy, anyhow (Masters and Johnson, 1966).

Sexual intercourse can be quite difficult to maneuver using the male-above position during the last several months of pregnancy. At that time, side-to-side positions are more convenient, especially where the man lies behind the woman. When a couple wants to avoid sexual intercourse, they can employ manual and oral caressing to orgasm.

Changes in sexual desire, response, and activity over the course of pregnancy have been the object of several research studies (Masters and Johnson, 1966; Solberg et al., 1973; Kenny, 1973; Morris, 1975; Tolor and Di Grazia, 1976). Most of these studies have found only a gradual decline in the level of a woman's sexual desire and activity, during the first two trimesters of pregnancy. Then, during the last trimester, a rapid decrease in sexual desire and activity occurs for most women. However, there are wide individual variations. Much may depend upon a woman's previous level of sexual interest, the extent of her physical discomforts, a woman's attitude toward her appearance during pregnancy, and a couple's affection for each other.

Another matter of concern for couples is the question of when sexual intercourse can safely be resumed after childbirth. Here again, doctors offer varied advice (Clark and Hale, 1974). Some doctors continue to offer the traditional advice of abstaining from sexual intercourse for six weeks. Others recommend waiting only until the episiotomy incision heals, which takes about two or three weeks. The primary considerations include the possibility of causing infection or damage to healing tissue in the uterus and episiotomy incision.

The return of sexual desire is more rapid in some women and slower in others. Women who breastfeed their infants usually experience a more rapid return of sexual desire (Masters and Johnson, 1966; Kenny, 1973). This may be because breastfeeding stimulates sensual, and even erotic, feelings in many women. Sexual desire may also return more rapidly to women who had a previously high interest in sexual activity. Many women experience a decrease in vaginal lubrication during a period of time after childbirth, making intercourse difficult. This can be corrected by use of a water soluable lubricant sold in pharmacies.

CONTRACEPTION

current contraceptive practice in the United States

Some form of contraception is used today by the vast majority of American married couples. A United States Department of Health survey found that as of 1976, only about 7 percent of white married couples and 14 percent of black couples, with women of childbearing age, were not using any form of contraception to avoid unwanted pregnancy (Ford, 1978). More important, the methods of contraception employed were overwhelmingly those which are most effective. In addition, contraceptive behavior is no longer different between major religious groups. The research also revealed that nearly the same percentage of Catholics and nonCatholics employ effective contraception (Westoff and Jones, 1977b). Birth control and family planning are now solidly rooted practices in the American lifestyle.

Effective contraceptive practice is one of the factors which accounts for the unprecedented decline of the American birth rate since the early 1960s. An increasing percentage of couples are choosing to remain childless or are postponing childbearing beyond their twenties. As of 1975, about 32 percent of married women under the age of 30 were childless compared with only 20 percent in 1960 (Silka and Kiesler, 1977). This is a rather dramatic social change.

There is an increasing difference in contraceptive practice between couples who desire no more children and those who may desire to have more children (Westoff and Jones, 1977a). The birth control pill is the contraceptive measure most commonly employed by couples who might want more children. However, as of 1975, sterilization had become the most common contraceptive measure among married couples who no longer desired more children. By that date, nearly half of all couples who had been married between 10 and 24 years were surgically sterilized. This is another indication of the American acceptance of family planning. It is a remarkable historical change when one considers that only three generations ago the distribution of birth control information was illegal in many states, and authors of birth control books were being arrested for publishing ''obscene literature.''

The objective of this section is to present an outline of the major advantages and disadvantages of different contraceptive methods. Detailed instruc-

METHOD	Combination Pill	Progestin-Only Pill	Intrauterine Device (IUD)	Diaphragm with Spermicidal Jelly or Cream	Condom
COST	Fee for office or clinic visit About $2 to $3.50 a month, by prescription Fee for annual checkup	Fee for office or clinic visit About $2 a month, by prescription	Fee for office or clinic visit $3 to $20 depending on device used Fee for annual checkup	Fee for office or clinic visit $3–$7.50 for diaphragm About $2 a month for spermicidal agent with average use	25¢ to $1 or more
EFFECTIVENESS (Expected pregnancies per 100 women annually)	Method failures: less than 1 User failures: 2 to 4	Method failures: 1 to 2 User failures: 2 to 4	Method failures 2 to 4 User failures: 5 to 10	Method failures: 2 to 4 User failures: 10 to 20	Method failures: 2 to 4 User failures: 10 to 20
PROCEDURE	Usually taken from first to 21st day of menstrual cycle, then 7 days off. Some brands of Pill are to be taken every day, reducing chance of skipping a pill	Pills are taken daily	Inserted into uterus. New types containing copper have to be replaced every two years. Hormone-containing devices are to be replaced each year.	Inserted several hours or just before intercourse. (Add additional spermicide before subsequent acts of intercourse.) Must be left in place for at least 6 hours after each use.	Rolled on before intercourse. Care should be taken that condom does not slip off before or after ejaculation.
REASONS TO AVOID (Ask your physician for complete list)	Not for women over 40. Not for women of any age with a history of cancer of reproductive system; thrombophlebitis (clots); serious liver disease (hepatitis	Nearly all of the side effects associated with the Combination Pill are linked to estrogen. While the "Mini Pill" contains no estrogen, it is suspected that	Not for women with pelvic infection (acute, chronic, or recurring); undiagnosed genital bleeding; cervicitis (inflammation of cervix); gynecologic malig-	Not for women not highly motivated to use diaphragm correctly before intercourse	Not for men not highly motivated to use condom correctly for each act of intercourse.

METHOD	Combination Pill	Progestin-Only Pill	Intrauterine Device (IUD)	Diaphragm with Spermicidal Jelly or Cream	Condom
REASONS TO AVOID (cont'd.)	and jaundice); heart disease; abnormal vaginal bleeding. May be contraindicated for women with varicose veins; diabetes; serious migraine-like headaches, and high blood pressure	progestin can be converted to estrogen within the body. Therefore, the contraindications may be the same as for the Combination Pill.	nancy; excessively heavy periods; anemia; fibroid tumors; heart disease. Be certain you are not pregnant before having device inserted. Copper devices not for women with known or suspected allergy to copper.		
COMMON EARLY SIDE EFFECTS (Ask your physician for complete list)	Nausea Breast tenderness Bloating Weight gain Irregular spotting or bleeding Headaches Depression	Bleeding irregularities (more common than with Combination Pill), from excessive bleeding to absence of menstruation Weight gain	Heavy periods Bleeding between periods Cramping pain (if excessive, device must be removed	Allergic reaction to spermicide or rubber in rare instances	Local irritation in rare instances
GENERAL HEALTH RISK	Abnormal sugar metabolism Changes in blood chemistry High blood pressure Change in libido Cystitis	General risk factors may be the same as those of the Combination Pill	2 to 20 percent expulsion rate (if unnoticed, pregnancy may result)	None known	None

RARE BUT POTENTIALLY SERIOUS SIDE EFFECTS	Thrombo-embolic disorders including strokes and blood clots in legs or lungs. Heart attacks among women over 35. Liver tumors. Report to physician immediately any unusual signs or symptoms, such as blurring of vision, migraine-like headaches, chest, leg, or abdominal pain, skin rash, pronounced emotional changes	Nearly all of the side effects associated with the "mini Pill" may be the same as those of the Combination Pill, but may occur less frequently. Risk of ectopic (tubal) pregnancy	Perforation of uterus. Severe pelvic inflammatory disease (infection). If pregnancy occurs, septic abortion (miscarriage) complicated by infection. Ectopic (tubal) pregnancy. See doctor immediately if you suspect you're pregnant, have severe pain, abdominal tenderness, suspicious discharge, or irregular bleeding. Device may have to be removed.	None known	None
SAFEGUARDS	If more than one Pill is missed, use another method as backup while continuing daily Pill use to end of cycle	If more than one Pill is missed, use another method as backup while continuing daily Pill use to end of cycle	At least once a month preferably after period, check to make sure device hasn't been expelled.	Check diaphragm regularly for holes or tears. You may require a different size if you have lost or gained more than 10 pounds, had a baby, miscarriage, abortion, or undergone a gynecological operation.	Use fresh one for each act of intercourse. Use contraceptive foam, for added protection if desired.

METHOD	Chemical Contraceptives (Foams, jellies, suppositories, tablets)	Rhythm (Calendar)	Rhythm (Temperature)	Tubal Ligation (Female)	Vasectomy (Male)
COST	About $2 to $3 or 20 applications	Special chart or calendar available at no cost from local Planned Parenthood clinics and from some doctors as well as from certain religious organizations	Cost of thermometer to record body temperature	$250 to $500 doctor's fee. If in hospital, add cost of stay. Cost of sterilization procedures often covered completely or in part by health insurance	$50 to $150 for doctor's fee (clinic rates may be lower)
*EFFECTIVENESS (Expected pregnancies per 100 women annually)	(Aerosol foam has the lowest pregnancy rate of chemical contraceptives) Method failures: 2 to 4 User failures: 10 to 20	Varies widely Method failures: 5 to 10.	Varies widely (more effective than calendar method) Method failures: 5 to 10. User failures: 20 to 30	Method failures: Less than 1 User failures: None	Method failures: Less than 1 User failures: None
PROCEDURE	Must be applied no more than 1 hour before intercourse. (It may take up to 10 minutes before suppositories and tablets are effective.) All must be re-applied before each act of intercourse.	A woman keeps a record of the date each menstrual flow starts and the length of time between periods. Using the number of days in the longest and shortest cycles, a woman can calculate the first and the last dates she's likely to be fertile within her subsequent menstrual cycle	A woman takes her temperature each morning before getting out of bed. A rather small but sharp rise occurs when the egg is released. After three days at the higher level, the unsafe period is past	Fallopian tubes are tied off or cut	Vas deferens (sperm-carrying ducts) tied or cut

REASONS TO AVOID (Ask your physician for complete list)	Not for women to whom pregnancy or abortion is unacceptable	Not for women for whom pregnancy or abortion is unacceptable. Not for women to whom sexual abstinence for certain number of days is undesirable	Not for women for whom pregnancy or abortion is unacceptable. Not for women to whom sexual abstinence for certain number of days is undersirable.	Not for women for who are unsure if they want children later.	Not for the couple who are unsure if they want children later.
COMMON EARLY SIDE EFFECTS (Ask your physician for complete list)	Allergic reaction in rare instances	None	None	Some soreness and pain for a few days after operation	Some soreness and pain for a few days after operation
GENERAL HEALTH RISKS	None known		None	Same risks as those associated with any surgery (bleeding, swelling, or infection)	
RARE BUT POTENTIALLY SERIOUS SIDE EFFECTS	None known	None	None	Women risk more serious although rare complications than men do.	Very slight risk of serious bleeding or infection
SAFEGUARDS	Always apply before each act of intercourse	Effectiveness of all rhythm methods is improved by always using at least two methods and by carrying out under the supervision of a physician or trained medical personnel		None required	Medical checkup after procedure to make sure that sterilization was achieved. Some contraceptives method must be used after vasectomy until it has been shown by lab tests that semen no longer contains sperm.

* Method failure means a pregnancy resulting from failure of the contraception itself (Pill, diaphragm, IUD, rhythm method, or whatever). User failure means a pregnancy resulting from failure of the couple to use the method or device properly.

Adapted from Judith Ramsey, "A Modern Guide to Birth Control," *Family Circle Magazine*, Nov. 1976, pp. 35-36. Reprinted with permission.

tions for using these contraceptive measures can be found elsewhere (Sanford and Perkins et al., 1976; Shapiro, 1977).

There are many factors that a couple may want to take into consideration when deciding which contraceptive method would be best for them to choose. No single method of contraception is best for everyone in all situations. The following chart provides a convenient reference for comparing the major contraceptives methods.

birth control pills

The most commonly used contraceptive method, as of 1976, was the birth control pill (Ford, 1978). In that year, about 22 percent of married, white and black women were using "the pill" to avoid conception. The birth control pills are also used by about one-third of unmarried teenage women, who have sexual intercourse (Zelnik and Kanter, 1977).

There are now two types of birth control pills: the combination pill and the "mini-pill." The combination pill contains a combination of the hormones estrogen and progesterone. It works essentially by chemically inhibiting the development of egg cells in the ovary. In addition, the progesterone makes the lining of the uterus inhospitable to the implantation of possibly fertilized eggs (Shapiro, 1977). The mini-pill contains only the hormone progesterone.

Birth control pills must be obtained by a doctor's prescription. A woman should first have a thorough medical examination because birth control pills are inadvisable and even dangerous for some women with special health problems (Sanford and Perkins et al., 1976). In addition, it is necessary for a doctor to make a careful medical judgement about which of the many chemically different pills is most appropriate for an individual woman (Shapiro, 1977). Obtaining birth control pills without having a thorough medical examination is unwise and can expose a woman to possible serious health hazards. Many doctors will not prescribe the pills for unmarried teenagers, possibly owing to moralistic considerations. As far as is known, however, birth control pills do not expose teenage women to any special health risks once they have begun menstruation (Shapiro, 1977).

Advantages. Birth control pills are the most effective means of preventing pregnancy. Although other methods can be nearly as effective when carefully employed, in actual practice, the ease and convenience of the pills add to their efficiency. They do not interfere with the spontaneity of sexual activity. Birth control pills also offer some women the added advantage of regularizing their menstrual cycles, reducing menstrual cramps, relieving premenstrual tension, and stimulating breast development (Sanford and Perkins et al., 1976).

Disadvantages. Birth control pills have not proven to be the universal solution to the problems of contraception, as was originally hoped.

Discomforting side effects of the pill occur to some women. They include possible nausea, breast tenderness, weight gain, irregular vaginal bleeding, and headaches (Sanford and Perkins et al., 1976). These discomforts are usually only temporary and often can be eliminated by switching to another brand of pills having a slightly different chemical balance (Shapiro, 1977). Depression is another possible problem. It is not clear whether depression is a consequence of psychological factors, such as anxiety or guilt, or whether it is due to the chemical effects of the pills on the nervous systems of some women (Glick and Bennett, 1972). Some biochemical research indicates that the pills interfere with vitamin B_6 metabolism in the nervous systems of some women, and that depression can be relieved by taking supplements of this vitamin (Shapiro, 1977). The experience of depression very often results in a loss of sexual desire. There has been a considerable amount of research on the effects which birth control pills might have upon a woman's level of sexual desire. Many of the findings are contradictory, but it appears that the pills are associated with decreased sexual desire only among a small proportion of users while there occurs either no change or increased sexual desire in most women (Bragonier, 1976).

The pill may have dangerous side effects. The most well-documented of these serious health risks is the possibility of blood clots forming in various parts of the body including the legs, eyes, lungs, brain, or heart (Shapiro, 1977). When blood clots block blood circulation to vital organs, the effects can cause severe pain, loss of body functions, or even death. The risk of dangerous blood clots for pill-using women increases significantly for women over age 30 who smoke (Tietze, 1977). Dangerous blood clots are much less likely to occur to such women who do not smoke. When the health risks of the birth control pills are compared with those of pregnancy and childbirth, however, the risk to life through childbearing is significantly greater than those of using pills, except for women over age 40 who smoke (Tietze, 1977c). Women who have had a history of abnormal blood clotting should not use the birth control pills.

Another disadvantage is psychological. Many women worry about the long range harm that the pills might have upon their bodies. In the light of recent findings about the dangerous long-range effects of a wide variety of chemicals, these worries are not unreasonable. Such worry causes anxiety, which itself can have discomforting effects upon the body (for example, depression, headaches, constant tension, muscular cramps, sleeplessness). Women who have such worries but still prefer the pill's advantages should read about them in detail and should then make a judgment on the basis of that knowledge (Shapiro, 1977). If currently unknown long range effects are a concern, a woman would be wise to avoid using birth control pills for more than ten years and to switch permanently to another method of birth control.

It is really very difficult to know if the health risks from the birth control pills have been minimized or exaggerated. Two recent studies have found that deaths to women from cardiovascular diseases have actually declined in 21 countries, since the introduction of the birth control pills, which would not have been the case if the pills increased women's risks to these diseases (Tietze, 1979; Belsey et al., 1979).

intrauterine device

According to the most recent survey, the intrauterine device, or IUD, was used by about 6 percent of white and black, married women in 1976 (Ford, 1978). It is also used by about 2 percent of unmarried teenage women, who have sexual intercourse (Zelnik and Kanter, 1977). The IUD consists of a small structure, usually made of plastic, which is inserted into a woman's uterus. It must be inserted by a doctor after a thorough physical examination.

There is no clear understanding of precisely how the IUD works to prevent pregnancy, but it is nevertheless very effective. It does not seem to prevent normal ovulation or fertilization. Instead, its presence in the uterus somehow prevents the egg from implanting itself in the wall of the uterus (Sanford and Perkins et al., 1976). New types of intrauterine devices have added copper or progesterone to aid contraceptive effectiveness (Shapiro, 1977).

Advantages. The IUD is a highly effective means of contraception. A woman does not have to remember to take certain actions each day, as she does with birth control pills. Yet, like the pills, an IUD doesn't interfere with the spontaneity of sexual interaction.

Disadvantages. Insertion of an IUD is often painful, although this is not always the case (Shapiro, 1977). After insertion of an IUD, during a period of 3 to 6 months some women experience severe abdominal pains and cramping, heavy bleeding during menstruation, and irregular menstrual cycles (Sanford and Perkins et al., 1976). These problems continue for a longer time among a small proportion of women. It is estimated that the IUD must be removed from 5 percent to 20 percent of women because of these discomforts (Sanford and Perkins et al., 1976). When undetected explusion occurs, it can result in an unplanned pregnancy. In addition, the problem of explusion is repeated in a majority of those women to whom it occurs, making replacement inadvisable (Shapiro, 1977). The problem of explusion is more common among women who have never been pregnant.

In rare cases, there are more severe complications. Some women with certain health problems should not use an IUD (see chart). In addition, serious infections can result when a woman's uterus is perforated by an IUD; perforation is almost always caused by a doctor's faulty insertion (Shapiro, 1977). This is estimated to occur in 1 out of every 1,000 women who use the IUD. Infections in a woman's reproductive tract, caused by using an IUD also occur for reasons other than perforation. It is estimated that such infections occur among 2 percent or 3 percent of women (Shapiro, 1977). These infections can have very severe consequences. However, when infections are detected early, they can be cured through the use of antibiotics. Recent research has also found that

Diaphragm insertion. (David A. Schulz, *Human Sexuality*, p. 106.)

dangerous ectopic pregnancies (occurring in the fallopian tube), although rare, are more common among women who use the IUD than among those who do not (Shapiro, 1977). Some doctors believe that these ectopic pregnancies are caused by infections which block the fallopian tubes.

An additional disadvantage of some of the new types of IUDs is that they must be replaced every year (hormone type) or every two years (copper type).

diaphragm

The diaphragm was used by only about 3 percent of white, and 2 percent of black married women in 1976 (Ford, 1978). Since that time there have been many journalistic reports that more married women are turning to the diaphragm as a contraceptive method, especially among those who have used birth control pills for many years. However, the diaphragm is used by less than one percent of unmarried teenage women, who have sexual intercourse (Zelnik and Kanter, 1977).

A diaphragm is a dome-shaped structure made of soft rubber and having a firm, flexible rim around it. It is fitted over the cervix and held in place behind the pelvic bone. It must, however, be used with spermicidal jelly or cream to be effective. The spermicide is what primarily serves to prevent conception, rather than the fact that it is a barrier against sperm entering the uterus. Diaphragms are available in various sizes and must be obtained by prescription from a doctor after a careful gynecological examination. The doctor should instruct a woman in the procedure for inserting her diaphragm. After some practice, a woman can usually insert the diaphragm properly in a matter of a few seconds. Insertion of the diaphragm must be done at least two hours or less before intercourse takes place. After intercourse, it must be kept in place at least six hours for spermicidal action to be effective.

Advantages. One of the main advantages of the diaphragm is that it doesn't have any discomforting or harmful side effects that can occur to some users. (The only exception is that in rare instances, women have an allergic reaction to the rubber or spermicide.) It is also a highly effective means of contraception when it is inserted properly with a spermicide. It is a particularly good method of contraception for women having a regular sex partner and a comfortable pattern of sexual interaction.

Disadvantages. The effectiveness of the diaphragm is sharply decreased by its improper use, especially among women who have some reason to be reluctant to use it. Some women feel that it interferes with the spontaneity of sexual interaction when it is inserted just before sexual activity. Some women often have unanticipated sexual activity, and don't like to plan ahead for it; or they may have an uncooperative and impatient sex partner. Other women don't like to have to touch their genitals, and may insert the diaphragm improperly.

Another inconvenience is that a diaphragm must be refitted when a woman's vagina changes shape. Therefore, it must be refitted after a woman gives birth or after a woman's first sexual experience. In addition, if a woman gains or loses more than 10 pounds, the diaphragm may need to be refitted. A diaphragm must also be changed at least once every year because the rubber may deteriorate with wear. In addition, a diaphragm may be perforated during insertion or removal by sharp fingernails. Inattention to any of these considerations increases the risk of pregnancy.

There are reports that in rare instances, a diaphragm may become accidentally dislodged during sexual activity, resulting in unanticipated pregnancy (Shapiro, 1977).

condom

In 1976, about 7 percent of white, and 5 percent of black married couples relied upon the condom as their method of contraception (Ford, 1978). The proportion of married couples who rely upon the condom has been decreasing rapidly, since the early 1960s. Use of the condom is also decreasing among unmarried teenagers and a twelve percent of teenage couples now employ it (Zelnik and Kanter, 1977).

A condom is a sheath, composed of latex rubber or animal membrane, which fits over the erect penis. It prevents sperm from being ejaculated into a woman's vagina. The effectiveness of the condom can be increased if it is used along with a spermicidal foam or jelly. Condoms are made in one standard size and are easily available from drugstores.

Advantages. One of the main advantages of the condom is that it can be used by men, unlike all other contraceptive measures except sterilization. In addition, it has no discomforting or harmful side effects. It is easily available to use by men who encounter situations of unanticipated sexual activity. Another advantage is that it prevents the spread of some veneral diseases. The condom can be a highly effective means of contraception, if it is used properly and in conjunction with a spermicide.

Disadvantages. Many men, and some women, feel that the condom dulls erotic sensations and interferes with manual and oral-genital sexual activity. As with the diaphragm, some couples regard the use of the condom as something which interferes with the spontaneity of sexual activity. Finally, pregnancy rates are reasonably high with the condom, because of improper use. It may slip off easily if the penis is kept in the vagina after penile detumescence.

spermicidal chemicals

Spermicidal chemicals are more effective when used along with a diaphragm or condom. However, they are used by some couples without the added protection. In 1976, about 3 percent of white, and 4 percent of black married couples relied upon a spermicidal foam as their method of contraception (Ford, 1978). An even lower percent of unmarried teenage couples use this method (Zelnik and Kanter, 1977).

Spermicides work mainly by immobilizing and killing sperm cells. Spermicidal chemicals are inserted into the vagina shortly before sexual intercourse. They are available in the form of suppositories, jellies, creams, and aerosol foams. The foam is considered to be the most effective form of spermicide used without a diaphragm or condom. They are all available without prescription at drugstores.

Advantages. Spermicidal chemicals are easily available. They also have no discomforting or harmful side effects, except in rare cases when people are allergic to the chemicals.

Disadvantages. Spermicidal chemicals are only a moderately effective means of contraception when they are used alone. In actual practice, according to some studies, failure rates are very high (Shapiro, 1977). Some people also feel that they are messy. In addition, some people feel that they interfere with the spontaneity of sexual activity.

rhythm

The rhythm method of contraception, or "natural family planning" as it is sometimes called, relies upon sexual abstinence during a period of time when a woman is most likely to get pregnant. Since the early 1960s, fewer and fewer married couples have chosen to rely upon this method. In 1976, only about 4 percent white and one percent of black married women were using rhythm as their method of contraception (Ford, 1978). Catholic couples were only a bit more likely to rely upon that method, with about 6 percent of Catholics employing it compared with about 2 percent of nonCatholics (Westoff and Jones, 1977b). Among unmarried teenagers, a higher percent of women report that they rely upon this method for contraception (Zelnik and Kanter, 1977). Those who report using rhythm may actually be using no method.

Women using the rhythm method employ certain procedures for estimating the time of ovulation during the menstrual cycle. The procedures for doing so are noted on the chart and explained in greater detail elsewhere. To avoid conception, a couple must avoid sexual intercourse during a period of five days before and five days after the woman's estimated time of ovulation. The actual period of fertility—when conception may occur—is shorter, or about six days. The additional days of sexual abstinence are a safeguard against variations in the time of ovulation. An attempt to rely upon an hypothetical standard of calculating ovulation at 14 days after the end of menstruation is useful for only about 8 percent of women; and even these women experience occasional variations in their time of ovulation (Shapiro, 1977). Such rough estimations have resulted in many unplanned pregnancies.

Advantages. The rhythm method has no side effects that are harmful or discomforting, unless sexual abstinence is counted as one. Actually, a couple can easily engage in manual and oral-genital sexual activity to orgasm while avoiding sexual intercourse during the fertile period. (They must, however, be careful that no semen has contact with even the external tissues of the female genitals since the semen can travel into the vaginal canal.) In addition, it offers an advantage for those Catholics (or members of other religious groups which restrict birth control) who want to conform strictly with the moral guidelines of their church regarding methods of family planning. This is the only method which, so far, meets the moral guidelines of Catholicism.

Disadvantages. The major disadvantage of the rhythm method is its high rate of failure in actual practice. It is rendered ineffective when a woman has an uncooperative sexual partner or when the couple does not strictly maintain the practice. This method also demands constant attention and checking to estimate the time of ovulation. Many couples simply cannot rely upon it because some women have highly irregular menstrual cycles. Some experiences, such as an illness, can cause variations in the time of ovulation and render calculations nearly impossible.

In addition, many couples feel that the rhythm method interferes with spontaneity of sexual activity. Those couples who practice strict sexual abstinence during ten days around the fertile period and then again during menstruation may find very limited time available for sexual activity because of the routine distractions of everyday life on ''safe'' days. Finally, reliance upon the rhythm method can cause anxiety caused by worries about whether or not it might result in an unplanned pregnancy.

ineffective attempts at contraception

In this review of contraception methods, two other techniques ought to be mentioned: withdrawal and douching. These methods are much more likely to be used by unmarried individuals, than by married couples (Zelnick and Kanter, 1977). Among white and black married couples in 1976, withdrawal was used by only 2 percent of couples. Douching was used by less than ½ of a percent of white couples, and 3 percent of black couples (Ford, 1978). However, among unmarried couples, the use of these methods is much more common. About 11 percent of unmarried teenagers rely upon withdrawal and about 2 percent rely upon a douche (Zelnik and Kanter, 1977). The tragedy is that these attempts at contraception are not likely to be very effective.

The withdrawal method is probably the one most commonly used worldwide, especially in societies where technological means of contraception are unavailable or too costly. In the withdrawal method, the man withdraws his penis from the woman's vagina just before ejaculation. It is often ineffective because it demands careful coordination of the couple and considerable self-control from the man. The failure rate is high because a man is sometimes unable to withdraw in time. In addition, the ejaculation of even a small amount of semen on the external labia can result in accidental impregnation. However, the belief that pre-ejaculatory fluid carries enough sperm to cause impregnation is now discounted by some researchers (Shapiro, 1977). Many couples find this method anxiety-provoking, sexually frustrating, and messy. There is also some evidence that frequent use of withdrawal can lead to the sexual dysfunctions of premature ejaculation in men and inorgasmic response in women (Masters and Johnson, 1970).

Douching is simply not effective at all. In this procedure, a woman washes out her vagina with soap and water or some solution immediately after having sexual intercourse. The procedure is ineffective, because sperm can enter a woman's uterus only a few seconds after ejaculation (Shapiro, 1977).

sterilization

Next to the birth control pill, sterilization was the most common method used by Americans to prevent conception in 1976. In that year, about 20 percent of white, and 13 percent of black married couples had undergone sterilization for contraceptive purposes (Ford, 1978). Sterilization was almost equally balanced between white women and men, with about 10 percent of wives and 10 percent of husbands having been sterilized. However, among black couples, it was mainly the wives who had been surgically sterilized; 11 percent of women versus 2 percent of men.

The term sterilization refers to any surgical procedure designed to terminate a person's ability to cause conception. There are a wide variety of surgical procedures which may be used to sterilize men or women. However, those which are most commonly used for contraceptive purposes include vasectomy in men and tubal sterilization in women. These procedures are almost always irreversible today, although techniques are being developed to permit reversibility. Some cases of successful reversal surgery have already been carried out (Shapiro, 1977). At any rate, the vast majority of men and women who undergo sterilization no longer desire any children and cases of change of mind are rare. Sterilization, through vasectomy and tubal sterilization, does not interfere with sexual desire. Actually, the available research indicates that sterilization often results in enhanced sexual desire because of the alleviation of worries about unplanned pregnancy (Landis and Poffenberger, 1965; Maschhoff et al., 1976; Shapiro, 1977). Sterilization is almost 100 percent effective in preventing conception, the rare exceptions being the result of surgical errors.

Tubal sterilization. Tubal sterilization is a general term used to refer to procedures designed to seal off a woman's fallopian tubes by tying them, cutting out a piece, or fusing them by heat. Tubal ligation has been the most common of these procedures in the past. It involves tying and usually also removing a piece of each fallopian tube. The surgery can be done either through an abdominal incision, or through an incision at the roof of the vagina (Shapiro, 1977). More recently, new techniques have been developed for tubal sterilization which involve fusing the fallopian tubes with heat, using a small instrument inserted through an incision. These techniques, called endoscopic techniques, can be carried out on a patient using only a local anesthetic and usually involve hospitalization of less than one day (Shapiro, 1977).

Advantages. The major advantage of tubal sterilization for women is that it is almost 100 percent effective as a contraceptive measure and requires no further action to be taken. It does not interfere with the spontaneity of sexual activity and requires no use of contraceptive devices or chemicals. Tubal sterilization also does not interfere with female hormone production or with the menstrual cycle.

Disadvantages. Some women cannot undergo surgery for tubal sterilization because of certain health conditions (Shapiro, 1977). A more serious concern is that of complications of surgery. There are possible dangers of infection, internal blood clotting which may obstruct vital organs, as well as hazardous surgical errors. While these complications are expected to be quite infrequent, some studies have reported them to be more common than should be expected (Shapiro, 1977). In addition, about 10 percent of women who undergo tubal sterilization experience irregular vaginal bleeding for a period of time (Shapiro, 1977). Finally, this method is not appropriate for couples who might desire more children.

Vasectomy.   In comparison with tubal sterilization, vasectomy is a very simple and safe operation. Vasectomy involves the blocking or cutting of both sperm ducts (or vas deferens) which carry sperm from a man's testicles. In the most common procedure, one or two small incisions are made in the sides of the scrotum. The doctor then removes a piece of each sperm duct, and ties off the remaining ends to block sperm transportation. The operation is carried out with a local anesthetic, and requires only about 20 minutes to complete. The operation does not require hospitalization and surgical complications are very rare. Sexual intercourse may be resumed about a week after a vasectomy. The amount of ejaculate that vasectomized men produce is reduced only by about 10 percent, which is that portion composed of sperm cells (Shapiro, 1977). In addition, a man's capacity to attain erection remains unchanged.

Advantages.   The advantages of vasectomy are the same as those for tubal sterilization in women. In addition, vasectomy does not expose a man to the risks of major surgery and complications are much more rare.

Disadvantages.   This method is not appropriate for couples who might desire more children.

THE SOCIAL PSYCHOLOGY OF PREMARITAL CONTRACEPTION

premarital contraceptive practice

In the early 1970s, the practice of effective contraception increased substantially among sexually active teenagers. A national interview survey of 15 to 19 year old women investigated contraceptive practice, among those who had sexual intercourse (Zelnik and Kanter, 1977). It found that some contraceptive measure was used, during their last occasion of sexual intercourse, by 63 percent of the women in 1976. Yet, the same study also found that 30 percent of sexually active teenage women experience a premarital pregnancy (Zelnik and Kanter, 1978a).

The potential for unwanted pregnancy is put in perspective by the finding that between 1971 and 1976, the percentage of sexually active teenage women who never used any contraception increased (Zelnik and Kanter, 1977). In 1976, the percentage of teenage women who reported that they "never" used any form of contraception during occasions of sexual intercourse was about 30 percent (Zelnik and Kanter, 1978b). The nonuse of contraception is particularly common when young people first begin having sexual intercourse. The survey found that 60 percent of the women who had sexual intercourse did not employ any contraceptive measure during their first experience (Zelnik and Kanter, 1978b). The situation among college students is remarkably similar (Fox, 1977).

cognitive factors in contraceptive practice

It is widely believed that the basic reasons for the lack of effective contraceptive practice, among the unmarried are: (1) inadequate contraceptive education, and (2) difficulties in the availability of contraceptives. Following this line of reasoning, the solution to the problem of premarital pregnancy is to be found by increasing adequate sex education and contraceptive accessibility (Furstenburg, et al., 1969). Unfortunately, the research on contraceptive behavior indicates that the psychology of contraception among unmarried young people is influenced by more than information and opportunity. Even though premarital sexual intercourse is widely approved among unmarried young people, it occurs within a social context of public and parental disapproval. Consequently, premarital contraception cannot be fully understood by simple analogy with marital contraceptive practice.

The communication of birth control information to teenagers may be impeded by their level of cognitive development. Several studies of sexually active teenagers have found that many of them do not comprehend the probabilities of getting pregnant, because of egocentric patterns of thinking (Kanter and Zelnik, 1973; Cvetkovich, et al. 1975). Many teenagers incorrectly believe that if they have sexual intercourse infrequently, their chances of getting pregnant are reduced. In reality, of course, the chances of getting pregnant are considerably higher during infrequent intercourse without contraception, than during frequent intercourse with effective contraception.

Indeed, it is quite likely that teenage girls who have only infrequent sexual intercourse are particularly likely to get pregnant. Teenage girls, who have frequent intercourse are much more likely to practice effective contraception than are girls who have only infrequent intercourse (Kanter and Zelnik, 1973). The complaint that, "I only did it a few times," is a common one among premaritally pregnant teenagers. A belief in the lowered risks of infrequent intercourse may also reflect a certain kind of moralistic thinking, which excuses infrequent offenses as being less damnable than frequent ones.

Many unmarried women who have sexual intercourse do so with great reluctance, because of guilt feelings, manipulation, feelings of powerlessness, or ambivalent desires to please their partner. Such feelings promote apathy about contraception. In contrast, some research has found that girls who are more highly motivated to pursue sexual activity tend to be more concerned about the use of contraception (Lindemann, 1974).

Similar findings come from a research project which compared a sample of college women who came to a university contraception clinic with a sample of college women who had never sought contraceptive materials (Reiss, et al., 1975). The contraception group of college women were significantly more self-assured and sexually assertive. Another study of sexually active college women compared women who used some form of contraception (mainly the pill) with women who either never employed contraception or relied upon their male partner to do so (Fox, 1977). The research found that the contraceptive using women were significantly more likely to hold more assertive attitudes and greater feelings of personal control over their own fate.

Personally and sexually assertive women are not timid or ambivalent about the use of contraception. They are likely to seek out information about effective contraception; to find ways of obtaining female contraceptive materials; to initiate discussion about contraception with their sexual partners; and to prepare consistently for the use of contraception, before occasions of possible sexual activity. Few women, even those who are assertive, employ effective contraception during their first experience of sexual intercourse (Fox, 1977). However, once assertive women begin having intercourse, they quickly take responsibility for preventing an unwanted pregnancy.

Finally, some important research has investigated the psychological relationship between sex anxiety and attitudes towards contraception (Byrne, 1977). The research indicates that people with high sex anxiety are less likely: (1) to plan ahead for sexual activity; (2) to communicate with their sexual partners about contraception; and (3) to use contraceptive measures which require them to touch their genitals. In essence, people with high sex anxiety may prefer the appearance of spontaneity in sexual activity in order to excuse themselves of the responsibility for their sexual behavior. Spontaneity is used much like alcohol, as an excuse for behavior which people consider immoral but practice anyhow.

In summary, unmarried women, who are most likely to practice contraception during sexual intercourse: (1) can fully understand the risks of getting pregnant; (2) are personally and sexually assertive, and willing to take responsibility for contraception; and (3) experience low anxiety, about sexual matters.

interpersonal factors in contraceptive practice

The factors which facilitate or inhibit the use of contraception among sexually active young people are not only cognitive ones. In addition, there are certain important factors in the relationship between sexual partners which affect their use of contraception.

It is quite likely that contraception between unmarried people is often neglected because many women expect men to take care of it, and many men expect women to take care of it. Consequently, in many cases, no one takes care of it. Among unmarried people, there is no clear male or female expectation concerning contraception.

One of the few studies of teenage male attitudes toward contraception found that about half of the boys questioned, expected their female sexual partners to be responsible for contraception (Finkel and Finkel, 1975). There are probably as many teenage girls who expect their male partners to take responsibility for contraception. This discrepancy between male and female expectations is most hazardous for women who experience infrequent sexual encounters.

Some research indicates that an affectionate sexual relationship is more conducive to the practice of contraception, than is a casual affair (Maxwell, et al., 1977; Reiss, et al.,1977). A conversation about contraception in a casual sexual encounter may destroy the mood of seduction and the appearance of spontaneity. When a couple affectionately care for each other, they can more easily communicate about contraception. The man involved is also most likely to care about whether his female partner may get pregnant.

It is widely believed that unmarried women who use the contraceptive pill will become "promiscuous." One recent research project tested this proposition, and found it to be untrue (Garris, et al., 1976). The research compared two groups of unmarried teenage women, who came to a medical clinic for contraceptive information and materials. One group had just begun using the pills, while the other group had been using them for at least six months. The contraceptively experienced group of teenage women did not have any greater number of sexual partners, than did the group beginning contraception. The experienced group did not increase their number of partners, but they did substantially increase their frequency of sexual intercourse.

It would appear that the increasing use of the pill does not change premarital sexual relationships, but only the frequency of sexual intercourse. This has been confirmed in another study, which investigated the sexual behavior of a sample of 213 unmarried teenage women, who had been using the birth control pill for a period of one year (Reichelt, 1978). These findings should not be surprising. Married women do not suddenly become "promiscuous," when they use the pill.

ABORTION

abortion as a social issue

Historical background.   The practice of inducing abortion is an emotionally heated political issue in American society today. This was not always the case. When the United States was first established, there were few laws governing abortion before the fifth month of pregnancy. However, by the 1860s, new legislation had outlawed all abortions except in cases necessary to save a woman's life. These new laws reflected a humanitarian response to the grave dangers to a woman's life posed by abortions carried out with crude instruments and without modern antiseptics and anesthetics. As medical technology improved, attitudes toward abortion changed. By the late 1960s, several states had already made the operation permissible under a variety of conditions.

Then, in January 1973, the Supreme Court declared all state laws unconstitutional which restricted a woman's right to choose abortion during the first three months of pregnancy. It also added that the states could only pass laws regulating the conditions of where and by whom an abortion could be performed after the first three months of pregnancy. The states could outlaw abortion entirely only after the point when a fetus had reached the point of viability (when it might live outside the mother, sometime after the sixth month) except in cases necessary to preserve the life and health of the mother. Later decisions of the Supreme Court further affirmed the right of a woman to choose abortion under these conditions without the consent of her husband or parents. The Supreme Court has made it clear that existing American law cannot count the fetus as a person until it is capable of living outside its mother's womb. The current legal situation of abortion reflects American and English common law, dating back to the thirteenth century.

The moral controversy. The abortion issue represents a conflict of moralities, with contending parties regarding each other as being immoral.

Proponents of legal abortion argue that it is therapeutic surgery, necessary for a woman's physical and psychological well-being. Further, they argue that it reduces the risks of mutilation and death as a result of crude, illegal abortions which occurred to a great many women when abortion was outlawed. In terms of social consequences, proponents argue that legal abortion helps reduce forced marriage caused by premarital pregnancy; helps economically distressed families avoid having unwanted children; and helps to reduce the number of unwed mothers with children on the welfare rolls. Finally, they argue that legal abortion affirms the privacy right of women to choose whether and when to have children.

Opponents of legal abortion, in contrast, argue that abortion sanctions the taking of a life, or murder. They argue that the legal tolerance of the murder of unwanted, unborn children will eventually lead to a tolerance for the murder of other categories of people, who might someday be considered undesirable (such as the deformed, retarded, severely ill, or infirm elderly). Some opponents also argue that legal abortion encourages premarital sexual permissiveness, because it eliminates the fear of pregnancy. They argue that women who get premaritally pregnant should accept the consequences of their behavior.

There does not seem to be much room for compromise between the opposing viewpoints. Public opinion polls indicate that a majority of Americans today support legal abortion. A study of eight public opinion polls found that by 1974, an average of 85 percent of Americans affirmed support for legal abortion in cases of danger to the mother's health, a defective fetus, or rape (*Intellect,* 1976). In terms of other reasons for abortion, an average of 48 percent of Americans, in 1974, approved of abortion in cases of poverty, premarital pregnancy, or when a mother desired no more children. A Harris poll conducted in 1975 found that 54 percent of Americans supported unconditional legal abortion during the first three months of pregnancy (*New York Times,* 1975).

An analysis of public opinion polls reveals that differences over the abortion issue reflect religious differences between Americans, but not really between Protestants and Catholics, as is widely imagined. Polls suggest that opposition to legal abortion is concentrated among those people who regard themselves as religious traditionalists and see themselves as affirming traditional moral values. On the other hand, a favorable attitude towards legal abortion is more likely to be held by people who affirm secular, humanistic moral values (*Intellect,* 1976).

Currently, opponents of legal abortion are much more effectively organized for political action than are those who favor it (Gratz, 1977). They are a very highly motivated minority, and are very well financed (*New York Times*, 1977). Opponents of legal abortion have employed a wide range of tactics to limit the availability of abortion services. These tactics include: lawsuits against doctors and hospitals providing abortions, passing local ordinances which obstruct abortion services, supporting legislators who oppose legal abortion, and even picketing abortion clinics. Consequently, legal abortion is simply not available in 80 percent of the counties in the United States (Sullivan et al., 1977).

Abortion in the United States.   The changes in American abortion laws have paralleled similar changes in many other countries. In the years between 1967 and 1976, seventeen nations eliminated their restrictive abortion laws. These nations included traditionally Protestant countries in Northern Europe, as well as traditionally Catholic countries such as Austria, France, and Italy. About one-third of the world's people now live in countries which permit abortion upon request of the woman (Tietze and Lewitt, 1977). Another third of the world's people live in countries where laws permit abortion for broad medical, psychological, or socioeconomic reasons. Clearly, the legal situation of abortion is not a consequence of any particularly American social forces.

In the United States during 1976, an estimated 1.1 million legal abortions were performed (Sullivan et al., 1977). About 95 percent of these abortions were performed in the nation's metropolitan areas because most rural and small town areas did not provide abortion services. In addition, over 60 percent of all legal abortions were performed in medical clinics because a majority of the nation's hospitals did not offer abortion services. (Abortions were provided by only 18 percent of public hospitals and 38 percent of private hospitals.) Thus, abortion services were not easily available for all women who might choose to use them. It is estimated that several hundred thousand American women, who might have chosen abortions, were denied abortion services in 1976 because they were simply unavailable near their area of residence (Sullivan et al., 1977).

Women who seek abortion services tend to be disproportionately young and unmarried. In 1975, about one-third of all women who had legal abortions were teenagers; another third were aged 20 to 24; and the remainder were aged 25 or older (*Family Planning Perspectives*, 1977). Only 26 percent of these women were married at the time of the operation. The proportion of married women seeking abortion services has steadily declined since legalization probably because of the practice of more effective contraception among married people.

Much concern and controversy focuses upon the time during pregnancy when abortions are performed. In 1975, the vast majority (88 percent) of women received their abortions before the thirteenth week of pregnancy (*Family Planning Perspectives*, 1977). Therefore, most American women who obtain abortions do so during the safest period to perform the operation and long before the fetus is viable. Teenagers and poor women are those who are most likely to postpone the time of seeking an abortion (Tietz and Lewitt, 1977).

The availability of legal abortion was reduced by new legislation passed by Congress in 1978 which prohibits the use of Medicaid funds for abortion services. It is estimated that at least 250,000 poor women are denied legal abortions each year as a consequence of this prohibition (Lincoln et al., 1977). According to a careful public health estimate, this action results in the deaths of at least 77 women annually, primarily because of complications arising from cheap, illegal abortions (Petitti and Cates, 1977).

abortion procedures

The following is a brief description of the most common medical procedures used for legal abortions. Women who might be considering abortion for themselves would be wise to consult sources for more detailed information to feel more secure about what to expect. Some excellent and readable sources include the works by Planned Parenthood (1973); Sanford et al., (1976); and Shapiro (1977). These works also offer useful information about where to find abortion services and how to evaluate their quality of medical care.

The suction method.   The suction method for abortion is also known by a variety of other names including: vacuum aspiration, vacuum currettage, and dilation and evacuation (D & E). Essentially, it involves using a source of suction to draw fetal tissue out of the uterus. First, the cervical opening may be dilated, if it is not large enough to admit the extraction tube (vacurette). Then, the fetal tissue is sucked out of the uterus through the extraction tube by a vacuum aspirator. The procedure takes about 5 or 10 minutes and normally doesn't require hospitalization. Contractions of the uterus afterwards may cause moderate to severely painful cramps for a period of a few minutes. Women can usually leave a clinic within a half hour after the operation if only local anesthetic has been used.

The suction method has become the most common abortion procedure. In 1975, more than 83 percent of all legal abortions were carried out through this procedure (*Family Planning Perspectives,* 1977). It is now used for most abortions during the first trimester of pregnancy. Dangerous complications which occur as a consequence of this abortion procedure are extremely rare. These complications include possible infection, excessive bleeding due to hemorrhage, and accidental perforation of the uterus. In balance, abortion by the suction method during the first trimester of pregnancy poses a lower health risk than childbirth (Tietze and Lewitt, 1977).

The suction method can be used during early abortion because of the small size of the fetus at that time. At about six weeks after the last menstrual period, the fetal material is only a pea-sized mass. At about ten weeks after the last menstrual period, it has grown to about an inch in length. However, by fourteen weeks, it has grown to about three inches in length, so that tissue may easily block the tube of the vacuum aspirator.

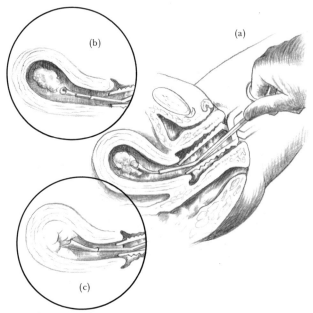

Vacuum curettage: A. the vacurette is inserted through the cervical canal; B. the suction is activated and material is processed through the tube; C. when the process is completed, the uterus pulls on the vacurette.

Dilation and curettage.   The dilation and curettage (D & C) method of abortion used to be the most common procedure until it was largely replaced by the suction method. It is still sometimes used for first trimester abortions by doctors who are more familiar with this procedure. In 1975, it accounted for 8 percent of legal abortions (*Family Planning Perspectives,* 1977).

In this procedure, the cervix is first dilated. Then, a doctor uses an instrument (curette), with a long, thin handle and a loop at the tip to dislodge the fetal tissue in a woman's uterus. The fetal tissue is removed with a thin forceps. This procedure is likely to be more discomforting and result in more bleeding than the suction method. It also causes a slightly higher rate of surgical complications (*Family Planning Perspectives,* 1977).

Intrauterine instillation.   The most common procedure for second trimester abortions is intrauterine instillation. In this procedure, a liquid is injected through the abdominal wall into the amniotic sac which surrounds the fetus. The solution induces uterine contractions after an interval of several hours (but sometimes lasting as long as 48 hours). This induced labor causes the fetus and placenta to be expelled. Unfortunately, the contractions are often severely painful to a woman. In the past, a salt solution was most commonly used. More recently, a fat-like chemical called prostaglandin has been used. It is believed to be associated with fewer complications (Shapiro, 1977). Prostaglandin is believed to be the chemical which is primarily responsible for commencing labor in normal pregnancies.

Possible health risks of abortion increase as pregnancy progresses, but especially after the first trimester (Shapiro, 1977). Therefore, if a woman chooses abortion, postponement progressively exposes her to a greater chance of dangerous complications. Intrauterine instillations should be carried out in hospitals where emergency facilities are available, even if they are rarely used during the procedure (Shapiro, 1977). Unfortunately, most hospitals prefer not to offer services for second trimester abortions because of political and moralistic concerns.

The health risks of intrauterine instillations include surgical errors during the injection. There is also a possible risk of major hemorrhage and excessive bleeding, as well as infection. These complications are rare, but another is more common: Sometimes the placenta is not expelled with the fetus, requiring curettage to remove this tissue. If that is not done, severe infection can result. In addition, when prostaglandin is used, nausea and vomiting is a common side effect.

The mortality risk of second trimester abortion is about the same as that for childbirth (Tietze, 1977b). However, women with certain health hazards, such as heart disease, liver and kidney problems, hypertension, and other ailments run a much higher risk and are usually advised against second trimester abortions.

psychological reactions to abortion

Negative emotional reactions to legal abortions are much less frequent than is widely imagined. In studies of psychological reactions to abortion, only a small minority of women who go through the experience have been found to have negative emotional reactions (Woods, 1975; Shapiro, 1977).

One study of 125 women who had legal abortions investigated both immediate emotional reactions and long term reactions a year after the experience (Smith, 1973). Only 22 percent of the women had immediate negative emotional reactions to the experience, such as mild depression or guilt feelings. Long term negative emotional reactions were even less common, with only 3 percent of the women having strong feelings of regret and another 3 percent having feelings of ambivalence. Those women who were most likely to have negative reactions to abortion were unmarried teenagers who lacked sources of emotional support from intimates.

Other factors, besides lack of reassurance from intimates, can promote psychological distress during the abortion experience and afterwards. These include initial ambivalence about the decision to have an abortion, moral reservations about abortion, and callous treatment by medical personnel during the abortion procedure. The social situation of an illegal abortion, in a culture which stigmatizes abortion, aggravates the distress which may be experienced by a woman.

the multiple causes of sexual dysfunction

The term *sexual dysfunction* was coined to identify problems which interfere with the ability to experience satisfying sexual response. *Sexual dysfunctions* refer to difficulties which involve an inability to experience sexual arousal or to participate in sexual intercourse to the point of orgasm. Male sexual dysfunctions include the inability to attain erection, premature ejaculation, and difficulty in reaching orgasm. Female sexual dysfunctions include an inability to become sexually aroused, difficulty in reaching orgasm, involuntary contractions of the vagina which prevent intercourse, and painful intercourse. The concept of sexual dysfunction focuses attention upon sexual response rather than upon broader aspects of personality and sexual interaction. However, this focus is merely a convenient starting point for research, analysis, and therapy.

Sexual dysfunctions may occur as a consequence of: (1) bodily malfunctions; (2) personal anxieties; (3) cultural expectations; (4) interpersonal conflict; or (5) any combination of these factors. However, the vast majority of cases of sexual dysfunction are not the result of any initial physiological malfunction or disease (Masters and Johnson, 1970; Kaplan, 1974).

Personal anxieties. A wide variety of personal anxieties may interfere with sexual functioning by distracting attention from erotic stimulation. One of the most common is called *performance anxiety* (Masters and Johnson, 1970). It derives from a person's fears of failure about adequate participation in sexual ac-

4 sexual dysfunctions and sex therapy

tivity. Performance anxiety usually causes individuals to carefully monitor their own sexual behavior, so that they become almost a spectator to their sexual participation. This distracts their attention from an enjoyment of their erotic feelings (Masters and Johnson, 1970). Another incapacitating fear is the fear of losing control of one's self during sexual activity (Fink, 1974). People who fear loss of control may be afraid that intense sexual arousal can cause them to behave in ways that they might later regret. Another distracting anxiety is the fear of displeasing one's sexual partner (Kaplan, 1974). This worry can cause a person to focus so much attention upon pleasing the partner that the person is unable to concentrate upon his or her own erotic feelings. Occasionally, sex anxieties derive from deeply disturbing experiences such as being raped or being humiliated during past sexual activity.

Cultural expectations.   Certain cultural expectations people learn may also contribute to problems in sexual functioning. Some people's sex anxiety derives from religious or conventional beliefs that sexual activity is sinful and disgusting. When such beliefs are strongly reinforced during early socialization, lasting feelings of displeasure in response to sexual stimulation may be imparted. Other inhibitions may occur as a consequence of learning rigidly traditional gender role expectations. A woman's sense of femininity may dictate that she restrain her sexual feelings and act only as a passive partner to sexual activity. A man's sense of masculinity may impede his uninhibited sexual expression with a woman he loves. In addition, sexual ignorance, which is a result of learning misinformation or inadequate information, can also create barriers to adequate sexual functioning.

Interpersonal conflict.   When sexual partners are in conflict, sexual interaction becomes an arena for the expression of hostility. Problems of sexual functioning are very often embedded in a web of interpersonal conflict. Sometimes sexual hostility and anxiety overflows from conflicting role expectations (for example, concerning companionship and expressions of affection, financial decisions, child discipline, or the division of household tasks). In other situations, sexual hostilities are an expression of a general power struggle for dominance and control of a couple's decision-making. Sexual hostility is also commonly a consequence of known or suspected infidelity. Inadequate or antagonistic communication about sexual matters is very often a side effect of long lasting conflict. Therefore, in cases where there is intense conflict between sexual partners, marital therapy in addition to sex therapy is usually necessary to treat people's sexual dysfunctions.

the treatment of sexual dysfunctions

Until the late 1950s, help for people with problems of sexual functioning was scarce. Low rates of success in alleviating these problems were obtained from medical treatments relying upon hormone therapy. Indirect psychotherapy relying upon self-insight into personality conflicts often required several years of treatment. Contemporary direct treatment methods for sexual dysfunctions have their origin in the techniques of behavior modification therapy, developed in the late 1950s by Joseph Wolpe (1958, 1973). Yet, it was not until the publication of Masters and Johnson's (1970) work with sexual dysfunctions that direct treatment sex therapy received widespread public attention. The importance of Masters and Johnson's previous physiological research, plus the high rate of success they obtained for a very large number of clients, added respectability to sex therapy. Sex therapy clinics began to be established around the country in the early 1970s.

Despite the very rapid development of sex therapy clinics, training programs, and new techniques, there has actually been little experimental research into the effectiveness of different techniques of sex therapy. Judgment of the effectiveness of various sex therapy techniques has been based mostly upon the evaluation of clinical case studies by the therapists who publish the studies. This is a notoriously unreliable method of evaluation. Replication of some of the techniques by different therapists, however, does offer some reassurance. Careful experimental research using control groups (comparing treatment with nontreatment groups) has been carried out only by a few behavioral scientists. Therefore, it should not be surprising to find wide disagreement about the effectiveness of various special programs of treatment.

Basic methods of sex therapy.   There are now a wide variety of special techniques used in different sex therapy programs however, most programs have the following seven procedures in common (LoPiccolo, 1977a):

1. *Involvement of Both Spouses.*   Sex therapists usually emphasize that sexual dysfunctions are mutual problems in the interaction between a couple. Therefore, most sex therapists try to involve both partners in treatment programs. This approach contrasts with the emphasis upon individual personality which is common in traditional psychotherapy. Some sex therapists do work with individual clients, however, especially if they are unmarried or divorced.

2. *Sex Education.*   Most clients of sex therapy are unaware of basic aspects of sexual physiology and effective sex techniques. Therefore, sex education is carried out through lectures, books, and films. In addition to the communication of useful information, this procedure often helps to reduce a couple's anxiety about certain sexual activities which may be prescribed in the treatment program.

3. *Attitude Change.*   In conjunction with sex education, therapists also try to change their clients' emotionally negative attitudes toward various forms of sexual activity. They especially try to enable both clients to take an active and assertive role in seeking sexual pleasure.

4. *Anxiety Reduction.*   Various direct techniques are used by sex therapists to reduce their clients' personal anxieties about sexual activity. Some techniques de-emphasize the immediate importance of sexual intercourse to orgasm, and instead, teach clients how to enjoy general bodily sensuality. Other techniques gradually desensitize clients' anxiety responses to specific forms of sexual activity.

5. *Communication Training.*   Most couples seeking therapy have difficulty communicating about their sexual preferences because of sex anxieties, fears of embarrassment, or restraining gender role expectations. Various techniques are designed to encourage couples to express clearly but pleasingly their particular sexual desires of the moment. Toward this goal, couples may be encouraged to share their private sex fantasies, to experiment with unfamiliar sex techniques, to guide their partner's sexual caresses, or to show their partner their preferred masturbation techniques.

6. *Restructuring Intimate Relations.*   Sex therapists often take an active, directive role in advising couples about how they may reorganize their relationship to achieve more enjoyable sexual interaction. They may suggest ways of arranging specific times for sexual activity, for example, when partners are not physically fatigued or distracted by household concerns. They may suggest ways of increasing companionship in recreational activities, as well as sharing of household tasks and financial and work responsibilities.

7. *Prescribing Changes in Behavior.*   Sex therapists also prescribe a graduated series of sexual activities for a couple to practice in the privacy of their own home. These activities are initially designed to encourage a couple's enjoyment of sensual body contact without holding any expectation for sexual intercourse. Only gradually are sexual activities prescribed which lead the couple to sexual intercourse. Few sex therapists prescribe sexual activities to take place in their clinics, although those who do so have received sensational media coverage.

The available research on the effectiveness of sex therapy indicates that successful treatment is closely associated with the characteristics of clients (Schumacher, 1976). Sex therapy is most effective with clients whose sexual dysfunction is a result of anxiety, fear, or sexual ignorance. The rate of successful treatment is also increased when a client has a loving and cooperative sexual partner. Sex therapy alone may be less successful with clients who have complex personal and interpersonal problems; psychotherapy may be more appropriate in such cases.

Controversial issues.   Beyond debates over the relative effectiveness of various sex therapy techniques, there are many professional and ethical issues. First, there is the issue of professional regulation. There is no special licensing or legal supervision for sex therapists (LoPiccolo, 1977b). Sex therapists come from diverse professional backgrounds. Many of them are licensed psychiatrists, clinical psychologists, or social workers, but many others have dubious backgrounds for such sensitive work. Presently, in most states, anyone can set up a practice in sex therapy, and many charletons may be capitalizing on the high fees charged (Masters, 1976). Indeed, the average fees charged range from $2500 to $4000 for a program of about fifteen hours of treatment (LoPiccolo, 1977b). Second, there is the related issue of adequate training for sex therapy. Few universities in the country offer intensive, supervised training programs for sex therapists (LoPiccolo, 1977b). Whether or not a few special graduate school courses or weekend workshop programs offer adequate training is a serious question. It is particularly questionable when aspiring sex therapists do not already have a university education in the counseling skills of one of the established helping professions (psychiatry, clinical psychology, and social work). There is also disagreement about whether a background as a medical doctor, nurse, educational counselor, or clergyman is sufficient.

In addition to disputes over professional qualifications, there are growing concerns about the ethics of certain sex therapy practices. Ethical questions center about such practices as: prescribed nudity in group therapy sessions, the use of surrogate sexual partners, and erotic contact between therapists and their clients (Lowry and Lowry, 1975; LoPiccolo, 1977b).

Sex surrogates are used primarily with clients who do not have a regular sexual partner. Most sex surrogates are women, but a few are men who work with unmarried female clients (Elias, 1977). Some sex surrogates are former prostitutes, but most are women who have some background in education, nursing, or social work (Elias, 1977). They usually have some formal training in sex therapy and work under the close direction of a therapist. Their work primarily consists of helping clients with "sensate focus" exercises which emphasize nongenital pleasuring and only gradually move toward full sexual intercourse. While therapists using sex surrogates have claimed high rates of successful treatment, the practice has an unclear legal standing.

Erotic contact between therapists and their clients is even more ethically controversial than is the use of sexual surrogates. Some sex therapists employ "sexological examinations." In these examinations, a therapist of one sex applies sexual stimulation to the body of a client of the other sex using hands or an instrument. The purpose is to test the client's sexual response and to offer feedback information about it. It has been reported that a few sex therapists actually engage in "therapeutic" sexual intercourse with their clients. Recent research involving psychiatrists and clinical psychologists has found that about 5 percent of these therapists (mostly male) have engaged in covert sexual intercourse with their clients, even though the behavior is considered ethically reprehensible by almost all helping professionals (Davidson, 1977; Holroyd and Brodsky, 1977).

MALE SEXUAL DYSFUNCTIONS

erectile dysfunction (impotence)

Erectile dysfunction, or *impotence* as it is traditionally termed, refers to the persistent inability of a man to attain an erection sufficient for sexual intercourse. Masters and Johnson (1970) made a useful distinction between primary and secondary impotence. *Primary impotence* refers to those cases in which a male has never been able to attain an erection sufficient for sexual intercourse, although erection may have been experienced through masturbation. These cases are less often successfully treated by sex therapy. *Secondary impotence,* which is much more common, refers to cases in which a male has previously experienced occasions of sexual intercourse. Secondary impotence may arbitrarily be considered to exist when the inability to attain an erection occurs on at least 25 percent of attempts at sexual intercourse (Masters and Johnson, 1970). It is necessary to make this judgment because most men experience occasions of erectile failure because of situational factors. Secondary impotence may be the most common male sexual dysfunction, although many older men do not seek treatment for it because they consider it to be an inevitable aspect of the aging process (Martin, 1975).

Although learned factors account for most cases of impotence, it has also been reported to occur as a result of a wide variety of physical ailments. The most common of these health problems is diabetes mellitus (Wabrek and Wabrek, 1976). However, any severe or debilitating disease can cause loss of sexual desire and impotence along with it. Therefore, a thorough physical examination is usually advised before a man begins sex therapy for impotence. The incidence of disease factors resulting in impotence is not known. However, it is estimated by physicians to occur in 5 percent to 15 percent of cases (Wabrek and Wabrek, 1976).

The immediate cause of most cases of impotence usually involves anxieties or displeasurable emotional responses associated with sexual intercourse (Cooper, 1969a; Lazarus, 1974). This is, of course, only a general precipitating factor representing the culmination of hundreds of diverse situations in which men learn to associate negative emotions with sexual arousal and/or sexual intercourse. These negative emotional associations may be fear of failure, shame, guilt, anger, disgust, or depression. Conflict within the relationship and sexual ignorance are often contributing factors. It is usually necessary in cases of impotence (as well as with other sexual dysfunctions) for sex therapists to carefully individualize the treatment program to deal with differences in the situations of clients.

Some examples will provide an idea of the diverse situations which may lead to persistent impotence as a conditioned response to sexual activity. A man may develop the mistaken fear that he is becoming permanently impotent after having several successive experiences of erectile failure. This may occur because of the continued consumption of too much alcohol, or because of the fatigue and tensions generated by occupational concerns, or because of normal physiological changes of aging. The fear of failure may be reinforced by bedroom quarreling or by humiliating sexual encounters. Sometimes guilt about an adulterous affair may render a man impotent with his partner. Sometimes a man's sexual arousal is diminished by constantly routine and uninspired sexual activity limited only to genital intercourse without manual and oral stimulation. In such cases, a man's sexual desire for his partner may be so low that erectile failure occurs on many occasions, particularly as the man begins to experience the aging process. In addition, some men regard sexual activity with disgust so that they find it difficult to become sexually aroused by a loving spouse. Such men are particularly likely to come from highly restrictive, orthodox or fundamentalist religious backgrounds (Masters and Johnson, 1970.)

Treatment procedures.   There are a variety of sex therapy procedures designed to alleviate erectile dysfunction. All of them, however, have two basic goals (LoPiccolo, 1977a). The first goal is to ensure that a man receives sufficiently intense sexual stimulation from his partner, in terms of both physical caresses and interpersonal relatedness. Both partners are given an intensive sex education in diverse techniques of sexual stimulation. Women are cautioned not to make any derogatory remarks about their partner's sexual abilities because this only reinforces performance anxiety. The second goal is to eliminate personal anxieties which interfere with erection despite the receipt of adequate stimulation. Particular attention is given to the alleviation of performance anxiety caused by fear of erectile failure. Toward this end, clients are explicitly discouraged from attempting sexual intercourse until the therapy program is near completion. At the same time, a man is encouraged to satisfy his partner's sexual desires through means of manual or oral caresses to orgasm, or through the use of a vibrator.

A variety of special techniques are used to gradually reduce performance anxiety and negative emotional distractions. One such technique is called *systematic desensitization* (Wolpe, 1958; Obler, 1973; Shusterman, 1973). Essentially, it involves teaching a man to associate a relaxation response with sexual arousal so that he can unlearn his previous anxiety response. A man is initially taught certain deep muscle relaxation exercises. He then learns to practice these relaxation exercises in homework assignments of gradually more elaborate foreplay with his partner. When he no longer feels anxiety in response to varieties of foreplay and is able to maintain an erection he is then encouraged to try sexual intercourse.

Masters and Johnson (1970) developed a procedure to treat erectile dysfunction which is very much similar to systematic desensitization. A couple is taught to engage in sensate focus exercises which involve relaxed bodily caressing and erotic exploration. These exercises are designed to stimulate general sensual enjoyment in the absence of performance demands for erection. Later, the woman employs genital manipulation using a teasing technique of successively stimulating her partner's erection and then letting the erection subside. This technique is designed to reduce her partner's fear of losing an erection and not being able to get it back.

Recently, there has been a renewed experimental interest in hormone therapy for impotence. However, a thorough review of the available data finds no clear evidence that the administration of hormones to impotent men has any lasting effectiveness (Schiavi and White, 1976). Initial changes in sexual response may be because of the effects of expectation in reducing sex anxiety.

premature ejaculation

Premature ejaculation is very difficult to define in terms of any concrete criteria. This is because any definition of prematurity must take into consideration both a man's sexual response and the mode of sexual interaction he experiences with his sexual partner. Superficially, premature ejaculation may be defined as a pattern of sexual response in which a man persistently reaches orgasm before entering the vagina or immediately afterward. Some therapists, however, define premature ejaculation as the inability of a man to exert voluntary control over his ejaculatory reflex. Other therapists define it as the inability of a man to participate in vaginal intercourse for a certain length of time in minutes. However, variations in patterns of sexual interaction render these definitions inadequate. A man's sexual partner may require long periods of foreplay before becoming sexually aroused, so that a man may consistently reach a high pitch of sexual arousal long before his partner is ready for intercourse. In other cases, both partners may enjoy long periods of manual and oral caressing before reaching orgasm in a short period of vaginal intercourse. In terms of sexual interaction, premature ejaculation may be defined as the inability of a man to delay his ejaculation for a sufficient length of time to satisfy a sexually responsive partner, on at least 50 percent of occasions of sexual intercourse (Masters and Johnson, 1970; Marmor, 1976). Premature ejaculation is the most common male sexual dysfunction treated by sex therapists.

While there remains much disagreement about the causes of premature ejaculation, there is a growing consensus that anxiety is the most common underlying factor (Marmor, 1976). It is noteworthy that persistent premature ejaculation has been experimentally induced in laboratory animals by mildly shocking them as they make efforts to copulate (Beach and Fowler, 1959). The origins of the anxieties which cause premature ejaculation in men are probably similar to those which cause impotence (Marmor, 1976). Indeed, cases of secondary impotence in men are very frequently preceeded by years of experiencing premature ejaculation (Masters and Johnson, 1970).

Cultural and interpersonal factors related to the double standard may also encourage some men to learn patterns of premature ejaculation. Some men, especially those who are poorly educated, share the cultural belief that a man cannot control himself once he is sexually aroused. This belief easily becomes a self-fulfilling expectation. Such men usually also feel that rapid movement to orgasm, without any constraint, is the most satisfying approach to sexual activity. Very often, these men have little concern about pleasing their sexual partner. These attitudes easily lead to patterns of sexual interaction which reinforce premature ejaculation.

In premarital sexual encounters, a man may be concerned only about pursuing his aggressive desire for sexual intercourse before his partner has a chance to change her mind. Anxiety over possible denial can promote tension which causes rapid ejaculation as soon as body contact occurs. A young man may also have sexual experiences with prostitutes who encourage rapid ejaculation in order to have a quick turnover of customers. Later, in sexual interaction with a loving partner, a man may have a partner who is sexually unresponsive and prefers a rapid termination of sexual activity, covertly reinforcing a pattern of premature ejaculation (Masters and Johnson, 1970). Alternatively, a man may have a loving and sexually responsive partner who initially tolerates his persistent premature ejaculation, but with the passing of years, grows increasingly embittered due to her own sexual dissatisfaction. She may come to regard his pattern of premature ejaculation as a sign of selfishness and lack of self-control. It is generally considered crucial to treat premature ejaculation as a problem in sexual interaction involving both partners, rather than a separate, personal concern of a man (Masters and Johnson, 1970).

Treatment procedures.   A variety of treatment procedures are used for premature ejaculation, usually in combination with each other. The systematic desensitization of anxiety, similar to that used in cases of impotence, has been employed. However, it has only a moderate rate of success when it is used without additional training procedures (Cooper, 1969b). A much more effective technique is the stop-start procedure (Semans, 1959). In this procedure, the penis is manually stimulated until a man feels orgasm to be imminent. Then, all sexual stimulation is stopped. After a pause, when sexual arousal is allowed to subside, the penis is again stimulated until orgasm is imminent. This procedure is repeated over and over again. When it is practiced over several weeks, a man learns to identify the feelings of approaching orgasm. He also learns to experience a considerable amount of direct stimulation without ejaculation. This technique may be employed in self-masturbation first, and then later by a sexual partner (LoPiccolo, 1977a). When it is employed with a sexual partner, it can be used to help restructure patterns of sexual interaction which have avoided genital fondling and sexual reciprocity.

Masters and Johnson's procedure (1970) of combining sensate focus exercises with the squeeze technique closely resembles systematic desensitization combined with the start-stop technique. In this procedure, the woman stimulates her partner's penis until he senses imminent ejaculation, and then she applies the squeeze technique to stop the ejaculatory reflex. In the squeeze technique the woman grips the tip of the penis by placing her thumb on the frenulum below the glans and her fingers above, and then firmly squeezes for a few seconds. This procedure is practiced repeatedly during daily homework exercises. During later exercises, the couple practices intercourse using slow thrusting movements in the female superior position until ejaculation becomes imminent; then when she removes his penis and again applies the squeeze technique. Eventually, the man is able to learn sufficient ejaculatory control for lengthy intercourse.

retarded ejaculation

Retarded ejaculation is a relatively rare sexual dysfunction in men. *Retarded ejaculation* is characterized by a persistent difficulty or inability to ejaculate during sexual intercourse. The developmental causes are thought to be similar to those leading to impotence with perhaps a greater likelihood of guilt associated with sexual activity. The dysfunction may be most common in men from religious backgrounds which stress anti-erotic beliefs. Occasionally, ejaculatory difficulties are caused by physiological malfunctions (Marmor, 1976).

The treatment procedure in cases where retarded ejaculation is a learned disorder consists of sensate focus exercises, followed by sessions of intense sexual stimulation (Masters and Johnson, 1970). The woman is instructed to apply concentrated stimulation to the penis—manually, orally, or with a vibrator—to bring about ejaculation initially outside the vagina. In later sessions, the penis is stimulated to a point of imminent ejaculation and then inserted into the vagina. Eventually, sex anxiety becomes desensitized, and ejaculation becomes easily associated with vaginal intercourse.

FEMALE SEXUAL DYSFUNCTIONS

general sexual dysfunction (sexual unresponsiveness)

There are currently no standard schemes for classifying sexual dysfunctions in women. Masters and Johnson (1970), for example, reject any use of the term *frigidity* because of its rather vague meaning. Nevertheless, it continues to be used by many scientific writers. This presentation will avoid use of the term *frigidity*. In addition, following Kaplan (1974), a distinction will be recognized between a woman's general inability to experience sexual arousal and the more specific difficulty of reaching orgasm.

General sexual dysfunction refers to the persistent inability to experience sexual arousal. On a cognitive-emotional level, it is characterized by an absence of erotic response to potential sexual stimuli. Such stimulation may be felt as a

tickling sensation, or as irritation, or regarded with disgust. Consequently, on a physiological level, a woman does not experience the bodily changes of sexual excitation (Kaplan, 1974). A woman usually does not experience genital congestion (vasocongestion) and her vagina does not become lubricated; or she may experience only slight lubrication during sexual intercourse (Kaplan, 1974). Many sexually unresponsive women have an aversion toward all sexual activity. However, others who have a loving relationship with their partners, do enjoy body contact and caressing, although they do not respond to it erotically. Some women with general sexual dysfunction have never experienced erotic response and sexual arousal. Other women have been sexually responsive in the past, as for example during premarital petting, but have lost ability to respond sexually.

The possibility that a similar sexual dysfunction may exist among some men has been neglected until recently. However, at least one sex therapist has suggested that some men have a similar inability to experience erotic response and sexual arousal (Apfelbaum, 1976). This general sexual unresponsiveness underlies some cases of impotence. The point is that general sexual dysfunction refers to an absence of sexual desire, more basic than difficulties in the sexual response cycle.

The developmental origins of female sexual unresponsiveness are diverse but essentially lie in experiences which cause a woman to associate anxiety and negative emotions with sexual arousal. A woman may carefully avoid sexual arousal as a result of acquiring the notion that femininity demands that a woman restrain her sexual feelings, or as a result of a puritanical devaluation of all sexual activity. Many sexually unresponsive women learn intense sex guilt because of religious anti-erotic upbringing and regard sexual activity with feelings of disgust (Masters and Johnson, 1970).

Fear is also a factor which inhibits sexual arousal in some women (Fink, 1974; Kaplan, 1974). Some women fear that sexual arousal will cause them to lose control. They worry that this imagined loss of control will cause them to act in such a way that they will be embarrassed, or rejected by their partner, or will allow themselves to be sexually mistreated. Some women's emotional restraint is such that they fear any intense feelings, not only those which are erotic. The fears of other women are more concrete. For example, they may fear becoming pregnant because of past unplanned pregnancies. Some women have had unpleasant sexual experiences which result in conditioned anxiety associated with sexual arousal. Such experiences may be rape, or sexual molestation, or frequent sexual aggression on dates.

The sexual unresponsiveness of many women is closely linked with their marital sexual interaction. Marital power struggles are often expressed in sexual activity. Some women react to dominating partners by becoming sexually unresponsive. Their sexual unresponsiveness is a means of expressing their hostility (Cooper, 1969c). Other women may be persistently depressed as a result of feeling trapped in marriage to their husbands. Depression usually renders people sexually unresponsive. Other women are simply not in love with or sexually attracted to their partners. Finally, many women do not experience adequate sexual stimulation from their partners. A great many women who are sexually dysfunctional also have partners who are sexually dysfunctional. Women who are sexually unresponsive or inorgasmic often have husbands who are premature ejaculators (Masters and Johnson, 1970).

In addition, in some cases of sexual unresponsiveness, women have a homosexual erotic orientation which impedes their arousal by heterosexual stimuli.

In the past, it was widely believed that sexual unresponsiveness was part of an overall personality problem. However, recent research has provided clear evidence that female sexual unresponsiveness and inorgasmic reactions are usually specific problems. These sexual dysfunctions are not necessarily an expression of a deeply distressed (neurotic) personality characterized by intense inner conflicts (Cooper, 1969c; Munjack and Staples, 1976). The belief that sexual unresponsiveness or difficulties in reaching orgasm are symptoms of an overall personality disorder only serves to intensify many women's sex anxiety.

The reactions of women to sexual unresponsiveness vary but are usually much less dramatic than the reactions of men to impotence. Many such women initially accept marital sexual activity, reluctantly and passively. Later, however, they increasingly seek subterfuges to avoid it by feigning fatigue, headaches, illnesses, or by provoking quarrels (Kaplan, 1974). Insufficient sexual arousal usually produces inadequate vaginal lubrication making sexual intercourse irritating or even painful at times. The lack of mutually pleasurable sexual activity causes many sexually dysfunctional women to regard it as worthless if children are no longer desired. Women are not under cultural pressure to perform sexually as are men, and they need not worry about erectile failure. Yet, sexually unresponsive women usually receive pressure from their partners to participate in sexual activity and to show enthusiasm for it. The lack of reciprocal pleasure often causes women to feel ''used'' and their partners to feel undesired.

Treatment procedures.   The treatment procedures designed to deal with general sexual dysfunction in women are similar to those used to help inorgasmic women.

The first step consists of sensate focus exercises designed to develop a woman's sensual and erotic feelings. A woman is directed to initiate gentle caressing of her partner before, in turn, being the recipient of his caresses. This may help to reduce her sex guilt and fears of rejection. It is also a technique which helps her to change from patterns of sexual passivity to sexual assertiveness (Kaplan, 1974).

The second step involves slow, teasing, stop-start genital stimulation offered by her partner manually, orally, or with a vibrator. He is, however, directed to avoid stimulation aimed at bringing about orgasm and to avoid sexual intercourse. She is instructed to bring him to orgasm through other means if he desires it. This genital play is designed to further enhance a woman's ability to enjoy erotic feelings and sexual arousal. It also helps to gradually desensitize her anxieties about loss of control in response to sexual arousal.

If genital play establishes a pleasurable response, a woman is instructed to initiate sexual intercourse when she feels like doing so at a time of high sexual arousal. This third stage of ''non-demand'' sexual intercourse involves slow, gentle thrusting rather than vigorous movements designed to bring about orgasm. When a woman desires to reach orgasm, she communicates this to her partner.

Besides teaching a woman to enjoy sexual arousal, these procedures help to modify previous patterns of sexual interaction. They open up avenues of communication about sexual feelings and preferences. These procedures also help a woman learn sexual assertiveness in giving and receiving sexual stimulation. She learns that sexual activity is for her own erotic pleasure and not simply something she does selflessly for her partner.

These procedures often have to be accompanied by extensive sex education and marital counseling in relationships that are beset by sexual ignorance and marital conflict.

orgasmic dysfunction

Orgasmic dysfunction refers to a woman's inability or persistent difficulty in reaching orgasm. Generally, women who are inorgasmic are sexually responsive and sometimes even experience intense sexual arousal. They usually experience erotic feelings, genital congestion, and genital lubrication (Kaplan, 1974). However, they have a difficulty going beyond the plateau level of sexual response.

Primary orgasmic dysfunction refers to cases in which women have never experienced orgasm from any source of stimulation (Masters and Johnson, 1970). *Secondary* or *situational orgasmic dysfunction,* in contrast, refers to cases in which women have persistent difficulties in experiencing orgasm through sexual intercourse, although they are able to experience orgasm through masturbation, or manual or oral caressing. It is also common, in cases of secondary orgasmic dysfunction, for women to have previously experienced orgasm in sexual intercourse but to have lost their orgasmic responsiveness. Orgasmic responsiveness in women can be highly situational. Some women cannot reach orgasm with their husbands, but can do so during extramarital encounters; the reverse occurs for other women. Some women can easily achieve orgasm through masturbation, but not through sexual intercourse.

As far as is known, the causes of inorgasmic responsiveness are similar to those which lead to sexual unresponsiveness. However, inorgasmic women are much less likely to suffer from sex guilt caused by anti-erotic upbringing (Kaplan, 1974). They are usually not severely inhibited sexually. On the other hand, they are more likely to suffer from performance anxieties, fears of losing control, or hostility toward their partner. The partner relationship is often a crucial factor in a woman's inorgasmic responsiveness (LoPiccolo, 1977a). A

great many women do not receive adequate sexual stimulation from their partners when sexual interaction is limited to brief sexual intercourse. In addition, a
conflictive, stressful, or depressing intimate relationship often leaves a woman
inorgasmic.

Treatment procedures. There are a wider variety of procedures used to
deal with orgasmic dysfunction than any other sexual dysfunction (Ascher and
Clifford, 1976; Sotile and Kilmann, 1977). All of them cannot be described
here. Basically, they are all aimed at eliminating sex anxieties and enhancing
erotic sensitivity. A crucial aspect of all treatment programs is that they teach a
woman to enjoy immediate sensuous stimulation rather than to concentrate her
attention upon achieving orgasm. One treatment program is the same as that
previously described for general sexual dysfunction.

Another effective treatment program involves the development of orgasmic
responsiveness through the use of masturbation training (LoPiccolo and Lobitz,
1972; Heiman et al., 1976). The rationale for the use of masturbation relies
upon the fact that it is the technique most likely to result in orgasm. First, the
woman examines her genitals with the use of a mirror and diagrams. At this
stage, also, a woman learns certain exercises which are believed to strengthen
her vaginal and pelvic muscles and help trigger orgasm (Kegel, 1952). Later, a
woman manually explores her genitals and learns how to stimulate those areas
which are most erotically sensitive. After these procedures, a woman intensively
stimulates her genitals while imagining erotic fantasies. If she still isn't able to
reach orgasm, a woman then uses an electric vibrator to apply stimulation. This
technique almost invariably results in orgasm.

Later stages involve sexual interaction between a woman and her partner.
First, she shows her partner how she masturbates so that he learns the most effective manner to manipulate her to orgasm. Finally, the couple have sexual intercourse after the wife has been manually caressed to the point of approaching
orgasm. This program is also augmented by sensate focus exercises, anxiety
desensitization training, and marriage counseling.

vaginismus

Vaginismus refers to involuntary spasms of the muscles at the entrance to the
vagina which usually prevent vaginal penetration. These spasms are often
severely painful and usually make sexual intercourse impossible. In many cases,
marriages go on unconsummated several years before assistance is sought. Most
women who suffer from vaginismus are otherwise sexually responsive and are
usually able to reach orgasm through manual and oral-genital caressing (Kaplan, 1974; Ascher and Clifford, 1976). Fortunately, the problem is relatively rare
and is now reasonably easy to alleviate.

The precise developmental origins of vaginismus are not known, but the muscular spasm is generally considered to be an anxiety response. Common background factors include severely anti-erotic religious training, or emotionally shocking sexual experiences such as rape (Masters and Johnson, 1970). Occasionally, the anxiety response occurs as a result of experiencing painful intercourse because of internal physical difficulties.

Treatment procedures.   Treatment procedures include those used to alleviate other female sexual dysfunctions with the addition of one special procedure. That procedure involves the use of a series of increasingly larger dilators which are progressively inserted into the woman's vagina over a period of weeks. The insertion may be done by the therapist, the woman herself, or her partner. Gradually, the woman is able to accept larger dilators without experiencing spasms until sexual intercourse can finally take place. Previous to this procedure, it is usually necessary to demonstrate to the man that his partner's physical difficulties are genuine and not faked.

other dysfunctions

Vaginismus is only one of the possible causes of painful intercourse. There are a great many biological problems which can cause sexual intercourse to be painful for women, and less commonly for men. These problems are collectively termed *dyspareunia* (Masters and Johnson, 1970). The sources of pain may derive from infections, internal injuries, physiological disorders, and even anatomical problems. A very careful gynecological examination is usually necessary to detect the origin of these sources of pain.

HOW COMMON ARE SEXUAL DYSFUNCTIONS?

No large-scale survey has yet tried to answer the question of how common sexual dysfunctions are between American married couples. This information would be very useful for marriage counselors, social workers and public health officials.

One small-scale study, however, does provide some insight into the magnitude of the problem. The researchers interviewed 100 married couples and asked them questions about their sexual interaction, as part of a study of marital adjustment among "normal", non-patient couples (Frank et al., 1978). About 40 percent of the men reported experiencing sexual dysfunctions, mostly that of ejaculating too quickly, and about 60 percent of the women also reported experiencing sexual dysfunctions, such as a difficulty in becoming sexually aroused or in reaching orgasm. If a similar proportion of married persons in the total population also experience sexual dysfunctions, these problems are indeed very common. Furthermore, the reseachers found that 50 percent of the men and 77 percent of the women reported other kinds of sexual difficulties, including an inability to relax for sexual activity, sexual disinterest, insufficient foreplay before sexual intercourse and lack of sexual attraction to their partner. It would appear that there is a great need for sexual counseling services.

part two

SEXUAL
BEHAVIOR

The study of personality is often considered to be the central concern of psychology. Yet, there are perhaps as many definitions of personality as there are psychologists. The difficulty in defining the nature of personality is not a result of professional whimsy; it is because the term *personality* is a very abstract concept. In simplification, the term *personality* refers to the qualities of individual persons as individuals. Yet, what qualities are those?

Some qualities of individuals may be observed, such as behavior, nonverbal expression of emotions, and verbal expression of thoughts. Other qualities of individuals cannot be observed directly and must be inferred, such as personal desires and goals. Some psychologists regard these inferred qualities as the deeper, inner essence of personality. However, other psychologists regard personality only in terms of qualities that can be observed.

Any definition of personality has its advantages and shortcomings. The following one will be used in this book. *Personality* refers to persistent patterns in a person's expressed thinking, emotional responses, and behavior which are reactions to the conditions of his or her life.

character and situational analysis

Psychologists have developed a great many theories of personality which can be used in attempts to understand the thinking, emotional responses, and behavior of individuals. These ways of understanding personality may be classified into two broad perspectives: (1) character analysis; and   (2) situational analysis.

5 sexuality in personality

Character analysis treats a personality as a closed system; in other words, personality is a consistent entity and not very responsive to changing environmental events. It attempts to identify the important parts of personality as a system and to understand the functional interrelationship of its internal parts. It focuses attention upon consistent personality motives and traits across specific situations.

In contrast, *situational analysis* treats a personality as an open system; in other words, personality is continually responsive to changing environmental events. It attempts to understand behavior as a response to specific situations without assuming much consistency in a person's behavior across situations (Mischel, 1973). It focuses attention upon the effects of varied situations and the personal meanings individuals attribute to a situation. The approach in this book emphasizes situational analysis.

This chapter will survey certain aspects of personality which are particularly important for an understanding of human sexuality. First, we will briefly explore the basic nature of thinking and emotions. Then, we will examine the most central aspect of a person's individuality: the self-concept. In relation to sexual aspects of the self-concept, guilt and shame will be a matter of particular concern. This chapter will then explore the role of subconscious processes in human sexuality, giving particular attention to sexual fantasies in daydreams.

THINKING AND EMOTIONS

the nature of cognition

In nontechnical language, *cognition* refers to thoughts and the processes of thinking. It is useful to consider cognition as the brain's processing of information. Cognition is analogous to a computer and the way it processes and stores data. Cognitive associations of ideas are processed as nerve impulses and stored in the form of neurological connections. These cognitive associations are coded into the brain primarily in the form of language symbols, and also in the form of mathematical symbols and visual images.

Yet, we must be careful not to push an analogy between cognitive processes and computer processes too far. Men are not machines. The brain can go beyond the information it is given by creatively reorganizing ideas. More important, human beings feel pain and pleasure—as no machine is capable of doing. In addition, human meaning can be attributed to anything when stimuli trigger a web of associated ideas. Some stimuli, for example, such as the words *sex* and *love* trigger a great multitude of cognitive associations.

Cognitive organization.   There are three basic kinds of cognitive associations: beliefs, values, and expectations. *Beliefs* are a person's descriptions of reality. They are experienced by a person as knowledge and convictions about the nature of human existence. *Values* are the desirable and undesirable goals a person has in relation to objects, events, and conditions. Values are a bridge between cognitive information and emotions. They are ultimately linked to personal feelings of pleasure and pain. In other words, they are linked to what people think is desirable or undesirable in life. When we evaluate something, we measure it in terms of pleasure and pain. The significance of values in human life accounts for the fact that thinking can never be a matter of dispassionate, cold-blooded information processing. Finally, *expectations* may be considered principles, or rules; they are a person's guidelines for predicting environmental events. Standards of conduct, for example, are rules for expected behavior. The *attitudes* of a person are a combination of all three components: beliefs, values, and expectations.

Cognitive associations can be compared to parts of a map. *Beliefs* are comparable to the representation of the terrain in shapes and colors, with lines connecting various points in relationships. *Values* are desirable and undesirable locations in the form of scenic routes, recreational places, restaurants, toll booths, and dangerous mountain roads. *Expectations* are the symbols concerning rules for driving speed, scaling and measuring distances, and color coding indicating whether a road is free or if one must pay a toll. Any map emphasizes certain concerns while it neglects other matters and distorts still others. So it is, also, with any person's cognitive map of the social world in which he or she lives.

These concepts can be applied to the cognitive mapping of sexual matters—a person's sexual attitudes may be more or less consistent or inconsistent. Unfortunately, inconsistent attitudes toward sexual matters are quite common in American society. This distressful situation exists because being raised as an American means being exposed to many contradictory viewpoints on the sexual nature of human beings. It is difficult for a person to "get his or her head together" about sexual matters. Many common sexual beliefs, moral values, and expectations for sexual conduct work at cross-purposes and pull people in different directions. The result is considerable personal and interpersonal tension. However, formal education about sexual matters can help to reduce some of this cognitive inconsistency. Learning makes it easier to reorganize thinking about sex and to straighten out inconsistencies in personal attitudes toward sexual matters. The more that people learn about sex, the less psychological strain they experience when they try to reconcile the many sexual contradictions existing in American society. One research study, for example, found that people who have high sex information tend to have low sex anxiety in comparison with people with inadequate sex knowledge (Wright and McCary, 1969).

the nature of emotion

Emotions are among the most widely discussed and least understood aspects of personality. There are a great many concepts of the nature of emotion among behavioral scientists as well as among laymen. Frequently, discussions about human emotions become a "dialogue of the deaf," as people use the same words with different meanings. The theory of human emotions offered here is one that is consistent with a cognitive social learning theory of personality. It stresses the unity of cognition and emotion, and their link to situational stimuli. First, it is important to note that the word emotion is not here intended to convey any implications of irrationality, immaturity, or blocked reasoning. An *emotion* is a combination of a physiological response to stimuli and subjective feelings of pleasure or pain which are interpreted through symbolic associations.

To understand emotion, it is useful to trace the sequence of emotional response, keeping in mind that such a response is instantaneous and only artificially divisible into parts. First, all emotional responses begin with situational stimuli (Arnold, 1960). These stimuli may be people, objects, events, or even internal ideas and fantasies (as in daydreams and sleep dreams). Second, such stimuli are perceived and appraised by a person experiencing an emotion. Appraisal involves making an instantaneous judgement of the benefit or harmfulness of a stimulus. Such an appraisal is based essentially upon learning from past experience and is not a matter of conscious decision-making. Some research provides evidence that the meanings a person attributes to a situation shapes the direction of his or her emotional response (Schachter, 1964). Third, appraisal triggers physiological changes in the body which are subjectively felt along a spectrum of pleasure or pain. These physiological changes are also felt at various levels of intensity in terms of bodily arousal (Plutchik, 1962). It has not yet been clearly established whether different physiological changes correspond to different emotional states, or whether differences simply exist in levels of arousal. Either way, it seems clear that the specific emotion experienced by a person (affection, jealousy, fear, hatred) is a reaction to situational meanings, rather than a reaction to bodily changes. Fourth, finally, emotional states are expressed by facial and bodily movements, verbal communications, and patterns of behavior. Emotional expression is exhibited in reaction tendencies of approach or avoidance toward a stimulus. *Emotions* are therefore both a response to stimulation and a source of activation for behavior.

When emotional states linger for a long time as a person's general predisposition for action, they are referred to as *moods*. In the case of moods, as distinguished from emotions, people react partly to a pre-existing state of physical feeling.

In emotional arousal, as well as in sexual arousal, cognition helps us to define and structure our internal feelings (Schachter, 1964). We rely upon external informational cues to guide our understanding of our internal feeling states. In isolation from external feedback information, bodily feelings are rather ambiguous in meaning.

An ingenious laboratory experiment provided evidence for the cognitive structuring of emotional responses (Valins, 1966). A sample of male subjects were asked to appraise and rate the attractiveness of several *Playboy* centerfold pictures. They were told that their heartbeats would be monitored and amplified as they viewed the pictures. Actually, what they heard was an amplification of false heartbeats. The experimenter wanted to test the effects of false feedback information, so the rate of the false heartbeats was systematically increased and decreased. This falsified information had a dramatic effect upon the subjects' appraisal of the pictures. Those pictures which were accompanied by increased heartbeats were rated as more attractive by the subjects. This experiment demonstrates that emotional and sexual responses are not simply physiological reactions detached from cognitive functioning. It also demonstrates the principle that the direction of emotional response follows from the cognitive attribution of meaning to environmental stimulation. Cognition and emotion are bonded together, rather than being separate processes.

Nonverbal communication.   What we observe between people is emotional expression. We use these cues to guess a person's emotional state, as well as the reasons for it. Since the early 1970s, there has been a flurry of research about *nonverbal communication.* These fascinating studies have investigated the sending and perception of "messages" in the form of facial expression, tone of voice, body posture and movement, touching, and distancing.

There appears to be increasing evidence that certain basic facial expressions (happiness, fear, surprise, anger, disgust, sadness) are universally given off and understood throughout the world as indicating particular emotional responses (Ekman, 1975). This suggests that there exists a physiological and unlearned component in emotional expression which can be recognized by all the world's diverse peoples. However, this does not mean that all people react to the same situation and the same ideas with similar facial expressions. Personal and cultural differences exist as a consequence of different learnings. In some parts of Africa, for example, people will respond with smiles and laughter to situations which provoke embarrassment and surprise, as well as amusement (LaBarre, 1947). Even in our own society, there are differences in the implications of facial expressions. Crying may be a response to intense joy as well as sadness. Some people learn to mask and inhibit their emotional expressiveness, while other people learn to exaggerate or falsely act out emotional expressions. Therefore, it isn't always easy to judge the implications of emotional expression in other people. Usually, we must rely upon the situational context in which emotions are expressed.

motives for sexual behavior

Personal motives might best be regarded as the goals of individuals. Individuals have a multitude of goals for their sexual behavior. They may, for example, use sexual acts to obtain erotic pleasure, expressions of affection, relief from daily tensions, conception for childbearing, approval from others, relief from loneliness, satisfaction of curiosity, a sense of power over another person, or money. These goals may be sought singly, or more commonly, in combination with others.

In general, a person's motives for sexual behavior are questioned only when his or her behavior is contrary to expectations held by other people. The unexpected is seen as unusual and requires explanation. On the other hand, when a person's sexual behavior conforms to expectations, it is usually regarded as having no need for explanation. It is taken for granted as routine. In contemporary society, people often do not know what to expect from each other sexually—even in marriage. People have also become more concerned about usual forms of sexual behavior. Why do some married people seek extramarital sex? Why do some adults seek sexual activity with children? Why do some men rape women? Why are some people sexually aroused by pain? Many people want simple explanations framed in terms of peculiar personal motives.

However, the concepts of motives is a very troublesome one in the behavioral sciences. A person may attribute certain motives (goals) to his or her own sexual behavior. Other people may attribute quite different motives to explain the sexual behavior of that person. It is a dilemma for scientific explanation when a person's reported motives differ from those attributed to him or her by other people. Who is correct? Motives are not something which can be observed. Only a person's behavior and their verbally reported goals for that behavior can be observed. In this book, people's reported motives are taken as their real motives. No attempt is made to uncover motives of people who may be lying to themselves or interviewers. Instead, an emphasis will be placed upon behavior as a product of past learning and situational pressures, rather than hidden personal goals.

SELF-CONCEPT AND SEXUALITY

the self-concept

In attempts to understand other people, we develop simplified impressions of them. We perceive people as behaving in consistent ways, even though they exhibit considerable variation between different situations. To simplify, we selectively focus our attention upon particular concerns, and classify people into a few categories. To simplify, we label people with personality traits much like we label objects in terms of color or texture.

We react to ourselves much like we react to other people (Mischel, 1973). When we reflect upon our own behavior, we seek to describe ourselves, evaluate ourselves, and label ourselves, forming a self-concept of our character. Our self-concept glosses over much of the variation in our behavior, so that we may more easily answer the question. "Who am I?" When we attempt to understand ourselves, we respond with our self-descriptions, self-ideals, and our personal standards. In other words, our self-concept consists of our attitudes toward ourself.

Dimensions of self-concept.   Several psychologists have attempted to identify the basic dimensions of self-concept by noting the various realms of experience in which a person relates to self (May, Angel, and Ellenberger, 1958). There are three basic dimensions of existence for each person: (1) the *biophysical dimension* of existence is the experience of our self as a physical and biological organism; (2) the *social dimension* of existence is experience of our self as an object of the responses of other people in interpersonal relations; (3) the *personal dimension* of existence consists of reflections upon ourself as a whole person during moments of solitude.

The sexual aspect of existence cross-cuts these three dimensions of existence. Therefore, it is an important aspect of self-concept. In the biophysical dimension, a person holds attitudes toward his or her bodily appearance and genitals, and toward masturbation, menstruation, intercourse, and pregnancy as bodily sexual functioning. In the social dimension, a person holds attitudes toward perceived sexual attractiveness for others, toward masculinity and femininity in behavior, toward the ability to be sexually pleasing to others, and toward the ability to be loved by others. In the personal dimension, a person relates to self as a whole person, part of which is his or her nature as a sexual being. For example, some people experience pervasive regret and guilt about sexuality which influence their self-concept as whole persons. (Such people may feel contempt for themselves in many ways other than sexual.) In other people, sexuality is an important source of feelings of self-esteem.

Our self-concept also has a *temporal (time) dimension*. The past and present, as well as the future of our experience, shapes our attitudes toward self. The past exists in the form of memories of ourself. A beautiful woman may continue to think of herself in terms of her acne-faced, "ugly duckling" childhood self. However, present circumstances often have a way of distorting and reshaping our memories. Finally, our aspirations project ourself into the future. That is to say, the concept of self is partly a product of future expectations. For example, a boy's expectation to be a husband and father will affect his self-description and self-evaluations, for example: "I am the type of person who will be a good husband and father." Anticipation of future events causes us to focus our attention selectively upon certain concerns of the present. As the circumstances of a person's life situation change, so does his self-concept evolve. It is, therefore, best to view a person's self-concept as continually evolving, rather than as a permanent, unchanging entity.

self-esteem and sexuality

Some people attract us, others repel us. When one doesn't know a person very well it is easy to like or dislike the person as a whole. Usually, however, the people we know as intimates cause us much pleasure as well as some pain. So too, when we turn our eye upon ourselves and evaluate ourselves, we react in pleasure and pain.

Self-evaluation involves a person's appraisal of his or her value to himself or herself. The experience which results is referred to as a person's level of *self-esteem*. It is the experience of either self-appreciation or self-rejection. Self-evaluation is dependent upon information (or misinformation) about one's personality. How do we obtain this information? Many behavioral scientists believe that we evaluate ourselves largely in response to the reactions of others to our behavior. Actually, we usually do not know what other people think of us (few tell us directly). Therefore we must base our self-evaluations upon our interpretations of other people's beliefs about us.

However, we are not equally sensitive to the reactions of all other people. Some people are more significant to us than are others. These *significant others* are usually our intimates: parents, spouse, or close friends. Significant others are also people whose ability or special knowledge we respect, or people to whom we attribute high status. Thus, our self-evaluations may also be influenced by the reactions to us of teachers, employers, clergymen, or psychiatrists.

Self-evaluations are also derived from the appraisal of success or failure at the tasks we perform. Even then, the reactions of other people remain crucial. Just as there are few games that a person can play alone, there are few tasks in which a person can be the sole judge of achievement. Whether the "tasks" are raising children, occupational performance, or relating to others sexually, it is difficult to base one's self-evaluations solely upon the expectations set for oneself. Persons, in the end, remain sensitive to the reactions of significant others.

Sexual matters are an important factor in most persons' levels of self-esteem. Personal sex problems are very often a consequence of low self-esteem (Schimel, 1974). Such problems may involve a person's concerns about masculinity or femininity, sexual ability, ability to be loved, bodily attractiveness, or even the ability to be a husband or wife. It may be recalled that *performance anxiety* is one of the most common causes of sexual dysfunction in both men and women.

shame and guilt

The emotional responses of shame and guilt are both products of the process of self-evaluation. It is useful to make a distinction between these two experiences, especially when they relate to sexual matters (Hsu, 1949; Victor, 1974). The cognitive as well as the emotional response aspects of these experiences are different.

Shame is the fear of social punishment and is experienced as embarrassment. The core emotional response of shame is fear—the fear of social disapproval, ridicule, and gossip. Most people are ashamed to speak publicly about their marital sexual activity even if they feel that their sexual conduct is not immoral or particularly unusual. A man may be ashamed to have his body seen by strangers even if he personally finds nothing wrong with his body. In many situations, we may feel embarrassed without necessarily also feeling guilty.

Guilt cuts more deeply into a person's self-esteem. The core feeling of guilt is anger, rather than fear. *Guilt* is anger directed at oneself. It is experienced as self-punishment in its many variations, such as self-condemnation and self-disgust. A person reacts with guilt when he or she perceives his or her self as violating personal standards of behavior. Such expectations are usually ones which are closely associated with a person's moral values and those of significant others. Guilt easily generalizes beyond specific situations because the individual evaluates himself or herself negatively as a whole person. When a person feels guilty about a sexual act, the person experiences self-condemnation not only about that specific act, but as a whole person.

Guilt is a form of low self-esteem. The guilty person experiences self-rejection consistent with a negative self-evaluation. In contrast, the embarrassment of shame is much more situational. Shame can be evaded by avoiding the embarrassment of public condemnation. Privacy protects a person against the eyes of would-be condemners. In guilt, however, it is difficult to evade the inner eye which focuses attention upon self-concept.

Research indicates that guilt reactions usually begin to be exhibited during late childhood or early adolescence (Kohlberg, 1969). The beliefs and values associated with the emotional response of guilt are learned. It takes many years for the implications of complex codes of behavior to be learned and internalized by a child.

The learning of guilt is encouraged when parents use "love-withdrawal" techniques of punishment, rather than direct physical punishment (Hill, 1960). In love-withdrawal discipline, guilt is promoted when parents make expressions of affection conditional upon "good" behavior. They label the child "bad" as a person (rather than labeling the specific behavior as "bad"), and then act as if they are "hurt" by the child's "badness." When they continue this procedure until the child asks to be forgiven, parents promote the learning of guilt as a form of self-contempt. The child then learns to respond to his "bad" conduct with self-contempt.

Sex guilt is another major source of personal sex problems. Clinicians treat a great many people whose sexual responsiveness is stifled by excessive feelings of sex guilt. Research indicates that people who experience high levels of guilt in response to sexual matters exhibit low sexual desire, inhibited sexual responsiveness, and difficulties in achieving orgasm (Kutner, 1971).

Sex guilt is experienced when a person anticipates engaging in, or actually engages in, sexual behavior which violates his or her moral standards (Mosher and Cross, 1971). In American society, sex guilt may still be experienced in response to masturbation, premarital intercourse, adultery, homosexual relations, and other acts which are widely disapproved.

Recent studies of responses to masturbation have found that a minority of young people experience sex guilt in response to that activity. One research project used questionnaires to investigate masturbation practices in a sample of over 400 male and female New York City college students (Arafat and Cotton, 1974). It found that while about 90 percent of men and 60 percent of women admitted currently practicing masturbation, only 13 percent of men and 10 percent of women experienced guilt in response to the act. (A much larger percentage—40 percent—of each sex were fearful of the embarrassment of being caught. This indicates the greater potential for shame, as compared with guilt, in response to masturbation.) Another research project investigated masturbation as part of a study of the sexual attitudes and behavior of adolescents using a questionnaire survey of over 400 teenagers across the United States (Sorenson, 1972). Of those teenagers who admitted to masturbation (60 percent of the boys and 40 percent of the girls), 50 percent said they never or rarely experienced guilt. The experience of guilt declined with age and came closer to that of college students.

Research investigating premarital sexual relations have come up with similar findings about sex guilt. One major study involved about 300 Iowa college students (Reiss, 1967). It found that about 60 percent of the women and about 25 percent of the men remembered feeling guilty about either kissing, petting, or intercourse. More important, as these people continued to engage in behavior which once made them feel guilty, they almost all gradually came to accept it without guilt. The investigator came to the conclusion that among most people, guilt feelings were gradually replaced by attitudes which were more consistent with the actual behavior of the person.

Some young people who are particularly predisposed toward sex guilt may avoid premarital intercourse entirely. One study of college students found that those men and women who had a high predisposition toward sex guilt in general were much less likely to engage in intimate sexual practices before marriage than were other men and women who had a low predisposition toward sex guilt (Mosher and Cross, 1971). The most common reason offered for avoiding premarital sexual intimacy was personal moral standards.

the neutralization of guilt

In the process of socialization, children (and adults) learn various ways of justifying their actions besides learning beliefs which promote guilt. These justifications, or rationalizations, function to neutralize guilt feelings when people engage in acts which they might otherwise condemn or which they think they *should* condemn (Sykes and Matza, 1957). In addition, some people *act* in ways that they condemn in *principle*. For example, many of today's parents condemn premarital sexual intercourse, even though a majority of them had such experience prior to marriage. Most people prefer not to live with perpetual guilt. People can evade self-blame if they are able to convince themselves that their particular situation is excusable.

One common way that people neutralize guilt is to deny responsibility for their own actions. (Children learn very early to say: "I didn't do it on purpose!") A boy who has had sexual relations contrary to his stated principles can convince himself that he was "drunk" and couldn't help himself. He can also shift responsibility for his actions by blaming the girl involved. The girl involved can convince herself that she was overcome by love. The *denial of responsibility* relies upon the beliefs that a person's actions are a result of forces beyond willful control (Sykes and Matza, 1957).

Another justification is the *denial of injury* (Sykes and Matza, 1957). It relies upon the belief that no harm comes from one's actions because there is no victim. For example, mate-swappers may justify their behavior as being only "fun" that does not break the bond of marital trust.

Another way people neutralize guilt is by claiming that any injury caused to others is justified because it is deserved by the victim. Many rapists, for example, justify their actions by convincing themselves that the victims were "sex teases'' who brought the rape upon themselves. They can feel guiltless with the *justification of revenge* (Sykes and Matza, 1957).

People can also neutralize guilt by *condemning their condemners* (Sykes and Matza, 1957). Prostitutes can justify their actions by condemning their condemners as hypocrites and by saying that many of them are also clients of prostitutes.

Perhaps the most powerful justification is to *appeal to a higher value* (Sykes and Matza, 1957). The strongest justification for some acts is justification by love: "When you are in love, anything is alright." For example, a great many teenagers continue to value virginity, yet feel that love is a higher morality. They have been taught the supreme value of love since childhood.

It is often taken as a matter of curiosity that many people who engage in socially condemned sexual activities (for example, prostitution or pornography) do not experience much guilt. Actually, given the ease of rationalizing guilt, and the support that can be obtained from others, the real wonder is that people still respond with guilt at all.

SEXUALITY IN VARIED STATES OF CONSCIOUSNESS

sex in subconscious processes

Contemporary behavioral scientists owe Sigmund Freud credit for recognition of the importance of subconscious process in human life. However, most behavioral scientists have a different interpretation of subconscious processes. Freudian personality theory regards the subconscious much like a second "inner personality" which directs a person's outward behavior (May, Angel, and Ellenberger, 1958). The newer approach stresses the unity of conscious and subconscious processes. It emphasizes that these processes do not constitute an anatomical "part" of personality (Ornstein, 1972); instead it emphasizes that the previous description of cognitive and emotional processes can be extended toward an understanding of their subconscious aspects.

In cognitive-emotional processes, *consciousness* involves focusing attention and awareness. Varied states of consciousness are a product of varied levels of attention and awareness of our external environment, our thought processes, and even our physiological functioning. Usually, we focus intense attention upon our social and physical environment and our own acts within it. Social pressures and environmental dangers demand that we focus our attention in that direction. Only in our daydreams, or in situations such as tedious classroom lectures, on straight-line highways, or during the twilight before sleep do we shift to an inner focus upon our own thoughts. (Beyond daydreams, in sleep, the focus of our attention is dominated by the stream of our own fantasy life.) Yet, even when we are physically active and alert to environmental stimulation, consciousness operates at various levels. Much goes on at the margins of our focus of attention. Conscious and subconscious processes operate simultaneously. Subconscious processes operate like the blurry background action which goes on at the margins of focus on a movie screen. The *subconscious* is not separate from the conscious, but merely at the margins of our attention and awareness. We perceive, learn, think, remember, and react at various levels of self-awareness, simultaneously. Thus, there are many specific cognitive-emotional processes which affect our lives at the margins of our immediate and intense attention.

If attention and awareness could be focused upon all external and internal sources of stimulation at once, our thinking would be overcome by a buzzing static of confusion. To be alert to everything is to be alert to nothing in particular. (In contrast, we can choose to focus our attention upon a single, special stimulus, such as one word in thought, and thus distract our awareness of almost everything else. This is the practice in various meditation and relaxation exercises.) *Consciousness* is always a matter of selective attention and inattention.

sexual fantasy in daydreams

A fascinating field of psychological research which has only recently received attention is the study of daydreaming. *Daydreaming* involves a shift of the focus of attention from an external source of stimulation to an internal source of stimulation provided directly by the brain. Daydreaming is best understood as a cognitive capacity, like the ability to use language or mathematical symbols. The phenomenon of daydreaming in human beings provides the best evidence that humans do not only respond to external stimulation but also actively provide their own stimulation. Daydreaming is a source of creative imagination which enables humans to extend and reorganize the information at their disposal.

Various types of daydream content have been identified in systematic research projects (Giambra, 1974b; Singer, 1975). In general, daydreaming reflects the ongoing, current interests, concerns, and problems of a person. They are usually not an escape into an imaginary world such as that of Peter Pan. This is indicated by the finding that the most common daydream content involves practical problem-solving and planning (Giambra, 1974a). Other kinds of content are sexual, achievement-oriented, heroic, religious, bizarre-improbable stretches of imagination, and unpleasant emotional fantasies of hostility, fear, and guilt. Research has revealed that some people are very much aware of their daydreaming and are able to use the process for purposes of examining problems, making plans, entertainment, and relaxation (Singer, 1975). In contrast, other people have daydreams which are fleeting, fragmented, and distracting. Such people are often unaware of the daydream process and find it difficult to use creatively. Still other people are aware of their daydreams but cannot put them to beneficial use because of the daydreams' emotional content. People in frustrating life situations often have daydream content permeated by hostility, fear, and guilt. Daydreaming is an inborn capacity in children and is first evidenced in their "make-believe" play. It may be encouraged by parents and schools. The material environment of toys is much less important than a social environment which provides a wealth of ideas and some privacy for children to play "make-believe." Research with children has found that such play helps their intellectual development by increasing their verbal ability, creative imagination, and ability to concentrate their attention (Pulaski, 1974; Freyberg, 1975). Adults who were more frequent daydreamers during childhood are found to be more creative, imaginative, and original thinkers (Singer, 1975). More research needs to be done, but at this point at least, it seems clear that daydreaming is neither a waste of time nor a simple escape from frustrating experience as has been a common assumption in the past. Also contrary to past assumption, it has been found that daydreaming declines in frequency with age. Adolescents daydream the most and retired elderly daydream the least (Giambra, 1974a,b).

Sexual fantasy in daydreams is quite common for most people throughout the adult years. One research project investigated the daydreams of 375 men (Giambra, 1974a,b). It found sexual fantasy to be the most common daydream content among men from age 17 to 23, and second most common among men from age 24 to 65. After that age, sexual daydreams became less frequent. It has also been found that throughout the life cycle, men's frequency of sexual daydreaming is closely correlated with their frequency of sexual activity. Men who are more sexually active also tend to have a more active sexual fantasy life than do men who are less sexually active (Giambra and Martin, 1977). Sexual fantasy in daydreams may be self-induced during tedious tasks or just before falling asleep. Such flights of fantasy may also be a response to people encountered, advertisements, pornography, masturbation, or even sexual intercourse. In early adolescence, sexual fantasies may not be very explicitly sexual in content, instead focusing upon romantic seduction, kissing, hugging, and petting (Oliven, 1974). As age increases through the teenage years, the content becomes more sexually explicit and imaginative.

The evolution of sexual fantasies may be a response to the breadth of sexual information (or misinformation) that becomes available to the imagination of a person. By late adolescence, or youth, many people have fantasies about socially forbidden sexual activities. Some young people feel needlessly guilty or worried about their sanity because of having such "dirty thoughts." Most of them, however, are less troubled in making the distinction between fantasy life and practical realities.

A careful research investigation of sexual fantasies was carried out on a sample of 141 suburban housewives, none of whom were psychiatric patients (Hariton and Singer, 1974; Singer, 1975). The research investigated the sexual fantasies that these women experienced during sexual intercourse. Almost all the women reported having sexual fantasies during intercourse—65 percent of them at least some of the time, and another 37 percent very frequently. The content of these daydreams is listed as follows, in descending order of their frequency of occurrence (Hariton and Singer, 1974):

1. Thoughts of an imaginary lover enter my mind.
2. I imagine that I am being overpowered or forced to surrender.
3. I enjoy pretending that I am doing something wicked or forbidden.
4. I am in a different place like a car, motel, beach, woods, etc.
5. I relive a previous sexual experience.
6. I imagine myself delighting many men.
7. I imagine that I am observing myself or others having sex.
8. I pretend that I am another irresistibly sexy female.
9. I pretend that I struggle and resist before being aroused to surrender.
10. I daydream that I am being made love to by more than one man at a time.

Data from questionnaires and intensive interviews were submitted to extensive statistical analysis so that conclusions could be drawn about the causes and effects of these sexual fantasies. The basic conclusion was that "the results indicated that general daydreaming frequency was associated with occurrence of fantasies during intercourse and that such fantasies were generally not related to sexual or marital difficulty, but rather with an enhancement of desire and pleasure" (Hariton and Singer 1974, p. 314). Also, women who daydreamed more frequently about other matters were also the ones more likely to daydream about sexual matters and to use fantasies to heighten their sexual arousal. One of the most important findings was that women who had positive thoughts about their husbands during sexual intercourse were just as likely to have sexual fantasies as were those women whose attitudes toward their husbands were negative. Sexual fantasies have long been regarded as dangerous and sinful in Western cultures, perhaps because of traditional religious teachings about sexual thoughts. The research does not support these negative beliefs, however.

It seems clear that sexual daydreams are similar in their causes, effects, and purposes to nonsexual daydreams. Any single interpretation of the nature of sexual fantasies would be incorrect. Sexual fantasies may be a diversion from boredom; or they may serve to heighten the intensity of sexual pleasure. They may serve individuals as a rehearsal and extension of sexual possibilities; or they may be passing flights of entertaining imagination. Sexual fantasies may, for some troubled people, be a source of guilt and for others, a source of frustrated aspirations.

Sexual fantasies of men and women.   There hasn't been very much adequate research comparing the sexual fantasies of men and women. However, that which is available seems to indicate that men and women have more similarities than differences in this aspect of sexuality, especially men and women in younger age groups. One national survey inquired into the sexual fantasies of men and women and found the following proportions of men and women reported these sexual fantasy themes (Hunt, 1974):

1. Intercourse with a beloved person.
   (men—75 percent; women—80 percent)
2. Intercourse with a stranger or acquaintance.
   (men—47 percent; women—21 percent)
3. Sex with several persons of the opposite sex at the same time.
   (men—33 percent; women—18 percent)
4. Being forced to have sexual activity.
   (men—10 percent; women—19 percent)
5. Forcing someone to have sexual activity.
   (men—13 percent; women—3 percent)
6. Having sexual activity with someone of the same sex.
   (men—7 percent; women—11 percent)

Men are more likely than women to fantasize about impersonal sex, group sex and forcing someone to have sexual activity. Women are more likely than men to fantasize about being forced to have sexual activity.

Many women have fantasies about being coerced, or forced, to have sexual activity, although almost always without any bodily harm imagined (tender coercion). Curiously, one study found that sexual force fantasies are more likely to be imagined by women who have learned to be sexually assertive with men (Hariton and Singer, 1974). An interpretation may be that such women are simply more sexually self-confident and feel secure enough to have such fantasy explorations. In women's coercion fantasies, it is the power of a woman's physical attractiveness that causes men to lose control (Haskell, 1976). It should be noted, however, that the existence of such coercion fantasies does not support the myth that many women actually desire to be raped and sexually abused (Haskell, 1976). The private world of "make-believe" is one in which imaginary actors can be carefully controlled by the daydreamer. Most people are well aware of the distinctions between fantasy life and actual behavior.

Sexual fantasies and forbidden sexual behavior.   An important research question concerns the relationship between sexual fantasy and socially disapproved sexual behavior. Do fantasies of socially disapproved sexual behavior have the effect of leading people into the actual behavior? Unfortunately, little adequate research has been carried out on this matter.

Daydreams about socially disapproved sexual activities, much like other sexual fantasies, may represent merely cognitive explorations of happenings prompted by nothing more than curiosity. At any rate, research indicates that the contents of fantasies (of any kind) are not particularly useful in predicting a person's actual behavior (Klinger, 1971).

sexuality and dreams during sleep

Questions about the nature of sleep and dreams have been the source of speculation for thousands of years. Many ancient mysteries have given way to scientific investigation, yet sleeping and dreaming remains a frontier of human experience. We still have more questions than reliable answers.

Sleep research. Investigations in sleep laboratories have greatly aided our understanding of the nature of sleep and dreaming. *Sleep is not a state of physiological and cognitive inactivity.* Indeed, there are many cyclical changes in physiological activity during sleep. There are variations in electrical brain wave activity, respiration rate, and heartbeat rate which can now be easily monitored. Perhaps the most important discovery has been that of variations in eye movements during sleep. It was the laboratory confirmation of this phenomenon

in 1953 which enabled the development of experimental methods for studying dreaming. Researchers found that a laboratory subject's experience of dreaming could be externally identified by rapid eye movements (REM) during sleep. When subjects are awakened at that time, almost all are able to report their dreams (Dement, 1974). This method is less affected by loss of memory and selective recall than are methods which rely upon morning-after diaries or recall in a psychiatrist's office.

We now know that there are several sleep states which alternate in cycles during a night of sleep (Dement, 1974). The two basic sleep states are *REM sleep (rapid eye movement)* and *NREM sleep (non-rapid eye movement).* NREM sleep, or deep sleep, is accompanied by slow, regular heartbeat and respiration rates. During NREM sleep, electrical brain activity is characterized by large, slow, irregular waves, very much different from those of an awake condition. In contrast, REM sleep is accompanied by much more bodily activity. During REM sleep, heartbeat and respiration rates are irregular, changing between slow and rapid. The sleeper's body is immobile, but there occur muscular twitches in the face and fingers. In addition, electrical brain activity during REM sleep is more like that in an aroused condition. When graphed, it is marked by short, rapid and irregular peaks. Finally, REM sleep is identified by the bursts of rapid eye movements from which its name is derived. The direction of these eye movements have been found to follow the direction of movements in a sleeper's dreams (Dement, 1974). It is as if the sleeper is watching the imagined activity of his dreams.

REM dreams are usually characterized by long sequences of related activity. These dreams involve visual imagery which often provoke considerable emotional reactivity. Such dreams are comparatively uncommon during NREM sleep. NREM dreams are most likely to be experienced as "thinking," or conversational thought. They are usually less emotional and may involve only short sequences of visual imagery (Dement, 1974; Faraday, 1972). NREM dreams are also much less likely to be recalled upon awakening.

If we examine REM dreams in terms of their cognitive processes, it becomes apparent that certain processes which exist in an awake state are missing during sleep (Hartmann, 1973). There is less of an ability to concentrate attention on a particular matter for any prolonged period and to avoid distractions. The feeling of making decisions and having free will are almost totally absent. Often the dreamer simply watches actions in which he is a participant. Visual attention often follows emotional responses, rather than the reverse (Klinger, 1971). Emotional responses are almost always flat and basic (such as anger, fear, joy), rather than subtle and complex in quality. Curiously, there is usually a lack of skepticism and surprise about the most bizarre occurrences. Space and time relationships are often distorted, as well as the forms of objects in a dream. Also, there is usually little depth perception. What occurs beyond the focus of attention is hazy. Unlike daydreams, sleep dreams are usually experienced "as if" they are really happening.

Sexual dreams.   Although there is much popular interest in the nature and meaning of sex dreams, there has been no systematic research focused upon sex dreams which provides for selective dream recall. The information which is available about the cognitive contents of sex dreams indicates a considerable similarity with what has been learned about sexual fantasies in daydreams. Kinsey (1948 and 1953) concluded from his data that the contents of sex dreams are usually a reflection of the sleeper's life experience. He found that the most common dream experience was heterosexual intercourse, with various socially disapproved sexual activities occurring less frequently. According to Kinsey, when socially disapproved sexual activities occurred in sex dreams, these activities had usually been experienced beforehand in life. When dreams involved unexperienced sexual activities, they may reflect the sexual fantasies of daydreams.

There has been some research on the effects of sex-related factors upon dream content, including pregnancy, menstruation, and psychological sex differences (Van de Castle, 1971). During pregnancy, women's dreams reflect concerns about their situation and tend to begin only in the forth or fifth month. By the sixth month of pregnancy, women's dreams become dominated by references to their condition. Their dreams frequently reveal fears of giving birth to a deformed or dead child. Dreams involving intense anxiety are, therefore, rather common during the latter part of pregnancy. During menstruation, women are more likely than at other times to experience dreams about babies and mothers. At that time also, they are more likely to have dreams about friendly relations with others.

The meaning of dreams.   Since prehistory humans have sought to find the meaning of dreams. The relevance and meaning of dreams depends much, if not entirely, upon the questions asked about them. In the end, dreams take on meaning in human life only when some preconceived line of interpretation is applied to them. Dreams are among the most private of experiences; yet dream interpretation is a "public" matter which is inevitably influenced by cultural systems of belief.

It is useful to compare efforts of dream interpretation with attempts to interpret modern painting. Both may be analyzed in terms of either (1) form and structure (phenomenological analysis), or (2) symbolic messages invested in the content (symbolic analysis). In phenomenological analysis, a modern painting may be analyzed and related to other visual experiences simply in terms of its visual structure—that is, as it appears directly to the consciousness without any preconceived notions of its meaning. In symbolic analysis, people prefer to seek deeper meanings in modern art by speculating about its symbolic content. Such an approach leads to many different "schools" of interpretation. In the end, the symbolic meaning of a painting, or dream, may be very personal and relevant only to the artist, or dreamer, herself or himself.

There are many different schools of dream interpretation. However, perhaps the most useful emphasize that the dreamer, using personal life experiences as a guide, is the most appropriate source of interpretation (Faraday, 1974). The dreamer may be the best authority on his or her own personal symbolism.

Sexual orgasm during sleep.   The existence of nocturnal erections and seminal emissions during sleep have been explained in many curious ways in the past. Sleep research has found that penile erections usually accompany periods of REM sleep and can even be used as one indicator of the beginning and end of REM sleep periods (Fisher, 1967). Dream content is not necessarily sexual during REM sleep. Instead, cyclical erections are simply a response to REM physiological arousal. Many men awaken with erections in the morning when they awaken from an REM period of sleep. These erections are not due to a "full bladder" as was previously believed. They are also not necessarily due to the experience of sexual dreams. Neither recency of sexual gratification nor long sexual deprivation affect the occurrence of REM sleep erections (Fisher, 1967). REM sleep erections occur even in infants.

Similarly, some research with women has found cyclical changes in nipple size and the volume of vaginal blood supply during sleep. These changes are also associated with the REM sleep cycle, but less closely coincident with the timing of the beginning and end of REM periods (Van de Castle, 1974).

Nocturnal orgasms begin to occur among boys during early adolescence, as early as 12 years of age, and may occur throughout adulthood. The experience occurs during REM sleep and involves the ejaculation of semen, usually accompanied by an erotic dream. The experience of orgasm usually awakens the sleeper. Nocturnal orgasms are also termed *nocturnal emissions* and are popularly called *wet dreams.* They have been found to occur in women as well. The precise physiological and cognitive mechanisms which trigger nocturnal orgasms are not known. They are not caused by the "pressure" from accumulated semen, as evidenced by their existence in women. Nocturnal orgasms are the first orgasmic experience for some boys and may provoke feelings of embarrassment among the sexually uninformed. Actually, in a majority of cases today, nocturnal orgasms are preceded by the experience of orgasm and ejaculation through masturbation (Oliven, 1974).

In men who abstain from any other sexual activity, nocturnal orgasms are experienced on the average of every 10 to 35 days (Oliven, 1974). However, a more frequent occurrence is not uncommon. Sexual activity without orgasm during the day, such as petting, increases the likelihood of occurrence. Nocturnal orgasms are most common among unmarried men in their late teens and early twenties, but even sexually active married men occassionally have the experience (Kinsey, 1948).

Women experience nocturnal orgasms less frequently than do men. Kinsey (1953) found that 70 percent of women in the study reported having experienced erotic dreams. However, only about one-third of women recalled dreams which resulted in orgasms. Among those women who recalled nocturnal orgasms, the frequency averaged about 3 or 4 per year. Also in contrast with men, women's experience with sexual activity tends to increase rather than decrease the likelihood of experiencing erotic dreams and nocturnal orgasms. Nocturnal orgasms are more common among women who are more sexually experienced.

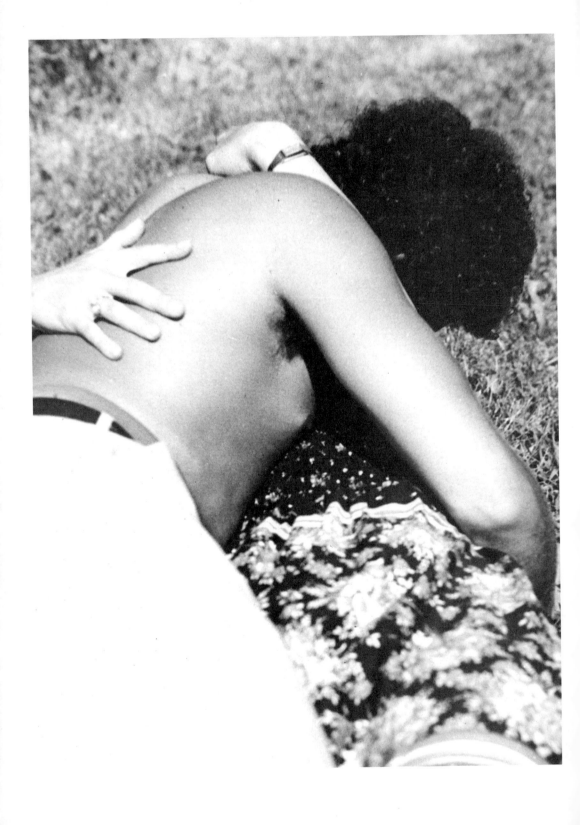

The focus of this chapter is upon that aspect of human sexuality most relevant to sensual pleasure: erotic sexuality. To understand the forces which shape erotic development, we must first have some notion of the basic factors which affect sexual arousal. First, the biological factors which influence sexual arousal will be presented followed by a presentation of interpersonal influences. These are closely interrelated and only distinguished as a matter of convenience.

SEXUAL DESIRE

the nature of sexual desire

It is useful to compare human sexual desire with hunger to gain insight into the nature of sexual motivation. Hunger results from a definite bodily tissue need. The need is for nutrient substances (proteins, carbohydrates, fats, vitamins, minerals) which enable the cells of the body to survive and reproduce. If a person is deprived of these nutrients, that person will die. No comparable situation exists in relation to sexual desire. If a person's sexual desire is deprived of gratification, no cell tissue is destroyed. People need not worry about death caused by sexual starvation. The many people who have trained themselves to live a celibate life such as monks, priests, and nuns (Christian, Buddhist, and Hindu) are a testimony to this simple reality. In addition, there is no conclusive evidence that such people suffer any terrible psychological consequences. The bodily sexual need—if it can be considered a "need" at all—is quite unlike the bodily need for food, water, air, or sleep.

6 sexual arousal in men and women

However, there are some interesting similarities between sexual desire and hunger. A person's feelings of hunger may be inflated or diminished as a consequence of what he or she learns. People can rather easily learn to diet or overeat. Similarly, feelings of genital sensitivity may be inhibited or intensified in response to what a person learns. Indeed, it may be very useful to begin by making a distinction between two dimensions of sexual desire: (1) a desire to experience sexual activity; and (2) bodily feelings of genital sensitivity, or what is popularly called "horniness." It is quite possible for a person to feel "horny," but reject any desire for sexual activity. (They may do so for a variety of reasons—practical and moral.) On the other hand, it is also possible for a person to desire sexual activity without feeling "horny." (Again, they may do so for a variety of reasons, such as desire to express affection, or to please a partner, or even as a result of curiosity.)

The effects of abstinence upon level of sexual desire is not entirely clear. A short period of abstinence appears to increase sexual desire in most people who are predisposed to enjoy sexual activity. However, abstinence from sexual activity alone does not in itself always result in an increase in sexual desire (Hardy, 1964). A crucial factor may be whether or not previous sexual activity has been experienced by a person as being pleasurable. In addition, the effects of a long-term sexual abstinence may be quite different from short-term abstinence. There are many reports that long-term deprivation of sexual stimulation actually diminishes sexual desire, resulting in sexual apathy. (A similar effect is found in cases of long-term food starvation.) Reports of sexual apathy caused by long-term sexual abstinence come from cases of people who are sexually isolated for long periods of time, such as in prisons or in remote military installations (Martin, 1976).

It should also be noted with caution that much sexual stimulation among humans is often indirect and in symbolic form (Victor, 1978). Indirect sexual stimulation encountered in conversation and the mass media may function to maintain a certain level of sexual desire in the absence of direct sexual activity. This may account for relatively high levels of sexual desire among some people who have very infrequent sexual activity, such as many teenagers.

variations in sexual desire

Sexual desire is not simply a response to an intense bodily need. Instead, it is very easily influenced by social forces in a society. Differences in level of sexual desire are found not only between individuals but also between different cultural groups. Anthropologists have found certain societies in which sexual desire is merely sufficient for reproductive purposes. One anthropologist studied an Irish village and found that—because of repressive moralistic traditions—any interest in sexual pleasure was consistently discouraged for both men and women (Messenger, 1971). In that village, premarital and extramarital sexual contact were almost nonexistent. Marital intercourse was expected for the sake of childbearing and was performed in a perfunctory manner which enabled quick release for the husband.

In contrast, other cultures encourage a constant preoccupation with sexual activity. Another anthropologist studied a society on a South Pacific island where premarital sexual activity begins during early adolescence (Marshall, 1971). Sex assumed the characteristic of a competitive athletic activity for both sexes who aimed at achieving prestige by exhibiting the ability to sexually please the opposite sex. The ability of a boy to provide a girl with several orgasms night after night as well as the ability of a girl to be very active during sexual intercourse were highly prized. Inadequate performance caused a loss of self-esteem as well as village gossip full of ridicule. After marriage, such ability continued to be esteemed by a couple, and marital intercourse was quite frequent even though frequency declined with age.

In the Irish village, any amount of sexual desire is a cause for regret whereas on the South Pacific island, insufficient desire is an embarrassment. As a personal goal, sexual activity can be given differing value-priorities. Obviously, the desire for such a goal is influenced by the kinds of learning and situational factors which similarly affect other human values. Sexual activity may have little value or great value in human life. In conclusion, sexual desire is a product of the biological capacity for sexual arousal and the value-priority a person learns to place upon sexual pleasure.

BIOLOGICAL ASPECTS OF SEXUAL AROUSAL

the effects of androgen

In both males and females, the same androgenic hormones create the bodily conditions which enable sensual, erotic pleasure to be experienced. These conditions include: (1) an intensified sensitivity of the genitals (penis or clitoris and labia) to stimulation; and (2) a build-up of sexual response to such stimulation until orgasm (Salmon and Geist, 1943). Without the presence of the necessary hormones and bodily conditions, a person cannot experience erotic pleasure.

Androgenic hormones, or simply androgen, is a family of chemically similar hormones which include testosterone. These hormones are produced in the testes of men and the adrenal glands of both sexes.

Various sources of evidence point to the conclusion that androgen is essential for the existence of genital sensitivity and the experience of sexual arousal in both sexes (Luttge, 1971). In women, removal of the ovaries does not bring about an elimination of sexual desire. However, the removal of the adrenal glands as a source of androgen does so almost always (Waxenberg, Drellich, and Sutherland, 1959).

In many cases, the administration of androgen to women increases their sexual desire, probably by increasing clitoral sensitivity (Luttge, 1971). (It also has the unfortunate side effect of increasing bodily and facial hair.) In adult men, removal of the testes (castration) does not always eliminate sexual desire and the capability of erection. This is probably because the adrenal glands continue to supply a small amount of androgen (Money and Ehrhardt, 1972). In most cases, however, castration does diminish or terminate genital sensitivity and the possibility of sexual arousal. The administration of androgen to castrated men usually reestablishes their sexual sensitivity and capability of erection (Luttge 1971). A drug has recently been developed which counteracts the bodily effects of androgen. When this anti-androgen drug was administered in Germany to male sex offenders who volunteered for the study, their sexual desire was greatly diminished or eliminated (Laschet 1973). There is no complete agreement among physiologists that androgen is the only hormone affecting sexual arousal, but no other bodily agent has yet been identified.

Since a bodily chemical must be present for a person to experience sexual arousal, it is necessary to ask about the effects of differing amounts. Do high and low levels of circulating androgenic hormones affect sexual desire and sexual behavior in any way? Only recently has there been adequate research into this question, primarily as a result of improved methods of determining hormone levels directly from blood samples. Basically, the research to date indicates that the relative levels of androgenic hormones circulating in the blood have no effect upon either sexual desire or sexual behavior.

One study, for example, compared the frequency of sexual intercourse of men having abnormally low testosterone levels with men having normal testosterone levels (Raboch and Starka, 1973). No significant differences in frequency of intercourse were found between these groups of men. Therefore, the researchers concluded that normal men produce a "superabundance" of testosterone, much more than is necessary to motivate sexual activity. More recent hormone research confirms that the actual level of testosterone in the blood of men has no relationship to their sexual interest or their frequency of sexual activity (Brown et al., 1978). The implication of the hormone research is that only micro-amounts of androgenic hormones are necessary for sexual activity to occur. A person's frequency of sexual activity is probably best accounted for by learning and interpersonal factors.

biological maturation and sexual arousal

Research on the effects of androgenic hormones is also important to an understanding of erotic development during childhood and adolescence. The available research indicates that androgen is present in very small amounts in boys and girls from infancy (Nathanson et al., 1941; Hamburg and Lunde, 1966). The existence of androgen in children may help to account for childhood masturbation and sexual play between children which is commonplace in some societies (Ford and Beach, 1951). Androgen production begins to increase markedly at about the age of 8 or 9 in both sexes (Root, 1973). Then, during early adolescence, androgen production levels off in girls but continues to increase in boys. Ultimately, adult men produce at least ten times more androgen than do adult men (Root 1973). The "superabundance" of testosterone in males is responsible for the development of male body characteristics rather than male-female differences in sexual behavior or desire.

In conclusion, it appears that the biological basis for sexual behavior exists from early childhood. The social environment inhibits or permits its expression below a certain age level.

It is unlikely that increased androgen production during puberty results in a sudden interest in dating and sexual activity. Instead, in American society, when adolescents begin to develop the outward appearances of an adult body, they begin to be seen by others as sexual persons. It is then that a young person begins to be exposed to a newly eroticized social environment. That new environment is composed of dating, petting, sex jokes, sex stories, sex information, and misinformation. Once a person is socially seen as a sexual being his or her erotic responsiveness becomes channeled by parents and peers in the direction of socially approved goals for sexual expression.

At the other end of the life cycle, popular belief holds that a decline in hormone production destines the elderly to sexual inactivity. This belief is simply not true. When this false assumption is held by an elderly couple, it may actually bring about a self-fulfilling prophecy by inhibiting sexual desire. As far as it is known today, the decline of sexual activity with advanced age is primarily a result of learning and interpersonal factors or health/disease factors.

Many people in their 60s, 70s, and even 80s, can and do enjoy sexual activity (Newman and Nichols, 1960). Certain physiological conditions of bodily aging may diminish sexual responsiveness. However, the termination of sexual desire is essentially a psychological matter. Men may experience a decreased skin sensitivity in their penis, less rapid erection, and less seminal fluid during ejaculation. Women may experience less vaginal lubrication and a relaxation of the vaginal muscles (Oliven, 1974). Yet, the ultimate inhibitions to erotic pleasure—or lack of them—derive primarily from the attitudes generated by an elderly couple's relationship with each other (Pfeiffer and Davis, 1972).

the effects of genital anatomy

Some psychologists have suggested that the difference between male and female genital anatomy has important implications in the learning of erotic responsiveness in both sexes (Bardwick, 1971; Shuttleworth, 1959). The erection of the penis is an obvious indicator of sexual arousal in males. It offers dramatic feedback information to a boy of his body's response to certain forms of stimulation. The larger size and external anatomy of the penis means that male children are more easily and consistently exposed to bodily excitation from genital stimulation. The erection of the penis also offers feedback information which localizes the source of that excitation in the genitals.

In contrast, the clitoris, which is the center of female genital sensitivity, is small and recessed into the body. Its erection in young girls may easily go unnoticed. Therefore, the suggestion is that women, particularly when young, are less easily aware of their genital excitation. They have less bodily feedback information (except from vaginal lubrication). Some women even have difficulty identifying whether or not they have experienced an orgasm (Perlmutter et al., 1975). Men do not experience this difficulty because of the information feedback from penile erection and ejaculation.

Few researchers have given any attention to the effects of the accumulation of semen in male sexual arousal. However, at least one psychologist has suggested that males behave as if they are under constant physiological tension to release accumulated seminal fluids (Shuttleworth, 1959). It is a widespread belief among men that genital tension derives from internal pressures of accumulated semen. As far as is known, the accumulation of semen does not generate any direct genital tension (Kinsey et al. 1948). Instead, men may learn feelings of pleasurable anticipation (tension) in response to subtle bodily sensations associated with the build-up of seminal fluids in the seminal vesicles.

cyclical changes in genital sensitivity

Considerable research controversy surrounds the question of whether or not there exist special times of heightened genital sensitivity during the menstrual cycle in women and whether such occasions are caused by hormonal changes. There is even disagreement over whether or not any changes in woman's sexual sensitivity derive from genital sources, mood alternations, or attitudes toward possible pregnancy. The available research offers quite contradictory findings. Some of the research finds no common pattern of sexual sensitivity among women over the menstrual cycle (Fisher, 1973; Griffith and Walker, 1975; Spitz, Gold, and Adams, 1975). Other research efforts have reported three different peak times of sexual sensitivity: (1) during ovulation at mid-cycle; (2) immediately preceding menstruation; and (3) immediately after menstruation (Udry and Morris, 1968; Morris and Udry, 1971; Cavanagh, 1969; Kane, Lipton, and Ewing, 1969; Luschen and Pierce, 1972).

These differences in findings may be a consequence of differences in research methodology. In addition, the differences in findings may be because of the difficulties of separating and interrelating interpersonal, psychological, and biological factors (Spitz, Gold, and Adams, 1975). At this point in the research, no definite conclusions can yet be drawn about the existence of cycles of genital sensitivity. There is no certainty about any cause and effect relationship between hormonal changes and sexual behavior. Also, individuals may have different cycles of sexual sensitivity so that any attempt to find a common pattern glosses over individual variations.

There has been little research into the possible effects of hormone cycles in men. One research project, however, did find that a majority of men studied had definite cycles of testosterone increases and decreases. However, the research found that these fluctuations in testosterone levels were not correlated with any increases and decreases in sexual activity (Doering et al., 1975).

It would appear that psychological and interpersonal factors, rather than hormonal factors, are those which best explain variations in human sexual activity.

PSYCHOLOGICAL ASPECTS OF SEXUAL AROUSAL

A complex interrelationship between biological and learned factors in sexual arousal exists. The body's anatomy and physiology provide the potential for sexual arousal. Ultimately, however, it is learned, interpersonal factors that activate the potential for sexual arousal and channel sexual behavior toward socially approved goals. The following section attempts to identity the basic social psychological mechanisms of sexual arousal. It focuses upon cognition, learning, and perception as they are influenced by interpersonal experience.

cognitive functioning

The cerebral cortex of the brain, with its cognitive (or symbolizing) functions, plays a central role in human sexuality (Money, 1961; Beach, 1969). Cognitive processes give erotic meaning to stimuli and sensations which a person may (or may not) regard as being sexually pleasurable. Cognitive learning is a distinctive and crucial aspect of human sexual learning. In addition, cognitive processes can inhibit or intensify human sexual arousal.

Some recent research provides evidence of the importance of cognitive processes in sexual arousal (Rook and Hammen, 1977). Several experiments have investigated the role of cognitive processes in the inhibition of sexual arousal. One study, for example, found that eight men who were shown a sexually explicit movie could voluntarily inhibit their erection when they were asked to think about nonsexual matters (Henson and Rubin, 1971).

Another experiment studied the hypothesis that cognitive distraction inhibits sexual arousal (Geer and Fuhr, 1976). In this experiment, 31 male college students served as volunteers. In private booths, the students heard an erotic tape recording in an earphone which described a scene of activities involving sexual foreplay, oral-genital contact, and intercourse. Their sexual arousal was measured with a penile strain gauge that indicated the degree of erection which each experienced. One special subgroup of men were also required to do complex mathematical calculations with instructions being given to them over an intercom. They were asked to do the calculations as they were simultaneously listening to the erotic tape. The students who had to concentrate their attention on the calculations experienced no sexual arousal while listening to the erotic tape. In real life situations, cognitive distraction during sexual activity may take the form of worries caused by a job, child discipline, or household care; or concerns caused by marital conflict; or even anxieties over adequate sexual performance. Sex therapists have long noted that these distractions interfere with sexual stimulation and reduce sexual arousal (Masters and Johnson, 1970).

In contrast, a concentration of attention upon thoughts of erotic pleasure appears to intensify sexual arousal. Interview research has found that women who concentrate upon erotic fantasies during sexual intercourse report that such imagery intensifies their sexual arousal (Hariton and Singer, 1974). Some sex therapists now advise clients who have problems in achieving orgasm to concentrate on erotic mental imagery. This enables them to avoid distracting thoughts which provoke anxiety, guilt, or fear of failure (Barbach, 1975). Men and women both experience sexual arousal in response to erotic fantasies alone without any body contact (Heiman, 1975). A few people are even capable of fantasizing to orgasm (Kinsey et al. 1953). In addition, sexual arousal in response to sexually explicit photographs, movies, and literature is ultimately a response to the stimulation of cognitive imagery. Lower animals do not exhibit sexual arousal in response to "pornography."

It is not at all unusal that brain functioning should affect other physiological processes in the human body. The effects of cognitive brain functioning on the body may include such distresses as ulcers, hypertension, gastric disorders, and even skin rashes. In certain neurotic disorders, cognitive affective reactions to life experiences may stimulate the bodily symptoms of blindness, deafness, or even paralysis. Therefore, it should not be surprising that cognitive brain functioning can intensify or inhibit genital sensitivity.

Behavioral scientists have developed a reasonably adequate understanding of the general principles of human learning in everyday social interaction (Bandura and Walters, 1963; Mischel, 1973). Three basic mechanisms of social learning can be recognized: (1) conditioning; (2) modeling; and (3) cognitive learning. These three mechanisms of learning usually occur simultaneously so that it is a bit artificial to focus upon one or another in an actual situation.

Conditioning. *Conditioning* involves learning which is the result of the effects of rewards and punishments. People are constantly being exposed to an environment which rewards and punishes their behavior. Generally, actions which are constantly rewarded tend to be continued, while ones that are constantly punished tend to be discontinued. These experiences of pleasure and pain may be direct, or indirect and symbolic. For example, giving candy to a child as a reward is a direct gratification, while praise is symbolic and indirectly satisfying. When a child receives a spanking, it is a directly painful experience, while receiving ridicule is symbolic and indirectly painful.

It is not only behavior which can be shaped by conditioning, but also bodily responses. Sexual arousal can be affected by rewards and punishments. When sexual arousal is frequently rewarded, sexual desire is intensified (Hardy, 1964).

However, when punishments are applied to sexual arousal, the effect can be the inhibition of sexual desire. Sexual desire, then, becomes associated with an unpleasant bodily state. For example, a child may find that stimulating its genitals provides it with pleasure. The reward of pleasure will enhance sexual desire as well as encourage the behavior which results in pleasure. If a parent often punishes a child for such behavior, it will occur less frequently. In addition, punishment will become associated with sexual desire. When both rewards and punishments become associated with sexual arousal, a person experiences sex anxiety (Bandura and Walters, 1963).

Modeling.   The second mechanism of learning is modeling. *Modeling* involves observation and imitation, usually of intimate associates. Children, especially, learn a great deal by imitating the behavior which they observe in their parents and close friends. They use the behavior of another person in certain situations as a model for their own behavior when they encounter similar situations. Rarely, however, is observational imitation a matter of conscious and deliberate planning. Usually, the model is cognitively programmed and remains latent in subconscious memory until a relevant situation activates it.

In our society, there is scarce possibility for children to observe adult sexual activity. However, modeling does play a very important role in sexual learning among children as they observe interpersonal behavior indirectly associated with sexual activity. A child may observe her or his parents embrace, caress each other, and express words of affection. Later on in life in male-female relations, that model will be repeated more easily than if it had never been experienced. A child who sees parents worried about nudity in the home will likely become anxious about nudity, even though the child may not know why (Sears, Maccoby, and Levin, 1957). In general principle, role models can provide positive or negative associations with sexual desire and arousal.

Cognitive learning.   *Cognitive learning* involves learning which depends upon language. Language consists of a code of spoken and written symbols which have no meaning in themselves. Instead, linguistic symbols represent human meanings which have become culturally associated with sounds and writing. Linguistic symbols are able to convey complex chains of associations which are only indirectly linked to concrete experiences. Cognitive learning about sexual matters derives from stories, jokes, direct explanation, and sometimes even from books. Such learning involves structuring the brain's pathways. It can be compared with learning the details of a very complicated map.

Certain kinds of abstract symbols are particularly important in sexual learning. These include beliefs, values, and rules for behavior. Many beliefs about the nature of sexual stimuli effect sexual arousal. Human values are constantly applied to evaluate sexual stimuli and sexual desire itself. These may be evaluated as a benefit or burden of being alive. In addition, sexual arousal is influenced by personal standards of conduct which can be the basis for feelings of self-esteem or guilt.

Some examples illustrate the influence of cognitive learning upon sexual arousal. In American society today, many men and women learn the value that sexual pleasure should be associated with love. Love is not directly experienced but is symbolized in expressions of affection. When this value is strongly internalized, it may be difficult for a person to respond sexually without anxiety to an interpersonal encounter which omits expressions of affection. The same person may react to an affectionate relationship with intense sexual arousal.

perception

The meaning of a sexual stimulus (person, object, or event) is not in the stimulus itself. Instead, human meaning is attributed to stimuli. *Perception* involves the brain's reception of stimulation as well as the interpretation of its meaning (Lindesmith, Strauss, and Denzin, 1975). In the human brain, the processes of perception (seeing) and cognition (understanding) are linked. We see with our brain as much as with our eyes. The brain attributes human meaning to the data of the senses simultaneously as it processes that data. Sexual stimuli are perceived as sexual only because erotic meanings are being attributed to them by the brain. This does not imply that perception involves conscious and deliberate judgments. Instead, most of the time perception is a response to ingrained learning and operates on a subconscious level of awareness.

Compared with other animals, humans are capable of being sexually aroused by an unusually wide range of stimuli (Ford and Beach, 1951). This is a consequence of the human ability to attribute erotic meanings to all sorts of stimuli. Erotic meanings may be attributed by some people, for example, to articles of clothing, particular body parts, special words, artistic creations, and even certain foods.

The term "erotic meanings" in this book is similar to that of "a sexual value system," as employed by Masters and Johnson. They state that "a sexual value system is derived from sensory experiences individually invested with erotic meaning, which occur under the choice of circumstances and the influence of social values which make them convertible to and acceptable as sexual stimuli (Masters and Johnson, 1970, p. 25).

Erotic meanings. Two levels of erotic meanings can be distinguished: (1) the cultural level; and (2) the personal level. The *cultural level* refers to widely shared meanings which are rooted in the common cultural heritage of a society. Such erotic meanings are rooted in traditional beliefs and expectations about sexual stimuli. When individuals attribute erotic meaning to any sexual stimulus they usually do so because of socially structured learning. The seductive mood music of our culture is not apt to seem erotic to natives of New Guinea, just as their cosmetic body scars would not be an erotic "turn on" for us. There is also a *personal level* of erotic meanings which are a product of relatively unusual experiences and learnings within a society. Personal erotic meanings are much like personal preferences. Just as personal taste in food differs somewhat within a society, so does erotic taste. However, it is an error to exaggerate the extent to which erotic meanings are personalized. Most people who share a culture share erotic tastes in common, just as they do their tastes in food.

Some examples will serve to illustrate the levels and types of erotic meanings. In American culture, lip kissing is primarily a symbolic expression of intimacy and a mild sensual pleasure. In some non-Western cultures, such as in traditional China and Japan or among the Eskimos, the custom did not exist. In such cultures, lip kissing was regarded as peculiar, vulgar, or amusing (Opler, 1969). In American culture, oral-genital kissing used to be considered unsanitary, perverted, and repulsive. Today, a majority of Americans have redefined it as an intensely sensual expression of intimacy (Hunt, 1974). Some people are sexually aroused by wearing the clothes of the opposite sex (transvestites). Such an erotic taste is an expression of very unusual, personal learning. On the other hand, it is not unusual for American men to be mildly sexually aroused by the sight of female underclothes. Yet, few, if any, women ever learn to be similarly aroused by male underclothes. Some people learn to regard stimulation of the anus as being erotic, while many others consider it to be ridiculous or repulsive.

Even the nude body is not a sexual stimulus in itself. Erotic definitions of nudity are attributed to nude bodies as a consequence of people's social learning. In many societies in hot climates, people may wear little clothing, while in other similarly hot places they may wear much clothing. Nudity and body modesty are a response to cultural expectations. Nude bathing beaches are becoming fashionable in some places in the United States and Europe (Kopkind, 1976). On such beaches, public nudity is not regarded as an occasion for sexual arousal except perhaps among nonparticipants. Research in nudist camps has found that various subtle customs serve to discourage people from attributing erotic meanings to public nudity (Weinberg, 1965). In public situations, sexual arousal in response to nudity can result in embarrassment, especially for men. Nudists and "skinny dippers" certainly continue to regard nudity as a stimulus for sexual arousal. But, they learn to respond to it erotically only in a situation of privacy.

In relation to the perception of erotic meanings, it is instructive to consider the American "breast fetish" (Morrison and Holden, 1974; Jesser, 1971). A fetish involves sexual behavior which has become especially focused upon a particular object or body part as an erotic symbol. After his research on male sexuality, Kinsey concluded that there "is reason to believe that more males in our culture are psychically aroused by contemplation of the female breast than by the sight of the female genitalia'' (1948, p. 575). Many American men believe that all women are sexually aroused by breast caressing, and that large breasted women are more sexually responsive than are small breasted women. Neither belief is true. At an early age, when sexual intercourse would evoke feelings of guilt and embarrassment, American teenagers commonly practice breast fondling as a substitute for genital contact. Breast fondling during petting reinforces the erotic significance of women's breasts.

Yet, in many societies, women are publicly bare-chested without having to be concerned about provoking sexual arousal in men. In many societies, the female breast is not an erotic symbol and breast fondling does not occur during sexual activity (Ford and Beach, 1951). In many societies, the female breast is a symbol of motherhood and maternal nurturance (unreplaced by bottle feeding). However, in American society, women who have breast-fed their babies in public have been arrested for public sexual indecency (Brack, 1975). The percentage of American mothers who breastfeed their infants is one of the lowest in the world (Brack, 1975), although this is changing. It is clear that women's breasts are a sexual rather than a maternal symbol among Americans.

Perceptual set.   There is, as yet, no clear understanding of the psychological factors which influence perception so that certain forms of stimulation come to be regarded as sexually arousing. Why are certain stimuli seen as erotic, and others not perceived as such? Social learning obviously accounts for the nature of perception in general terms. However, more specific perceptual mechanisms are relevant.

People learn certain psychological predispositions to see stimulation as being sexual. Such predispositions are technically known as a person's *perceptual set.* In other words, people learn to respond to particular ''cues'' in a social situation with a readiness for sexual arousal. For example, the naked breasts of women are such a cue for many men. Yet, the meaning of cues are judged from their social context. Nudity and even genital manipulation are not generally defined as cues for sexual arousal when they occur in a doctor's office (Emerson, 1970).

A person's perceptual set operates within the context of the particular *definitions of the situation* shared by participants in that situation. Nudity in a bedroom may be a cue for sexual arousal if a married couple define the occasion as being appropriate. They may not do so, and the occasion may not result in sexual arousal. In contrast, the definition of the situation in nudist camps and public nudist beaches is such that nudity is not a cue for sexual arousal. The possibility always exists, of course, that participants may not share the same definition of the situation. A woman who invites a male friend to her apartment for a few drinks may find that he has a perceptual set to see the situation in terms of erotic meanings, rather than as an occasion for friendly conversation. In summary, sexual arousal occurs when a person attributes erotic meaning to a situation.

EROTIC RESPONSIVENESS IN MEN AND WOMEN

erotic response

Two basic dimensions of sexual arousal can be distinguished: (1) physiological sexual response; and (2) psychological erotic response. *Sexual response* is indicated by such bodily changes as erection in men, genital lubrication in women, and increasing muscular tension in both sexes. Sexual response in the body follows a cycle of physiological changes from initial excitement through orgasm to bodily relaxation (Masters and Johnson, 1966). *Erotic response* is a psychological readiness for sexual arousal. It occurs as a consequence of a person's attribution of erotic meaning to stimulation. Certain emotional reactions, like affection, confidence, and curiosity can enhance sexual arousal. Certain emotional reactions, such as guilt, disgust, anger, or embarrassment, can inhibit sexual arousal. The underlying psychological mechanisms of erotic response involve disinhibition and anticipation.

Disinhibition is a form of relaxation which occurs at the same time as the physical nervousness of sexual arousal. Disinhibition lets down the barriers of conventional social reserve. The disinhibited person relaxes his or her worries about potential embarrassment, shame, guilt, or distraction. That is what gives sexual activity its seemingly spontaneous quality. This relaxation response enables a receptivity to sensual stimulation more than that which is usually possible in most ongoing everyday activities. Certain conditions, such as privacy, familiarity with partner, and mutual affection, promote disinhibition for most people. Some people in some situations use alcohol to relax before sexual activity.

Anticipation focuses attention upon sensual feelings and intensifies the build-up of physical tension toward orgasm. It is the expectation that sexual activity will result in a pleasurable emotional state. Anticipation is intensified by such conditions as a short abstinence from sexual activity and variety in sexual activity. Anticipation is strengthened by past experiences of pleasure and weakened by displeasurable associations (Logan and Wagner, 1965). In summary, both relaxation and tension are necessary aspects of erotic response.

Most of the recent research has found no clear cut difference between men and women in their erotic responsiveness. Instead, all the erotic differences which exist between men and women are matters of degree. There is considerable overlap between males and females in any factor which influences erotic responsiveness. Indeed, the research indicates an increasing convergence of male and female sexual behavior especially among more recent generations of Americans and Europeans. Even today, the differences in erotic response and sexual behavior are greater among males and among females rather than between the sexes. In contrast to much speculation, no biological difference has been found that can account for male-female differences in erotic response. There is increasing agreement among sex researchers that male-female differences in erotic responsiveness are a consequence of differences in erotic socialization.

Most of the research on erotic response has been since the late 1960s, and there is not enough of it to allow any definitive conclusions. Many of these investigations have relied upon laboratory experiments in which relatively small and unrepresentative samples of volunteers are exposed to vicarious sexual stimulation. The stimuli usually consist of photographs, slides, movies, tapes of stories, or selections of readings in which explicit sexual activity is depicted. The laboratory research has proven to be very useful. Nevertheless, some caution must be maintained in appraising the findings drawn from such research. First of all, people's responses in laboratory conditions may differ considerably from that in actual interpersonal situations. In addition, most of the subjects in these experiments have been college students. Therefore, the findings may tell us very little about the responses of people who are older and not college educated. Finally, past measurements of sexual arousal have usually had to rely upon self-reports. More recently instruments have been developed to directly measure penile erection and vaginal swelling (Heiman, 1975). These are now being used in conjunction with self-reports of attitudes and the meanings which people attribute to stimuli.

A variety of personality factors have been found to be associated with an enhancement, or inhibition, of erotic responsiveness. The most important of these include feelings of love, previous sexual experience, sexual variety, and sex guilt.

Love. Feelings of love in response to an affectionate relationship are among the most potent intensifiers of erotic responsiveness for men as well as women. An affectionate partner who enthusiastically enjoys sexual activity is probably the single most sexually arousing "stimulus" for the vast majority of people of both sexes. Men and women have been found to be equally responsive to erotic stimuli when they are presented in an affectionate context in sexually explicit movies and tape recordings (Sigusch et al., 1970; Schmidt, Sigusch, and Schafer, 1973; Heiman, 1975; Fisher and Byrne, 1978).

An intensive study of the factors associated with orgasm in a large sample of women found that a woman's feeling of love for her partner was the most important predictor of a woman's consistency in experiencing orgasm (Fisher, 1973). On the other hand, a woman's lack of confidence in a love relationship was the factor found to be most predictive of problems in achieving orgasm.

Unfortunately, similar studies have not yet turned attention to the relationship between affection and male orgasmic problems. However, increasing numbers of young men now associate love closely with sexual arousal (Peplau et al., 1977). In many older men, feelings of being unloved by a marital partner may be an important source of early impotence. It is likely that for many men sexual activity is a nonverbal symbol of affection offered by the partner. If that is so, rejection of sexual initiative may be taken by some men as rejection of affection.

If we shift attention to erotic responsiveness in an impersonal sexual context, it is possible that a greater percentage of men than women are erotically responsive to impersonal sex. There is some counterevidence, however, that both men and women are capable of being erotically responsive to impersonal sex in the form of sexually explicit movies and tapes (Heiman, 1975; Fisher and Byrne, 1978). Studies of group sex also indicate that some women are capable of being sexually aroused by that form of relatively impersonal sex (Bartell, 1971). Nevertheless, the existence of prostitution around the world, catering to men rather than women, seems to suggest a more common male taste for impersonal sex. Many more men than women also continue to seek premarital and extramarital sex with partners for whom they have no affection (Hunt, 1974).

What could explain the seemingly more common male responsiveness to impersonal sex? It is possible that men in general are less sexually inhibited than are women. Yet there are probably other reasons. Perhaps impersonal sex offers some men the prospect of avoiding anxieties about pleasing their partners which inhibit self-centered pleasure-seeking. Concerns of pleasing a partner are, of course, those which are necessary in a love relationship.

Past experience and variety.   There is some evidence that enjoyable participation in a sexual activity may serve to strengthen erotic responsiveness to future involvement in the activity. Research with middle aged and elderly couples has found that past enjoyment is the most important determinant of the persistence of sexual attraction and activity (Pfeiffer and Davis, 1972). Other research has found that men and women are more sexually aroused by slides and movies depicting sexual activities when they have had past experience with the acts portrayed than when they have not had such experience (Mosher, 1973; Griffitt, 1975).

However, simple participation in a sexual activity may not be sufficient to reinforce erotic responsiveness. Participation in any sexual activity must be emotionally enjoyable for the experience to strengthen erotic responsiveness. The meanings which people attribute to their sexual experience are crucial. There are millions of sexual partners with long sexual experience together who are troubled by erotic unresponsiveness, difficulties in reaching orgasm, and impotence. There are a great many teenagers who reluctantly participate in sexual activities without the experience strengthening their erotic responsiveness to sexual acts.

An aspect of past experience is variety and routine in sexual activity. Many sex therapists advise the practice of some degree of variety in long-term sexual relationships. The suggestion is based upon the assumption that sexual variety intensifies the anticipation of sexual activity while constant repetition often erodes erotic responsiveness. Many men who visit prostitutes do so to experience variety in sexual activity. Sexual variety between partners might include: varying positions of intercourse, changing locations and times of sexual activity, oral-genital sex, anal intercourse, sexual activity while bathing, or while listening to romantic mood music.

Sex guilt.   The effect of sex guilt upon sexual arousal has been a topic of frequent discussion and controversy but unfortunately little research until recently. *Sex guilt* is a form of self-condemnation which results in feelings of disgust when persons transgress their personal standards of sexual conduct. Several investigations have found that college students who scored high in tests of sex guilt reported themselves as engaging in less socially disapproved sexual behavior than did college students who scored low in sex guilt (Mosher and Cross, 1971; Abramson and Mosher, 1975). The high guilt students were less likely to engage in masturbation, any form of heavy petting, or in premarital sexual intercourse. They gave moral reasons, rather than practical ones, for their abstinence. They also condemned cunniligus and fellatio in any sexual relationship as being "abnormal." These findings confirm the hypothesis that the sexual behavior of high guilt persons is much more self-restricted than is that of persons with low sex guilt.

Are people who have high sex guilt unable to become sexually aroused? Other research throws some light on this question. Studies of reactions to sexually explicit literature and films have found that both high and low sex guilt subjects respond with sexual arousal to such erotic stimulation (Mosher and Greenberg, 1969; Mosher, 1973). However, the subjects who were high in sex guilt responded with significantly greater feelings of guilt, disgust, and embarrassment, and with lower arousal. It is not known whether high sex guilt persons are erotically inhibited in marital sexual relations. It is most probable that variety in their marital sexual relations is severely inhibited and limited to sexual intercourse in conventionally accepted positions. In summary, it would appear from the available research that high sex guilt does not extinguish erotic responsiveness, but it does result in unpleasant emotional states in response to unconventional sexual behavior.

Are women more likely than men to learn sex guilt, as is popularly believed? There is no direct evidence that this is so, but the indirect evidence suggests that it is true. Several experimental studies have shown that as many women as men react to sexually explicit photographs, films, and literature with sexual arousal, but many more women have negative emotional feelings about it (Sigusch et al., 1970; Schmidt and Sigusch, 1970; Schmidt, Sigusch, and Schafer, 1973; Mosher, 1973; Heiman, 1975; Herrell, 1975). Several of these studies have also found that more women than men react negatively to presentations of unconventional sexual practices such as unusual intercourse positions and oral-genital caressing (Schmidt and Sigusch, 1970; Mosher, 1973). Research focusing upon sexual behavior has found that more women, than men, respond with guilt to masturbation and to premarital intercourse (Reiss, 1967; Abramson and Mosher, 1975).

The higher sex guilt of women than men may be disappearing rapidly in the United States. One study of 45 married women found that the younger the women were, the lower was their sex guilt about various sexual practices and the more diverse was their actual sexual experience (Keller et al., 1978). Younger women have been exposed to a society which is increasingly less restrictive toward female sexuality, while older women have learned inhibitions which affect their sexual behavior even in marriage.

visual responsiveness

Much research appears to contradict any assumption that there are sex differences in visual responsiveness to erotic stimuli. It has been found that men and women are about equally aroused sexually by explicit photographs and movies of people engaging in sexual activity (Schmidt and Sigusch, 1973; Mosher, 1973; Schmidt, 1975). This is particularly true when such movies do not convey a contemptuous attitude toward women.

It would appear that photographs of mere nudity are less stimulating for women, but that visual presentations of sexual activity do elicit women's sexual arousal. Isolated nudity may have little erotic meaning for most women. Instead, nudity within an interpersonal context is more likely to be erotically meaningful for women. Perhaps, also, the gradualness of movies functions to moderate women's anxiety, in response to erotic stimulation (Gebhard, 1973), whereas abrupt sexual stimuli having little association with interpersonal relationships may more easily evoke anxiety among women.

If we shift the focus of attention to the erotic responsiveness of men, these differences in visual reactions to nudity may indicate that more men continue to be sexually aroused by stimuli which are relatively impersonal. The greater male responsiveness to impersonal contexts of erotic stimulation is revealed in a number of ways. Men's erotic fantasies, in contrast with those of women, are more likely to focus upon genital gymnastics than interpersonal relationships (Barclay, 1973). Much pornography which is made by men for men illustrates such fantasy by giving disproportionate attention to genitals (rather than people) in action. Facial expressions, emotional reactions, and interpersonal relationships are matters given little consideration (Smith, 1976). Sexual activity in pornography usually commences abruptly with few preliminary enticements, rather than offering a gradual unfolding of increasingly intense intimacies.

In one research project, a group of college women were asked to describe an erotic movie which would be the most sexually arousing for them (Steele and Walker, 1976). Their responses agreed upon a script in which a man and woman gradually proceeded from undressing to kissing, having a great deal of foreplay, displaying much affection, and including intercourse in a variety of positions. In this female "ideal" script, both partners treated each other with gentleness, the woman was an active participant and both expressed feelings of satisfaction. The emphasis was upon a total, rather than a genital, relationship. The evolution of the relationship was gradual, rather than abrupt.

The foregoing research findings about erotic response to visual stimuli may be applied to actual interpersonal situations. They imply that men and women can be equally responsive to the sight of their partners in the nude and during sexual activity. However, women's visual responsiveness may be more dependent upon an interpersonal context which involves expressions of affection and gradual movement toward greater intimacy. The visual responsiveness of men is more likely than that of women to be stimulated by past fantasies of impersonal sexual activity directed primarily toward their own orgasmic pleasure.

intensity of sexual desire

There is one question which constantly arises in considerations of male-female erotic differences: Are there differences in sexual desire between men and women?

The basic difficulty with this question centers on exact meaning of "sexual desire." The referents for empirical observation and measurement are quite unclear. Usually, a person's level of sexual desire is measured in relation to their frequency of orgasm through sexual intercourse and masturbation (Kinsey et al., 1948; Kinsey et al., 1953). However, a person certainly could experience sexual desire and arousal without proceeding to orgasm or even without engaging in any sexual activity.

On the average, American men are more sexually active than are American women as measured by their frequency of orgasm over the life cycle (Kinsey et al., 1953). However, there is no evidence that any one particular underlying factor accounts for this difference. No biological "push" has yet been found. Women are likely to have more unpleasant emotional associations with sexual activity: fears of pregnancy, feelings of being used rather than loved, feelings of being degraded and shamed by engaging in socially disapproved practices, and lack of orgasmic relief in sexual intercourse. In addition, the erotic socialization of women as compared with that of men results in less self-confident sexual assertiveness and lower expectations for erotic pleasure in male-female relationships. Sexual satisfaction is more important to the self-esteem and therefore more central to the self-concept of the average American male than female. Beginning at puberty, with warnings and fears of pregnancy, girls learn to regard sexual activity as being less important than do adolescent boys. Women learn to develop much more ambivalent attitudes toward sexual activity than the more enthusiastic attitudes of men (Bardwick, 1971). This becomes clear when we examine erotic socialization in American society.

There does not seem to be any biological factor which could account for the male-female difference in the valuation of sexual activity. Research on the physiology of sexual response indicates that men and women have equal capacities for enjoying erotic pleasure in sexual arousal (Masters and Johnson, 1966). No differences in male and female genital sensitivity have yet been found. It is possible, as previously noted, that differences in genital anatomy (clitoris versus penis) may enable men to be more easily *aware* of milder levels of sexual arousal (Bardwick, 1971). Yet, in most cases, past pleasurable experience probably enables women to learn to sense mild genital arousal when it occurs also.

It should be noted that any male-female difference in sexual desire as a value-priority is not an absolute contrast. A high value-priority given to any activity is essentially a high level of interest in that activity. Studies of marital preferences for frequency of intercourse still find more husbands than wives reporting a higher level of preference (Hunt, 1974). One study of a national sample of men and women, for example, found that about 50 percent of husbands aged 45 and older desired sexual intercourse more frequently while about 25 percent of wives aged 55 and older reported the same desire for a higher frequency (Hunt, 1974).

What effect, if any, does intensity of sexual desire have upon erotic responsiveness? There is no direct research on this question, partly because of the difficulties of defining and measuring "sexual desire." However, if high sexual desire can be taken to mean a high value-priority or interest in sexual activity it is quite possible that high sexual desire enhances erotic responsiveness. It is likely that a high interest in sexual activity intensifies a person's anticipation, and thereby, readiness for sexual arousal.

Between human beings, sexual activity is initiated, performed, and coordinated by interpersonal expectations. In that way, it is just like any other form of social interaction. The expectations which guide interpersonal behavior are referred to as *roles*. Much like roles in a theater script, sexual interaction is "scripted" by erotic role expectations (Gagnon and Simon, 1973). The expectations sexual partners hold for particular patterns of sexual activity may be mutually shared or may be a matter of conflict. When erotic role expectations are in conflict, the result is what has been called *sexual incompatibility*.

Americans are developing rising expectations for more frequent and more diverse sexual activity in marriage. Rising expectations have their costs, however, leaving some couples with unfulfilled daydreams, emotional difficulties, and interpersonal conflict. Yet, there are also rewards for many couples who are able to find a deepened enthusiasm for the love and pleasure which they share.

In a long-term sexual relationship, variety is not something which simply occurs automatically. It is likely that a great many married couples become set in a boring sexual routine which they find difficult to change. Couples easily develop erotic role expectations for a rigid sexual "script," with which they become very comfortable. Thereafter, any variation in it becomes difficult to initiate. In sexual activity, as in any other social activity, a convenient routine is very difficult to alter.

There is much research evidence that married couples expect and practice much greater variety in their sexual activity than they did a generation ago

7 erotic roles of men and women

(Hunt, 1974; Travis and Sadd, 1977). Some people, however, find it difficult to enjoy sexual practices which only decades ago were considered perverse and abnormal. Social change in sexual behavior is rarely accepted easily. New erotic role expectations are likely to generate emotional difficulties and interpersonal conflict. The fact that married couples now have more frequent and diverse sexual activity than in the past does not mean that couples are more sexually compatible. Sexual compatibility is not a matter of what bodies do with each other but a matter of what partners expect of each other.

MALE AND FEMALE EROTIC ROLES

preferred frequency of sexual intercourse

Recent research indicates that substantial changes are taking place in long-term sexual relationships. Married couples of all ages are having sexual intercourse more frequently than in the past.

One large-scale research project investigated the frequency of sexual intercourse in a nationally-representative sample of over 5400 married American women between the ages of 19 and 45 (Westoff, 1974). The study was able to compare its findings in 1970 with those of similar research carried out during 1965. It found that a substantial increase in the frequency of marital sexual intercourse had taken place over the preceding short five-year period. What is more, this increased frequency of sexual activity was not limited to younger groups only, but occurred across all age groups. The average frequency of intercourse reported by the women was: 11 times per month at age 20; 9 times per month at age 25; 7 times per month at age 35; and 5 times per month at age 45.

The investigators were able to check two factors which might help to explain the increase in marital sexual activity: (1) the influence of more effective contraception; and (2) the influence of the changing female gender role (Westoff, 1974). Increases in sexual intercourse were found among women who practiced all types of contraception as well as among women who did not practice birth control. However, significantly greater frequencies were found among women who practiced the most effective techniques of contraception (that is, the pill, the IUD, and the diaphragm). In relation to women's changing gender role, the research found that college-educated women had higher frequencies of sexual intercourse than did non-college-educated women. It also found that women who agreed with modern gender role expectations had higher frequencies of sexual intercourse than did women who were more traditional.

There is a circular relationship between quantity and quality of sexual intercourse. Couples who get more pleasure out of sexual intercourse have sex more frequently; and the more frequently they have sex, the more satisfied they are with their sexual relationship. A questionnaire survey of 100,000 women found that the more frequently wives had sexual intercourse, the more satisfied they were with their sexual relationship (Travis and Sadd, 1977).

Conflict over preferred frequency.   Differences between sexual partners in their preferred frequency of intercourse can easily become a source of conflict and sexual incompatibility. How common are such differences between men and women in a long-term sexual relationship? Unfortunately, very little research has actually investigated the question using large samples of couples and interviewing each partner separately.

One study of a sample of 581 married couples found that the most common sexual problem reported by the partners was a difference in their preferred frequency of sexual intercourse (Landis and Landis, 1973). A recent investigation of this issue in a sample of 210 marriages found that 37 percent of the men and 35 percent of the women reported that the man desired sexual intercourse much more frequently than did the woman (Carlson, 1976). Only about 8 percent of men and 7 percent of women reported that the woman had a higher preference level. It is quite likely that the average frequency of intercourse between a couple having differing expectations is closer to that of the partner with lower expectations.

Other research offers evidence that a difference between husbands and wives in their preferred frequency of intercourse is reasonably common. One research project investigated recreational preferences, in a sample of 227 husbands and 233 wives, living in middle-class areas of a Southeastern city (Mancini and Orthner, 1978). They were given a list of 96 possible leisure activities, from which to choose the five that they "enjoyed the most." One of the choices was "sexual and affectional activity." This was one of the five favorite activities of 45 percent of the husbands, but only 26 percent of the wives. In addition, a greater proportion of husbands, than wives, indicated a preference for sexual activity, at all lengths of marriage, from one to fifty years.

Another study investigated sexual attitudes and behavior in a sample of 161 couples who had been married twenty years (Ard, 1977). The research found that after twenty years of marriage, sexual relations was still a source of "great enjoyment" for 70 percent of the husbands as compared with 57 percent of the wives. The husbands and wives were also asked about their preferred frequency of intercourse. Here the research found that the husbands on the average preferred to have sexual intercourse more frequently than did the wives. Curiously, it also found that the husbands tended to underestimate their wives' preferred frequency, while the wives tended to overestimate their husbands' preferred frequency. The perceptual difference exaggerated the real difference.

There is insufficient research to answer the question of how common or serious are marital differences over preferred frequencies of sexual intercourse. In many cases, both spouses may desire more frequent sexual activity. The desire for more frequent sexual intercourse is not always a consequence of any conflict over preferences between sexual partners. Husbands and wives may both desire more of a good thing but have their desires hampered by fatigue, inconveniences, or distractions. An indication that shared desires for more frequent sexual intercourse may be common can be found in two surveys conducted by *Redbook Magazine,* which questioned 100,000 women and 40,000 men. The surveys found that 53 percent of the men and 38 percent of the women said that they had sexual intercourse "too infrequently" (Travis and Sadd, 1977; Travis, 1978b).

sexual assertiveness and initiative

Mutual sexual pleasure is now a shared goal of most sexual partners. No longer is sex in marriage regarded as it had been in the past as a man's pleasure and a woman's burden. A man and woman are both expected to show concern for the sexual pleasure of the other in a loving sexual relationship. One national survey of young people between the ages of 16 and 25, for example, found that 80 percent of young women now expect a man to be concerned with his partner's sexual satisfaction (Yankelovich, 1974). In turn, do men now share this expectation? Some research indicates that the answer is a definite "yes." In the study of 40,000 men who responded to a questionnaire in *Redbook Magazine,* almost every man reported that much of his own pleasure comes from the sexual pleasure he is able to offer his partner (Travis, 1978b). Clearly, it is now an erotic role expectation thåt men show a concern for the sexual pleasure of their partners as well as an ability to offer it.

However, the goal of mutual sexual pleasure between loving partners has given rise to a curious paradox. Many women now feel under pressure to be more sexually pleasing to their male partners.

Several studies of marital sexual interaction have found that husbands commonly complain that their wives do not take sexual initiative frequently enough (Carlson, 1976; Rubin, 1976). These studies also indicate that a great many wives now feel social pressure from their husbands to take a more assertive role in sexual activity. In the Victorian past, women were expected to take a passively responsive disposition during sexual activity—reacting to male sexual initiative, responding to suggestions, and being the recipient of erotic stimulation. Most women accepted these expectations. Increasingly, however, many women feel under the pressure of new expectations—to initiate sexual activity, to suggest their own sexual preferences, to give erotic stimulation to their partners, and to move about more actively during sexual intercourse.

The question of women's sexual assertiveness raises several issues: (1) How do men react to women who are sexually assertive? Do men expect women to take sexual initiative frequently? (2) Do many women now expect themselves to take sexual initiative? (3) In actual sexual behavior, do men and women both feel comfortable taking a sexually assertive erotic role?

In terms of men's attitudes, some research does indicate that most men accept and appreciate a woman who is sexually assertive. The *Redbook* study of 40,000 men, for example, found that over 80 percent of the men reported that it is exciting for them when a woman takes the sexual initiative (Travis, 1978a).

Indeed, the men collectively reported that this possible characteristic of women is more sexually arousing to them than any other stimuli. One study investigated sexual initiative in a sample of 125 unmarried college students (Jesser, 1978). The research found that women who directly requested sexual activity were no more likely to be rebuffed by their male partners than were women who used subtle signaling to indicate their sexual desire. However, the men in both of these studies were disproportionately younger and more educated than is the whole male population.

Another study, in contrast, indicates that many less educated, working-class husbands may have quite contradictory attitudes toward sexually assertive women. Many of the working class husbands, in the study, reported that they wanted their wives to take sexual initiative more frequently; yet they broadly criticized women who behave "like men" in sexual relations (Rubin, 1976). It seems that some men at least hold contradictory expectations for the sexual behavior of the women they love.

Turning attention to the attitudes of women, some research indicates that young women now claim the right to take sexual initiative when they so desire. One opinion poll of a nationally representative sample of young people 16 to 25 years old, for example, found that 83 percent of college women and 67 percent of non-college women believe that "women should be as free as men to take initiative in sexual relations" (Yankelovich, 1974). This research would seem to suggest that a majority of young women now reject a sexual partnership restrained by the traditional erotic roles of male sexual assertiveness and female passive receptiveness.

However, women (or men) who reject traditional erotic roles are not necessarily able yet to feel comfortable with new expectations for their sexual behavior. A great many women still do not feel quite comfortable taking an assertive role in sexual activity. One recent study of sexual intimacy between unmarried college couples found that their sexual relationships continued to be guided by traditional erotic roles (Peplau et al., 1977). Even between sexually liberal couples, the men almost always took initiative in indicating a desire for sexual activity and the women responded by either accepting or rejecting their advances. Another study of 59 college women found that 40 percent of them did not feel comfortable enough to take sexual initiative or even to tell their sexual partners exactly what "turned them on" (Burstein, 1976). Finally, an intensive interview study of working class marriages found that many of the wives simply preferred their husbands to take the traditional assertive role in sexual relations (Rubin, 1976).

Sexual assertiveness in actual practice is probably most common among younger, more educated women. One study of 2372 wives, for example, found that among women age 25 years and younger, 41 percent reported taking sexual initiative at least half of the time (Bell, 1976). However, only 25 percent of the women who were past the age of 50 reported doing the same. Many of the older women even felt inhibited in talking to their husbands about their sexual desires. Yet, sexual assertiveness may directly enhance a woman's level of sexual satisfaction. One study of 45 professional women found that the more sexually assertive a woman was with her husband, the greater was her level of reported sexual satisfaction (Whitley and Paulsen, 1975).

Only one research project has investigated the interpersonal dynamics of sexual initiative between marriage partners (Crain and Roth, 1977). It administered separate questionnaires to 113 young married couples, most of whom were college educated and had no children. The research found that the men usually initiated sexual activity, but they preferred their wives to play a more equal role. The husbands reported that their greatest sexual pleasure was experienced when their wives initiated sexual activity. On their part, however, most of the wives preferred the more traditional erotic role of simply responding to male initiative. Importantly, the research went further. It found that the more often that a woman took sexual initiative, the more she was perceived by her husband as expressing personal desire rather than a sense of obligation to participate. In contrast, the more exclusively a man was relied upon by his wife to take sexual initiative, the more a man felt that expectation to be an obligation. Many of the husbands indicated having difficulties in taking sexual initiative, but few of the wives seemed to realize that was the case. Instead, most of the wives perceived their husband's sexual initiative simply as a preference which expressed their husband's personal desires.

foreplay

The term *foreplay* is usually used to refer to sexual activity which precedes sexual intercourse. However, foreplay can be enjoyed for its own sake. It can be a means of heightening sexual arousal and expressing feelings of intimate relatedness.

There are indications from the research of an increasing use of noncoital techniques of sexual stimulation, especially among younger married couples (Hunt, 1974).

Today, oral stimulation of the woman's nipples is practiced by almost all men (Hunt, 1974). Similarly, almost all women have engaged in the manual stimulation of their partner's penis (Hunt, 1974). Among men and women under the age of 35, about half have engaged in manual stimulation of their partner's anus (Hunt, 1974). A minority of this age group employ the practice fairly often.

There are additional ways that couples introduce variety into foreplay. According to recent research, many young couples augment sexual stimulation with vibrators, pornography, and marijuana (Travis and Sadd, 1977). Alcohol also continues to be used prior to sexual activity by many couples. Increasing numbers of young couples also vary the location for sexual intercourse from the bedroom to other rooms, motels, and outdoors (Bell, 1976).

The duration of foreplay can be a matter of shared or conflicting erotic role expectations. While the expectations of sexual partners have not been the subject of much research, the actual timing has been. The 100,000 women who responded to the *Redbook Magazine* questionnaire were asked: "On the average, how long must foreplay last for you to become sexually aroused?" (Travis and Sadd, 1977). The answer was 1 to 5 minutes for 29 percent of the women; 6 to 10 minutes for 43 percent; 11 to 15 minutes for 20 percent; 16 to 20 minutes for 5 percent; and more than that duration for the remaining 3 percent of women. These responses indicate that almost three-fourths of women can become sexually aroused with 10 minutes or less of foreplay.

However, many men and women now prefer to prolong their foreplay to elaborate their sexual pleasure. There is some research evidence that most couples are spending more time in foreplay today than did couples in the 1940s when Kinsey collected his data (Hunt, 1974). American husbands in general seem to enjoy foreplay as much as their wives and are less insistent upon reaching a quick orgasm than were men in the past. The study of 40,000 men responding to the *Redbook Magazine,* for example, found that 30 percent of the men wished foreplay would last longer than it did (Travis, 1978b). Foreplay is no longer as it was previously viewed: a form of kindness, offered by a man to his sexual partner, while he struggles to control his desire for orgasmic relief. It would appear that men and women now commonly share an erotic role expectation for extensive foreplay before vaginal penetration.

In some cases sexual partners may hold conflicting expectations—either the man prefers quick penetration with few preliminaries or the woman has difficulty becoming sexually aroused with very elaborate foreplay. It is unknown just how commonly such sexual problems actually occur between marriage partners. An indication of the possible extent of such problems comes from a 1970 national opinion poll of American women (Harris, 1970). It found that 14 percent of American women reported that a sexual problem which bothered them in their relationship was that they were not ready for intercourse at the same time as their partner. The actual incidence is probably a little higher given the tendency of people to under-report sexual problems.

The problem of contradictory expectations regarding the pacing of sexual arousal is best handled through direct sexual communication. Unfortunately, a great many sexual partners are unable to communicate about such matters. Their dialogue of the deaf may leave them saddened by silent reproaches. She may be likely to misperceive him as only being interested in his own sexual satisfaction, while he may be likely to misperceive her as being sexually unresponsive.

In the scripting of sexual activity, some couples have lengthy foreplay with short intromission (intercourse), while other couples rely upon lengthy intromission for sexual stimulation. Some couples often have orgasms separately, through coital and noncoital stimulation, while other couples exclusively expect simultaneous, mutual orgasms through sexual intercourse. However, there is some evidence that when a couple relies upon lengthy intromission for sexual stimulation, the female partner often finds it difficult to experience orgasm. One questionnaire study of about 3000 women, for example, found that only about 30 percent of the women could achieve orgasm regularly through sexual intercourse alone without any additional genital stimulation (Hite, 1976). Many of the women also reported that their sexual partners relied almost exclusively upon sexual intercourse for sexual stimulation.

In the past, many American men regarded it as a matter of male pride to be able to have lengthy sexual intercourse before ejaculation. Many of these same men also avoided foreplay. Their reliance upon the movements of sexual intercourse for sexual stimulation probably made it difficult for their partners to have equal sexual pleasure. This male erotic role expectation in the absence of sexual communication between partners helps to explain why many women in the past rarely or never experienced orgasm.

Some misunderstanding between sex partners is a result of the expectation for mutual orgasms during sexual intercourse. To achieve such a goal sex partners must share a similar mood for sexual activity and have good communication and coordination. The experience of mutual orgasms offers intense feelings of sharing and has a certain poetic symmetry. Yet, oftentimes, it is more realistic for the partners to take turns in bringing their sexual tension to climax.

Variations.   Certain areas of the body tend to be particularly sensitive to erotic tactile stimulation. These body surfaces have been termed *erogenous zones.*

Erogenous zones in men include: (1) the glans of the penis, especially along its rim; (2) the frenum, a small area of skin on the front of the penis, immediately below the glans; and (3) to a somewhat lesser extent the skin of the shaft, especially along the urethra. In addition, the surface between the anus and testicles, the scrotum, and the inner surface of the thighs may also be erotically sensitive to gentle caresses.

In women, erogenous zones include: (1) the clitoris, and the area immediately surrounding it; and (2) the inner surface of the labial lips and the entrance rim to the vagina. (However, the interior of the vagina is rather insensitive to tactile contact.) The nipples of the breasts, in both women and men, also contain a concentration of nerve endings and may become erotically sensitive. Whether or not a person develops erotic breast sensitivity probably depends more upon psychological conditioning than upon physiological factors. Many women are quite unresponsive to breast stimulation, while in contrast, about 10 percent can achieve orgasm directly through such stimulation (Kinsey, 1953; Masters and Johnson, 1966). The size of a woman's breasts are entirely unrelated to their erotic responsiveness.

The timing of different kinds of caresses can heighten, or mute, orgasmic feelings. Caressing may be gentle or vigorous, interrupted or continuous. In general, the process which most intensifies sexual arousal begins with very gentle caresses, interrupted in a stop-and-start teasing fashion, and moves gradually toward more vigorous and continuous stimulation. Individual and situational differences, however, are important.

The main physiological center of erotic sensitivity in a woman is the clitoris. However, direct manual stimulation of the clitoris is usually quite discomforting or even painful to a woman (Hite, 1976). Stimulation of the woman's genital region can be done by gently caressing the entire area, including the inner thighs. Once sufficient lubrication has taken place, the fingers can be used to caress gently the inner side of the labia and the area immediately surrounding the clitoris. In most women, the clitoris is much too sensitive to be caressed directly with fingers. As orgasm begins to approach, many women prefer vigorous caressing of the whole genital area.

When a woman manually caresses her male partner's genital region, the most arousing initial approach is a slow and gentle approach. (Some men rapidly build such a pitch of intense anticipation, especially when young, that they are quickly brought to orgasm by such stimulation.) Manual caressing of the penis can begin with a gentle touch of the fingers to the frenum, just below the glans. After the penis is erect, the woman can apply the palm of her hand to the front of its shaft providing slow and gentle up-and-down friction. As sexual arousal increases, many men prefer a firmer grasp which pulls the skin of the penis up and down. However, stimulation which is too rough often dulls sensation. Some men find a teasing, feather-light touch of the fingers to the scrotum very exciting. Others are not aroused by such stimulation.

Whether or not manual caressing leads to orgasm outside of the vagina is simply a matter of a couple's preference. Experiencing orgasm through mutual caressing may be quite satisfying as an occasional variation. It can be employed during pregnancy or when one spouse is too tired for sexual intercourse.

Oral caressing during sexual activity offers several advantages over manual caressing in terms of its ability to enhance sensual feelings. The mouth is a source of lubrication which enhances feelings of gentle friction over the skin. It also offers greater warmth than the hand. Any concern about giving or receiving germs is easily managed by the usual practice of body and mouth hygiene.

The lips and tongue are filled with nerves which are sensitive to tactile contact. That is one reason why kissing can become sexually arousing. In addition to our custom of rubbing the lips together, more intimate kissing is possible. The tip of the tongue may be used to caress the other partner's tongue and roof of the mouth. The latter approach renders a tickling sensation, which many people find quite exciting. This kind of kissing is popularly called "French kissing" (although it is probably more common between Americans than between French people).

The breasts may be stimulated orally in various ways. The nipples may be licked or teased with the tongue by rapidly flicking it over the nipple for a period of time. The sensation of warmth may be added if the breasts are gently sucked into the mouth.

oral-genital sex

Just a few short decades ago, oral-genital sex was widely considered a perversity in American society. It remains illegal according to the laws of most states even when practiced between consenting marriage partners. Yet sex surveys since that of Kinsey have revealed that oral-genital sex is rapidly becoming a regular practice in the sexual repertoire of a majority of American couples. In technical terms, *fellatio* means the oral stimulation of the penis, while *cunnilingus* means the oral stimulation of the female genitals.

Oral-genital sex is rapidly becoming an erotic role expectation between sex partners. One recent national sex survey found that oral-genital sex is at least an occasional practice among 80 percent of married couples under the age of 35, and 90 percent of those under the age of 25 (Hunt, 1974). Another study of 2000 women found that 29 percent of the women regularly practice fellatio with their partners, and 31 percent often receive cunnilingus from their partners in sexual foreplay (Bell, 1976). Very similar findings come from the *Redbook Magazine* survey of 100,000 women (Travis and Sadd, 1977). Cunnilingus was often experienced by 39 percent of the married women and an additional 48 percent experienced it occasionally. Fellatio was often performed by 40 percent of the married women and occasionally by another 45 percent.

Oral-genital sex is most commonly and most frequently practiced by college-educated people and by those who were born more recently. The difference may be because such people are more aware of mistaken beliefs about oral-genital sex. The national sex survey, for example, found that fellatio was practiced by 72 percent of college-educated wives, compared with 52 percent of those having only a high school education; and cunnilingus was practiced by 66 percent of college-educated husbands, compared with 56 percent of those having only a high school education (Hunt, 1974). In terms of age differences, the study of 2000 married women, for example, found that while 13 percent of 30-year-old women never engaged in fellatio, almost half of the women over the age of 50 never did so (Bell, 1976).

These research findings about the commonality and frequency of oral-genital sex, of course, cannot tell us much about the personal meaning of the practice between sexual partners. When once-forbidden sexual practices become commonplace, the change does not occur without causing some people emotional difficulties. One intensive interview study of 50 working class and 25 professional married couples revealed some of these difficulties (Rubin, 1976). Oral-genital sex was a source of subtle conflict between many of the working class couples. Many more of the husbands than wives indicated a desire to engage in the practice. Many of the working class women were troubled by feelings that oral-genital sex was still somehow a bit perverse. Even though about the same percentage of these women engaged in oral-genital sex as did the professional wives, they did so without enthusiasm. They reluctantly consented to their husbands' desires for oral-genital sex without regarding it as something they personally enjoyed. The women expressed particular reluctance to engage in fellatio, perhaps because it required them to take a more active and assertive erotic role. When they experienced cunnilingus, they could do so more easily because it required them to be only a passive recipient of sexual stimulation. The emotional difficulties of many of these wives were further aggravated by the ambivalent attitude of many of their husbands toward women who engage in fellatio: The obscene appellation "cock-sucker" remains one of the worst insults in the English language.

Women's reactions to cunnilingus were investigated in one questionnaire survey of about 3000 women (Hite, 1976). Many of the women reported that the experience was intensely pleasurable. Other women were distracted by a variety of anxieties. Some of the women felt that their genitals were unattractive or even "dirty." Others were very concerned about possibly disagreeable vaginal odors and tastes. Some of the women were also disturbed by feelings that their male partners were reluctant to perform cunnilingus or really didn't enjoy doing so. Therefore, even some of the women who enjoyed cunnilingus held quite ambivalent attitudes toward the practice.

How widespread is conflict about oral-genital sex between sexual partners? We do not know with any certainty. The *Redbook Magazine* questionnaire asked women about their enjoyment of oral-genital sex (Travis and Sadd, 1977). Cunnilingus was reported to be "very enjoyable" by 62 percent of the women and "somewhat enjoyable" by another 28 percent. In contrast, fellatio was reported to be "very enjoyable" by only 34 percent of the women and "somewhat enjoyable" by another 38 percent. Apparently many women find it more blessed to receive than to give oral-genital sex. Although there is no evidence, the same difference may exist for many men. The possible extent of conflicting expectations is revealed by a finding in the Redbook Magazine survey of 40,000 men (Travis, 1978b). One-third of the husbands reported that they wished their wives would perform fellatio more often than they do. These unfulfilled desires were expressed in sex fantasies about fellatio which were found to be common among the men.

A further indication of the possible extent of unfulfilled male expectations for fellatio can be found in studies of sex acts requested from prostitutes. One sex researcher, for example, was able to observe over a thousand contacts between sixty-four call girls and their clients in New York City (Stein, 1974). Fellatio was by far the most frequently requested sexual service (by 83 percent of the men). A sizable minority of the men (29 percent) reached orgasm through fellatio rather than through sexual intercourse. Many of the men complained to the call girls that their wives would not perform fellatio or showed no enthusiasm for it. The researcher suggested that the high frequency of this practice indicated a common desire of many men to step out of their traditional assertive erotic role and assume a passively receptive erotic role while the prostitute did the sexual "work." Ultimately, the common American male desire for fellatio may reveal an underlying desire for occasional relief from a rigidly sterotyped erotic role. Additional evidence for this explanation is the finding from the same research that almost half the men took a passive role during sexual activity (Stein, 1974).

Variations. One study asked about 3000 women to describe the oral-genital caresses which they found to be particularly pleasurable (Hite, 1976). In one very pleasurable oral-genital caress, the tip of the man's tongue is used to make circular movements around the clitoris and flicked in rapid vibration over its top surface. In addition, the man's tongue can be run along the inner surface of the inner labial lips and flicked into the entrance of the vagina. Another oral caress which may be very pleasurable involves the man sucking the woman's labia into his mouth. However, the man must be careful not to cause any pain with his teeth.

Oral-genital caressing of the penis involves flicking the tip of the tongue over the frenum and around the glans. The penis can be drawn into the woman's mouth and moved slowly up and down while she applies gentle suction. These oral-genital caresses can bring a man with little self-control very quickly to orgasm. Therefore, here as in other matters, communication is essential to the pacing of sexual arousal.

In mutual oral-genital caressing, both partners can play an active role as well as receive intense stimulation. The positions for it offer considerable body contact and enable both partners to engage in manual, as well as oral, caressing. This practice is euphemistically called "sixty-nine." Actually, it is often difficult to concentrate on one's own sensuous pleasure while at the same time offering effective oral-genital stimulation. Therefore, while practicing "sixty-nine," many couples find it preferable to alternate between giving and receiving stimulation.

The question of achieving sexual orgasm directly through oral stimulation is a delicate one because of the negative symbolic meanings traditionally associated with such activity. Many women find it particularly satisfying to obtain one or several orgasms through oral-genital caressing before proceeding to genital intercourse (Hite, 1976). This is also the easiest way for a man to provide his partner with multiple orgasms. Many men also find it intensely gratifying to experience orgasm directly through oral stimulation. Some women find the taste and texture of semen to be disagreeable while others do not (Hite, 1976). Again, there is nothing inherently abnormal, unnatural, or unhygienic in such a practice.

positions of sexual intercourse

In Western societies in the past only one sexual position was considered "normal" for decent people. Because of the religious sanction it received, it has come to be referred to as the "missionary position." Kinsey's research found that the male-above position was the one most frequently practiced among Americans born before 1930 (Kinsey et al., 1953). A small proportion of couples (9 percent) never even strayed from it in their lifetimes. However, most couples did practice some variation, especially those who were brought up more recently.

A recent national sex survey found evidence that since the time of Kinsey's research, variation in sexual positions has become common practice between marriage partners (Hunt, 1974). The research found that the female-above position is frequently used by 75 percent of married couples (versus only 45 percent in Kinsey's research). A side-to-side position is frequently used by 50 percent of married couples (versus only 31 percent in Kinsey's research). The rear-entry position is frequently used by 40 percent of married couples (versus only 15 percent in Kinsey's research). Finally, a sitting position is frequently used by 25 percent of married couples (versus only 9 percent in Kinsey's research). Frequent variation in sexual positions is found to be most common among younger couples.

Research studies of male and female attitudes toward different sexual positions is virtually nonexistent. One study, however, did investigate attitudes toward the female-above position in a sample of 119 unmarried college students (Allgeier and Fogel, 1978). Half of the students were shown slides of a couple having sexual intercourse in the female-above position and the other half were shown slides of a couple having sexual intercourse in the more conventional female-below position. All the students were then asked to give their impressions of the personalities of the man and woman using a scale of descriptive adjectives. Surprisingly, the research found that the female students (but not the male students) rated both the man and woman in the female-above position quite negatively. Specifically, the female students regarded the woman as "dirtier, less respectable, less moral, less good, less desirable as a wife and mother," when she was above the man during sexual intercourse. The female students rated the man in the female-above position in a similarly negative way. This research seems to indicate that young unmarried women as compared with men tend to hold more traditional erotic role expectations regarding positions of sexual intercourse. Negative emotional responses to the female-above position may reflect the reluctance of women to accept a role of sexual assertiveness. That position allows a woman greater control over the pacing of her own sexual arousal (Allgeier and Fogel, 1978). It is possible, of course, that such a clear-cut difference between men and women might not have been found if the research had been done with married couples.

Men may still be more interested than women in varying their sexual activity. The *Redbook Magazine* questionnaire study of 40,000 men found, that 65 percent of the men were not satisfied with the amount of sexual experimentation which they experienced (Travis, 1978b).

Variations. Much too much importance can be attributed to positions for sexual intercourse. An over-concern about positions can easily result in a minimization of foreplay.

There are hundreds of possible positions for intercourse. However, as a practical matter, the positions found to be most pleasurable for continual pursuit are those which: (1) are comfortable and relaxing; (2) do not cause muscular strain; and (3) enable a reasonable freedom of movement (Masters and Johnson, 1966). Choice of position is also affected by a couple's body size and weight as well as their athletic ability at the end of a tiring day's work. Each position has certain practical advantages and disadvantages. In addition, each offers somewhat different kinds of sensations of bodily movement and touch.

The most common position for sexual intercourse among Americans as well as among most other peoples is the *face-to-face, man-above position* (Ford and Beach, 1951). This may be because it is convenient and relaxing especially for the woman. It also allows for some possibilities of manual and oral caressing while offering a maximum of body contact. The face-to-face relationship facilitates communication and easily observed expressions of pleasure providing a greater sense of intimacy. Finally, it may provide greater friction to the clitoris than is possible in some other positions. On the other hand, this position presents difficulties for some people. It may present difficulties for people who are very obese, or for women in the last stages of pregnancy. It also may not be sufficiently relaxing for some men who ejaculate too quickly. The muscular tension needed to balance and move and the considerable body contact can provoke premature ejaculation.

There are numerous variations of the man-above position. Instead of resting her legs straight or holding open at the sides, a woman can rest her legs on her partner's shoulders by folding them upward so that her thighs rest on her stomach. This can offer variation in feelings of skin contact and motion. Another alternative is for the man to kneel between the woman's legs, holding her buttocks and bringing her to him for adequate support. This position is the one which is most common in many Pacific island societies (Ford and Beach, 1951).

A *sitting position* involves the use of a chair without arms. With one partner resting against the back of the chair for support, the couple can have intercourse seated face-to-face with their legs overlapping the sides of the chair. In this position, the couple's hands are free for caressing while they are also able to kiss.

Penile penetration is deep, and there is considerable skin contact in the genital area. However, the deep penetration may be painful for some women if their partner's penis bumps against their cervix.

The most common alternative to the missionary position is one in which the couple are *face-to-face, with the woman above.* This position offers advantages similar to the missionary position but is more relaxing for the man. He can lie back comfortably exerting little energy to maintain himself in that position and use his hands to caress his partner's body. In so doing, he can concentrate more easily on his own sensations. It may also offer certain advantages to a woman. If her partner is exceptionally heavy, this position literally takes the weight off of her. In addition, she can more easily regulate the pace of movement toward orgasm in rhythm with her own build up of sensations. Finally, it may be very useful for a couple in which the man tends to ejaculate too quickly. The man's relaxed position is less likely to promote rapid orgasm. It is for this reason that the woman-above position is often counseled in cases of frequent premature ejaculation.

The woman-above position also has certain disadvantages. It is more fatiguing for the woman. She may have to kneel in a position which causes muscular strain in her thighs. In addition, when there is vigorous movement with deep penetration in this position, some women find that it is internally discomforting or even painful.

The most common arrangement for the woman-above position is for the woman to kneel astride her partner's hips and squat down on his penis. She can then use her kneeling legs to move herself up and down. Her partner can make her more comfortable and relieve some of the strain by holding her by the waist to assist her up and down movements. There are numerous variations of the woman-above position. The woman can lie flat on top of her partner. Unfortunately, movement in such a position may be difficult. She may have to use her elbows as a balance point to create movement, or her partner may have to move her with his arms. A more unusual variation is for the woman to squat above her partner, but face toward his legs. Such a position offers less friction to the clitoris unless it is provided manually. It is also less psychologically intimate because the man faces his partner's back.

Another set of variations are *side-to-side positions.* A couple may have intercourse lying on their sides and facing each other. The woman can raise her upper leg and rest it across her partner's hip, enabling him to enter her vagina. In this position, both partners are free to use their hands and mouth in caressing the other. In this position, also, it is easy for a couple to maintain their contact after orgasm as they fall asleep.

Yet the side-to-side position also presents some difficulties. It may be very difficult to manage if the body shapes of a couple are inappropriate for it. In addition, such a position does not allow for vigorous genital movement because the couple's bodies are locked into a constricted position.

An alternative side-to-side position is one in which the man lies on his side facing the woman's back. This position is, perhaps, the one which is most relaxing for a couple. It is a variation particularly appropriate for times when a couple are very tired or on sleepy mornings or when there is illness or pregnancy. However, in cases where one, or both, of a couple are obese this position may be very difficult to manage. In addition, while this position enables the man to have a maximum of possibilities for manually caressing his partner, she is left with few possibilities for active participation. If manual caressing is not provided, she may feel little sensuous contact and inadequate friction to her clitoris.

The final set of variations are *rear-entry positions*. One arrangement is for both partners to kneel with the man behind the woman and between her legs. This positions provides the man with considerable freedom to move his hands in caressing his partner's body. It also provides the man with a full-bodied feeling of motion during the thrusting movements of intercourse. (This increases stimulation to the kinesthetic sense—the sense of body movement.) In addition, the soft pressure of his partner's buttocks against his whole genital region may provide exciting tactile stimulation.

Unfortunately, the rear-entry position doesn't offer many advantages for women. Friction to the clitoris may be inadequate and may have to be provided manually during intercourse. Body contact for her is minimal and possibilities for active participation are limited to thrusting backward. The deep penetration for some women may result in discomfort or pain. Finally, such a position may not provide a sense of intimacy for a couple because partners are unable to view each other's facial expressions. This position is, perhaps, the most tabooed in American culture. It is attributed symbolic associations with animal behavior as well as the degradation of women.

A variation of the rear-entry position is a sitting arrangement. The man can sit in a chair, or on the edge of the bed, with his partner seated on his lap, her back toward him. He is free to move his hands in manually caressing her. However, genital movement in this position is difficult. A variation of the rear-entry position, for the more athletic, is a partial standing arrangement. The woman stands and bends the upper part of her body at the hips, grasping the back of a chair or some other support for balance. The man stands behind her, holding her by her waist for balance. Such a position can be very difficult to manage if the sizes and body shapes of the couple are inappropriate for it. Such positions are for most people only a rare amusement, when circumstances and mood permit some good humored sex play.

There are a great many other possible positions for sexual intercourse. However, the basic patterns have been described here and others are simply modifications of them.

other sexual activities

Anal intercourse.   Anal intercourse involves the insertion of the penis into the anus and rectum, rather than the vagina. This practice has been, until recently, the subject of a strong cultural taboo in Western societies. It remains illegal according to the laws of most states, even when it is practiced between consenting marriage partners.

The practice of anal intercourse continues to be relatively rare between sexual partners in American society. Nevertheless, it appears to be a form of sexual experimentation which is beginning to occur more frequently among younger generation Americans. This probably reflects the declining moral disapproval of it by younger people as compared with older people (Hunt, 1974). One national sex survey found that anal intercourse is an occasional experiment among 25 percent of married couples under the age of 35 (Hunt, 1974). Yet only 6 percent of people in this age group report experiencing the practice from "sometimes" to "often." The *Redbook Magazine* survey of 100,000 women, also investigated the incidence of anal intercourse (Travis and Sadd, 1977). Among the women who responded to the questionnaire, 57 percent had never tried it, 22 percent had tried it once, 19 percent did it occasionally, and only 2 percent did it often. Younger women were more likely to have tried it. These data are consistent enough to indicate that anal intercourse is not a shared erotic role expectation except between a very small number of couples. It is a very occasional diversion in the sexual repertoire of perhaps one-fifth of couples.

Anal intercourse can be extremely painful for the woman if she is not completely relaxed about it and if her partner does not proceed very gradually and gently. The Redbook Magazine survey questioned the women who had experienced anal intercourse about their reactions to the practice (Travis and Sadd, 1977). Only 10 percent of the women reported that their experience was "very enjoyable," with another 31 percent noting that it was "somewhat enjoyable." In contrast, 42 percent of the women reported that it was "unpleasant" and for another 7 percent, it was "repulsive." For most of the women, anal intercourse was not a practice enjoyable enough for consistent pursuit. Most of the women who tried it probably did so out of curiosity, or to please their husbands.

Medical doctors urge certain precautions for couples who might experiment with anal intercourse. First, the penis should never be inserted into the vagina after anal penetration. Doing so is quite likely to result in a transfer of bacteria which can cause severe vaginal infections (Neubardt, 1975). Second, anal penetration should never be attempted without sufficient use of a lubricant (Feigen, 1975). Forcing anal entry of the penis is not only likely to be extremely painful for the woman, but also to result in physical injury to the anal canal. Finally, it is necessary for the woman to deliberately relax the anal sphincter muscle, and for her partner to avoid any vigorous thrusting movements.

Considering its physical limitations and its low potential for mutual sexual pleasure, anal intercourse is not likely to become a common sexual practice.

Autoeroticism.   Recent research indicates that the frequency of masturbation among couples has increased substantially since the time of Kinsey's

research. This is a bit surprising, especially in the light of the fact that the frequency of marital sexual intercourse is also increasing.

One national sex survey, for example, found that 70 percent of husbands and wives admitted to having engaged in self-stimulation since being married (Hunt, 1974). The *Redbook Magazine* survey of 40,000 men had consistent findings (Travis, 1978b). It found that 80 percent of the men reported that they had masturbated occasionally during the previous year. The companion *Redbook Magazine* survey of 100,000 women asked if they had ever engaged in masturbation since being married (Travis and Sadd, 1977). Seventy-four percent admitted doing so, with 16 percent doing it "often," 52 percent doing it occasionally, and 7 percent only once. What these data appear to indicate is that private masturbation as an occasional practice is not uncommon among married people.

Some studies have also investigated the reasons married people offer for self-stimulation (Hite, 1976; Travis and Sadd, 1977; Travis, 1978b). The most common reasons offered are: (1) a temporary absence of their spouse; (2) a way to release tensions; (3) additional source of sexual satisfaction; and (4) an alternative to unsatisfying marital sex. There appear to be diverse and probably multiple motives for the practice.

Some attempts have also been made to probe the emotional reactions of married people to self-stimulation. In the Redbook Magazine survey, 31 percent of the women said that the experience was "always satisfying," 49 percent noted that it was "sometimes satisfying," and 20 percent reported that it was "not satisfying." Another questionnaire survey of about 3000 women investigated this question in much greater detail (Hite, 1976). It found that most of the women who masturbated to orgasm felt physically satisfied, but still emotionally unfulfilled. Some of the women experienced painful regret caused by guilt feelings, although others did not, even though almost all of the women had been brought up to regard masturbation as being immoral and abnormal. Some of the women also said that self-stimulation helped them to learn more about their body's sexual response. In addition, some of the women said that the practice enabled them to feel less sexually dependent upon their partner, because they could relieve their sexual tensions whenever they were in the mood to do so. There has been no similar research with married men, but the findings would probably be similar.

Private self-stimulation is rarely a shared erotic role expectation between sexual partners. Although a small minority of couples report the practice of watching each other engaged in simultaneous masturbation (Travis and Sadd, 1977; Travis, 1978b). Some studies have attempted to probe the relationship between self-stimulation and marital and sexual satisfaction (Travis and Sadd, 1977; Travis, 1978b). The findings suggest that masturbation is more frequent among those people who report being maritally and sexually dissatisfied, even though it is also an occasional practice among people who are happy with their marriage and sexual relationship. It may be inferred, then, that private masturbation is usually an alternative to sexual intercourse in an unhappy marriage, but a supplement to sexual intercourse in a happy marriage.

EROTIC ROLES AND ORGASM

Orgasm is not simply a physiological event which may or may not occur during sexual activity. It is a goal which may or may not be shared between sex partners. Male orgasm has a very high probability of occurring during sexual intercourse. However, this is not so for female orgasm. If both sex partners do not expect the woman to reach orgasm during sexual activity, it may be unlikely to occur.

In some societies, the physiological possibility for women to experience orgasm is unknown or is widely doubted. This is the situation according to anthropological reports in rural Ireland (Messenger, 1971). Because of traditional hostility toward sexual pleasure in Irish society, sexual intercourse takes place quickly with little previous foreplay. Male orgasm is regarded as an unfortunate, but necessary release of sexual tension. The traditional role for women is to passively submit for the sake of procreation. Given these erotic roles, it is likely that very few rural Irishwomen ever experience orgasm. The doubt about female orgasm leads to a self-fulfilling expectation. For the rural Irish, it doesn't exist (except perhaps for unusual women).

Sex therapists report that the most common complaint they encounter among their female clients is difficulty reaching orgasm (Masters and Johnson, 1970). Many possible factors may contribute to this difficulty. Some of these factors include high sex anxiety and guilt, marital conflict, and lack of love for their sex partner, or an over-concern about pleasing their sex partner. Another common contributing factor is a reliance upon genital intercourse as an exclusive source of sexual stimulation. In countering this expectation, couples are usually taught new erotic roles in which they learn how to enjoy leisurely sensuous foreplay. The training is called "sensate focus."

It was formerly believed that men and women had physiologically different rates of sexual arousal to orgasm, with men being more rapid and women being slower to reach orgasm. However, Kinsey's research cast doubt upon this popular belief (Kinsey et al., 1953). He found that many women reported that they were able to masturbate to orgasm in a matter of only a minute or two. Women need an average of 4 minutes to reach orgasm through self-stimulation, yet women need an average 10 to 20 minutes of sexual intercourse to reach the same point. Kinsey's research, and that of others, indicates that sexual intercourse alone may not provide many women with sufficient clitoral stimulation to reach orgasm (Hite, 1976).

An additional complication is that genital intercourse provides much more intense stimulation for men. One research project estimated that most men ejaculate after only 2 to 7 minutes of intercourse, but a majority of women need more than 15 minutes of intercourse to reach orgasm regularly (Gebhard, 1966). If a couple's usual sexual script involves only 1 or 2 minutes of foreplay followed by 3 or 4 minutes of intercourse, it is not likely to be very satisfying for the woman. This may be the usual sexual script in societies where there is little concern for women's sexual pleasure.

In conclusion, the evidence appears to indicate that there is no innate difference between male and female rates of sexual arousal to orgasm. Women who experience intense anticipation of sexual activity and receive adequate clitoral stimulation can reach orgasm as rapidly as men. Whether or not a woman consistently reaches orgasm during sexual activity is not so much a matter of correct sexual "technique," but a matter of shared erotic role expectations.

male erotic role expectations

Do most men now expect their sex partners to reach orgasm regularly during sexual activity? Do they see themselves as partly responsible for helping their sex partners reach orgasm? The answer seems to be that female orgasm has become a considerable matter of concern for a majority of American men. The Redbook study of 40,000 men found that almost every man who responded to the questionnaire said that it was important for him that his partner reach orgasm with some regularity (Travis, 1978b). Almost all the men also said that they would be upset if their partner simply faked orgasm to please them.

The erotic role expectation of men, that their partners experience orgasm, is a double-edged sword. On one hand, it indicates that many men are genuinely concerned about the sexual enjoyment of their partner. On the other hand, it indicates that many men now regard their partner's orgasm as a mark of sexual achievement. In the absence of adequate sexual communication, regular expressions of orgasmic responsiveness may be more important to many men than it is to their partner.

Several research projects have found that many women feel under pressure to fake orgasm to please their sex partner (Hite, 1976; Rubin, 1976). This is evidence that many men now regard their partner's orgasm as a symbol of their own sexual ability. The traditional male erotic role emphasis upon sex as achievement has returned in a new guise. It can be quite irritating for women who may desire sexual activity at times when they are fatigued and do not wish to be stimulated to the point of orgasm (Rubin, 1976).

At the same time, there are still many men who remain unconcerned about whether or not their partners reach orgasm. Their script for sexual activity may be described in the crude slang: slam-bam-thank-you-ma'am. According to some research, many women still find their sex partners taking such an approach (Hite, 1976). In addition, there may be many men who rely upon sexual intercourse to stimulate their partners, unaware that such stimulation may be inadequate for many women. Their lack of communication can easily be misperceived by their female partners as evidence of unconcern.

female erotic role expectations

What do women expect in relation to their own experience of orgasm? Obviously, if a woman has never experienced orgasm, she can have no idea about what she is missing. Women who have never experienced orgasm during sexual activity are not likely to expect it. This is so unless some information leads a woman to believe that there is something valuable missing from her sex life. However, when women become familiar with the intense pleasure of orgasm, they are likely to expect it frequently during sexual activity. One study of 540 wives, for example, found that a majority of the women said they did not experience complete sexual satisfaction when they were unable to reach orgasm (Wallin, 1960). More important, the research found that college-educated women were more likely than noncollege-educated women to expect their husbands to help them achieve orgasm during sexual activity. These college-educated women were also more likely to feel sexual frustration when they did not experience orgasm. The implication is that a woman's expectation for orgasm increases her likelihood of feeling sexual frustration if she does not experience orgasm during highly arousing sexual activity.

The more frequently a woman reaches orgasm, the higher she will rate her enjoyment of sexual activity. The *Redbook* study of 100,000 women, for example, found that 85 percent of the women who rated the sexual aspect of their marriage as being "very good" also reported experiencing orgasm "all" or "most of the time" (Travis and Sadd, 1977). The frequency with which the overall sample of women reached orgasm was as follows: 15 percent did "all of the time," 48 percent did "most of the time," 19 percent did "sometimes," 11 percent did "once in a while," and only 7 percent "never" did so (Travis and Sadd, 1977). Other recent survey research has had remarkably similar findings (Hunt, 1974). What these data indicate is that a majority of American wives now experience orgasm regularly during sexual activity. Consequently, it is likely that orgasm is now an erotic role expectation for a majority of American wives.

What is the reaction of women who do not experience orgasm regularly during sexual activity? The reaction may depend upon a woman's personal expectations and the level of sexual arousal she experiences during sexual activity. A woman who has sexual activity and never or only occasionally experiences orgasm is likely, after some months or years, to develop an aversion to sexual activity. If she does not become highly aroused sexually, she is likely to feel that the experience is a bit tedious and simply irritates her vagina (due to insufficient lubrication). On the other hand, if she does become highly aroused sexually, she is likely to feel that the experience leaves her with unrelieved bodily tension and painful sexual frustration (resulting from genital congestion and expansion of the vagina). She may have many restless nights of insomnia unless she relieves the sexual tension through masturbation. Either way, a woman is likely to feel that sexual pleasure is not reciprocal and that she is simply being "used" as a sex object.

Women who do not regularly experience orgasm are likely to find sexual intercourse unpleasant. Yet it is possible to exaggerate the importance of orgasmic responsiveness in women. There are occasions when many women prefer not to experience orgasm, but may still desire sexual activity (Butler, 1976). A woman may feel too fatigued to experience highly arousing sexual activity, but may still desire the emotional pleasures of being caressed and fondled. A woman may desire such body contact to enjoy expressions of affection without sexual intercourse. Yet a great many men regard such activity in bed as a preliminary to intercourse and expect it to lead there. Here again, differing erotic role expectations in the absence of adequate communication can easily result in mutual misperception and antagonism. She misperceives him as being single-mindedly concerned with his own sexual pleasure, and he misperceives her as being teasing, yet sexually unresponsive.

Sexual compatibility is not a product of similarity in bodily functioning or even of correct sexual "technique." Instead, it is a product of adequate sexual communication which enables a couple to coordinate their personal sexual preferences. In that way, they may come to share erotic role expectations for each other.

Society exists for humans like the sea exists for fishes. We live in it; we live by means of it; and it shapes our ways of thinking and acting. Yet we would barely notice it if it were not called to our attention. The intention of this chapter is to call attention to the role which society and its impersonal social forces play in our sexual lives. Our sexuality seems so personal that society would seem to have little relevance in terms of our understanding of self. Yet it is a surrounding and penetrating sea which ought not to be ignored. It influences our sexual attitudes, our sexual behavior, and even our sexual functioning.

The previous chapters have indicated how American society exerts an influence upon sexual arousal and erotic roles. This chapter offers a broader view of our society by taking a look at it in comparative perspective with other societies, and then, in historical perspective with its past. In addition, it offers a brief overview of American attitudes toward certain controversial sexual issues.

Society is a core concept in behavioral science. Much like the core concepts of other disciplines, "society" is an abstraction which can be defined in various ways. Like the concept of "energy" in physics, or "life" in biology, there is considerable debate over the precise meaning of "society." Society is indeed an abstraction, probably incapable of being precisely defined; yet it is real in its consequences. It has been said that one does not realize the reality of society until one tries to change it.

Society is something more than a mere collection of separate individuals in a population. Society cannot be understood by counting people. It is most useful to regard a society as an association of people who are able to carry out all the ac-

8 sexuality in society

tivities necessary to perpetuate themselves and to maintain themselves independent from other groups. In this sense, a society may be any association of people from a small isolated tribe to a nation state. Any society has the potential for subdividing into smaller independent units. However, the result is usually civil war (as has been the American experience). Ultimately, social processes of both cooperation and coercion maintain the social bonds of people in association with each other.

Behavioral scientists distinguish between two dimensions of society: culture and social organization. *Culture* refers to the shared understanding of reality maintained in a society. More specifically, the term culture refers to shared beliefs, values, and norms. *Sexual beliefs,* for example, are descriptions of the nature of human sexuality. *Sexual values* are the criteria for evaluating aspects of sexuality as desirable or undesirable. *Sexual norms* are formal and informal social rules for the conduct of sexual interaction. The culture of people is interwoven with their patterns of social organization.

Social organization refers to the systematic arrangement of patterns of interaction which prevail in a society. Culture and social organization are closely tied to each other in the sense that the ways people sexually interact with each other generate shared conceptions of human sexuality. In a reverse sense, the shared sexual beliefs, values, and norms of a people can establish cultural traditions which guide future sexual interaction.

THE SOCIAL ORGANIZATION OF SEXUAL BEHAVIOR

the cross-cultural diversity of sex norms

There is a special viewpoint which influences Western attempts to understand the sexual behavior of people in non-Western societies. Out cultural heritage begins with the unstated assumption that all sexual rules are restrictions upon sexual conduct. The assumption arises from the outdated belief that sexual desire is a powerful and dangerous force in human life which must be restricted by society. Actually, cross-cultural investigations have found that a great many sexual norms are not prohibitions, but guidelines for sexual conduct.

For behavioral scientists to understand the sexual norms of people from societies different from their own, it is necessary for them to employ the principle of cultural relativism. *The principle of cultural relativism* is the assumption that no social norm is morally superior to any other. Even rules for sexual conduct must be seen simply as a component in a system of social relations. Without the principle of cultural relativism, meaningful scientific research into sexual behavior cannot exist. Without it scientific analysis becomes moral argumentation. The principle of cultural relativism enables behavioral scientists studying other cultures to overcome cultural provincialism. Using this principle, behavioral scientists can study the sexual behavior of human beings with the same impartiality that biologists bring to the study of animal sexual behavior.

Anthropologists have made several attempts to bring together the vast amount of information collected about the sexual behavior of people in societies around the world—in industrial, developing, and tribal societies (Ford and Beach, 1951; Stephens, 1971). One useful scheme for comparing cross-cultural differences in sexual norms recognizes three basic types of rules: (1) prohibitive; (2) permissive; and (3) obligatory (Murdock, 1949). *Prohibitive norms* forbid certain sexual practices under certain conditions. The rule that "thou shalt not commit adultery" is an example in some Western societies. *Permissive norms* allow certain sexual practices but do not require them. A social rule that it is permissable for unmarried people who are in love to have sexual intercourse is an example. *Obligatory norms* require certain sexual practices under certain conditions. An unstated social rule that marriage partners are obligated to have sexual intercourse is an example.

Until recently, Western societies were rare examples of extreme restrictiveness. The dominant Western sexual norms of the past attempted to prohibit all sexual activities outside of marriage, as well as some sexual acts within marriage. However, this narrow restrictiveness existed in very few other societies (Murdock, 1949).

It would not be at all possible here to survey the vast diversity which exists in sexual norms. Instead, we can only summarize some cross-cultural comparisons in relation to several sexual issues of concern to Americans. The wider limits of the world's sexual diversity could be shown further if space allowed for some examination of cross-cultural customs for bodily decoration, foreplay techniques, and sexual positions (Ford and Beach, 1951). Almost any form of sexual behavior which is regarded as being abnormal, unnatural and perverted in any society is a customary sexual practice in some other society. The difference is not one of prohibited perversion in one society and sexual indulgence in another. As judged from the sexual norms of any one society, the sexual practices in another society are apt to appear to be a bit bizarre. (The names of societies are not given, in the following section, because many of them are unfamiliar.)

Childhood sexuality.   Only a small number of societies attempt to prohibit all forms of sexual expression in children including masturbation, sex play, and childhood sexual intercourse (Ford and Beach, 1951). Most societies are relatively permissive toward childhood masturbation and heterosexual play without positively encouraging it. A few societies have sexual norms which actively encourage childhood sexual activity to the extent of making it obligatory. In such societies, early sexual experience in masturbation and sex play is considered necessary for the "normal" development of adult sexuality (Ford and Beach, 1951).

In societies which permit or encourage childhood sexuality, there exists a wide variety of sexual customs (Ford and Beach, 1951). In some societies, young children are deliberately masturbated by their parents because of the belief that this will stimulate their proper sexual development. In a few societies, children are even allowed to watch their parents engage in sexual intercourse. In most tribal societies, and among most of the world's poor people where families live in one room, it is a common occurrence for children to observe adults in sexual activities (Stephens, 1971). In a few societies, children even witness ceremonial sex orgies (Stephens, 1971). In some societies, parents deliberately arrange for their children to practice heterosexual intercourse.

Permissiveness toward childhood masturbation is more common than its prohibition. In a few societies, it is obligatory because girls are expected to enlarge their labia through constant friction as a way of improving their sexual attractiveness (Stephens, 1971).

In the minority of societies which prohibit all forms of childhood sexual activity, a variety of sexual customs are common (Ford and Beach, 1951). In some societies, children who are caught masturbating are severely beaten. In other societies, such children may only be ridiculed. Some societies prohibit all sexual activity until puberty and then encourage premarital intercourse. In other societies, sexual restrictiveness continues until marriage. Most societies which prohibit childhood sexual activity also try to maintain a conspiracy of silence in matters of sexual information for children.

Premarital sex. A major survey of anthropological studies found that about 70 percent of societies permit premarital sexual relations under varying conditions (Murdock, 1949). The finding that only a minority of the world's societies prohibit premarital intercourse is consistent with the previous finding that a majority of societies are permissive toward childhood sexual expression. In societies where premarital intercourse is permitted, children born to unmarried women are usually cared for by relatives, according to pre-arranged custom. In such societies, also, premarital sexual activity is very often restricted to certain distant kinship relatives, rather than being open to personal inclination.

In societies with a prohibition upon premarital intercourse, enforcement usually falls more strongly upon females rather than males (Murdock, 1949). In such societies, the justification for the prohibition is usually expressed in terms of religious values and concerns about women's childbearing out of wedlock.

Societies which prohibit premarital intercourse attempt to enforce that prohibition through a variety of sexual customs. The most common custom consists of the close supervision and seclusion of unmarried girls. Women who are nonvirgins at marriage may be socially disgraced, returned to their parents, or even killed in a few societies (Ford and Beach, 1951). In a few Middle Eastern societies, the customs of clitorectomy and infibulation of young girls are still sometimes used to protect female chastity (Patai, 1973). *Clitorectomy* involves the surgical removal of the clitoris, usually carried out because of the belief that this will reduce female sexual desire. *Infibulation* is a procedure for sewing together the labia, leaving only small outlets for urination and menstruation to prevent sexual intercourse. Obviously, American society does not go to extremes in trying to maintain a prohibition against premarital sexual intercourse. Our society depends mainly upon appeals to guilt.

Extramarital sex.   Unlike premarital sexual intercourse, sexual intercourse after marriage with persons other than one's spouse is prohibited in a majority of the world's societies. A survey of anthropological studies found that about 80 percent of societies have norms prohibiting extramarital sexual relations (Murdock, 1949). However, a great many of these same societies have norms which do permit extramarital sex on special occasions or with certain in-law relatives (such as with the husband's brother or wife's sister).

Another anthropological survey found that only 60 percent of societies prohibit extramarital sex under any condition and with any category of persons (Ford and Beach, 1951). Yet, even in these societies, enforcement of the prohibition varies considerably. In most of these societies, the burden of punishment falls upon women rather than men. Male adultery is often informally tolerated, especially when it occurs with prostitutes. In a few societies, the punishment for adultery is execution (Ford and Beach, 1951; Stephens, 1971).

In the minority of societies which have permissive norms toward extramarital sex, jealousy and resentment are still common (Stephens, 1963). Delicate negotiations and fears of provoking marital friction limit the actual frequency of extramarital sex. In only a few societies is extramarital sex experienced by either spouse, upon permission from the other, without resulting in animosity.

If the perspective is broadened to include any nonmonogamous sexual practice, then it is found that a majority of non-Western societies have such customs. A great many societies permit men to marry several women (*polygyny*), and a few permit women to marry several men (*polyandry*). It is also customary in many societies for men to have concubines who are sexual partners without legitimate recognition as wives.

Homosexual behavior.   A survey of anthropological studies found that homosexual behavior is unconditionally prohibited in only a minority of the world's societies (Ford and Beach, 1951). It found that about 65 percent of societies have social norms which permit homosexual activity, usually under specific circumstances. A few of these societies even make it obligatory during certain ceremonies. These findings are a considerable contrast with the Western beliefs that homosexual behavior is a rare aberration.

In no society is homosexual behavior given preference to heterosexual behavior or is it a more common practice than heterosexual intercourse. Nevertheless, in some societies which permit homosexual behavior, the vast majority of the male population has experienced homosexual relations at one time or another (Ford and Beach, 1951; Bullough, 1976). In a few societies, strong social pressures encourage homosexual practices, especially where men and women are strictly separated for long periods of time (Bullough, 1976). In a few societies, also, homosexual anal intercourse is an obligatory rite during puberty ceremonies (Ford and Beach, 1951). A majority of societies simply tolerate male homosexual activity without especially approving it. In some societies, bisexual behavior is fashionable, as it was in ancient Greece and Rome (Bullough, 1976).

There are only a few anthropological studies which provide information about female homosexual behavior. However, there are reports from a small number of societies in which female homosexual practices are permitted (Ford and Beach, 1951). In addition, there are numerous reports of tolerated homosexual behavior among wives of large polygamous harems (Bullough, 1976).

social forces affecting sex norms

There have been few attempts to identify the underlying social forces which shape the development of the social norms (rules) regulating the organization of sexual interaction in a society. The great world-wide diversity of sexual customs can easily lead one to conclude that any particular organization of sexual behavior is a mere accident of a society's cultural history. However, a few attempts have been made to find principles which can explain the underlying sources of sex norms around the world. These explanations focus upon the effects of: (1) religious doctrine; (2) male-female power relations; and (3) the biophysical environment and technology.

Religious doctrine. Throughout the world, even in the most sexually permissive societies, sexual activity has been encompassed in an aura of mystery and taboo. Only in modern industrial societies has human sexuality become an object of systematic scientific investigation. In the past, beliefs about human sexuality (as well as moral values) were derived from traditional authority, usually invested in religion. Religious doctrines concerning human sexuality could not easily be challenged.

Archaeological research indicates that ancient civilizations had more permissive sex norms than those which prevail in societies influenced by the transcultural religions (Stephens, 1971). *Transcultural religions* are those which are not limited to any particular tribe or nation. Such religions include Christianity, Islam, and Buddhism. These religions all emerged during a time of revolutionary religious ferment when many new ascetic (pleasure-condemning) religions competed for followers. They spread beliefs about human sexuality which became a source of sex norms in societies throughout the world (Stephens,

1971). These religions taught that sexual pleasure-seeking was a cause of much human misery. Consequently, they promoted a great many sexual prohibitions which restricted childhood sexuality, premarital sex, extramarital sex, and homosexual behavior, as well as clothing, techniques of foreplay, and positions during intercourse.

These ascetic transcultural religions placed procreation at the center of beliefs about human sexuality and regarded it as being the only moral purpose for sexual activity. Perhaps, because of their emphasis upon procreation and childbearing, these religions were particularly restrictive of female rather than male sexuality.

Male-female power relations. The social norms which regulate sexual interaction cannot be separated from male-female power relations. Male-female power relations are inevitably linked to the overall structure of power and authority which prevails in any society. An extensive cross-cultural analysis of sexual practices came to the conclusion that, in general, female sexual behavior tends to be most greatly restricted in societies characterized by hierarchical dominance relations between members of that society (Stephens, 1971). In such societies, dominance and subordination characterizes the political relations between men and also the relations between men and women. In these societies, women are subordinated to the political and economic control of men. In contrast, societies with generally permissive sex norms tend to be characterized by relatively equal male-female power relations (Stephens, 1971).

In advanced industrial societies, women have been able to gain greater equality through employment and economic independence from men. It

becomes less necessary for women to bargain their sexual attractiveness for economic rewards. Therefore, female sexuality has become freed from economic dependence upon men and can be guided by other considerations (such as, love, companionship, curiosity, pleasure). In addition, women's occupational involvement reduces the importance of their reproductive role and makes procreation and motherhood less central to stereotypes of femininity.

The biophysical environment and technology.   Another underlying influence upon sex norms is the biophysical environment and the technology which a people use to reshape their environment. The effects of these sets of factors upon sex norms are usually very subtle.

Certain indirect influences of biological aspects of human sexuality upon sex norms can be recognized. It has been found that throughout the world, female sexuality has been put under more social constraint than has male sexuality (Murdock, 1949; Stephens, 1971). It is often argued that the more common social restriction of female sexual behavior is a consequence of the fact that women can get pregnant. Therefore, they must learn to be more cautious than men about the possible consequences of their sexual behavior. Without contraceptive technology female sexuality is bonded to procreation and motherhood. Contraceptive technology frees women from fears of unwanted pregnancy. Contraception enables female sexuality to become as independent of childbearing and parental expectations as is male sexuality. In an advanced industrial society, birth control enables women to have a much wider choice in their life activities (employment, careers, volunteer work, political office, advanced education). Women can now have these options without having to abstain from sexual intercourse to prevent unwanted pregnancies.

A biological factor which is related to birth control is the death rate of children in a society (Sullerot, 1973). Child mortality is high in societies where effective medical practice is unable to prevent many children from dying of childhood diseases. This situation is most common among the rural poor, even in the United States. In rural-agricultural societies, male children are needed to assure farm productivity and economic security. In many rural societies, the procreative ability of women to have many children is a crucial survival value. This condition limits women's gender role and sexuality to procreation and motherhood (Sullerot, 1973).

THE AMERICAN SEXUAL HERITAGE

colonial new england and puritanism

Most early Christian writers of theology were intensely hostile toward sexual pleasure. They developed a dualistic conception of human nature divided between animalistic "flesh" and angelic "spirit." The teachings of Paul, Augustine, Tertullian, and Thomas Aquinas all viewed sexual desire as animalistic and essentially evil. They regarded sexual intercourse, even in marriage, as a necessary evil for the sake of procreation (Bardis, 1964; Queen and Habenstein, 1974). St. Paul set the moral tone when he declared: "It is good for man not to touch a woman. Nevertheless, to avoid fornication, let every man have his own wife and let every woman have her own husband" (I Corinthians 7: 1-2). Life-long celibacy and virginity were esteemed as supreme virtues. The early Christian theologians viewed sexual intercourse as the means through which the innate sinfulness of human beings was transmitted, generation to generation.

The Puritans (Congregationalists) brought with them to Colonial New England one version of the early Christian conception of human sexuality. As religious and social reformers, the Puritans were reacting to the corruptions of aristocratic England and its established Anglican church. These reformers emphasized sexual sins more than most other Christian sects of the time. Their punishment for sexual sin could be severe. Adulterers could be branded or executed for the offense. At least three such executions actually did take place in Massachusetts, according to available records (Frumkin, 1961). However, such severe punishment was rare. In most cases only fines and public confessions were demanded. Premarital intercourse ("fornication") could be punished by public flogging. Again, in most cases where offenders were discovered, usually due to a premarital pregnancy, only public confessions and fines were exacted (Morgan, 1942). For the most part, the Puritans depended upon public shaming and preventing opportunities for sexual temptation. In some cases, certain unfortunates were made public examples so that the limits of sexual deviance could be reaffirmed for the whole community (Erikson, 1966).

The Puritans were not really as "puritanical" as that term has come to mean. They revealed none of the sexual prudery of later day Victorians. Their records reveal a candid attitude towards sexual matters. In addition, unlike the early Christians, they affirmed the value of sexual pleasure in marriage especially when love was part of that relationship (Morgan, 1942).

In Colonial New England, the double standard was never as widely tolerated as it was in the Colonial South. Slavery and prostitution did not offer men sources of premarital and extramarital sex. However, the use of indentured servants was an important factor in the shaping of Puritan sex attitudes. Most young men, and many women, sold their labor for years to masters of households (Morgan, 1942). They had little independence from their masters and were allowed scarce time for courtship. They could not even marry without their masters' consent and that was very unlikely during their period of contracted labor. Consequently, with so many young men unable to marry early, premarital intercourse was a constant temptation. Female servants, anxious to find husbands, were the chief co-conspirators with male servants. In addition, masters of households committed adultery with maidservants. The prevalence of much errant sexuality tempered the restrictive sexual codes of the Puritans

(Morgan, 1942). There were just too many young men and women who would have to be shamed by fines, whipping, and public confessions.

The precise extent of premarital sexual intercourse in Puritan New England is not known. However, several historical studies suggest that it was quite prevalent. The records of a church at Groton, Massachusetts, for example, show that among two hundred parents coming to baptize their babies between 1771 and 1775, one-third confessed to having had sexual intercourse before marriage (Calhoun, 1917). They confessed so that the baptism could take place, and because they had the misfortune of a premarital pregnancy. Many couples did not have that incentive to record their sexual deviance for posterity. Other research studies report similar findings about the prevalence of premarital sex in Colonial New England (Morgan, 1942; Oberholzer, 1956; Smith, 1973).

the frontier and evangelicalism

America was until comparatively recently a land dominated by frontiers and farming. Beginning with the early settlement of the Eastern coast, farming was the dominant source of livelihood. Farms on the frontier had to be carved out of rough wilderness. The harsh life on the frontier and heavy labor gave primacy to physically strong and adventurous men. Hunting, housebuilding, and land clearing were distinctively the muscle work of men. Consequently, the first waves of settlers along the frontier always had a surplus population of young men and a relative scarcity of women (Moller, 1945; Demos, 1970). Many husbands set out for the frontier leaving their wives and families in Europe or back East until they could establish a decent existence.

As the frontier moved westward, many young unattached men sought employment in railroad building, mining, and ranching. The predominance of men in frontier areas was such that men outnumbered women, sometimes by 2 or 3 to 1. As late as 1880, for example, Colorado had 129,131 males to 65,196 females; Oregon had 103,381 males to 71,387 females; and Montana Territory had 28,177 males to 10,792 females (Bartlett, 1974).

Frontier towns, with their surplus of young men, had a constant problem of social control (Moller, 1945; Bartlett, 1974). As is the situation in "boom towns" today, many unattached young men found temporary amusement after hard labor in alcohol, prostitutes, gambling, and fighting. Prostitution and venereal disease were prevalent (Martin, 1974). Saloon girls provided more than social hospitality. Adultery was a major concern because of the surplus of unattached men. This was particularly true for husbands whose work took them far away from their wives for long periods of time. In areas where men were overwhelmingly isolated from women, as at mining camps and army bases, homosexuality was also prevalent (Rickey, 1963). A high incidence of homosexual behavior among "manly" frontier men may also have been a product of the unique biophysical environment of the American frontier.

It was not Puritan Congregationalism which was to become the dominant religious influence along the frontier, as it spread westward over the Allegheny Mountains. Instead, it was Methodism and Baptism which attracted the greatest following (Sweet, 1952). These evangelical churches did not emphasize complicated church doctrines or the necessity of lengthy study for the conversion of the poor and illiterate. Instead, they emphasized the personal experience of religious conversion as the path to salvation. It was necessary to feel guilty and repent past sins to achieve that conversion experience. Thus, evangelical religion helped to shift the social control of sexual behavior from public shame to private guilt.

The various evangelical sects had quite a bit of "sin" with which to work on the Western frontier (Sweet, 1952). The social fabric was disorganized. Initially, there was little in the way of government, courts, or churches. Men and women both made heavy use of whiskey. Petty feuds and violence were commonplace. So were fornication, adultery, and prostitution. As the evangelical churches became established, they set up moral courts to police their own members. The use of alcohol was condemned as a major menace. Sometimes, also, so were dancing and the use of tobacco.

The evangelical churches brought with them the attitudes of Puritan reformism and sought to eradicate sexual relations outside of marriage. Established families seeking a secure environment regarded these churches as islands of stability in a hazardous sea. Although most families did not become converted members of any church initially, the churches did set the moral tone as settled communities began to develop (Sweet, 1952).

In the South, the evangelical churches encountered a similar situation. Religious practice and interest among most of the population was not active (Ahlstrom, 1972). The evangelical churches easily attracted a large following with their appeal to the poor, illiterate, and underprivileged. The converts, with their new found religious moralism, could condemn the wicked ways of both the "white trash" and the "hypocritical" wealthy.

urbanization and victorianism

As industrialization and urbanization developed in American society, a new moral vision took shape and spread. Victorian moralilty prevailed among the newly emerging urban, middle class of the nineteenth century. It was not a formal religious doctrine, but a secular code of moral conduct. However, it was rooted in the early Christian conception of human sexuality and it did influence almost all religious groups of American society. The peculiar morality of the Victorians is what later came to be known as "puritanism."

In reality, Victorian morality was an extreme form of the ancient male-dominated double standard of sexual conduct. It was founded upon a conception of male and female sexuality set apart by sharp contrasts. It was also characterized by much hypocrisy in contradiction between public preachment and private practice.

Victorian morality probably arose as an ideological means for new urban, middle class families, to express their self-righteous sense of superiority toward both the lower and upper classes. The concern for "respectability" was most intense among those families which were only modestly better off than the poor. These families lived close enough to the poor that their more economically stable lifestyle could be easily threatened.

Most contemporary Americans find the sexual attitudes and practices of their Victorian ancestors to be a bit quaint and curious. Women were seen as being of two distinct varieties: "good" women, who had little sexual interest; and "bad" women, who were corrupted by their own "lust." Premarital virginity in women was seen not only as a practical matter, but also as a symbol of "purity" of character. Respectable women were romantically idealized as dependent, frail, and untouchable. This enabled some women to feel a sense of superiority toward men whose "animal sexual instincts" gave them a more "bestial" nature (Welter, 1966).

Sexual matters were not supposed to be discussed between "respectable" women or between adults and children. Anything related to human sexuality had a great potential for embarrassment. Conventional prudery went to the extreme of avoiding all words with sexual connotations (Rugoff, 1971). For example, a pregnant woman was spoken of as "in a family way"; menstruation became a "female malady"; genitals became "private parts"; syphilis became a "social disease"; and a prostitute became a "fallen woman." There were, of course, countless euphemisms for copulation, including "carnal knowledge," or just simply "relations." Speaking about parts of the body was also taboo, even when they were not human parts. A leg became a "limb" even when part of a table and a breast of chicken became "white meat."

The unclothed body was also considered obscene. Women went to bathing beaches covered from neck to ankle. A woman's naked calf was seen as sexually provocative. In some places, ancient Greek statues were clothed or put into closets to be seen only by responsible authorities.

The prudery made sexual companionship in marriage quite difficult. Victorian marriage manuals warned readers against the dangers of having sexual intercourse too frequently. They were told that it was especially debilitating to the energies of men—energies which men needed for more important tasks. Medical authorities advised that the proper interval between occasions of intercourse was once per week to once per month (Gordon, 1971). Daughters were usually advised by their mothers shortly before marriage to bear the unpleasant burden of their new sexual responsibilities out of love for their husbands.

Masturbation was seen as being particularly evil. Masturbation ("self-abuse") was widely believed to be the cause of insanity in both men and women. Many of the writings of medical doctors affirmed this erroneous belief (Barker-Benfield, 1976; Neuman, 1975). In some extreme cases, women who were considered insane or alcoholic had their clitorises or ovaries surgically removed (Barker-Benfield, 1976). In some cases, insane men were castrated (Bullough and Bullough, 1977). The erroneous belief that masturbation could cause mental illness presisted among a sizable minority of medical doctors up to the 1950s (Greenbank, 1961).

Another Victorian curiosity was the suppression of birth control information. The Comstock law, named after the moral crusader Anthony Comstock, defined birth control information as obscene literature. The law made it illegal to send contraceptive information through the mail, even when it was in medical books (Gordon, 1971; Rugoff, 1971). This law caused a considerable problem for married couples who wanted to limit the size of their families for economic reasons. Consequently, doctors usually advised sexual abstinence (politely termed "continence" or "self-restraint") as a birth control method. This further inhibited marital sexuality.

The middle class repression of female sexual desire had some other troubling consequences. The sexual prudery among middle class women limited their involvement in premarital and extramarital sex (Smith, 1973). However, it also functioned to strengthen a secretive double standard of morality among middle class men. The quiet evasion of Victorian morality was especially fostered by the emphasis upon pretense. Deviance from sexual expectations among men was tolerated as long as men could pretend propriety in public and conceal their private delinquency. The prudery made pretense more important than actual practice.

Prostitution flourished in the Victorian era because there were enough middle class men to support it in style (Rugoff, 1971). Some "houses" were expensive entertainment parlors which offered music, alcohol, and gambling, in addition to sex. Prostitution first became established in America during the latter part of the seventeenth century in seaport cities along the Eastern coast (Dingwall, 1956). It was poor women, of course, who were the source of most prostitution. In the Victorian era, this could easily be rationalized because it was believed that the poor were naturally "lustful" and could not control their sexual desires. The large families of poor people were seen as proof of this sex myth (which still persists). Members of poor ethnic groups, such as blacks, Irish and Italians were especially stigmatized as being "lustful," because of the racist and anti-Catholic prejudice which was common among other Americans.

Victorian attitudes towards human sexuality were already changing by the end of the nineteenth century when scientific research into human sexuality began to be attempted by a few courageous investigators. Victorian morality reached the height of its influence by the 1860s and began to decline as people reacted to its repressiveness and hypocrisy. By the turn of the century, some middle class women were pursuing college educations and careers; many couples were practicing contraception and limiting their family size; and many wives admitted to enjoying sexual pleasure (Degler, 1974; Gaylin, 1976).

Victorian morality created a contradiction in American culture between unreal, romanticized, and anti-erotic ideals on one hand and fears about the sexual unknown on the other hand. This contradiction continued to linger in the sex attitudes of Americans well into the twentieth century. Kinsey's research evidence published during the late 1940s and early 1950s was one of the factors that began the process of demolishing the pretense that deviance from restrictive sexual ideals was rare in American society. He showed that many strongly condemned sexual behaviors were widespread, including masturbation, oral-genital sex, premarital, and extramarital sexual intercourse. A little later, in the 1960s, the physiological research of Masters and Johnson showed that many traditional beliefs about female sexuality were simply incorrect. They provided evidence that women were very similar to men in their sexual responses, no slower to respond, no less orgasmic (actually multiorgasmic), no less likely to find erotic pleasure in sexual activity. Yet many Victorian sex attitudes remain alive in vast segments of the American population caught between anti-erotic ideals and a fear of the unknown in human sexuality.

from folklore to science

Since the decline of Victorian morality, it has become increasingly easy for people to discuss, write about, and read about human sexuality. However, a deeper, underlying change has also developed. It is a change which is without historical precedent. This change is a result of the intrusion of scientific research into debates over the nature of human sexuality.

In the past, authority in determining the accuracy of beliefs about human sexuality was socially recognized as being invested in religious officials. These authorities functioned as interpreters of past tradition. Increasingly, however, authority has shifted away from reliance upon past tradition to a reliance upon scientific research methods for testing sexual beliefs. Increasingly, people seek sexual knowledge from sex researchers and sex therapists rather than religious officials. Authority for determining the meaning of human sexuality has shifted to biological and behavioral scientists and their processes for finding truth through empirical research.

A fundamental dilemma in thinking about the nature of human sexuality flows from this shift to rational scientific authority. The central concern of traditional authority has always been about questions of sexual morality ("what should be"). In contrast, scientists are primarily concerned with obtaining basic knowledge ("what is") and information useful for people's health and happiness. Religion and tradition can no longer function as sources of sexual knowledge. Yet science does not and cannot offer a morality for sexual conduct. The split between sources of moral guidance and sources of basic knowledge gives rise to much personal confusion about sexual matters. The dilemma is intensified when scientific findings create doubts about sexual beliefs which have been traditionally accepted without question.

Today, many people look to a variety of helping professionals to bridge the gap between sexual knowledge and moral guidance. Some of these counselors are tempted to offer moralistic guidance disguised as advice about sexual health and normality.

SEX IN AMERICAN CULTURE: CONSENSUS AND CONFLICT

research on sex attitudes

When anthropologists want to investigate the culture of a people in a tribal society they seek to interview a great many people about their beliefs, values, and standards of behavior. They carry out careful observations of the lifestyle of those people in a great variety of situations. If a foreign anthropologist came to American society with the goal of understanding sex in American culture, the

research problems would be tremendously magnified. American society has an extremely large, complex population of people having many social distinctions based upon religion, ethnic group, occupation, education, urban-rural residence, and even regional difference. It would be easy for that foreign anthropologist to develop a distorted picture of American culture unless the researcher was able to interview thousands of people who were drawn from these diverse groups. The expense of interviewing such a representative sample of Americans would be enormous and it might take many years to complete the research.

One method of investigating the meanings of human sexuality in American culture relies upon surveys of sex attitudes in representative samples of Americans. Attitudes reveal underlying beliefs, values, and standards of behavior. Unfortunately, most surveys of sex attitudes have relied upon only small samples of special populations, such as college students. Such samples are far from being representative of the total population. College students, for example, are younger and more educated than is the general population. An added methodological problem can occur if attitude surveys rely upon self-selected volunteers and questionnaires which are anonymously answered. Volunteers for survey investigations of sex attitudes are likely to hold more liberal views on sexual matters than are nonvolunteers (Kaats and Davis, 1971). Consequently, because of the expense which necessitates the employment of a large, well-trained survey organization, there have been few scientifically adequate surveys of American sex attitudes.

Fortunately, in recent years, a few national surveys of sex attitudes have been commissioned. One of these was carried out between 1970 and 1973 by the Institute for Sex Research which was founded by Alfred Kinsey (Levitt and Klassen, 1973). Another survey of young people, ages 16 to 25, was carried out by a national opinion poll research organization (Yankelovich, 1974). Although it did not carry out interviews with people older than 25, the results were still useful. They are representative of the age group surveyed.

american sexual attitudes

Sexual matters in American society are a constant source of social controversy. One reason for this widespread social conflict is that there is little consensus about many sexual issues in American culture. American sexual attitudes continue to be framed by agreement or disagreement over moral issues defined by concerns which reach back through centuries of Western, Christian thought. However, increasing numbers of people, especially those born since World War II, appear to be adopting attitudes which dissent from traditional Western morality (Yankelovich, 1974). The social controversy over sexual matters is not a consequence of any "sexual revolution," but merely a gradual evolution of changing attitudes. The potential for controversy becomes clear when we examine the research findings about American sexual attitudes.

Premarital sex.   The findings of the Institute for Sex Research in 1973 indicated that a majority of adult Americans continue to affirm the traditional disapproval of premarital sexual intercourse under any set of circumstances. About 50 percent of American adults regarded premarital sex between adult men and women as being "always" or "almost always wrong" even if they love each other (Levitt and Klassen, 1973). If the relationship does not involve love, about 65 percent of Americans in 1973 would condemn the man and about 70 percent would condemn the woman (Levitt and Klassen, 1973).

In addition, if premarital sex involves teenagers who are in love with each other, about 60 percent of Americans in 1973 would condemn the boy and girl (Levitt and Klassen, 1973). A large majority of Americans in 1973 disapproved of teenagers who have premarital sexual relations without being in love. About 70 percent of Americans in 1973 would condemn the boy and about 80 percent would condemn the girl (Levitt and Klassen, 1973). These findings reflected the attitudes of the entire adult population. However, when we investigate the attitudes of young people on this matter, the findings are quite different.

Young people between the ages of 16 and 25 are those people who are most likely to be unmarried and to have the possibility of experiencing premarital intercourse. Recent surveys reveal that this age group tends to be quite accepting of premarital sex. One national survey carried out in 1973, for example, found that only 34 percent of non-college youth and 22 percent of college youth regard casual premarital sexual relations to be "immoral" (Yankelovich, 1974). A more recent national opinion poll among teenagers, 13 to 18 years old, found that only 22 percent of the boys and 32 percent of the girls regard premarital sex to be "wrong" (Gallup, 1978). In the South and Midwest, teenagers are somewhat more likely to regard premarital sex as being "wrong" than are teenagers in the East and West. Obviously, there exists a sharp conflict of moral opinion between adults and young people over premarital sex, as well as between people of different regional backgrounds.

Extramarital sex.   Extramarital sexual relations continue to be strongly disapproved by a large majority of Americans. The findings of the Institute for Sex Research in 1973 indicated that about 85 percent of adult Americans disapproved of sexual intercourse between people who are married to someone else (Levitt and Klassen, 1973). Similarly, young people between the ages of 16 and 25 also disapprove of extramarital sex. The national survey of young people found that 65 percent of non-college youth and 60 percent of college youth disapprove of extramarital sex as being "immoral" (Yankelovich, 1974).

Compared with the extent of difference between adults and young people over the issue of premarital sexual relations, there is much less conflict of opinion over extramarital sex. Nevertheless, these findings may indicate a gradual shift in attitudes toward extramarital sex in the direction of less unconditional disapproval. However, such a conclusion would be premature until today's younger generation has been married for several decades.

Masturbation. A great many Americans continue to regard masturbation as being morally wrong. The findings of the Institute for Sex Research in 1973 indicated that about 50 percent of Americans consider masturbation to be "always wrong" (Levitt and Klassen, 1973). Younger people are somewhat less likely to condemn masturbation. One national survey found that about 40 percent of people in their 20s would forbid or attempt to discourage masturbation by teenage children (Wilson, 1975).

Prostitution. A substantial majority of Americans continue to disapprove of prostitution. The Institute for Sex Research found in 1973 that about 70 percent of Americans regarded prostitution as being "always" or "almost always wrong" (Levitt and Klassen, 1973). The strength of this disapproval is indicated by a second finding, about the attitude of Americans toward prostitution. About 65 percent of American adults support laws, which make prostitution illegal.

Homosexual Behavior. Homosexual behavior remains one of the most strongly condemned sexual practices, in American society. The Institute for Sex Research has carried out an extensive investigation of American attitudes toward homosexual behavior. About 86 percent of Americans regard homosexual behavior as being "always" or "almost always wrong" (Levitt and Klassen, 1974).

A majority of Americans, about 60 percent, support laws which would make homosexual behavior illegal (Levitt and Klassen, 1973). About 40 percent of Americans would mandate involuntary treatment to change homosexual behavior, and about 8 percent would put homosexuals in prison for at least one year (Levitt and Klassen, 1973). About 85 percent of Americans regard homosexual behavior to be sexually obscene; and a majority (62 percent) also, regard it as usually being a psychological sickness (Levitt and Klassen, 1973). Majorities of Americans (from 67 percent to 77 percent) would prevent homosexual men from employment as judges, government officials, school teachers, ministers and medical doctors (Levitt and Klassen, 1974).

However, the attitudes of younger Americans, 16 to 25 years of age, appear to be considerably different on this issue. Only about 50 percent of non-college educated young people regard homosexual behavior, as being morally wrong (Yankelovich, 1974). College educated young people are even less disapproving of homosexual behavior, with only 25 percent of them regarding it as being morally wrong (Yankelovich, 1974).

Some research has tried to identify the specific groups of Americans who are most strongly hostile towards homosexuals (Levitt and Klassen, 1974; Nyberg and Alston, 1977). An attitude of excessive hostility towards homosexuals has come to be termed *homophobia* (Lehne, 1976). In general, homophobia is most common among people: 1) who have not finished at least a high school education; 2) who are older; 3) who say they are traditionally religious and attend church regularly, and 4) who reside in rural and small town areas. Only a small minority of Americans are tolerant toward homosexuals, or even ambivalent towards them. In contrast, the greatest tolerance for homosexuals is found among people: 1) who are college educated; 2) who are younger; 3) who say they are not religious, or who don't attend church regularly, or who are Jewish; and 4) who live in large cities (Irwin and Thompson, 1977).

in american society, sex is political

What kind of society do we live in? Is it one, which is best described as sexually repressive? Or, is it one which is characterized by rather permissive sexual pleasure-seeking?

There is ample evidence for either point-of-view. The judgement that a person makes about the sexual character of American society usually reflects their underlying value-priorities. On one hand, sexual traditionalists are likely to frame the issue, in terms of an affirmation of sexual morality versus a tolerance for immorality. In contrast, sexual humanists are likely to frame the issue, in terms of an affirmation of individual freedom versus sexual repression. People who associate mostly with sexual traditionalists are liable to view our society as being ruined, by a breakdown in morality. In contrast, people who associate mostly with sexual humanists are likely to view our society, as slowly awakening from a nightmare of sexual repression.

Sex in American society today reveals much continuity with its heritage of the past. There continues to be a strong and persistent condemnation of all sexual pleasure-seeking outside of a marital relationship. Yet, today as in the past, there continues to be extensive deviance in actual behavior from that restrictive ideal. Human sexuality in American society remains a source of much personal anxiety, prudishness and intolerance toward other human beings. Yet, alongside these troubling predispositions, there is also much compulsive sexual hedonism. Perhaps, extreme ideal standards give rise to an equal and opposite extreme reaction. The sexual contradictions in our society, between public preachment and private practice, in the nation's capital and in one's hometown, can be disturbing to people who dislike hypocrisy. The contradictions encourage quite a bit of cynicism, as well as some moralistic fanaticism.

In American society, sex is political. It is political, because we have more laws governing private sexual behavior, than any other industrial society. It is political, because contending factions of the population wish to use social power, to impose their moral vision upon everyone else, or to defend themselves against such imposition. Sex is political, because divergent sex attitudes turn sexual matters into controversial social issues. Premarital sex, abortion, sex education, pornography, prostitution, and homosexual behavior are likely to remain emotionally-heated social issues, far into the future.

part three

SEXUAL
DEVELOPMENT

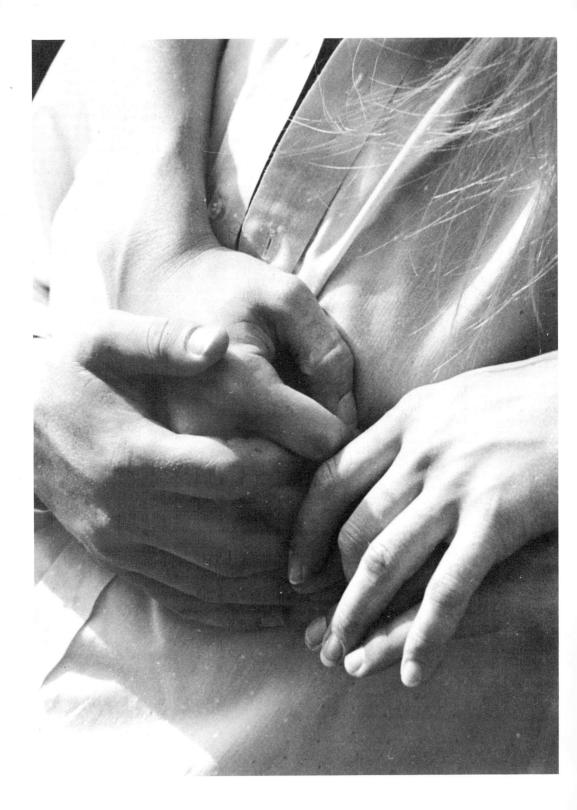

childhood sexuality

Erotic socialization refers to the process of learning about the meaning of sexual pleasure in human relationships. It is a product of the experience of rewards and punishments for sexual behavior as well as the sexual information and values encountered from others. In a sense, mechanisms of society guide every child's capacity for sexual arousal toward socially approved forms of behavior. However, a child takes an active part in this learning process. A child is no mere passive recipient of programming instructions like a computer—as any parent knows! Curiosity may motivate a child to explore sexual matters which parents would prefer to remain hidden. Contradictions between the sexual information provided by parents and by friends can lead a child to doubt either or both sources of "knowledge." Thus, personal curiosity and social contradictions serve to encourage a certain amount of independent thinking about sexual matters in many children and adolescents.

It is in the area of childhood sexuality that Victorian conceptions of human sexuality have been most persistent. The Victorians viewed normal children as essentially nonsexual beings. Children's "innocence" of sexual matters had to be protected from corruption. The Victorians believed that any sexual information had to be carefully hidden from the world of the child. Any childhood behavior which appeared to be sexual had to be quickly punished and discouraged.

Masturbation, for example, was considered a grave threat to the sexual

9 erotic sexuality during childhood and adolescence

"innocence" of children. The 1914 edition of the United States government publication *Infant Care,* for example, claimed that childhood masturbation could "wreck"a person for life. It recommended that responsible parents who suspected this corruption in their child should tie the infant's legs to opposite sides of the crib so that the child could not rub its thighs together (Wolfenstein, 1951). A gradual evolution in thinking has occurred since 1914. The 1951 edition of the same child guidance book encouraged parents to regard childhood masturbation as a petty nuisance and simply to ignore its occurrence. However, this viewpoint still did not regard sexual behavior in children as being quite normal. Even today, a great many American parents remain anxious about how to guide the sexual development of their children.

erotic socialization in other societies

In the half-century since Freud provoked public consciousness of childhood sexuality, adults in Western societies still find it difficult to conceive of normal children as sexual beings. Elsewhere in the world—in many non-Western, nonindustrial societies—very young children are indeed viewed as having the capacity for sexual activity. Parents in a large number of societies tolerate or even encourage sexual activities among children (Ford and Beach, 1951). Consequently, children in such societies are sexually active from early childhood, sometimes as early as five years of age. Eskimo children of the East Arctic, for example, experiment with sexual intercourse when they are only five or six years old (Briggs, 1974). They do so with the encouragement of their parents and even talk about their exploits.

Where childhood sexual expression is encouraged, sexual activities usually follow a sequence of development. Sexual play proceeds from self-stimulation, to mutual masturbation between members of the same and opposite sex, to attempts at heterosexual intercourse (Ford and Beach, 1951). By the age of ten, before they are capable of conception, children in these "permissive" societies have acquired extensive sexual experience.

There exists considerable variation in the kinds of sexual guidance given children in sexually permissive societies. In some societies, parents and other adults directly tutor young children in matters of erotic pleasure and even arrange sexual encounters for their children. This is because parents in some societies believe that childhood sexual experience is necessary for adequate sexual adjustment in adulthood. In most of these same societies, parents and children sleep in the same room. The incomplete privacy enables children to view their parents having sexual relations (Ford and Beach, 1951). When children are prepared with foreknowledge, such an experience is encountered as a "natural" aspect of their environment rather than as an emotional shock. In these societies, an open and free discussion of sexual matters between children and adults is common practice (Ford and Beach, 1951).

The anthropological evidence clearly confirms the reality of childhood sexuality as an aspect of normal development in societies which permit its expression. Very young children have the capacity of experiencing erotic pleasure if their social environment guides them towards that goal.

the sexual behavior of american children

During the first year of life, infant boys experience erections and infant girls experience vaginal lubrication (Martinson, 1976). Almost all five-year-old children are capable of achieving orgasm (Kinsey et al., 1948). Children's sexual responses are similar to those of adults. They experience a build-up of bodily excitation due to genital stimulation and respond with increasing pelvic thrusting. Ejaculation of semen in boys does not occur until sometime during puberty. However, the existence of this childhood capability for sexual arousal does not mean that it will be experienced persistently or in any particular frequency. The persistence and frequency of childhood sexual arousal depends to a great extent upon the amount of sexual stimulation children receive from the social environment, from parents, and from playmates.

The available research about the sexual behavior of children in American society indicates that sexual activity is continuous throughout childhood, at least among boys (Broderick, 1966; Elias and Gebhard, 1969). There may be a decrease in sex play among girls during early adolescence at the beginning of puberty (Gebhard, Roboch, and Giese, 1970). Childhood sexual activities tend to be sporadic, haphazard events. Yet there does not appear to be any period of termination (or sexual "latency" period) between early childhood and adolescence (Rutter, 1971).

Masturbation. The research findings using children as subjects indicate that the occurrence of erotic self-stimulation is substantially less common among girls than among boys. The most common masturbation technique used by children involves rubbing themselves against soft objects. One study of 432 children from ages 4 to 14 found that only 30 percent of the girls reported deliberate autoerotic activities, but 56 percent of the boys reported they did so (Elias and Gebhard, 1969). This sex difference is consistent with data derived from the memories of adults (Kinsey et al., 1953). Therefore, it is not likely that this finding results from a greater reluctance of girls to report masturbation. Instead, the sex difference in masturbation is probably real and probably results from differences in genital anatomy (the recessed clitoris).

In terms of social learning relevant to sex differences in childhood masturbation, one study of children from ages 3 to 6 found that only 14 percent of the girls could offer any word for the female genitals. Yet half of the boys could do so (Moore and Kendall, 1971). It would appear that very young girls have a limited body consciousness of their genital area. An even more curious finding was that more girls had a word for the penis than for their own genitals.

Sex play.   Children engage in many secretive games involving genital exhibition, exploration, and experimentation. These may be in same-sex or mixed-sex groups. Children call these games by various names, such as "doctor and nurse," "playing house," and "show it" (Martinson, 1973). In these games, children pursue their curiosity about each other's bodies. This sometimes may lead to mutual genital fondling and even attempts at sexual intercourse.

One study found that 34 percent of boys and 37 percent of girls reported involvement in some form of heterosexual play before the age of 14 (Elias and Gebhard, 1969). The average age at which heterosexual play first occurred among boys was at about 9 years. The same study found that 52 percent of boys and 35 percent of girls reported involvement in some sort of homosexual play (Elias and Gebhard, 1969).

parents and childhood sexuality

In American society, a child's sexual learning involves learning how to manage feelings of anxiety and guilt (Bandura and Walters, 1963; Gagnon and Simon, 1973). In general, American parents tend to be anxious about childhood sexual behavior and confused about how to guide their children's sexual development. This anxiety, in turn, is transmitted to their children's sexual curiosity and exploratory behavior. American parents commonly deal with sexual matters through patterns of avoidance or punishment (Bandura and Walters, 1959). These are described in detail in the following section. Children quickly realize that the world of what adults consider "sexual" is a world set apart and hidden from them (Martinson, 1973). It is laden with fearful and exciting possibilities. They are, therefore, likely to pursue their sexual curiosity in privacy and secrecy.

There does exist considerable variation in the sexual attitudes of parents. Some parents are very traditional and restrictive; others are very progressive and permissive. Yet, powerful social pressures converge upon parents to produce many similarities in their reactions to the sexual curiosity and experimentation of their children. Many parents worry that sex information "too early" will stimulate sexual curiosity and experimentation (Libby and Nass, 1971). They may fear possible emotional harm to a child from "premature" sexual information and experience. They may worry about the reactions of neighbors and school teachers to their child's sexual exploration. Parents may also be concerned that stimulating a child's sexual curiosity could lead to invasions of the privacy of their own sexual relationship. The heritage of American society makes it difficult to have a relaxed and easy sexual communication between parents and children. Yet, this should not seem too surprising, since many sexual partners also have great difficulty in communicating about sexual matters.

One fascinating research project compared the sex knowledge of the children from an American second grade class (in Pittsburgh) with that of the children from a similar class in Sweden (Koch, 1978). Although the sample of children was rather small—22 Americans and 16 Swedes—the findings are quite thought-provoking. The children in each country were asked to draw a series of pictures showing "where babies come from and how babies are born." Afterwards, the children used these pictures in an interview with the investigator about human reproduction. The Swedish children were found to have significantly more factual information. None of the American children, for example, knew about sexual intercourse. In contrast, all of the Swedish children did so and some even drew scenes of parents in bed to start their stories of human reproduction. In the American pictures, fathers were almost entirely left out of the stories and the only men present were doctors. Even more provocative were differences in the emotional tone contained in the children's drawings. Many of the American children's drawings had fearful scenes, such as those showing doctors with long knives ready to cut the mother open to get the baby out of the mother's "stomach." The research concluded that American children had less accurate sex information, more misinformation, and greater sex anxiety than Swedish children, who were better informed because of the intensive sex education provided in Swedish elementary schools. The American children were dependent upon information from parents and peers. The Pennsylvania school system specifically prohibited any teaching about "sexual techniques" or birth control.

The goal of most American parents for the sexual development of their children is similar, regardless of their different ways of trying to achieve it. The essential goal of American parents is to postpone their children's erotic development as long as is possible, or at least until adolescence (Sears, Maccoby, and Levin, 1957; Bandura and Walters, 1959). The reason is that in American society there is no acceptable form of sexual expression for children. Childhood sexuality cannot be channeled into childhood play or even childhood affections. The only acceptable path of development is to postpone a child's capacity for sexual activity until adolescence.

A recent large-scale study interviewed 1,400 parents of children 11 years old and younger in Cleveland and found that there has been little change in parental sex education over the last several decades (Roberts et.al., 1978). While 75 percent of the mothers and 50 percent of the fathers reported that they had discussed pregnancy with their children, most had discussed reproduction only in relation to animals or plants rather than among humans. Sexual intercourse was "mentioned" by only 15 percent of mothers and 8 percent of fathers, leaving an information gap between pregnancy and the mode of impregnation. Fully 40 percent of the daughters had not yet learned about menstruation from their parents by their eleventh year. And, only 1 percent of mothers and 2 percent of fathers had ever discussed the experience of first ejaculation with their sons. A sizable minority of 40 percent of the parents felt that masturbation by their children was wrong, most because of religious prohibitions or beliefs about its harmfulness. More than half of the parents also felt that it was not right for children to see their parents nude, especially parents of the other sex. In addition, many of the parents felt inhibited about expressing open affection for each other, in front of their children. Most parents took no initiative in offering sex information, but waited for their children's inquiries. However, by age eleven, most of the children had simply stopped asking questions about sex.

sex and child-rearing practices

The various child-rearing methods used by parents are all designed, directly or indirectly, to discourage the emergence of erotic interest. Three basic strategies are used by parents, no matter how haphazardly they are employed: (1) preventing sexual stimulation; (2) discouraging overt sexual behavior; and (3) information control.

Avoidance techniques.   Parents may attempt to prevent sexual stimulation in the form of bodily experimentation or ideas obtained from others. They try to accomplish this by means of a wide variety of avoidance techniques including: distracting a child from sexual experimentation, exercising close supervision, and preventing situations which could provoke sexual curiosity (Sears, Maccoby, and Levin, 1957; Martinson, 1973). For example, parents may divert a child's attention to something else when the child appears to be exploring his or her genitals. Parents may carefully supervise their children when they are playing "too quietly," with opposite-sex playmates in the bedroom. They may censor the TV watching of their children so that they do not encounter "adult" programs. They may carefully avoid any discussion of sexual topics which their children may overhear.

As a rationale for avoidance, a great many parents manage to convince themselves that "normal" children have no sexual feelings or curiosity (Bandura and Walters, 1959). This belief enables them to allay their own anxieties about having to discuss sexual matters with their children.

Punishment techniques.   Parents may also attempt to discourage the exhibition of any sexual behavior in their children through the use of a variety of punishment techniques such as: spanking; scolding, ridicule, or isolation. These practices are most likely to be employed by traditional and restrictive parents. However, progressive American parents are less likely to use these direct approaches in punishing childhood sex play (Sears, Maccoby, and Levin, 1957). They are more likely to employ verbal appeals to fear and guilt. Yet, these are still forms of punishment. A child who is found masturbating might be scolded and spanked by his or her parents or frightened by being told that he or she will become sick if such behavior is continued.

One research finding is that no difference has yet been found in the parental punishment of boys and girls for sex play (Maccoby and Jacklin, 1974). Other research suggests that differences in parental treatment begin to occur when children reach adolescence (Roberts, et al., 1978).

A significant finding about parents as sex educators is that the higher their sex anxiety (the more "uptight"), the more punitive they are toward expressions of sexuality in their children (Sears, Maccoby, and Levin, 1957). Parents who have a relaxed attitude towards their own sexuality are much more likely to take a tolerant attitude towards their children's sexual expression.

Information control.   American children are usually encouraged by their parents to ask them for information on all sorts of matters in which parents possess the wisdom of experience. However, when it comes to inquiries about reproduction, sex differences, and especially erotic pleasure, many parents respond quite differently. A child's sexual curiosity is often met with evasion, deliberate misinformation, nervousness, obscure references to birds and bees, and sometimes even insult or punishment (Martinson, 1973). Few American parents offer adequate sex information which is geared to a child's level of understanding (Roberts, et al., 1978).

When sex information is offered, it is usually too little and too late (Elias and Gebhard, 1969; Lewis, 1973). Information which is considered "sex information" is almost always about reproductive sexuality. Rarely does "sex information" as conceived by parents (or schools) refer to matters of erotic pleasure or even to love relationships. These matters are viewed by parents as even more delicate and difficult to explain.

Many parents are embarrassed about discussing sexual matters with their opposite sex children. Fathers may feel inadequate and anxious about discussing menstruation with their daughters. Mothers may feel similarly about discussing erection, ejaculation, and nocturnal emissions.

It is difficult to communicate accurate sex information geared to the child's age-level of comprehension, even if parents desire to do so (Bernstein, 1975). Too much irrelevant detail may only confuse a child. Too much simplicity may underestimate the child's real ability to understand sexual matters. However, the greatest difficulty of many parents may be their own anxiety about provoking a child's sexual curiosity and experimentation. (Parents, for example, can find adequate ways of "explaining" how a rocket is sent to Mars.)

Another difficulty for parents is an absence of an adequate sexual language to use with children (Sears, Maccoby, and Levin, 1957). American parents do not offer their children an adequate vocabulary to discuss genital parts, sex differences, sexual activities, and sensual feelings (Martinson, 1973). Linguistic deprivation makes it very difficult for the child to express his or her curiosity and to understand bodily feelings (Bandura and Walters, 1963).

Eventually, the child is forced to rely upon the sex language learned from older playmates. The child quickly realizes that the use of this "obscene" language will be punished by parents. Since that language becomes the only relevant language in which a child can express sexuality, it is reserved for secretive use with playmates.

As boys reach adolescence, "obscene" language becomes a symbol for acceptance in the male peer group. Girls are much less likely to learn and use such language (Kutner and Brogan, 1974). This difference is probably because obscene language is permeated with connotations of male superiority and contempt for women. As an example, to "fuck" or "screw" a girl connotes a somewhat hostile act which symbolizes male superiority. Girls do not "fuck" boys. They "make love" to them. It is not surprising, then, that research finds that males are more likely to use the terms "fuck" or "screw" as synonyms for intercourse than are females (Kutner and Brogan, 1974).

EROTIC SOCIALIZATION DURING ADOLESCENCE

The child's capacity for physiological sexual arousal begins very early in life. In American society, the discouragement of heterosexual activity tends to postpone erotic development until adolescence. The child's capacity for sexual arousal results in sporadic and unfocused sexual experimentation. Beginning sometime during adolescence, the person's social environment becomes more distinctively eroticized. At that time, the young person is increasingly exposed to erotic stimulation. This increases the frequency of sexual arousal and channels erotic behavior in socially approved directions.

There exists much greater variation in the sexual experience of adolescents than in the experience of children. The erotic socialization of adolescents varies greatly between communities, religious groups, and ethnic groups. A world of different cultural meanings of sexuality exists, for example, between a Mormon community in Utah and an inner-city black community. Also, during adolescence, the erotic environments of boys and girls begin to diverge in different directions (Gagnon and Simon, 1973).

Adolescence is the time of concentrated learning about the social meanings attributed to sexual acts. The major sources of this learning include: (1) parents; (2) self-directed learning; (3) the male and female peer groups; and (4) heterosexual relationships.

parents and adolescent sexuality

When parents see the emerging signs of puberty in their children, their concerns often become intensified. It is difficult for parents to gradually change their child-rearing from caring for a child assumed to be devoid of sexuality to caring of an obviously emergent sexual person. It is difficult to change from patterns of avoidance, punishment, and information control. Most American parents regard puberty as an announcement of the beginning of sexual desire and are unsure about how to guide its evolution. The influence of parents is usually aimed at: (1) restricting sexual expression; and (2) teaching moral values to their adolescent children. The sex information which they offer is commonly either very limited or very general (Sorenson, 1973).

One nationwide study of adolescent sexuality found that the parent-adolescent discussion of sexual matters continues to be difficult (Sorensen, 1973). It found that 72 percent of the boys and 70 percent of the girls, ages 13 to 19, felt that their parents did not talk freely about sex. Yet a majority of the adolescents wanted to discuss sexual matters with their parents. Only 30 percent of them reported that such discussion with their parents "makes them feel very uncomfortable" (Sorensen, 1973). Some topics were particularly avoided. These included: techniques of sexual intercourse, how to choose a sexual partner, and how to get more pleasure from sexual activity. Some of the parents, however, did offer information about birth control. About 31 percent of the girls and 18 percent of the boys received some information about birth control from their parents (Sorensen, 1973). On the other hand, many young people desired such information from their parents but were unable to speak with them about it. About 39 percent of the boys and 26 percent of the girls wanted to be able to ask their parents for birth control information.

Abstract sex information is one thing, while personal sex information is quite another. A majority (60 percent) of the adolescents said that they did not want to discuss their own sexual activity with their parents because they felt it was a private matter (Sorensen, 1973). This reluctance to engage in sexual self-disclosure was probably also shared by their parents. It is not likely that parents can expect sexual self-disclosure from their children without communicating about their own sexual intimacies in exchange.

In the ideal, parents could offer their adolescent children much helpful sexual guidance. Parents can communicate accurate sex information to correct misinformation from "the streets." They can communicate about the joys of sex in a love relationship. They can help their children avoid unnecessary fears about sexual functioning and sexual relationships. At the same time, they can encourage an ethical attitude toward sexual relationships. They can achieve these goals by various means. They can offer simple, direct and honest answers to their children's sex questions, starting at whatever age the questions arise. There are now many popular sex information books for children which parents can buy and have easily available in their homes (for example, see Pomeroy, 1968 and 1969). Such books are often a useful intermediary between parents and their children in sexual matters which either may find embarrassing to bring up for discussion. And, parents should not expect to be able to answer all sorts of sexual questions. They may have to do some reading on their own. When a parent is asked by an adolescent daughter whether or not it is safe for teenagers to use the birth control pill, the parent may have to consult the most recent information available in the library. (See the section on contraception in Chapter 3.)

Young people today obtain sex information (and misinformation) from a variety of sources. Several research projects have found that parents are still not the primary source of sex information for a majority of adolescents (Thornburg, 1970; Libby and Nass, 1971; Hunt, 1974). In the past, same-sex friends played the predominant role of sex educators. However, in the last 30 years, there have been some gradual changes. Among boys, same-sex friends continue to be the major source of sex information (Gebhard, 1977; Spanier, 1977). Among girls, however, the mother has now become as important or even more important than same-sex friends as a source of sex information (Gebhard, 1977; Spanier, 1977). The role of the mother as communicator of sex information has increased in importance even for boys over the last 30 years (Gebhard, 1977; Spanier, 1977). Fathers appear to serve as sources of sex information for only a limited percentage of adolescents. The mass media and independent reading are also important sources of sex information for a substantial proportion of young people. Other possible sources of sex information include: older brothers and sisters, relatives, school instruction, and more rarely, clergymen and medical doctors.

Some parents believe that sex information will stimulate a teenager's sexual curiosity and lead them into early sexual adventures (Libby and Nass, 1971). Yet two recent research projects have found that when parents (usually mothers) are the main source of sex information, their children are less likely to have premarital sexual intercourse at an early age, than are adolescents who obtain their sex information from their peer group (Lewis, 1973; Spanier, 1977). This effect of parental sex education is particularly true for adolescent girls; and especially when the communication covers many sexual topics.

self-directed learning

Sexual curiosity.   During the pre-adolescent years, sexual arousal is frequently experienced in a variety of play activities. This is true of both sexes but especially so for boys probably because of their external genitals. Sexual arousal is commonly experienced in reaction to activities which result in genital friction such as wrestling, climbing trees, or sliding down bannisters (Kinsey et al., 1948). It may also be experienced at times of emotional or romantic excitement. Girls are likely to have more difficulty than boys in distinguishing between sexual arousal and general bodily excitation (Heiman, 1975). Males may be more easily aware of the genital dimension of their excitement, because of the feedback information of erection.

During early adolescence, occasions of sexual arousal become more and more frequent and more genitally focused. Sometimes, when a boy has an erection in an inappropriate situation such as in a classroom or on a beach, it can be a source of embarrassment. These experiences can be especially anxiety-provoking for pre-adolescent boys who are sexually uninformed and fearful about making sexual inquiries (Martinson, 1973).

Sexual curiosity stimulates an exploration for bits and pieces of sexual information during late childhood and early adolescence. Among boys, these are gathered from older friends in the form of sex stories, sex jokes, and "girlie" magazines (Martinson, 1973).

The effects of sex information control are probably greater among girls. Consequently, fewer girls encounter these indirect forms of sexual stimulation (Elias and Gebhard, 1969). One study, for example, investigated exposure to written and pictorial erotica among a sample of 400 high school students from a midwestern community (Elias, 1971). A much higher proportion of boys compared with girls had read descriptions of sexual activity or had seen it in photographs or movies.

One recent study investigated the sexual interests of 14-year-old boys and girls in a sample of 65 boys and 65 girls from five different schools (Rubenstein et al., 1976). The boys and girls had the same primary sexual concerns. Both sexes were especially curious about the interpersonal context and consequences of sexual intercourse. They were much less curious about reproductive anatomy and physiology (contrary to what many adults might assume). In terms of the context of sexual intercourse, the young people were concerned about whether they would enjoy, fear, or feel guilty about sexual intercourse. They were also interested in the nature of love relationships and information about birth control. In terms of the possible consequences of sexual intercourse, they expressed an interest in pregnancy, venereal disease, and abortion. Surprisingly, there were only a few gender differences in sex interests. The girls were significantly more interested than were the boys in such issues as birth control, abortion, and rape. (These findings are similar to those obtained in surveys conducted by this author in human sexuality classes where the students range from late adolescence to middle age.)

Sexual fantasy.   Sexual fantasy during adolescence extends imagination to new erotic possibilities. In a sense, adolescent sexual fantasies serve to eroticize more of a person's environment (Simon and Gagnon, 1969).

Clinical observations suggest that the erotic daydreams of girls tend to focus upon romantic relationships with boys, emphasizing their magnetic attractiveness (Pomeroy, 1969). The erotic fantasies of early adolescent girls usually involve only a minimum of body contact, such as caressing or kissing. On the other hand, the erotic daydreams of similar-age boys are usually more explicitly genital. They are also much more frequent in occurrence (Pomeroy, 1968). These male-female differences in adolescent fantasy life probably reflect differences in the subcultural environments of the two sexes. (The male and female adolescent subcultures are described in the following sections.)

Some young people experience feelings of anxiety or guilt when having erotic daydream fantasies (Simon and Gagnon, 1969). They may fantasize, for example, about sexual involvement with a relative or teacher or total stranger. They may fantasize about forbidden sexual behavior newly learned from sex stories, such as oral sex or group sex. An early adolescent boy or girl may believe that he or she is the only person having such erotic fantasies. They may believe that they are somehow destined to have psychological problems as a consequence. Such distress may be compounded by religious teachings that "dirty thoughts" are sinful and by an inadequate sex education.

Eventually, adolescent sexual fantasies are employed as an imaginary stimulus to accompany self-stimulation. One nationwide study of adolescents between the ages of 13 and 19 investigated common adolescent fantasy themes during masturbation (Sorensen, 1973). Only 11 percent of the boys and 7 percent of the girls who admitted masturbating said that they never fantasized during masturbation. The vast majority of adolescents used sex fantasies to heighten sexual arousal from sometimes to most of the time. Common adolescent male fantasy themes included: (1) sex with someone who is forced to submit; (2) sex with more than one female; (3) group sex; (4) sex when one is forced to submit; (5) varying degrees of violence to the other person; and (6) oral and anal sex. Common fantasy themes among adolescent girls included: (1) sex with a male who is much admired; (2) sex with one or more males when one is forced to submit; (3) inflicting mild violence on the other person; and (4) receiving oral sex (Sorensen, 1973). It might be noted that themes of hostility and coercion appear to be common in adolescent sex fantasy life. Perhaps this reflects the tensions evoked by personal and interpersonal conflicts over sexual conduct during adolescence.

Masturbation.   Recent research has found that the average age of first masturbation is now earlier than it was when Kinsey did his research in the 1940s (Elias and Gebhard, 1969; Hunt, 1974). One nationwide study found that 63 percent of males and 33 percent of females could recall deliberate masturbation to the point of orgasm before the age of thirteen (Hunt, 1974). Similar research findings in Germany and Sweden suggests that this same change is also occurring in other industrial societies (Linner, 1972; Schmidt and Sigusch, 1972).

Perhaps even more important, recent research has found a much greater increase in the percentage of adolescent girls who masturbate at every age level than the increase in boys (Hunt, 1974). This finding may signal gradual changes in the erotic development of women in American society. By the end of adolescence almost all boys and a majority of girls have practiced self-stimulation to orgasm.

Past research has found that the frequency of masturbation is much greater among adolescent boys than it is among adolescent girls (Kinsey et al., 1953). However, some recent research findings indicate that this difference between males and females is becoming less marked, particularly among older adolescents. One research project, for example, investigated the autoerotic behavior of a sample of 435 college students in New York City who were an average age of 20 to 22 (Arafat and Cotton, 1974). It found no significant differences between male and female frequencies of masturbation even though fewer women did masturbate (60 percent versus 90 percent). The average frequency found was between several times a week and several times a month.

In recent years, several research projects have investigated the autoerotic behavior and attitudes of college students to determine whether a person's frequency of masturbation is related to other aspects of personality. The research has found that higher frequencies of masturbation are associated with a higher interest in sexual matters (Abramson, 1973), and a greater desire for sexual pleasure (Arafat and Cotton, 1974). Higher frequencies of masturbation have also been found among adolescents who are more heterosexually involved in dating and petting (Gagnon, Simon, and Berger, 1970).

These findings seem to contradict the popular belief that masturbation is caused by social and sexual isolation. In contrast, greater social involvement with the opposite sex may actually stimulate autoerotic behavior when regular opportunities for orgasmic satisfaction are blocked (Gagnon, Simon, and Berger, 1970). Masturbation is often used to release the sexual tensions built-up from the genital congestion which results from petting. It is sometimes deliberately used by young people who desire to avoid premarital intercourse. It should be noted that no frequency of masturbation has been found to be "excessive" in the sense of causing any bodily harm (Masters and Johnson, 1966).

One research project found that a person's level of self-esteem (high or low) is not related to frequency of masturbation (Greenberg and Archambault, 1973). Another research project found that "emotional instability" is not related to a person's frequency of masturbation (Abramson, 1973). These findings are also contrary to the popular belief that masturbation is more common among adolescents who have low self-esteem and are socially timid.

Two personality characteristics have been found to be related to lower frequencies of masturbation. These are frequent church attendance and increasing age (1953; Greenberg and Archambault, 1973).

Masturbation has been, until recently, one of the most strongly tabooed sexual practices in Western societies. One research project, for example, found that many parents are more anxious about adolescent masturbation than they are about premarital petting (Bandura and Walters, 1959). Until recently, the condemnation of masturbation was encouraged especially by religious officials and medical doctors (Neuman, 1975; Barker-Benfield, 1976). The root of this condemnation probably grows from the historic Western disapproval of all nonreproductive sexual behavior (Sagarin, 1968).

Many traditional myths supported the masturbation taboo by spreading fear and provoking guilt about the activity. These beliefs held that masturbation could make people insane, that it encouraged homosexual tendencies, and that it impeded a person's ability to express affection in a sexual relationship. None of these beliefs have been found to be true (Kinsey et al., 1948; Kinsey et al., 1953). Nevertheless, one surprising study of medical doctors done as recently as 1959 found that 50 percent of the graduates of five medical schools and 20 percent of the faculty believed that masturbation is a common cause of mental illness (Greenbank, 1961).

In sharp contrast with past concerns about the dangers of "self-abuse," current sex therapists have found that directed masturbation is a very effective treatment for women who are unable to achieve orgasm (LoPiccolo and Lobitz, 1972; Kohlenberg, 1974). There is even some evidence that masturbation experience in girls can assist early adjustment to heterosexual intercourse. The

Kinsey research, for example, found that girls who had experienced orgasm during masturbation were also more likely to experience orgasm during initial sexual intercourse in comparison with girls who did not masturbate to orgasm (Kinsey et al., 1953). Indeed, several recent "sex manuals" advise masturbation exercises as a technique for women to develop their bodily erotic responsiveness and orgasmic capacity (Heiman, et al., 1976). In relation to men, it has also been suggested that slow masturbation aimed at delaying orgasmic build-up is an effective means for adolescent boys to learn ejaculatory control to avoid premature ejaculation during heterosexual relations (Pomeroy, 1968).

Many young people continue to experience feelings of anxiety, guilt, and depression in response to masturbation (Greenberg and Archambault, 1973; Arafat and Cotton, 1974). Moral self-condemnation, fears of discovery, fears of psychological problems, and fears of being unmasculine or unfeminine all contribute toward unpleasant emotional after effects in many people (Simon and Gagnon, 1969). Masturbation is simply contrary to many peoples' concept of themselves as normal sexual beings. One study found that self-stimulation tends to evoke more negative feelings in women than in men (Arafat and Cotton, 1974). It may be more inconsistent with the traditional self-image that many women hold of themselves as being receptive rather than assertive in the pursuit of sexual pleasure. It may also symbolize impersonal sex without affection for many women.

the male and female peer group

An adolescent's peer group very often exerts a greater influence than that of parents on sexual attitudes and behavior. This is particularly true where parents offer little sexual information and where there is little family communication about sexual matters (Lewis, 1973; Spanier, 1977). Parent-adolescent conflict over sexual matters continues to be common in American families (Wake, 1969; LoPiccolo, 1973).

A distinction can be noted between male and female peer groups. The different peer groups emphasize different kinds of activities and interests. These male-female differences in lifestyles are termed male and female *subcultures* (Ehrmann, 1959; Udry, 1974). Male and female subcultures ultimately arise from the social segregation of adolescent men and women. In the past, the male subculture emphasized such matters as auto mechanics, sports competition, comaraderie, and the pursuit of sexual pleasure (Udry, 1974). In contrast, the female subculture focused attention upon social popularity, clothes, physical attractiveness, and romantic involvement with boys (Udry, 1974).

The male and female subcultures may now be declining as important agents of erotic socialization. This is because friendship relations have become less sex-segregated. Some research has found that cross-sex companionship has increased since the 1940s (Kuhlen and Houlihan, 1965). Other research has

found that dating now begins at an earlier age than it did 30 years ago (Broderick and Fowler, 1961). These social changes reflect the increasing similarity in the sex-role socialization of boys and girls. Yet, the male and female subcultures continue to influence the erotic socialization of many adolescents, according to some recent research (Berg, 1975).

Sex in the male subculture. Sexual activity is a dominant concern in the male subculture. Boys engage in much conversation concerned with the pursuit of sexual pleasure. "Obscene" vocabulary is often used as an expression of masculinity. It filters down from older adolescents to pre-adolescent boys, as each learns to emulate more "informed" elders. The content of the conversation emphasizes two basic themes: sex as play and as achievement (Udry, 1974). In the male subculture, men learn to regard the pursuit of erotic pleasure as a major form of recreational activity. Perhaps more important, the male subculture still teaches men to regard sexual activity as an arena for achieving prestige.

Many adolescent males brag to each other in explicit detail about their sexual prowess. Much of this bragging is an elaboration of aspirations, rather than of actual events (Ehrmann, 1959). This emphasis upon sex as achievement encourages a view of women as objects of sexual sport to be seduced, mastered, and victimized. The context of much conversation and joking about women is sometimes openly hostile and contemptuous. Such conversation may be designed to neutralize feelings of empathy and romanticism towards potential "victims." The attitude evoked is: "they deserve it."

Today, however, a great many adolescent boys never develop an exploitive attitude toward women. Their desire for affectionate relations counters the effect of the male subculture.

The male subculture intensifies the sexual curiosity and erotic fantasy life of adolescent boys. Techniques of sexual arousal are a prominent topic of conversation (Ehrmann, 1959). They are given considerable attention in sex stories, sex jokes, and "girlie" magazines.

Sex in the female subculture.   In the female subculture the pursuit of sexual pleasure is not a prominent concern. This continues to be so even though sexual conversation between girls has become more common in recent years (Udry, 1974). In the past, when sexual matters were discussed between girlfriends, the content commonly involved themes of romantic affairs and self-defense against the sexual demands of boys (Udry, 1974). Today, there is more open discussion about such matters as premarital sex, contraception, and abortion (Konopka, 1976). Yet, few girls give verbal approval to casual sex without an affectionate relationship.

Among girls, sexual activity cannot be a simple source of "play." Adolescent girls must worry about being sexually "victimized," about becoming pregnant, and about being shamed. Most girls quickly learn that sexual encounters with boys can lead to the exaggerated bragging of former boyfriends and to malicious gossip among girlfriends. Sexual involvement evokes much more anxiety in adolescent girls than it does in boys (Bardwick, 1971). Consequently, many early adolescent girls do not learn to develop a strong sexual curiosity or sexual desire (Simon and Gagnon, 1969; Bardwick, 1971).

In later adolescence, many girls desire to please the boys that they love and comply with the male desire for sexual activity (Bardwick, 1971). Only gradually, with increasing sexual experience, do most girls learn to enjoy sexual pleasure for themselves. It may be argued that during adolescence many girls learn to regard sexual pleasure with feelings of ambivalence (Bardwick, 1971).

the double standard

The main source of sexual politics in American culture is the traditional double standard of sexual behavior. On the level of abstract ideals, Americans have traditionally expected complete abstinence from all sexual activity before marriage of both females and males. Actual practice was quite to the contrary. In reality, women were (and sometimes are) much more strongly condemned for any nonmarital sexual expression. Men were treated with much greater permissiveness. Women were expected to be not only virginal but also without erotic interest until their wedding night. "Pure in spirit as well as body," was the cliché taught to women.

Even today, remnants of the double standard continue to make permarital sexual relationships an area for interpersonal conflict. One research project, for example, found that college men are more likely to talk about their sexual involvements than are college women (Carns, 1973). It is necessary for them to "spread the word" to obtain prestige in the male subculture. Another research project found that a high frequency of premarital sexual involvement is correlated with high self-esteem in college men but not in college women (Berman and Osborn, 1975). Adolescent girls who report more frequent premarital sexual involvements also report lesser feelings of happiness (Gagnon, Simon, and Berger, 1970).

The situation is clear. It is adolescent girls, not boys, who still have to worry about being sexually victimized being exposed to public ridicule as a consequence of the double standard.

The double standard tends to be propagated in the male subculture where men are segregated in all male groups, such as in the military, college dormitories, and sports teams (Arkin, 1978). Some fathers even tolerate their son's, but not their daughter's, youthful pleasure-seeking as being "natural" (Bandura and Walters, 1959). However, today this attitude is most common among lower class men (Rainwater, 1966).

the sexual behavior of american adolescents

Petting.   Petting is the most common form of heterosexual activity practiced by American adolescents. The term "petting" is rather inexact. It refers to any kind of sexual caressing which does not lead to sexual intercourse. The sexual caresses are the same as those used in *foreplay*. Indeed, it is during petting that a repertoire of sexual caresses may be learned for use in later life. Men who have their first intercourse at an early age tend to have less extensive experience at petting. They are also more likely to prefer little foreplay with their wives (Kinsey et al., 1948).

A distinction is commonly made between "light petting" and "heavy petting," although the terms do not clarify much. Light petting may involve: kissing, tongue kissing, hugging, and manual stimulation of the woman's breasts while clothed. Heavy petting may involve such sexual caresses as: the manual and oral stimulation of the woman's unclothed breasts, manual stimulation of the genitals, mutual masturbation, horizontal imitation of the movements of coitus, and oral stimulation of the genitals (Harper, 1961). Sexual caressing to the point of orgasm is often experienced under conditions of "heavy" petting. In most of the world's societies, these sexual practices would be regarded as bizarre. Extensive sexual caressing without sexual intercourse is rare practice anywhere else in the world, other than in America and Europe.

Adolescents gradually move from light petting to heavier petting with increasing age. One recent large-scale investigation of adolescent sexual behavior found that about 50 percent of adolescent boys and girls had experienced light petting before the age of sixteen (Miller and Simon, 1974). Only about 25 percent of both males and females had experienced heavy petting by that same age.

Those young people who remain unmarried through their late teenage years and early twenties tend to have increasingly frequent experiences with heavy petting. (Those people who marry later in life are also more likely to be college students than youths employed at jobs.) One national research survey found that by age 24, unmarried men and women had extensive experience with heavy petting (Hunt, 1974). More than 50 percent of the women and 66 percent of the men had experienced petting to orgasm, mainly via mutual masturbation. Another study found that about 60 percent each of college men and women had practiced mutual masturbation (Packard, 1968).

One study of college students in a Southern university found that oral-genital sex was experienced by 66 percent of the males and 54 percent of the females (Robinson, King, and Balswick, 1972). These findings about oral-genital sex during petting are similar to those obtained in the nationwide survey which found that 72 percent of men from the youngest age group had experienced fellatio before marriage (Hunt, 1974). Other research with college students from a Midwestern university found that many unmarried young women now practice fellatio and experience cunnilingus before first having sexual intercourse (Curran, 1977). Perhaps these young women do so to enjoy intense sexual stimulation while avoiding possible pregnancy and preserving a feeling of still being a virgin. In the sequence of erotic development, it is much more rare for men to engage in oral-genital sex before first experiencing sexual intercourse (Curran, 1977). The available research indicates that petting has become much more common and now involves more intimate caresses than it did in the 1940s when Kinsey did his research.

The level of petting (light to heavy) is also related to the level of psychological intimacy which a couple share. The sexual caresses that are more intensely arousing and more condemned outside of marriage tend to be reserved for relationships bonded by greater affection and security (Bell and Blumberg, 1960). Light petting has now become a rather routine practice in casual dating relationships (Miller and Simon, 1974). A majority of adolescent girls still resist demands for heavy petting unless they feel secure in an affectionate relationship (Hunt, 1974). However, a growing minority of older adolescent girls do occasionally engage in heavy petting without having any strong affection for their partners (Hunt, 1974). They do so for sexual satisfaction, or to please their partners, or to boost their feeling of attractiveness. A study of college women at a university in Colorado found that 55 percent of them had engaged in heavy petting at least once with someone they did not love (Davis, 1971).

In the past, petting functioned as a substitute for sexual intercourse among American youth who feared inpregnation or who valued female virginity. This is still often the case. One study of international differences in premarital sexual behavior found that American college students as compared with students in England, Germany, and Norway were more likely to regard heavy petting as an end in itself (Luckey and Nass, 1969). The research found that American students had comparatively more experience with various sexual caresses, but less frequent sexual intercourse than students in the other three countries. Recent research, however, indicates that American adolescents are now moving rapidly from involvement in heavy petting to an acceptance of sexual intercourse (Hunt, 1974).

Adolescent erotic socialization in American society exposes youth to much interpersonal conflict and personal anxiety. The adolescent years are ones of struggle to develop a satisfying and balanced sexuality. The adolescent is exposed to conflict over sexual matters with parents, dates, and lovers. Adolescents may also experience painful personal conflict over standards of wise and proper sexual conduct.

(Premarital sexual intercourse is explored in Chapter 12.)

the transition from virginity

The new premarital transition.   In the American past, it was rather common for spouses to be virgins on their wedding night (or, at least, it was common for wives). Today this is no longer true. A substantial majority of today's young people are not virgins as they begin marital cohabitation.

The percentage of adolescents who have premarital sexual intercourse increased greatly during the late 1960s and early 1970s. According to the most recent and respected national survey of adolescent sexual practices, about 55 percent of women (and a much higher percentage of men) have experienced sexual intercourse by the end of their 19th year of age (Zelnick and Kanter, 1977). A much greater percentage of post-adolescent women and men make a premarital transition from virginity before their wedding night.

A majority of parents continue to disapprove of premarital sexual intercourse. Yet the transition from virginity is now more common before marriage than it is after the wedding ceremony. The historical change from a marital to a premarital transition from virginity has created an important change in this life-cycle transition. It is now relatively rare for the first experience of sexual intercourse to occur simultaneously with the beginning of "living together."

Reactions to first intercourse.   One study of first intercourse in a sample of about 100 college students found that the women reported having had many inhibiting worries during the experience (Eastman, 1972). A majority of the women said that they had felt fear of pregnancy, or anxiety about whether their parents would find out, or guilt about behavior they considered immoral. Many women also worried about painful intercourse or about what their friends might think of them. The men had fewer such worries. Therefore, it is not surprising that more of the men (96 percent) than the women (51 percent) reported that they had "enjoyed" their first sexual intercourse. None of the men reported having disliked the experience. However, 40 percent of the women did consider it to have been an emotionally negative experience.

Medical authorities estimate that the penetration of the intact hymen is severely painful for one-third of women, with another one-half experiencing only brief and moderate pain, and 20 percent experiencing no pain at all (Oliven, 1974). It should be noted that high anxiety on the woman's part, and carelessness on the man's part can aggravate any painful feelings.

A nationwide study of the sexual behavior of adolescents between the ages of 13 and 19 also found substantial differences between males and females in their reactions to first intercourse (Sorensen, 1974). The most common feelings of boys, in descending order, were: excited, satisfied, thrilled, happy, and joyful. In contrast, the most common feelings of girls, in descending order, were: afraid, guilty, worried, and embarrassed. However, the more negative emotional reactions of the girls were usually not long-lasting. A majority of them continued to have sexual intercourse with their first partner and felt that their relationship and sexual experience had grown more satisfying (Sorensen, 1974).

The location of first sexual intercourse among the unmarried has received little research attention. It is widely assumed that the location continues to be in the back seat of the mammoth American automobile. However, the evidence is that the recent generation of youth rarely have their first experience there. Instead, the most common location is now in the home of one of the sexual partners or at the home of a friend (Zelnick and Kanter, 1977). It is quite likely that the increased employment of both parents has now made it rather easy for young people to find a convenient and comfortable location for their sexual activity.

Is the experience of first sexual intercourse on the wedding night more or less stressful and emotionally satisfying than when it occurs before marriage? One large scale research project carried out in England compared the experiences of people who had premarital sex with those of people who were virgins at marriage (Schofield, 1973). It found that neither set of circumstances enabled greater or less enjoyment of the "first time."

Even when the first experience of intercourse occurs after marriage, a couple may still have certain worries and stresses. Research evidence suggests that the notion of a wedding night "psychological trauma" is only a myth. It is an exceedingly rare occurrence (Kanin and Howard, 1958). Nevertheless, women and men may both worry about being sexually inadequate because of their inexperience. Women may worry about painful penetration and whether they will be treated with care by their new husbands. Both may worry about doing something awkward and embarrassing themselves. In addition, the wedding night may be a rather emotionally intense one in which to initiate sexual intercourse. A couple may be harrassed, fatigued, and possibly also inebriated.

A great many young people today continue to worry about what will happen during their transition from virginity. They look forward to the transition, anxious to make this symbolic passage into sexual adulthood. Yet many young women are still worried about the interpersonal circumstances of the occurrence. In balance, the situation is less frightful for them than it was during their grandmother's youth.

Many young women and men are now going through the transition from virginity during early and middle adolescence. It is a time when the psychological stresses of that period in life can bring additional problems. At the heart of any life-cycle transition is a transformation of a person's self-concept and the meaning they attribute to their lives. The anxiety over creating a satisfying identity for one's self can be intensified by a particularly early transition from virginity.

The transformation of self-concept.   A young person's transition from virginity can bring about a transformation in the way he or she views the sexual self. Most obviously, they may change from a view of self from sexually inexperienced to "experienced." There are other subtle changes in self-concept which are possible. They may feel quite positive about the "new" self, or they may feel quite ambivalent when beset with regrets.

Some research has found that the transition from virginity gives rise to more identity problems for women than for men (Waterman and Nevid, 1977). Women are much more likely to feel ambivalent about the sexual self. They have more questions about the validity of their personal sex standards, their self-worth, and their future sexual expectations.

Many young women today are caught in a double bind of pressures. They can easily lead themselves to believe that "all" of their female friends are sexually experienced. Yet they still worry about their reputation and about transgressing the moral standards which they held during early adolescence. Most women resolve the dilemma by seeking first intercourse in a love relationship (Kleinman, 1978). Having premarital intercourse with a beloved partner allows a young woman to define herself as a loving person. The emphasis is shifted from sex to love.

However, when a love relationship breaks up, as so many do, a young woman may be plagued by doubts about her self-worth (Kleinman, 1978). Is she now to be considered by her self and others as being "easy" and promiscuous? In retrospect, what was seen as love now becomes seen as a mere infatuation. She may redefine her sexual experience as unjustified and regrettable. After becoming sexually "experienced," a young woman can continue to define herself as an affectionate person, searching for a committed relationship. Or, she may justify her previous behavior by changing her attitude toward premarital intercourse (Kleinman, 1978). She may reject the idea that love is a necessary prerequisite for sexual intercourse and begin to accept sexual activity in pursuit of personal pleasure. This position puts her "on the other side of the fence" from her early adolescent romantic daydreams. It may be accepted with feelings of ambivalence and fatalism.

body consciousness

Our body consciousness refers to our attitudes toward our physical form and functioning. It consists of the visual images that we carry in our memories drawn from wall mirrors as well as the mirrors of our own imagination. It consists of the characteristic ways in which we experience our bodies as receptacles of our selves. The body image which an adolescent formulates during the crucial years of puberty may persist well into adulthood. A young person who experiences himself or herself as ''chubby'' during the early teenage years may retain the visual imagery of the experience, long after they have become more streamlined.

The persistence of past body consciousness is demonstrated by a curious phenomena known as the *phantom limb*. People who have had a leg or arm amputated continue for some time to experience themselves as if they still had the appendage. They will absent mindedly reach for things with the missing arm or try to walk on the absent leg. Our bodies become lasting elements in the cognitive map we hold of the world in which we live.

puberty

Perhaps the most crucial period in the development of a person's body consciousness occurs during puberty. *Puberty* is the period of time in which the male and female reproductive systems begin to be capable of causing conception. There is no particular point which can be recognized as the beginning of puberty

10 puberty and body consciousness

nor can any be taken as its end. The first menstrual period (menarche) in girls and the first ejaculation in boys are conventionally used to pinpoint the beginning of puberty in an individual. At the age when these physical events first occur, a capacity for conception is not guaranteed. Insufficient sperm and no ova may yet be produced. Many physical changes occur previous to and after those events.

While the term *puberty* refers to bodily changes, adolescence is entirely a matter of social construction. *Adolescence* is the social situation of people between childhood and adulthood. Its beginning and end are even more difficult to gauge than is that of puberty.

The mechanism of the biological clock initiating puberty remains unknown. We do not know why puberty is early in some people and later in others. However, some basic outlines of the hormonal mechanisms are now understood. Scientists believe that some kind of triggering mechanism lies in the *hypothalamus* at the base of the brain. It delivers a message to the *pituitary gland* which then secretes hormones that stimulate rapid growth. The pituitary gland, in turn, also sends chemical messages—carried by gonadotropic hormones—to the sex glands. *Gonadotropic hormones* regulate the production of the other key hormones in reproductive development: testosterone, estrogen, and progesterone.

The sex hormones are produced in the ovaries, testes, and adrenal glands of both sexes. It was formerly believed that different hormones distinguish men and women. However, the hormonal differences between the sexes are now understood to be a matter of the relative proportions of sex hormones, rather than the presence and absence of hormones (Rose, 1972). Males produce much more *androgen,* which masculinizes the body. Females produce much more *estrogen,* which feminizes the body.

There is no sudden increase in gonadotropin messages and the production of sex hormones. Rather, there is a gradual build-up of production several years before any outward signs of puberty. Puberty is not a "raging storm" of sudden hormonal changes. There is no concrete evidence that hormonal changes during puberty cause any psychological distress, even though the notion is taken for granted (Rose, 1972). Instead, emotional difficulties may occur as a result of a maturing person's rapidly changing body consciousness and self-concept.

The sequence of bodily changes in males during puberty usually begins with the enlargement of the testicles and scrotum (Tanner, 1970). At about the same time, rapid growth in stature may begin followed by the growth of pubic hair and enlargement of the penis. Within a year of this growth spurt, the first ejaculation usually occurs. This event may occur in nocturnal emissions, but more commonly occurs as a result of self-stimulation (Kinsey, Pomeroy, and Martin, 1948). However, sperm production in the testicles may still be insufficient for impregnation. Over the next several years, secondary sex characteristics gradually begin to appear. These include: the deepening of voice, development of facial and bodily hair, and enlargement of muscle tissues. Such characteristics are termed *secondary* because they are not necessary for reproduction. They are linked, however, in the sense that all these changes are brought about by *androgen*.

Female puberty involves much more complex bodily changes. Gonadotropic hormones from the pituitary gland act on the ovaries to stimulate the secretion of *estrogen*. In turn, the increased estrogen flowing through the blood stream stimulates the growth of breast tissue. The budding of breasts is usually the first sign of puberty (Tanner, 1970). (The milk producing mammary glands do not become fully mature and functional until childbirth.) At about the same time, an increase in *androgen* production stimulates the development of pubic hair. The *menarche* (first menstrual flow) usually occurs after these two events. At first, menstrual periods occur at unpredictable intervals, and ovulation does not take place. It may take six months to a year or more before a regular cycle develops and ovulation starts. Most women's menstrual cycles occur in a range of 26 to 34 days, with 28-day cycles being the average. The *menstrual cycle* is hormonally regulated by increasing and decreasing levels of estrogen and progesterone secretion. Menstrual cycles can become irregular for a great variety of reasons, and some women's cycles are perpetually irregular. *Menstruation* involves the discharge of blood, mucus, and old cells from the lining of the uterus. This process maintains the receptivity of the uterus to the implantation of fertilized eggs. Additional changes occur in the female genitals during puberty. Estrogen stimulates the enlargement of the labia, while androgen causes the clitoris to enlarge slightly. Estrogen also slows skeletal growth and causes a redistribution of body fat, resulting in the shorter more rounded appearance of woman.

the timing of puberty

The timing of puberty is often a matter of concern for parents as well as their children. It is not an easy task to determine the average age of the beginning of puberty. As already noted, there is no sudden change which announces its beginning. The gradualness and ambiguity of puberty permits the social labels of "maturity" and "immaturity" to be applied easily to individuals, especially by adolescent peer groups. Such judgments impart social inequalities of greater and lesser prestige to young people.

The menarche, which occurs after puberty has already begun, is easier to recognize than anything which occurs in boys. The first ejaculation is less of a public event than menarche, and not likely to be matter of family, school, or medical attention. In boys rapid growth in height and emergence of secondary sexual characteristics are more likely to be used as indicators of puberty. Any specific age given for the average commencement of puberty can only be an approximation because of the wide range of individual differences. A recent study by the United States Public Health Service indicates that in American society, the average age range for female puberty is between ages 9 and 16, with an average menarchial age of 13 (U.S. Public Health Service, 1973). The average

age range for male puberty is between ages 11 and 17. The average age of first ejaculation is estimated to be at about age 14 (Kinsey, Pomeroy, and Martin, 1948).

Recent studies have come up with the finding that the average age of menarche has been decreasing in industrial societies, over the last one hundred years (Tanner, 1968). Records of other indicators of puberty (such as rate of growth) also provide evidence of an increasingly early puberty in both girls and boys. The average age of the beginning of puberty may be as much as 2½ to 3½ years earlier today than it was 100 years ago (age 13 versus 16). No conclusive explanation is yet available. However, the most reasonable hypothesis holds that improved nutrition is probably the key element (Tanner, 1968). Industrialization and economic improvement have resulted in healthier diets with less starch and more protein for more people. The suggestion is that retarded puberty, resulting from inadequate nutrition, has usually been the case in the past. Now puberty is arriving for the well-fed at the earliest possible age. Corroborative evidence for the nutrition link comes from studies which report earlier menarchial dates: (1) in higher socioeconomic groups compared with lower socioeconomic groups; and (2) in wealthier, industrial societies compared with poorer, developing societies (Diers, 1974; Tanner, 1968). There is no evidence that girls in hot tropical climates mature earlier than those in temperate zones as was popularly believed. The reverse may be more accurate, because the wealthier, industrial societies are all in temperate climatic regions.

Further evidence that better nutrition during fetal growth and childhood is linked to earlier puberty comes from the recent finding that the onset of menstruation is associated with body weight (Frisch and Revelle, 1970). It has been found that menarche occurs when body weight reaches about 106 pounds in girls. This critical weight correlates with menarche whether girls are slightly early, average, or slightly late in arriving at it. Better nutrition has enabled children to grow faster in height and weight, within certain biological limits. Scientists hypothesize that the critical body weight triggers metabolic changes which in turn increase the secretion of estrogen. Critical body weights may also be associated with the beginning of puberty in boys, but evidence for that is not yet available.

the social meanings of puberty

Puberty marks a person's entrance into adulthood. Yet it is not clear just when a person becomes an "adult." Adulthood is not attained by physical size and reproductive maturity, nor by qualities of character. Instead, adulthood is essentially a social status. In other words, *adulthood* is attained when a person gains the social recognition that he or she is accountable to certain social expectations and has certain rights. An *adult* is a person who is socially recognized as having the rights and expectations of employment, marriage, citizenship, and legal protection and accountability.

In American society, there exists no rite of passage, or ritual ceremony, which symbolizes the change in a person's social status from that of a child to that of an adult. However, many other societies do have such ceremonies (Brown, 1969). They mark a life-cycle transition and make public announcement of a person's new status in the community. (Jews, for example, practice the rite of the Bar Mitzvah, which symbolizes this message.) The absence of a symbolic passage into adulthood causes the physical indicators of puberty to take on an unusual public importance among American adolescents. The physical changes of puberty are socially recognized as symbols of an oncoming adult status. Bulging muscles in boys and emerging breasts in girls take on a symbolic function, much like insignias of rank. They are status symbols.

Some behavioral scientists believe that adult sexuality is more greatly influenced by the experiences of adolescence than by those of childhood (Gagnon and Simon, 1973). Adolescence is the time when the self-concept of a child is transformed into that of an adult. This psychological transformation occurs simultaneously with puberty, when a young person's body is also rapidly being transformed. During this time, sexual matters take on new meaning. A hidden world of information (and misinformation) about human sexuality is unveiled to them. And, perhaps most important, it is during this time of life that social relationships become eroticized.

A central aspect of a person's self-concept consists of the person's attitudes toward the body. As puberty reshapes an adolescent's body, it is inevitable that his or her attitudes toward his or her body are also transformed. Adolescents must adjust to changes in bodily functioning. Equally important, they must adjust to the new social meanings attributed to their adult male and female bodies.

BODY CONSCIOUSNESS AND REPRODUCTIVE PROCESSES

menstruation

An adolescent's reaction to his or her body's new reproductive functioning is even more direct and immediate than the reaction to the transformation of the body's physical appearance. For young women the emergence of monthly cycles plays a central role in feminine body consciousness.

Culturally transmitted attitudes toward menstruation differ considerably, even between various ethnic groups within the American population (Abel and Joffe, 1950). Among some people, bizarre myths still prevail about the nature of menstruation and it remains unmentionable in polite conversation. In such groups, menstruation is still regarded as a form of illness (''being unwell''), and girls may be given little, if any, family preparation for its occurrence. Among other groups, a more casual and relaxed attitude is taken by parents who psychologically prepare their daughters for the bodily events of menstruation.

Many pre-pubescent girls probably still do not receive enough accurate information about menstruation in a reassuring parent-daughter emotional relationship. This neglect is most common in poorer, less educated families. One study of a large group of middle class women found that 94 percent of those who were teenagers received some information about menstruation from their family, while 4 percent were totally unprepared (Larsen, 1961). In contrast, another study of women with similar middle class backgrounds found that 21 percent had no advance preparation (Shainess, 1961). Another study reported that 25 percent of 8- to 10-year-old girls from middle class backgrounds, and 75 percent of working class daughters had no menstrual information (Elias and Gebhard, 1969). Whatever proportion of girls receive information from their parents, we have even less research data about the accuracy of the information and the emotional context of parent-daughter relations. One study, for example, found that a majority of mothers (60 percent) reacted negatively to the first sign of their daughter's menstruation (Shainess, 1961). Some of these mothers even criticized their daughters, as if they had done something wrong. The question of psychological preparedness works in two directions. It seems that some mothers are psychologically unprepared to deal with their daughter's new reproductive maturity.

Proper studies of girls' reactions to menarche should derive from research with girls who have recently experienced that event. Unfortunately, because of remaining social taboos, that sort of research is not available. Most studies involve older adolescents, or women, working from their memories of the event. As always, memories may be colored by interceding life experiences. What research is available tends to indicate that reactions to the beginning of menstruation are ambivalent combinations of positive and negative attitudes (Rothchild, 1967; Bardwick, 1971). These attitudes may involve a pride in new bodily maturity, fear of embarrassment, and worry about pain and bleeding. Because of the usual association of bleeding with bodily damage, it may be difficult initially for girls to conceive of menstruation as a normal bodily function (Bardwick, 1971). Many adolescent girls experience anxiety in anticipation of menstrual bleeding. One study, for example, reported that even among girls who had received advance information, a majority still anticipated menstruation with anxiety and fear (Shainess, 1961).

An additional stimulus for anxiety is the pain which is commonly experienced during initial menstrual periods. *Menstrual pains* (called *dysmenorrhea*) may be mild to severe and may be occasionally or persistently experienced even by adult women. The exact cause of menstrual cramps has not been clearly determined. It is most likely that they derive from strong muscular contractions of the uterus, but the evidence is far from conclusive (Sherman, 1971; Goldstein, 1976). What is even less clear is why some women do not experience them at all. The basic source of menstrual cramps is probably physiological (Dalton, 1969). However, anxiety can add additional discomforts, such as headaches, backaches, and muscular tensions. (These are common bodily reactions to anxiety, even in the absence of any recurring organic pain, among men as well as women). Whether the pains have their origin in physiological changes, anxiety, or a combination of these factors, they are experienced as very real and are not simply imaginary complaints.

Premenstrual tension. Even greater controversy surround research on the premenstrual tension and mood swings experienced by many women. Various research studies indicate that from 25 percent to 100 percent of women experience unpleasant feelings during some days previous to their menstrual flow (Parlee, 1973). (It is important to distinguish these symptoms from those experienced during the menstrual period.) The combination of sensations has been termed the *premenstrual syndrome* by many researchers (Dalton, 1969). Unfortunately, the particular sensations included under this rubric vary so widely that precise research is made nearly impossible (Parlee, 1973). The most common denominator seems to be anxiety in its many forms (fears, tensions, irritability, nervousness, headache, muscular aches, and insomnia).

One explanation of premenstrual tension is that it is an anxiety reaction in response to the anticipation of the onset of menstruation (Paige, 1973). It is possible that premenstrual anxiety is a conditioned response to subtle bodily changes, such as tissue swelling, which indicate the approach of menstruation. If menstruation is itself anxiety-provoking (because of menstrual pains, bleeding, or embarrassment), then the bodily sensations which indicate its approach can provoke the same anxiety. Many anticipatory worries are subconscious experiences, particularly when they are associated with recurring pain (Logan and Wagner, 1965). Such tensions are not easily alleviated by a person's deliberate efforts to relax, even when the distress felt is painful (such as headaches or muscular aches).

Other investigators believe that unpleasant feeling states (such as irritability, depression) may be caused directly by hormone fluctuations in the estrogen-progesterone balance (Dalton, 1969). A close association has been found between hormone changes and changes in mood (Ivey and Bardwick, 1968). Yet, this association may also be a result of monthly cycles of anticipatory anxiety.

One recent research project provides some evidence that cultural background and learning strongly influence the degree of premenstrual tension and menstrual pain experienced by a woman (Paige, 1973). This research compared the menstrual responses of a sample of women who differed in religious background and attitudes toward menstruation. Catholic women were most likely to experience severe anxieties and pains. (This may be more relevant to the particular ethnic backgrounds of some Catholic groups.) Protestant and Jewish women were much less likely to experience such discomforts previous to or during menstruation. More important, women who were most conventionally feminine in self-concept—whether Catholic, Protestant, or Jewish—were those most likely to experience menstrual distress. (These women were identified as those who never used tampons, highly valued virginity before marriage, stressed marriage and motherhood as exclusive life goals, and regarded menstruation as a form of illness.) One conclusion that can be drawn from this research is that when menstruation is culturally regarded as a distress which must be suffered by women, the consequence is to aggravate feelings of anxiety.

There are many traditional beliefs about mood swings, fragility, and "irrationality" in women as a consequence of hormonal changes in the menstrual cycle. These beliefs are often used to buttress the traditional stereotype of feminine personality. They are also used to prevent women from finding employment in certain occupations considered more appropriate for men (such as surgeon or airline pilot). There is no adequate evidence of the inevitability, or great prevalence, of disruptive mood swings among women (Parlee, 1973). Nor, is there adequate evidence which can confirm beliefs about the physical fragility of women.

In this light, any recommendations that women should avoid strenuous and stressful activities may only be presumptions derived from the traditional feminine stereotype. (In balance, these same suggestions might also be offered as health measures for certain men.) In this relation, a study of a group of female Olympic athletes is interesting to note (Timonen and Procope, 1971). It found that during training and competition, menstrual pains were absent or reduced in about 60 percent of cases. Only 12 percent, mostly swimmers, always stopped training during their menstrual period. Current medical advice for early adolescent girls is to avoid strenuous exercise during only the first day or two of their menstrual period, if they experience severe menstrual cramps (Oliven, 1974). There is even some evidence that exercise can actually serve to reduce menstrual pains.

In terms of employment concerns, it is also interesting to note that there is accumulating evidence of mood cycles (associated with circadian rhythms) in men, as well as women (Luce, 1971). A few industries have even taken these cycles into account when planning work schedules (Ramey, 1972). Investigations of testosterone cycles in men, however, have found no correlation with mood changes (Doering et al., 1975).

ejaculation

If the research on psychological aspects of menarche is inadequate, research focusing upon the psychological reactions of boys to their first ejaculation is virtually nonexistent by comparison. Boys usually receive no advance information from their parents. One study of young people's sources of sex information, for example, found that only 12 percent of boys received any advance information about nocturnal emissions from their parents (Lewis, 1973). Among themselves, adolescent boys are likely to discuss ejaculation in the context of sex jokes and stories. However, many boys receive little accurate information and experience surprise, embarrassment, and guilt in response to their first ejaculation (Oliven, 1974). Most boys experience their first ejaculation during masturbation, rather than as a nocturnal emission (Kinsey et al., 1953; Levin, 1976). If a boy's first ejaculation occurs during sleep, he may easily fear that an embarrassing affliction has beset his body (Oliven, 1974). The bedwetting that results from "wet dreams" is usually held as a shameful secret when a boy discerns that the matter is a taboo topic. Very few boys tell anyone else about their first ejaculation (Levin, 1976). It is widely speculated that feelings of shame and guilt are commonly experienced by adolescent boys in association with ejaculation (Rothchild, 1967). Such reactions may be because of the association of ejaculation with masturbation. However, any conclusions about the psychological attitudes of adolescent boys toward their new bodily experience is severely limited by the absence of adequate research.

BODY CONSCIOUSNESS AND PHYSICAL SEX STEREOTYPES

The social environment has a great effect upon the development of a person's body consciousness. If it can be said that "anatomy is destiny," it is primarily caused by the social environment which people experience. People whose appearance is not very different from the average can be made to feel quite "different" when they are socially labeled as such. This is because physical sex

stereotypes function to structure differing social environments for people. The differing environments, in turn, bring about differing self-concepts and life-cycle paths for males and females, as well as persons having differing bodily characteristics. An evaluation of the physical attractiveness of a man or woman is ultimately, derived from the physical sex stereotypes which are cultural ideals in a society. In addition, desirable personality traits are attributed to people whose appearance happens to fit the sex stereotypes. Bodily appearance and personality are tied to each other perceptually by conventional social expectations.

It seems to be unjust that people should judge the character of others by their physical appearance. We would like to believe that "beauty is only skin deep." Yet, dramatic research evidence indicates that people do not act according to that belief. A group of psychologists set up a laboratory experiment to determine if people attribute more socially desirable behavior to physically attractive individuals and more unfavorable behavior to less attractive individuals (Dion, Berscheid and Walster, 1972). Thirty men and thirty women were asked to judge the personality traits of individuals only from photographs they were shown. They were presented with photographs of individuals who were considered physically attractive, average, and relatively unattractive, according to outside judges. (The judges, of course, had to rely upon the guidelines of physical sex stereotypes.) The results of this experiment confirmed that people's character is socially labeled in relation to their physical appearance. The subjects judged the attractive individuals to have more socially desirable personality traits. They also judged the less attractive individuals to have fewer desirable traits. In additional studies, these researchers found the same social labeling based upon physical appearance to be applied by children in nursery school and by teachers in elementary school (Berscheid and Walster, 1972). Physical appearance as judged from physical sex stereotypes may not be the only factor that people use in forming impressions of others. Yet it remains a potent influence upon perception, especially when people do not know each other very well.

It is important to keep in mind that a person's body consciousness is largely a response to the way in which he or she is judged by other people. An adequate understanding of body consciousness is achieved only by finding the cause and effect relations between body, society, and self-concept. Lists of personality "traits" of people who are fat, skinny, tall, or short contribute little towards an understanding of body consciousness.

People who suffer from obesity, body deformities, and physical disabilities often suffer more from social stigma than from physical difficulties (Goffman, 1963; Clinard, 1974). They are regarded as undesirably different and treated as if their "spoiled identity" defines their total personality. Their reaction is usually one of resentment of others. The informative value of understanding unusual cases of bodily shortcomings is that almost everyone has a "spoiled identity" in one way or another. The appearance of most people falls short of the cultural ideals of the physical sex stereotype. Where physical stereotyping is rigid, resentment will run high.

Many adolescents suffer concerns about their bodies and express a desire to change some aspect of their physical appearance. Both sexes may worry about pimples and acne, about being overweight, or wearing glasses. Girls worry about the size of their hips and breasts, their height, and facial complexion. Boys worry about their muscularity, height, and lack of body hair. Their feelings of inadequacy derive from comparisons between themselves and the prevailing physical sex stereotypes (Jourard and Secord, 1955; Calden, et al., 1959). These body ideals are communicated in magazines, movies, television, and advertisements. They show the female ideal as being slender of leg, thigh, and waist, with narrow hips, moderately large breasts, and fair, unblemished skin. They show the male ideal as much taller, with moderately bulging biceps and broad shoulders, sprouting hair at the chest. Adolescents whose physical appearance come closest to these cultural ideals are usually the most popular in the dating-rating game of high school. It is no wonder that many average adolescents perceive themselves as having physical inadequacies where none actually exist. Their sensitivity about their physical appearance is aggravated by teenage rivalries and conformity pressures (Schonfeld, 1969). Adolescents frequently treat each other with much more intolerance and much less compassion than do adults. The social climate of the high school generates a constant fear of being the object of backbiting ridicule.

body consciousness and maturation rate

There exists no demarkation line between average maturation, and early and late maturation. Most commonly, early maturation is considered to occur when secondary sexual characteristics emerge and the growth spurt occurs before the

age of 10 years. Late maturation is considered to occur when these visible indicators of puberty begin to develop after the age of 16 (Schonfeld, 1969). During adolescence, late and early maturers also tend to be distinguished by particular physiques, due to differing growth patterns. Early maturers usually develop broad and stocky builds (Bayley, 1956). Late maturers tend to develop more slender, less muscular body builds (McNeill and Livson, 1963). The height of late maturers catches up to the average height, after their delayed growth spurt.

body consciousness in men and women

Early maturing girls.   Initially these girls experience certain disadvantages, because they appear to be physically mature before most other girls of their age. Their parents may be pointedly unenthusiastic about their early development. They may be encouraged to date at an early age by older boys, who view them as sexually mature. This can result in their being labeled as ''promiscuous'' by other girls their age (Jones and Mussen, 1958). These circumstances can lead early maturing girls to become an object of ridicule and gossip in elementary school. However, by the beginning of high school, the situation changes, as their mature physique becomes an advantage in the competition for dates. (Faust, 1960). At that time, they gain prestige due to their desirability as dates. One research study found that early maturing girls tend to get married earlier than other women (Buck and Stravraky, 1967). The earlier dating offers them greater opportunities of finding mates, and probably leads many of them to desire to marry earlier.

Late maturing girls.   The social environment of late maturing girls offers them certain advantages also. As girls, their short and slim figures are an advantage. They may be regarded as attractively ''petite'', and closer to the feminine stereotype than many average maturers (Weatherby, 1964). They can camouflage their late development in mature appearing clothes, and fake having their menstrual periods. However, if they are particularly child-like in appearance at 15 and 16 years of age, they may have difficulties in getting dates.

Early maturing boys.   These boys experience social advantages, which may persist through their lives. Their early physical development causes them to be regarded as more attractive and mature in character than other boys, at an early age (Hanley, 1951; Mussen and Jones, 1957). They gain social prestige by being popular with girls and desired as dates. This situation is largely a consequence of the fact that their tall, broad and stocky physiques are most consistent with the male sex-stereotype. In addition, their earlier muscular development enables early maturing boys to do well in competitive sports (Biddulph, 1954; Reichert, 1958). This further enhances their prestige, because athletic rivalries dominate the social life in most American schools (Coleman, 1961).

Early maturing adolescents of both sexes also reveal more conventional masculine or feminine self-concepts and interest patterns, than do late maturers (Conger, 1973). These findings reflect the greater conformity of early maturers to conventional social expectations. They are more highly rewarded than others of their age, because their appearance comes closest to the physical sex-stereotypes of adult men and women.

Late Maturing Boys.   The most disadvantageous situation is that of late maturing boys. At age 16, their bodies still appear child-like. Their small stature and undeveloped secondary sexual characteristics cause them to be regarded as "immature" and childish in character by their peers, and often by adults as well (Schonfeld, 1969). In adolescent peer groups they are often objects of ridicule from both sexes. They are regarded by girls as undesirable for dates (Mussen and Jones, 1957). Their lower physical ability makes them unable to compete in the sports rivalries, which determine the prestige heirarchy among high school boys (Reichert, 1958). It is among late maturing boys that a body stigma and spoiled identity, often have lasting harmful consequences in adult self-concept and behavior (Ames, 1957; Jones, 1957).

body consciousness in men and women

Female body consciousness.   Women's body consciousness is more intense than that of men (Fisher, 1973c). Women's lives are more centered around bodily concerns. Therefore, women are more easily aware of their bodily functioning and bodily changes than are men. Unfortunately, physical attractiveness is a key measure of the social prestige of women in American society and perhaps most others. It is physical attractiveness which brings rewards in the forms of dates, mates, jobs, and compliments. Women's self-concepts are also more body centered than those of men because of the more dramatic physical changes they experience in the course of their lives. These bodily changes include menstruation, pregnancy, childbirth, nursing, and menopause. It is no wonder, then, that women focus much greater attention and concern upon their bodies.

One consequence of women's more intense body consciousness is that they are more easily aware of bodily sensations and emotional responses than are men (Fisher, 1973c). Calling it "intuition," women may rely more than men upon their feeling states to make judgments. Men may learn to regard such judgments as "irrational." But, often feeling states can be wise guides for action. Women, on the average, make more accurate judgments of other people than do men (Dymond, 1949). Women are also less likely than are men to ignore bodily ailments, or mounting stress, until a point when severe disorders occur (Jourard, 1971).

Another consequence of women's more intense body consciousness is that they are more likely than men to use clothing to express their self-concept and their feelings about themselves (Fisher, 1973c). Men are more likely to feel that clothing is only a material, practical concern. In American society today, clothing and body adornment are still sex stereotyped even though unisex blue jeans have become fashionable. American culture discourages men from showing obvious concern about their bodily appearance. Attention to clothes, body adornments, cosmetics, and perfumes are still stereotyped as feminine concerns. However, these differing social expectations are changing rapidly.

One illustration of women's body consciousness and its effects upon behavior occurs in cases of women who undergo *mastectomy* (removal of a breast). Such surgery is often carried out in women who have breast cancer. Many women who have a mastecomy experience serious adjustment problems because they feel less attractively feminine (Maguire, 1975; Woods, 1975). After having a mastectomy, a substantial proportion of women fear loss of love from their husbands and experience a sharp decline in sexual desire (Hotchkiss, 1976).

Women may have more positive attitudes towards their breasts than their genitals. Although there is little adequate research on the matter, sex therapists report that many of their female clients hold emotionally negative attitudes towards their genitals (Heiman, LoPiccolo, and LoPiccolo, 1976). Some women feel that their genitals are ugly, a potential source of unpleasant odors, and an embarrassment to reveal to a lover. Our culture reinforces these negative attitudes. There are many degrading, obscene jokes about female genitals which commonly circulate among some men, but are heard by adult women. There are a lot of advertisements for vaginal deodorants which play upon the anxieties of some women. Parents often provide their son with cute nicknames for his penis, but no label at all for their daughter's genitals (except perhaps for the ambiguous "bottom"). Some pubescent girls are alarmed when they become aware of the growth of their inner labia, believing it to be some kind of deformity. Many women are unfamiliar with their genital anatomy (except from clinical drawings) because of its hidden location. Consequently, many sex therapists request their female clients to examine their genitals with the aid of a mirror so that they may feel more comfortable about this part of their bodies. Some women are initially repulsed by the experience, but others find it reassuring. Many sex therapists believe that if a woman regards her genitals to be disgusting, these feelings will inhibit her participation in some forms of sexual activity, such as oral-genital sex.

Male Body Consciousness. The social prestige of adult men is derived primarily from their occupation, rather than from their physical attractiveness. In an industrial society such as our own, the more prestigious occupations are those which demand intellectual and decision-making abilities, rather than physical abilities. Industrialization has, therefore, reduced the social significance of men's bodies. Manual laborers, such as farmers and factory workers, retain much of the former concern about the physical symbols of masculinity such as muscular strength and size (Gagnon, 1971). However, for men with less physically demanding jobs, muscle power is increasingly irrelevant.

The situation is different among adolescent boys. Adolescent boys do exhibit great concern about their masculinity as symbolized by physical characteristics such as height, muscular development, body and facial hair, and even penis size (Schonfeld, 1969). In the community of adolescent boys, as compared with that of adult men, physical attributes remain important carriers of social prestige. In a sense, the adolescent male emphasis upon muscular size, physical strength, and physical aggressiveness is a remnant of the social world of pre-industrial America.

Certain aspects of the male body continue to shape men's feelings of masculinity. Height remains important as a symbol of masculinity. One research project investigated relationships between men's attitude towards their height and other aspects of personality. It found that the more a man had the need to feel bigger, the more committed he was to the idea that men are superior to women (Fisher, 1973c). Many men, especially among the poorly educated, also associate penis length with masculinity. In addition, American men continue to associate a sense of masculinity with vague notions of bigness, strength of character, and "toughness" even though muscular prowess has lost its practical significance in our society (David and Brannon, 1976).

part four

SEXUAL RELATIONSHIPS

romantic love beliefs

It is important to make a distinction between beliefs about love and the actual interpersonal experiences of individuals in a love relationship. There is a cultural fund of beliefs about love in folk wisdom and philosophical thought, just as there are beliefs about any other significant human experience. Since the times of the ancient Greeks, love has been the frequent topic of writers including novelists, philosophers, theologians, and song writers. In Western societies today, beliefs about love permeate the mass media in ''pop'' songs, mass circulation magazines, movies, and television. Love is a dominant theme in these diversions. They are part of almost everyone's social environment and create personal expectations about love relationships.

Until quite recently, the beliefs about love presented in the mass media were dominated by the heritage of Victorian romanticism. These beliefs have been termed the *romantic love complex*. They represent idealized aspirations for male-female intimacy. As that was conceived in Victorian society, it omitted sexuality and emphasized intense emotionality instead.

There exist variations on the theme of romantic love, but several beliefs are relatively consistent: (1) love consists of an intense emotional feeling of pleasure (euphoria) and desire for another person; (2) the feeling of love is monogamous and exclusive for one person (at a time); (3) mutual love solves most interpersonal problems (in other words, serious conflict between lovers does not occur; the relationship between lovers is almost always harmonious);

11 sex in an intimate relationship

(4) people in love with each other are unselfish and seek only to serve the needs of the other—lovers lack self-enhancing goals in their relationship; (5) the experience of love is primarily for the young and is somehow eroded by the cynicism of psychological aging (however, some middle-aged people and older are able to remain young in spirit).

Such beliefs about love may currently be in the process of passing into history. Since the late 1960s, the mass media have increasingly presented modifications of these love themes. This is evident in the content of popular songs, movies, and even romance magazines. One sociologist, for example, carried out a content analysis of the lyrics of popular love songs of 1966, as compared with those of 1955 (Carey, 1969). He found that substantial changes in beliefs about love had occurred in the lyrics. Love was increasingly seen as a product of a mutual relationship, rather than a product of unpredictable emotions and mysterious forces of fate. People were much less likely to "fall in love" but instead deliberately searched for a love relationship. Also, in contrast with the 1950s, sexual attraction and activity was openly regarded as an expression of love. Similar changes have been found in a content analysis of romance magazines read by teenage girls (Hurowitz and Gaier, 1976).

In their attempt to understand the nature of male-female intimacy, young people have few sources of guidance. The mass media offer one source, whereas their parents' relationship offers another possibility. It may be fortunate that much of the mass media is turning away from an oversimplified Victorian romanticism. The newer mass media focus upon love as a difficult human relationship may sadden many Americans who hold nostalgia for the romanticism of the past. Yet, it may offer firmer ground for realistic expectations about long-term male-female intimacy.

the problem of defining love

Any attempt to seek a definition for the word *love* runs into immediate problems because the word has become so ubiquitous in modern America. The word has been applied so broadly and means so many different things that it has come to mean nothing specific. People are said to love God and mashed potatoes; to love rock and roll music and their pet dog; to love humanity and sometimes their spouse. It is quite useless to make lists of types of love. The main result of making typologies of love is to get lost in a game of semantics. To avoid such a dilemma, it seems best to try to focus research attention on the interpersonal experiences which people commonly refer to as being love.

There are two basic approaches to an understanding of love used by behavioral scientists. One focus is upon *love as an emotional response of an individual*, whereas the other is upon *love as a relationship between two individuals*. The next section will discuss love as an emotional response, although this chapter is concerned primarily with love as an interpersonal relationship. Focusing attention upon love as a relationship was formerly less common than viewing it as an emotional response because of the heritage of Victorian romanticism. However, love as a relationship is a common viewpoint today.

love as an emotional response

Recently, social psychologists have begun to apply the principles gained from experimental laboratory studies in attempts to understand the nature of love as an emotional response (Berscheid and Walster, 1974). Recalling principles from Chapter 5, *emotions* are a combination of physiological responses to stimuli and feelings of pleasure or pain. They are given meaning by cognitive (symbolic) associations. In other words, we rely upon external cues to guide our understanding of our feeling states. We derive these cues from our interpretations of social situations in which we experience an emotional response.

One social psychologist has proposed that we experience the emotion of ''love'' when we: (1) are physiologically aroused; and (2) conclude that love is the appropriate label for our aroused feelings (Walster, 1971). This particular interpretation of love as an emotional response makes scientific sense because emotional arousal is essentially ambiguous, until it is given cognitive meaning by a person's beliefs.

In actual social situations, there are a great many circumstances which may evoke emotional arousal. Rarely, however, do people label their emotional arousal as being love. We need to know much more about the particular cues which lead people to label their emotions as love. In this relation, two considerations are particularly important. Cultural beliefs about love (romantic and otherwise) encourage a person to identify certain interpersonal situations as being appropriate for labeling their feelings as love. In addition, a person's romantic (and sexual) daydreams can promote ''falling in love'' when the fantasies seem to match the situation.

love as a multidimensional relationship

If certain interpersonal conditions can evoke feelings of love in an emerging relationship, so can certain interpersonal conditions maintain the emotions of love in a long-term relationship. When we shift our concern from the emergence of love to the maintenance of love, it would seem best to shift our focus from what goes on in an individual to what goes on in the relationship between individuals. Focusing upon a love relationship is particularly useful if we want to understand the place of sex in a long-term relationship.

Love as an intimate relationship is a continuously evolving process. It is a systematic pattern of behavior between people. Several behavioral scientists have suggested guidelines for conceptualizing love as intimate relations (Reiss, 1960; Davis, 1973). Four basic dimensions of a love relationship can be identified as:

(1) mutual attraction; (2) self-disclosure; (3) behavioral interdependence; and (4) emotional interdependence. *Mutual attraction* occurs when two people like each other and desire each other's companionship. *Self-disclosure* occurs when two people reveal intimate information about themselves to each other. *Behavioral interdependence* occurs when two people exchange favors in the form of services and become dependent upon each other for the accomplishment of many tasks. *Emotional interdependence* occurs when two people exchange favors in the form of emotional pleasures they can offer to each other.

These dimensions of love have a cyclical effect. Each preceding dimension facilitates the next. Mutual attraction enables self-disclosure, while that enables behavioral interdependence which strengthens emotional interdependence. We can understand the evolution of an emerging intimate relationship in this cyclical way. In the same sense, we can understand how intimacy breaks down when a relationship unfolds in reverse order. Difficulties in behavioral interdependence, for example, will inhibit self-disclosure.

Regarding love as an intimate relationship is a way of seeing it as essentially similar to a close same-sex friendship relationship, the differences being that few same-sex friends live together, plan a future together, and share a sexual relationship. When people live together and plan a future as a couple, it is easier for them to engage in the process of intimate relatedness. When sex is

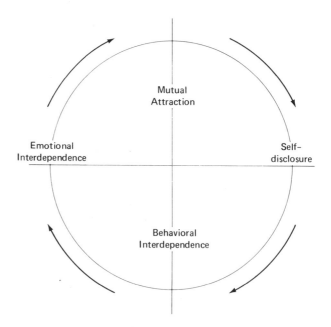

Diagram of love as a multidimensional intimate relationship. (Adapted from Ira L. Reiss, *Premarital Sexual Standards in America,* New York: Free Press, 1960, page 140.)

added to an intimate relationship, it can symbolize mutual affection and function as a further social bond.

The idea that love and close friendship are essentially similar forms of intimate relatedness does not mean that they are exactly the same. A heterosexual love relationship has the potential for being the most inclusive and exclusive form of intimacy for individuals (Simmel, 1906). Few people can know much about us as persons. Most people come to know us only in isolated circumstances and can know only segments of our lives. No one can know us as whole personalities. However, more of our selves may be included in a love relationship with another person than in any other relationship (Borland, 1975). In such an intimate relationship, one person may come to know more about another's past biography, present life situation, and future aspirations than any other. In that sense, the one may share a concept of the other's self similar to his or her own self-concept. This is what is meant by *understanding*. A love relationship is also more exclusive than are most superficial relations for the very reason that persons invest more of their selves in it than in their relations with other people. In it, we have a special and rather unique relatedness with another person.

MUTUAL ATTRACTION

physical attractiveness

The role of physical attractiveness in love relations has been the subject of speculation since ancient times. Yet it has only been the topic of scientific research since the late 1960s. There has already accumulated a reasonably large body of research findings about physical attractiveness.

In contrast with popular belief that physical attractiveness is merely a matter of individual taste, much research evidence indicates that shared physical stereotypes are used as measuring rods of beauty (Berscheid and Walster, 1974). While such stereotypes vary between cultures and ethnic groups, there does seem to exist considerable agreement within social groups about physical attractiveness.

In a sense, high physical attractiveness is much like a scarce commodity. That is probably why highly attractive people are attributed high prestige. Many studies have found that the prestige of high physical attractiveness creates an aura of desirability which goes beyond mere appearance (Berscheid and Walster, 1974). People commonly assume that highly attractive others are not only desirable dates and mates, but also more successful, talented, sociable, self-confident, and virtuous than are less attractive people (Berscheid and Walster, 1974).

One research project, for example, investigated the erotic meanings attributed to physically attractive women by asking subjects (male and female) to speculate about the sexuality of women whose photographs were shown to them (Sarty, 1975). The highly attractive women in the photographs were assumed to have greater sexual desire, to be more sexually active, and to enjoy sex more than those who were less attractive. These findings help to explain the link between physical attractiveness in women and their erotic appeal to men. Although beliefs about the sexual desirability of attractive women may not be true, they heighten men's anticipation of possible erotic pleasure. Perhaps this is why several studies have found that physical attractiveness is given higher priority in the dating choices of men than of women (Stroebe et al., 1971).

One research project found that highly attractive college women are more likely to have experienced heavy petting and premarital intercourse than college women of average or low attractiveness (Kaats and Davis, 1970). However, these findings may indicate only the greater opportunity and social pressure for sexual activity experienced by highly attractive women, rather than any greater sexual desire or enjoyment. The research found that such women are not different than other college women in their sexual attitudes.

In a sense, high physical attractiveness in women can be both an advantage and burden. Highly attractive women may be assumed, at least by men, to have more desirable personality traits. Yet they may also be consistently regarded by men as a sex and prestige symbol, which may promote superficiality in intimate relations.

Dating choices are related to a person's self-esteem. There is evidence that when a person has low self-esteem, he or she will choose to date less attractive people than will a person with high self-esteem (Kiesler and Baral, 1970). Research has found that although most men ideally would prefer to date the most attractive women, they cautiously choose to date only those women whom they believe will not reject their initiative (Huston, 1974). Men who consider themselves to be highly attractive tend to take initiative with the most attractive women. Men who judge themselves as being unattractive tend to choose others who are not highly attractive (Stroebe et al., 1971).

Reactions to the social prestige ranking of physical attractiveness encourage people to date others of similar attractiveness. Research comparing the photographs of engaged couples with randomly matched men and women found the engaged couples to be remarkably similar in their physical attractiveness (Murstein, 1972). In conclusion, it seems that similarity of physical attractiveness makes it easier for two people to "fall in love." Conspicuous differences in physical attractiveness discourage mutual attraction.

The dating advantages obtained by youthful attractiveness do not carry over into long-term relationships. Intimate relations may be less affected by the prestige of physical attractiveness than are more superficial relationships. There is even some evidence that women who were highly attractive during their youth report less marital satisfaction by midlife (Berscheid and Walster, 1974). The decline of physical attractiveness with aging may be most troublesome for those women who were highly attractive in their youth.

We know practically nothing about the role of physical attractiveness in long-term relations. It does seem likely, though, that mates who maintain a concern for their physical appearance can offer each other some degree of visual pleasure over the years. Most people are of average physical attractiveness by definition so the question is not one of prestige. Long-term partners may be so gratified to find refuge from the invidious comparisons of dating that they neglect their appearance with each other. Visual displeasure can repel people from each other in a sexual relationship. Bedding down in unattractive night clothes year after year can certainly diminish mutual sexual attraction. On the other hand, it is possible that mutual sexual satisfaction may reinforce the physical attraction between a couple.

consensus

Another factor that can promote mutual attraction is consensus. *Consensus* occurs when people hold similar attitudes toward a matter which concerns them. There is a substantial amount of research which indicates that people who hold similar attitudes are attracted to each other while people who hold different attitudes tend to avoid each other (Griffitt, 1974).

Some research has found that acquaintances seek out other people with similar attitudes to form friendships (Newcomb, 1961). In addition, some studies of dating have found that couples who progress toward a more serious relationship tend to hold more similar attitudes than those who discontinue dating (Coombs, 1966). There are also several studies of married couples who have investigated the role of consensus in marital relations (Barry, 1970). Many, but not all, of these studies indicate that high consensus between married couples is associated with marital satisfaction.

A key to understanding the role of consensus in an intimate relationship is that different matters are emotionally important to different people. Disagreement over insignificant matters is less crucial than disagreement over matters that people hold to be important. Partners who happen to be artists may regard agreement in artistic taste as being important, while for most other couples disagreement over such an issue may be considered to be a trivial concern. Agreement about religious belief is a matter of concern between some intimates, yet other people are relatively unconcerned about religious differences in their intimate relationships. The particular attitude component which is most crucial to mutual attraction is that of *values*. When partners in a couple hold similar basic values, they may share consensus even though they may also have a great many individual differences in personal attitudes.

Consensus and sexual interaction. In an intimate heterosexual relationship, consensus in sexual attitudes is likely to be an emotionally important matter of concern. When lovers hold similar sexual attitudes, they are able to feel more comfortable with each other than if they anticipate disagreement. The rap-

port which derives from consensus enables a couple to be more spontaneous in their sexual behavior. They can communicate more openly, honestly, and directly about sexual matters.

There are a wide range of sexual issues in which disagreement between a couple can provoke antagonism. These issues include beliefs about the role of sexual activity in an intimate relationship and the personal value-priority given to sexual pleasure. There are also a great many potentially divisive specific issues concerning such matters as premarital and extramarital sex, the frequency of intercourse, sexual preferences, contraception, and family planning.

empathy

Every couple has at least as many differences in attitudes as they have similarities. The existence of empathy between lovers helps to account for the mutual attraction between people who maintain their distinctive individuality.

Empathy occurs when one person imaginatively participates in the experience of another so that he or she is able to understand the other's point-of-view and experience similar emotional feelings. The essence of an empathetic response between people does not exist in agreement about beliefs, but instead, mutuality of feeling. An empathetic response is founded upon an ability to use another person's verbal and nonverbal communication as a means of imagining their inner experience in a situation. Empathy is not a matter of knowledgeability about or sympathy for another person. Instead, empathy has its source in an ability to translate memories of one's own past pleasures and pains into the experience of another person (Hoffman, 1976).

An illustration of an empathetic response is the common experience people have while watching a movie when they feel similar emotions to those they imagine are being experienced by the characters on the movie screen. In such a case, the emotions experienced are real, even though the characters are not! In one laboratory research study, subjects who watched another person receiving electric shocks or money were found to experience physiological reactions to the punishment or rewards received by the other person (Krebs, 1970).

Empathy facilitates mutual attraction in several ways. When a couple is mutually empathetic with each other, feelings of being "understood" are fostered. Empathy is essential to an "I-thou" relatedness in the sense that it links the uniqueness of individuality to mutuality in a relationship. In addition, empathy aids compromise in disputes. It cannot settle differences of opinion, but empathy does help to avoid unnecessary misunderstandings. Empathy helps each person to understand the viewpoint of the other even if they do not agree with it.

There has unfortunately been little research into the role of empathy in courtship and marriage. One study did find that greater empathy between dating couples was associated with greater satisfaction with the dating relationship (Stewart and Vernon, 1959). Another study of married couples found that couples who reported greater marital satisfaction were more empathetic, as determined by their ability to accurately predict each others' responses to a personality questionnaire (Dymond, 1954).

Empathy and sexual interaction.   Empathy has not been investigated in relation to sexual interaction, but some speculations are in order. It is quite likely that empathy helps a couple understand male-female differences which are a consequence of sex-role socialization. Empathy can also facilitate mutual understanding of differences in sex attitudes and sexual preferences. Finally, mutual empathy may play an important role in heightening mutual sexual pleasure. Empathy can enhance a lover's capacity to give pleasure by enabling him or her to be sensitive to variations in the erotic responsiveness of the partner. An empathetic response to the other person's expression of pleasure can also intensify the pleasure-giver's own erotic responsiveness.

expressions of affection

In long-term intimate relations, expressions of affection between lovers are an important factor in maintaining mutual attraction. Expressions of affection take verbal form in the words "I love you." But there are also nonverbal signs of affection, such as a kiss or caress. Affectionate communications convey several meanings: (1) an expression of pleasurable feeling in response to the other; (2) a positive personal evaluation of the other; and (3) a symbolic affirmation of intimate relatedness.

Experimental investigations of people's reactions to others who express a "liking" for them have generally found that it results in a reciprocated liking for the other (Berscheid and Walster, 1969). Nevertheless, there are important contingencies. The expression of affection must be perceived to be sincere rather than an attempt at ingratiation (Berscheid and Walster, 1969). When the expression of affection is perceived to be an attempt to manipulate a person to obtain certain benefits from them, it is likely to provoke animosity. An example is an insincere expression of affection during a seduction attempt. Another contingency is a person's self-esteem. There is some laboratory research evidence that people who have low self-esteem, often misinterpret expressions of affection, especially when the message is not clear (Jacobs, Berscheid, and Walster, 1971). When the intent of an affectionate expression is ambiguous, people with low self-esteem are apt to regard it as being insincere.

Some research indicates that American men may be more reserved about expressing affection than are women (Balswick and Peek, 1971; Balswick and Avertt, 1977). This gender difference may create dissatisfaction in heterosexual intimacy. There is some evidence that married couples who express their affection for each other are more likely to be satisfied with their relationship than are couples who do not express affection (Levinger and Senn, 1967). The effects of marital satisfaction and the expression of affection work both ways. Dissatisfied couples do not express much mutual affection. The communication of affection offers a couple important feedback information about each partner's satisfaction with the relationship. Wives who do not receive much husbandly expression of affection, may easily be led to believe that there is some unstated problem in the relationship. Love is not self-evident, but must be expressed in some way.

Expressions of affection and sexual interaction.   Expressions of affection may play an important role in maintaining mutual attraction in long-term sexual intimacy. During sexual activity, expressions of affection serve to symbolize the association of love and sexual pleasure. Such expressions acknowledge each partner's pleasure with the other and affirm a positive evaluation of the other's sexuality. However, when expressions of affection become limited to the bedroom, they easily become ritualized and artificial. When kisses, caresses, and admissions of love are linked exclusively to sexual activity, they lose the appearance of spontaneity and are easily perceived as a technique of ingratiation.

SELF-DISCLOSURE

the duality of self-disclosure and privacy

Self-disclosure may be defined as the communication of personal information to others. In recent years, this process has become an important topic of social psychological research. Initial investigators were particularly concerned about understanding the relationship between psychotherapists and their clients, but attention has shifted increasingly to the study of intimate relations. The dilemmas of self-disclosure have long been recognized to be at the very heart of intimacy (Simmel, 1906).

The element of self-disclosure called *level of intimacy* is difficult to distinguish. Essentially, intimate personal information is that which a person regards as being private. Therefore, most people are excluded from this knowledge. The more exclusive is the personal information, the "deeper" its level of intimacy. Intimate information is, then, a kind of secret shared between people which bonds them in trust to each other (Simmel, 1906). An intimate relationship is ultimately a relationship between confidants. *Intimacy* involves an exclusive relationship in which personal information is protected and limited from people outside that relationship.

It is often difficult for researchers to distinguish the level of intimacy in self-disclosure. The particular contents of intimate information vary between different personalities. The kind of self-information which is expected to be shrouded in privacy even differs in various societies. A person's intimate information need not be dramatic or incriminating. It may even seem trivial to other people. The distinctive quality of intimate information is that a person regards it as a source of vulnerability and defines it as being private (Davis, 1973).

In Western societies, sexual information about one's self is usually regarded as being private. However, there are a wide range of other kinds of intimate information. A person may regard his or her body as a source of vulnerability because of real or imagined bodily pecularities. A person's self-perceived shortcomings may also be guarded by privacy, as well as certain opinions and emotional responses. It is also common for people to want to conceal their financial affairs, at least from acquaintances. In many circumstances, people may want to conceal information about their social identities, such as their ethnic group origin or religious affiliation. Certainly, also, people sometimes wish to conceal information about behavior which other people consider immoral.

In everyday life, acquaintances must maintain a certain discretion (or personal reserve) about their self-disclosure (Simmel, 1906). When interpersonal relations are not bonded by confidentiality and trust, the communication of intimate information is always potentially threatening. The reasons for discretion in self-disclosure are numerous. A person's self-disclosure may result in ridicule, hostility, gossip, envy, and conformity pressures to change. This is particularly so in a society where interpersonal relations are characterized by competition, rivalries, and conflicts of opinion. Therefore, people employ a variety of social distance mechanisms to preserve their privacy. Common social distance mechanisms include the suppression of spontaneous emotional expression, the ritualistic communication of superficial pleasantries, the avoidance of controversial matters in conversation, and formalistic good manners. In American culture, these social distance mechanisms take the form of maintaining a disposition of agreeable "friendliness" without presuming the trust and confidentiality of actual friendship (Kurth, 1970). This "friendliness" cannot be mistaken as an invitation for deeper involvement. Instead, it functions as a barrier to genuine intimacy because it embodies an implicit expectation that serious self-disclosure should not take place.

The satisfactions of self-disclosure and privacy. The satisfactions of privacy and self-disclosure are often mutually exclusive and pull people in opposite directions (Simmel, 1906). Privacy protects an individual from ridicule, vicious gossip, conformity pressures, and conflict with others. Privacy may play an important role in maintaining a person's sense of individuality (Victor, 1974). Yet, self-disclosure offers alternative satisfactions, especially within the confines of an intimate relationship: (1) it enables a person to obtain useful feedback information about themselves from other people which may enhance their self-knowledge (Derlega and Chaikin, 1975)—in self-disclosure, we learn more about ourselves often by "thinking out loud" with an intimate; (2) self-disclosure to an intimate may relieve the stresses of constantly maintaining a superficial public mask in contradiction to one's own self-concept (Davis, 1973)—we can confess our self-perceived vulnerabilities to our intimates and release the tensions generated by unexpressed self-doubt, guilt, and fear; (3) finally, in self-disclosure to an intimate we build a bridge of trust to another person. In a relationship bonded by trust, lovers can find security from the uncertainties caused by being excluded from the intimate circles of others (Weitman, 1970).

The duality of privacy and self-disclosure becomes clear once it is realized that privacy is also necessary to protect self-disclosure (Westin, 1967). When intimates engage in the communication of intimate information, that communication must be protected by a circle of privacy. The bonds of trust are shattered once people communicate the "secrets" of their intimates to others outside their confidential relationship. There is nothing more disruptive to a friendship or love relationship than when one of the participants learns second-hand that their "secrets" have been shared with strangers. There is nothing more distressful in love than the suspicion that one's lover has been unfaithful with one's confidences. (The real meaning of "unfaithfulness" may have more to do with intimate information than sexual contact.)

self-disclosure in male-female relations

Research studies of marital relations contribute useful information toward an understanding of self-disclosure in an intimate relationship between men and women. One intensive study of 58 blue-collar marriages found some differences between husbands and wives in their amount of self-disclosure (Komarovsky, 1964). About two-thirds of the husbands and wives engaged in self-disclosure about equally as often. This finding is consistent with much other research which indicates that an informal social rule of reciprocity operates in self-disclosure (Derlega and Chaikin, 1975). However, in the other third of couples where there was unbalanced self-disclosure, the wives tended to engage in more frequent self-disclosure than the husbands (Komarovsky, 1964).

Another study of self-disclosure between 189 married couples where the husband was a professional found that the majority of husbands and wives engaged in the frequent disclosure of personal problems and tensions (Burke, Weir, and Harrison, 1976). The wives, however, tended to be more open with such personal information. The longer a couple were married, the less likely they were to engage in this kind of self-disclosure. On the other hand, couples where both partners were employed were more likely to engage in self-disclosure than couples in which the wife was a full-time homemaker. Most importantly, the research found that the couples who shared self-disclosure about personal problems and tensions reported greater marital satisfaction than did couples who avoided self-disclosure in these matters.

The available research tends to indicate that the amount of self-disclosure between a couple does not predict marital satisfaction (Gilbert, 1976). Unhappily married couples report either extremely frequent or extremely infrequent self-disclosure. It appears that the amount of positive versus negative self-disclosure serves to promote marital satisfaction. One investigation of self-disclosure between married couples found that the couples who reported greater marital satisfaction were those who also reported more expressions of pleasing than displeasing self-disclosure (Levinger and Senn, 1966). The maritally satisfied spouses reported fewer displeasing disclosures such as criticisms, complaints, and negative feelings about each other. These findings are consistent with other research, which indicates the existence of high amounts of negative self-disclosure in conflict-ridden marriages (Gilbert, 1976).

On the other hand, many unhappily married couples appear to suppress the expression of negative feelings about each other because of fears of endangering their marriage. Several research projects have found the existence of very meager self-disclosure between couples who report considerable marital dissatisfaction (Gilbert, 1976). In summary, the available research seems to indicate that frequent pleasing self-disclosure is associated with satisfaction in intimate relations.

There have been increasing reports from family study specialists that a great many American marriages suffer from inadequate communication. Some psychologists have argued that this problem can be remedied if couples would be willing to engage in a maximum of self-disclosure (Jourard, 1971). This argument may be too simple. It may be that the satisfactions of self-disclosure in intimacy ultimately depend upon a couple's ability to deal with issues of conflict.

Nonverbal Communication.   In recent years, there has been a great amount of speculation about the possible "inexpressiveness" of American men as husbands. Unfortunately, it is not quite clear exactly what is meant by the term "inexpressive." The term may be used to refer to an inability to express positive feelings, such as affection or a sense of beauty. It may also refer to an inability to express negative emotions, such as sadness and grief. In addition, it can refer to a disposition toward low self-disclosure.

There is not yet any clear-cut research evidence that men are substantially less likely to engage in self-disclosure within the context of an intimate male-female relationship. In terms of self-disclosure, there may also be a great many American women who are reserved about self-disclosure in intimate relations.

It is most likely that informal observations of male inexpressiveness point to certain male-female differences in nonverbal communication. There is some laboratory research evidence that men with traditionally restrictive sex-role attitudes are less likely to exhibit nonverbal expressions of positive emotions than are men with more liberal sex-role attitudes (Weitz, 1976). Perhaps traditionalist American men conform more closely to the sex-role stereotype of men as being "strong and silent."

Some research has provided clear evidence for the common observation of gender differences in emotional expressiveness. One laboratory research project investigated male and female abilities to send and receive nonverbal communication (Buck, Miller, and Caul, 1974). A closed circuit television camera focused upon the senders' faces as they attempted to communicate their emotional reactions to a series of slides. In another room, the receivers were asked to guess the slide category being described and the senders' emotional responses to it from their facial expressions shown on a television monitor. The verbal expressions of the senders were tape recorded to test the accuracy of the receivers' judgments. In addition, measurements were taken of certain physiological changes in the senders' bodies. The research found that the men were more likely to internalize their emotional expression, while women were more externally expressive. In summary, the research indicates that men exhibit less overt facial expression but greater internal physiological reactivity than do women. (The greater inhibition and internalization of emotional expression by men may be one cause of the frequent incidence of stress related diseases, such as ulcers.)

The evidence that expressive differences between men and women are learned rather than inherited is provided by the finding that young children do not exhibit these sex-related differences (Buck, 1973). It appears that socialization pressures beginning during adolescence inhibit male emotional expressiveness and encourage female expressiveness (Weitz, 1974).

Unlike many other peoples, Americans traditionally condemn a wide range of emotional expression in men. Even the male expression of anger, while more easily accepted than expressions of affection, grief, sadness, or fear, provokes easy suspicions of a "loss of control." Emotional expressiveness in American men is often labeled something akin to a "sickness" (disturbed, immature, unrealistic). One well-televised national occasion provided an example. In 1972, Senator Edmund Muskie's campaign for the Presidential nomination came to a sudden end when he was moved to tears in public, expressing his sadness over malicious accusations against his wife. Yet American attitudes toward male expressiveness are changing, and it is becoming more acceptable for men to express emotion without being labeled "weak" or "unmanly."

sexual self-disclosure and sexual reserve

Intimate sexual self-disclosure in Western cultures has a high potential for shame and conflict. Consequently, sex is an area closely guarded by much personal reserve. What, precisely, are the contents of sexual self-disclosure between intimates?

1. Bodily self-disclosure.   Bodily self-disclosure in erotic activities is the most obvious form of sexual self-disclosure. It can be a source of concern and personal reserve for people during initial sexual encounters. However, excessive modesty or body prudery can create difficulties for couples who have had sexual relations over decades. It is quite likely, for example, that many husbands and wives remain unfamiliar throughout their lives with the details of each other's genital anatomy. Because of sexual reserve, they may remain unaware of genital areas of particular sexual sensitivity and the kinds of genital caresses which maximize erotic pleasure. Many couples even avoid sexual intercourse in the nude and neglect possible pleasures of erotic body exploration (Bell, 1969). Sexual reserve may also inhibit the sensual pleasures of touching and being touched as an expression of affection outside the confines of the bedroom.

2. Signaling sexual receptiveness.   The signaling of sexual receptiveness involves the use of both verbal and nonverbal communication to indicate a desire or lack of desire for sexual activity. This is often a subtle and difficult matter when spouses do not have mutually frequent sexual desire. Many couples develop special codes of expression to indicate their receptiveness.

3. Communicating sexual responsiveness. The communication of sexual responsiveness involves verbal and nonverbal expressions of erotic pleasure. Such expressiveness can intensify the mutual pleasure of sexual partners via the effects of empathy.

4. Communicating sexual preferences. The communication of sexual preferences involves the communication of desires for kinds of careses, sexual positions, and environments. Such communication is crucial in pacing the build-up of sexual excitement. It also provides feedback information which enables sexual partners to maximize each other's pleasure.

5. Communicating sexual fantasies.   At an even more intimate level of sexual self-disclosure, sexual partners can disclose their personal sex fantasies. Some sex therapists suggest that the sharing of sex fantasies, even when involving socially condemned practices, can intensify mutual sexual arousal. It is doubtful that many married couples release their sexual reserve as far as sharing sex fantasies. Many individuals cannot openly face their own fantasies. Such intimate self-disclosure can be very threatening to many couples.

6. Communicating past sexual experiences.   Finally, sexual self-disclosure may also involve the communication of past sexual experiences with others in premarital or extramarital affairs or in a previous marriage. This sort of self-disclosure may be particularly threatening, because it is likely to evoke feelings of sexual jealousy.

Self-disclosure and erotic roles.   It is quite likely that a great many married couples are too reserved to engage in much sexual self-disclosure (Gochros, 1972). Many married couples probably do not engage in sexual communication other than in a joking and superficial manner, even though they have regular sexual activity.

Several factors contribute to sexual reserve between intimate heterosexual partners. The most important of these factors are the erotic roles which men and women are socialized to play in sexual activity. Men are expected to know all they need to know about sex, or at least to present a facade of sexual competence. Therefore, men often act as if there is little useful information they can learn, especially from their female partners. It is contrary to the traditional male erotic role for a man to ask his partner about what pleases her. Many men may be shocked out of their complacency by the sexual self-disclosures of their lovers. On the other hand, women are traditionally socialized to be reserved about their sexual selves. Taking initiative in sexual activity, indicating their preferences, and offering helpful suggestions may be contrary to many women's self-concepts of their femininity. The combination of female reserve and male complacency promotes a conspiracy of silence in matters of sexual communication, even when a couple is able to maintain effective communication about other matters.

BEHAVIORAL INTERDEPENDENCE

the exchange of favors

Adequate communication between intimates enables them to cooperate more effectively and coordinate their activities. *Behavioral interdependence* refers to the coordination of social interaction in cooperative activities between intimates. The essential basis for cooperation is an exchange of favors.

However, the social bond of interdependence between lovers goes beyond practical exchange (Davis, 1973). Lovers are bonded by a mutual assistance alliance in the face of external threats. Lovers expect each other to represent their interests in quarrels and disputes with others outside their relationship. A close friend or lover is thus an ally and not merely a co-worker. It is not objective appraisal that intimates expect of each other in their external affairs but subjective, empathetic allegiance. In addition, lovers share responsibility for each other's lives. They expect to depend upon each other for economic support and health care when the situation requires it. Finally, lovers usually share each other's property in communal living.

Reciprocity between intimates. An informal rule termed the *norm of reciprocity* forms a bond in relations between intimates (Gouldner, 1960). This rule is the mutual expectation that favors will be reciprocated in the long run of a relationship. Intimates feel obligated to return favors bestowed onto them. The exchange need not be one of an immediate return of the same sort of favor. Instead, intimates feel an obligation to meet each other's needs in the general conduct of their relationship. Failure to achieve a mutually agreeable balance of exchange over a period of many years results in feelings of resentment and guilt.

While American culture places great value upon personal independence, the necessities of intimacy demand the support of mutual dependence. It can be argued that this cultural emphasis upon independence, even within the context of intimate relations, is a significant threat to cohesive family life. The intimate situation of dependence and obligation may be more difficult for those persons who prefer independence and autonomy.

When intimates live together, they become mutually dependent upon each other for the performance of many activities. American spouses are expected to cooperate with each other in economic support, household maintenance, home repairs, child care and training, health care, recreation, and sexual relations. In the traditional family, different roles were assigned to each sex. More recent cultural values encourage wide ranging marital companionship and the interchange of roles in these activities. The performance of distinct gender roles, which designate certain behavior as being masculine or feminine, are increasingly considered inconvenient and unjust. Research studies of American families have, indeed, found increasingly that various patterns of sharing family activities now characterize family role relations (Blood and Wolfe, 1960).

the exchange of sexual favors

The exchange of sexual favors is a somewhat unique form of exchange. Sexual pleasure may be given and received simultaneously in the same act. Mutual sexual pleasure can promote strong bonds between lovers because of the rather direct pleasure they are able to offer each other. Mutual sexual pleasure is, to a great extent, dependent upon shared expectations and the effective coordination of sexual activity. The pacing of sexual arousal to orgasm, for example, is easier if sexual partners are familiar with each other's sexual preferences and responses.

Sexual bargaining. In the relationship between some couples, the exchange of sexual pleasure is subject to bargaining (Bell, 1970). In such relationships, sexual pleasure is used as an incentive or withheld as a form of coercion. Sexual bargaining of this sort is most likely to occur between partners who do not share a similar desire for sexual pleasure.

Sexual bargaining is also promoted by the traditional erotic roles of men and women. In the past, sexual access was believed to be "given" by women as a favor for other considerations and "taken" by men. The traditional discouragement of female sexual initiative served to create an imbalance in sexual exchange. Sexual favors, like gifts, must be offered and received in some sort of balanced reciprocity. If one partner in a sexual relationship must continually initiate requests for sexual favors, that partner is likely to feel humiliated and resentful. The situation is much like that of poor relatives who constantly receive gifts from their rich kin, with mixed feelings of both gratitude and hostility.

Sexual play and sexual performance. Elements of play and work interpenetrate many human activities, including sex (Foote, 1954; Lewis and Brissett, 1967). This becomes clear when we see how recreational activities can be transformed from entertainments into tests of achievement. Children's participation in many sports, for example, is transformed from an enjoyable pasttime into a frustrating task when they become more concerned with their performance skill than their pleasure.

Sex is a form of play when it is an uninhibited expression of feelings of the moment. It is playful activity when it is not burdened by any need to achieve or to demonstrate skilled performance. On the other hand, sexual activity can be transformed into work by excessive anxieties about employing skillful technique. It may also become work when one partner is fatigued but still feels obligated to offer sexual favors to the other. Sexual activity can become work, too, when one partner is anxious to exert self-control over the build-up of their sexual excitement, in an effort to restrain their movement to orgasm. In addition, sex can be work when one partner feels obligated to be active when he or she would rather relax, lie back, and be entertained.

In the Victorian past, sexual activity was regarded as a man's play and a woman's work (a "release" for him and a "duty" for her). The new egalitarian goal of mutual pleasure demands a degree of knowledge, skill, and concern for the other which was previously unnecessary. There are increasing reports from marriage counselors and sex therapists about clients who have sexual difficulties caused by anxieties over their sexual performance. It is ironic that the new goal of mutual pleasure may be making sexual activity a frustrating task for some couples who try too hard to make sex a form of mutual play.

EMOTIONAL INTERDEPENDENCE

emotional pleasures in intimate relations

When intimates develop a well-coordinated, cooperative relationship, they become sources of emotional gratification for each other. *Emotional interdependence* refers to a relationship in which intimates become mutually dependent upon each other for their emotional well-being. They are then, particularly able to offer each other psychological favors in the form of emotional gratifications.

Many theoretical schemes have been proposed to analyze the basic categories of emotional gratifications. One useful scheme suggests four broad, basic categories of emotional gratifications: (1) response; (2) recognition; (3) security; and (4) new experience (Thomas and Znaniecki, 1927). This scheme is particularly useful in attempts to understand the kinds of emotional pleasures which people may find in interpersonal relationships.

Response. *Response* refers to the emotional pleasures that a person receives from expressions of affection and care. Response may be found in parent-child love, sexual partner love, and close friendship. It is experienced by a person through verbal and nonverbal expressions of personal liking by others.

When a person receives insufficient affection and care from others, he or she experiences the pain of *loneliness*. People vary considerably in their ability to deal with loneliness. Some people even learn not to be deeply troubled by the experience. Loneliness may be quite common in American society. The frequent changes of residence of so many Americans has created a ''nation of strangers,'' at least in urban and suburban areas. It takes time to develop genuine intimate relatedness with others.

Recognition. *Recognition* refers to the sense of emotional well-being generated by adequate self-esteem. A person's self-esteem is dependent to a greater or lesser extent upon the notice, acceptance, and approval of others. Recognition, then, is the affirmation by other people that one is a valued individual. (This should not be confused with expressions of affection.) There are many social forms in which recognition is communicated: direct praise; a prestigious position; public admiration; an achievement in art, science, or business. In intimate relations, recognition is communicated in words of praise and approval. In the larger social sense outside of intimate relationships, recognition is usually attributed to a person in a more impersonal manner.

The deprivation of sufficient recognition results in the emotional pain of *low self-esteem.* Most people do not need the acclaim of widely heralded achievements. Nevertheless, all people do need some sources of recognition to ward off a sense of inadequacy. When these sources are limited to the family circle, a person's self-esteem may be quite fragile. This may be the case particularly of wives who have limited social contact outside of the nuclear family.

Security.   *Security* refers to the emotional satisfaction gained from stability and order in one's life. Stable circumstances are reasonably predictable, and as such, comfort anxieties about the unexpected and unknown. On the other hand, *insecurity* involves experiencing the anxiety and fears of uncertainty. In relations between intimates, security is found in familiarity, predictability, and some degree of routine. Perhaps this is what intimates mean when they say that they feel ''comfortable'' with each other.

New experience.   *New experience* is the opposite of security. The pleasures of new experience are those found in change, novelty, and adventure. New experience satisfies a person's curiosity. People who are deprived of sufficient new experience have the painful feeling of *boredom.*

In relations between intimates the emotional satisfactions of security and new experience exist in continuous tension. Too much routine can result in a cancerous growth of boredom. Familiarity doesn't necessarily breed contempt, but it certainly can propagate boredom. In relations between intimates, new experience is most vitalizing when they are learning more about each other through self-disclosure. As intimates settle into a routine with each other, they may become all too familiar with each other's stories. Yet, over a life cycle, new situations are continually emerging: children growing up, adventures on vacations, changing jobs, retiring to a new life. Perhaps intimates who grow and change together are those who can best offer each other the pleasures of new experience. One person's self-development, then, enriches the other. People whose interests and experiences are diverse can most easily offer emotional gratification to their intimates.

emotional pleasures in sexual relations

The four categories of emotional gratifications can be useful in attempts to identify the particular kinds of emotional pleasures which lovers may find in their sexual relationships. The first are the emotional pleasures of *response* which are found in sexual activity accompanied by verbal and nonverbal self-disclosure and expressions of affection. An affectionate sexual relationship affirms an "I-thou" relatedness between partners who enjoy each other's unique identities. Second, the satisfaction of self-esteem may be found in words of praise which offer *recognition* of one's masculine and feminine sexual desirability. Third, *security* is found in each partner's familiarity with the other's sexual preferences and response. Fourth, the pleasures of *new experience* can be experienced by sexual partners who avoid routine and practice variety in sexual caresses, positions, timing, and environments. It may be an unfortunate psychological reality that a sexual relationship maintained over decades can easily become boring and muted. (Even a favorite food eaten continuously can diminish one's appetite.) Therefore, deliberate attempts to introduce sexual variety in a relationship may be necessary to refresh a couple's sexual appetites.

Some research has found that some people have a particularly strong desire for emotion-provoking novel experiences. These "sensation seekers" are found to be drawn to diverse and often socially tabooed sexual activities in search of new sexual experiences (Zuckerman, 1974).

Whether or not a couple finds these emotional gratifications in their sexual relationship depends upon their mutual attractiveness, self-disclosure, and behavioral interdependence. A sexual relationship is vested in an over-all interpersonal relationship. The emotional gratifications found in sexual activity are interwoven with the character of that interpersonal relationship.

LOVE AND CONFLICT

the inevitability of conflict

Conflict is not the opposite of social harmony. Instead, conflict is a condition in all human relationships, including love (Simmel, 1955). There is a constant potential for disruptive conflict in an intimate relationship. Indeed, an intimate relationship is the ground upon which the most intense antagonism is often generated (Coser, 1956). Conflict, therefore, ought to be viewed as an intrinsic aspect of an intimate relationship rather than as a lapse from genuine intimacy. It is artificial to regard love as the harmonious absence of conflict. The emotional rewards of intimate relatedness depend considerably upon a couple's ability to manage the inevitable conflicts between them.

Conflict in an intimate relationship can easily escalate and spread to more and more aspects of the relationship. The antagonism generated by spreading conflict can make the emotional balance of a relationship more painful than pleasurable. When this happens, love will undergo a reverse evolution (Reiss, 1960). The reverse evolution of love can continue over a period of many years until intimates have become virtual strangers in each other's presence. It is likely that more love relationships are terminated by indifference than by dramatic antagonistic confrontations. The reverse evolution can be so insidious that a love relationship can fade away before a couple realizes what has happened to them. There may be few dramatic incidents which they can point to as causes of their demise.

One highly respected marriage counselor has suggested that the potential for conflict in marriage causes a great many couples to settle for a superficial kind of coexistence (Mace, 1976). He suggests that the anger and pain generated by conflict causes many couples to fear intimacy. Many marital partners protect themselves with a shield of psychological reserve, even though they hunger for a deeper relationship.

Recently, some behavioral scientists have tried to analyze the nature of conflict as part of an intimate relationship, rather than as a separate condition which is distinctive of troubled marriages (Bach and Wyden, 1968; Scanzoni, 1972). Various types of conflict have been identified. Some kinds of conflict can actually enhance intimate relatedness by bridnging disputes out into the open, clarifying underlying issues, and stimulating compromise. This type of conflict has been termed *functional conflict* because it promotes interpersonal bonds. On the other hand, many conflicts weaken interpersonal bonds by generating excessive hostility and an unwillingness to compromise. Such conflicts are termed *dysfunctional.* Often conflict is not openly expressed between a couple, but lies latent in their relationship. Such *repressed conflict* occurs when a couple desperately attempts to avoid confrontations over unresolved issues by avoiding self-disclosure of disagreeable reactions or by constantly postponing discussion of disagreements.

Some conflicts between intimates are not rooted in disputes over specific issues that can be compromised. Instead, many occasions of conflict result from personal tensions and fears. Such conflicts may be termed *personality conflict.* It is not uncommon for intimates to use each other as lightning rods upon which they release pent up tensions. The triggers for such bursts of displaced hostility are usually trivial, but the anger generated can easily escalate to more serious matters. This is particularly true when there are concealed issues of repressed conflict in a relationship.

An intimate relationship is constantly evolving. Intimates must constantly manage their conflicts to avoid a deterioration of their relationship.

some sources of sexual conflict

Conflicts over sexual matters appear to be quite common in American marriages, at least as judged from the reports of marriage counselors about their clients (Gochros, 1972; DeBurger, 1975). It must be kept in mind, however, that conflicts over other matters quickly overflow into the sexual arena. Several common sources of sexual conflict can be identified, including: (1) disagreement over sexual preferences; (2) nonreciprocal sexual satisfaction; and (3) sexual jealousy.

Disagreement over sexual preferences. A lack of consensus about sexual preferences and practices affects many couples. Such conflict usually lies repressed in a relationship, rather than being openly expressed. One example is the rather common dispute over the practice of oral-genital sex (Deburger, 1975; Rubin, 1976). Fellatio and cunnilingus are still considered to be sexual perversions by some Americans, espcially those who are not well educated. Repressed conflict over oral-genital sex is most common in blue collar families, where it is most likely to be rejected by women (Rubin, 1976). Conflict may also occur because of differences in preferred frequencies of sexual intercourse. When there is a difference in perference level between sexual partners, the husband is more likely to have the higher preference level, although the reverse is the case for many wives. One study, for example, found that 54 percent of spouses reported unequal preferred frequencies for sexual intercourse, with 29 percent of husbands and 15 percent of wives having a higher preference level than their spouses (Levinger, 1966).

Nonreciprocal sexual satisfaction. A second situation which easily generates sexual conflict occurs when sexual pleasure is one-sided. A lack of reciprocity in experiencing sexual pleasure may occur for a great many reasons. Included among the causes are a lack of adequate sexual knowledge, excessive anxieties and inhibitions, and the traditional erotic roles of men and women.

Sexual jealousy. Perhaps the most disruptive sexual conflicts involve sexual jealousy. As important as jealousy is to an understanding of intimate relations, few behavioral scientists have attempted to investigate its nature until recently (Clanton and Smith, 1977). Part of the problem involves attempts to define sexual jealousy in the absence of adequate research.

Perhaps jealousy may best be regarded as a cognitive-emotional response. The cognitive component of jealousy is shaped by subtle learning processes. Beliefs learned by a person which encourage sexual jealousy include beliefs about monogamy and beliefs about the exclusiveness of sexual intimacy. Research into the emotional components of sexual jealousy have found reactions to be quite varied betwen individuals; reactions include fear, anger, and depression (Bryson, 1976).

Sexual jealousy most commonly involves fears of losing a loved one or fears of being excluded from intimate self-disclosure (Clanton and Smith, 1977). Such fears, whether based upon imagined or actual transgressions of the bonds of trust, can trigger bitter conflict between intimates. Conflict generated by jealousy may be particularly difficult to manage because it is a form of personality conflict where there may exist no specific issue of contention.

There have been some attempts to investigate possible male-female differences in jealousy (Bryson, 1976, 1977). The research indicates that women are more likely to respond with depression and actions designed to maintain the relationship. On the other hand, men are more likely to respond in ways designed to protect their self-esteem, such as seeking an alternative sexual relationship. The difference may be a result of traditional power relationships between the sexes, with women being more dependent upon men, and men being more autonomous outside of the marital relationship.

Nonmarital sexual interaction is a general category of sexual relationships between men and women who are not married to each other. It includes: (1) sexual relations between people who are not yet married (premarital sex); (2) sexual relations involving people who are married to someone else (extramarital sex); (3) sexual relations involving divorced and widowed people (postmarital sex); and (4) sexual relations involving never-married adults. These forms of sexual interaction occur between people who are not spouses. They all also occur in a social context of widespread disapproval in American society. This chapter deals with premarital and postmarital sex; Chapter 14 deals with extramarital sex. Marital sex will be discussed in Chapter 13.

ATTITUDES TOWARD PREMARITAL SEX

premarital standards of sexual conduct

The existence of contradictory rules setting contradictory guidelines for behavior is a rather common occurrence in any society. Such a social condition is what sociologists term *anomie*. The situation may seem illogical, but it is social reality nonetheless. Consider, for example, the rules governing maximum driving speed on the highways. There is an "official" speed limit which is clearly posted. However, most people drive faster than the official limit, closely watching other

12 nonmarital sexual interaction

drivers to learn the informal rule of the road. This informal limit is usually a bit lower than the speed limit at which police will give out speeding tickets. The police among themselves have an informally agreed upon enforceable speed limit. In addition, there may also be informal speeding rules for special groups, such as truck drivers, political officials, local notables, and unsuspecting out-of-towners. The result can be a bit confusing for people seeking to determine "the rule."

Attitudes toward premarital sexual intercourse are best understood as a reflection of a similar anomic social condition. The social contradictions are often quite confusing and distressing for adolescents. Yet this anomic condition is not recent. It has its roots in ancient contradictions between the value of female virginity and the double standard. The popular notion that premarital sexual abstinence was the dominant morality of the past is a creation of nostalgia for a past which actually never existed.

In Chapter 8, it was noted that attitudes toward premarital sex differ considerably between unmarried young people and married adults. A majority of married adults disapprove of premarital sexual relations. Yet a majority of young people do not. The sex attitudes of unmarried young people are the most directly relevant to an understanding of premarital sexual interaction. Therefore, this section will focus upon the premarital sex attitudes of young people under the age of 25.

Premarital sexual traditionalism. The *standard of sexual abstinence* has been the cultural ideal for premarital sexual conduct in Western societies since at least the arrival of Christianity. As an ideal, it influenced society's collective conception of "what ought to be" even when people deviated from it in everyday life. However, the standard of premarital abstinence was always more important as a public profession of ideals for men than it was for their private sexual practice. It was primarily female virginity that was esteemed and not that of men. Some men did value premarital abstinence for themselves, but most did not take that ideal as seriously as did women. The *double standard* has been, until recently, the actual standard of sexual conduct in Western societies.

For the double standard to persist, women must value virginity. However, the attitudes of young women toward premarital sex have been changing rapidly. One recent nationally representative survey found that only 40 percent of young women considered premarital sexual intercourse to be immoral (Roper, 1974). Another nationally representative survey found that among women college students, only 29 percent regard it as being immoral (Yankelovich, 1974). Clearly, a majority of today's unmarried women no longer consider virginity to be a moral imperative.

The most curious thing about the double standard is that it lasted for so many centuries without modification. Under the double standard, men were expected to obtain premarital sexual experience. Yet they were also expected to guard the viriginity of their sisters and daughters against men like themselves. Most men would only marry a virgin. How was the double standard able to work? If all women remained virgins, how could men obtain their premarital sexual experience?

The double standard was able to exist through a variety of discrete social arrangements. Certain women were set aside as prostitutes to serve the sexual needs of men. In addition, other women were socially labeled "bad" women and were regarded as targets for sexual exploitation. Such women were those who behaved in a disreputable or nonconformist manner. Finally, most men were also quite willing to exploit women who were members of social out-groups. It was usually a matter of honor for men to avoid the sexual exploitation of women from their own ethnic group, religion, or social class. However, men held no such scruples toward women from other social groups. They had no intention of marrying them anyhow.

It was also necessary to obtain the collusion of "respectable" women for the double standard system to work. Respectable women took pride in the esteem attributed to them because they remained virgins until marriage. They regarded "fallen women" with contempt, as losers in the battle of the sexes. Many respectable women were able to play the role of "sexy virgin" only because of the double standard. Such women practiced the subtle art of sex teasing behind a facade of innocence. They could be sexually attractive to men without being sexual or even while feeling disgust for sexual activity.

The basic change which has occurred in attitudes toward premarital sex is a decline in the double standard. Recent research indicates that fewer and fewer women are willing to tolerate it and fewer men profess it (Kaats and Davis, 1970; Ferrell, et al., 1977). In many circles of young people today, a male who openly affirms the double standard is held in contempt by others.

The double standard system has come apart for a variety of reasons. Increasingly few young women now regard premarital virginity as a moral value. Increasingly few young men now demand that the woman they will marry must be a virgin. The double standard system began to break down during the 1920s when the value of love began to become more important than that of female virginity. During that period of rapid social change, increasing numbers of engaged couples had sexual intercourse justified by their love.

Premarital sexual permissiveness.   The increasing acceptance of premarital sexual intercourse is basically an expression of a sexual standard which has been termed *permissiveness with affection* (Reiss, 1960). It holds sexual intercourse to be acceptable between unmarried people if they are simply "in love." This standard is essentially an outgrowth of the past acceptance of sexual intercourse during engagement. It goes one step further, by not requiring any commitment to marriage.

There are, however, certain complications. Love means different things to different people. Ultimately feelings of love must be reflected in symbols. The need to symbolize love in some visible form is particularly important when people are insecure about the permanence of their relationship. Some young people are likely to regard themselves as being "in love" only if they share a commitment to marry (symbolized in a promise and a ring). However, most young people today do not require a definite commitment to marry as symbolic evidence of a love relationship. A "going steady" dating arrangement may be sufficient evidence of love. Even more flexible young people may need only expressions of affection in the form of emotion, word, and deed. That may be enough to justify the belief that "if you are in love, sex is okay." The standard of permissiveness with affection holds the same expectation for men and women. However, it still stirs up confusion. Young people must now struggle with the question of whether or not they are "really" in love.

Regardless of all the talk about "free love," there are still relatively few young people who hold a premarital standard of mutual sexual desire on a casual level (Hunt, 1974). Few teenage girls feel comfortable with casual sexual encounters lacking an affectionate relationship. Even most women in their 20s find "one night stands" to be disagreeable, in contrast to a more intimate sexual relationship. Many teenage boys preach a code of causal sex. However, they do not really respect girls who behave as "easy lays." These boys are actually exploitive, double-standard males in a new "swinging" disguise.

premarital attitudes and other aspects of personality

Moral judgment. In recent years, an important topic of psychological research has been the question of how people develop their concepts of morality. One research project investigated the premarital sex attitudes of college students using a technique to measure the basis of their moral judgments (Jurich and Jurich, 1974). The research used a sample of 160 students from eight different colleges. Some of the students simply based their judgment on the pursuit of personal needs. However, most of them did not. The research found that students whose moral judgment was based upon external authority tended to hold the traditional standard of abstinence or the double standard. If their moral judgment was based upon religious belief, they affirmed the standard of abstinence. If their moral judgment was based upon beliefs about "natural" male and female sexual behavior, they affirmed the double standard. These two different kinds of moral judgment are actually similar in some ways. They both reflect a moral judgment based upon a form of authority (religion, or custom in the male peer group). Both are similar in the sense that they reflect moral judgment based upon conventionally accepted, "natural" expectations for sexual relationships. In contrast, the students who held sexually permissive standards tended to base their moral judgment upon certain personal ethical principles such as mutual commitment, affection, or respect. Their judgment reflected a moral evaluation of human relationships, rather than particular sexual acts, as being "right" or "wrong." It was based upon shared expectations which two individuals might hold for each other's behavior.

This research points to the possibility that concepts of sexual morality are emerging from beyond the bounds of traditional religion. It is also interesting that standards of both sexual abstinence and sexual exploitation (the double standard) were found to be more common among young people who considered themselves to be traditionally religious (Jurich and Jurich, 1974). Most important, such research offers evidence that standards of premarital sexual permissiveness often derive from serious moral judgment rather than simple egocentric pleasure-seeking. When they are exposed to a variety of competing premarital sex standards, the choice made by young people is not one in which they simply either accept or reject the traditional standard of abstinence. Instead, their choice reflects a selection from alternative moral judgments.

Religious and political belief. An important research question has always been whether attitudes toward premarital sex are associated with different social background factors and personal beliefs. One recent research project was able to investigate this question using a very large national sample of freshman entering colleges during 1974 (Bayer, 1977). The freshmen were asked if they agreed or disagreed with the statement: "If two people really like each other, it's allright for them to have sex, even if they've known each other for only a very short time." An intricate computer analysis of the data found that the factor which was most able to distinguish the students holding sexually permissive attitudes was religion. This was true for both men and women. Students who identified themselves as being either Jewish or having no religious preference were most likely to agree with the sexually permissive statement. Students identifying themselves as being Protestant or Catholic were much less likely to endorse, premarital sexual permissiveness. Among Protestants and Catholics, however, those students who identified themselves as being politically liberal were more likely to accept sexual permissiveness. Protestants and Catholics who identified themselves as being politically conservative were least likely to accept sexual permissiveness. (In addition, the research found that students from different socioeconomic backgrounds did not show any significant difference in their acceptance or rejection of sexual permissiveness.)

In summary, attitudes of premarital sexual permissiveness are found to be most common among young people who identify themselves as being either: (1) nonreligious or Jewish; or (2) politically liberal, if they are Protestant or Catholic. Premarital sexual traditionalism is found to be most common among young people whose religiosity is closely linked to sociopolitical conservatism (Joe et al. 1976).

premarital sexual intercourse: the increase

The increasing incidence of premarital sexual intercourse has been the focus of considerable research attention. There is little reliable data about the frequency of premarital sexual intercourse prior to the twentieth century. However, social historians have gathered information about the extent of premarital pregnancies in America since 1640 (Smith and Hindus, 1975). The information suggests that the percentage of young people having premarital sexual intercourse increased during the Colonial period. The increase reached a high point shortly after the American Revolution. Later, during the Victorian era, premarital pregnancies declined. This indicates a return to a low incidence of premarital intercourse, by the mid-1800s. Then, again after the Civil War, the incidence of premarital pregnancies gradually began to increase.

More reliable data about actual sexual behavior is available for the twentieth century. According to Kinsey's research, the proportion of Americans having premarital sexual intercourse did not increase very sharply until shortly after World War I (Kinsey et al., 1948). During the 1920s, there was a great increase in the percentage of couples having premarital sexual intercourse. The incidence did not accelerate very much again until the late 1960s during the Vietnam War era. The 1970s have been another period of rapid change in premarital sexual behavior, comparable to the 1920s.

There is now substantial research evidence that a sharp increase in the proportion of young people having premarital sexual intercourse began to occur during the social turmoil of the late 1960s (Vener and Steward, 1974; Bauman and Wilson, 1974; Udry et al., 1975). One of the most important of these studies was done with nationally representative samples of teenage women between the ages of 15 and 19, under a grant from the Department of Health, Education, and Welfare (Zelnick and Kanter, 1977). The research employed teams of interviewers who questioned two samples of over 4000 teenage women during 1971 and again in 1976. It found that the proportion of unmarried teenage women who had premarital intercourse increased 30 percent in just that five-year period. By 1976, 18 percent of 15-year-old girls had sexual intercourse while 55 percent of 19-year-olds did so. These findings mean that a majority of unmarried young women now have sexual intercourse by the time they turn 20 years of age.

Another major study of teenage sexual intercourse was carried out under the auspices of the Public Health Association during 1975 (Brown, Liebermann, and Miller, 1975). In a survey of teenagers in four communities, it found that by age 17, sexual intercourse was experienced by 45 percent of the females and 67 percent of the males. It appears that a considerably larger percentage of unmarried teenage men than women have experience with sexual intercourse.

There is a substantial difference in the incidence of premarital intercourse between white and black teenage girls (Zelnik and Kanter, 1977). About 14 percent of the white girls and about 38 percent of the black girls had premarital sexual intercourse by age 15, in 1976. By age 19, about 49 percent of the white girls and about 84 percent of the black girls had the experience.

If young people do not marry while they are still in their teenage years, their likelihood of engaging in premarital intercourse continues to increase with every year they remain single. The available research indicates that the vast majority of single young men and women in their 20s during the decade of the 1970s had sexual intercourse prior to their marriage.

One national sex survey carried out in 1972 found that 70 percent of single women and 80 percent of single men in the age group of 18 to 24 had some experience with premarital sexual intercourse (Hunt, 1974). A great many people first have sexual intercourse shortly before getting married. Therefore, it is not surprising that the incidence of premarital intercourse was found to be even higher among married people in that same age group. Among 18 to 24 year olds who were already married in 1972, 81 percent of the women and 95 percent of the men had sexual intercourse before their marriage (Hunt, 1974). Other research also provides evidence that the vast majority of young people who married during the 1970s had sexual intercourse prior to their marriage (Travis and Sadd, 1977). This, of course, is a substantial change from the experience of people who are now grandparents.

There has indeed been a great change in the proportion of people who have had premarital sexual intercourse. However, the change has been primarily among women rather than among men. According to Kinsey's data, among women born before 1900, only about 14 percent of the women who were still unmarried by age 25 had experienced premarital intercourse (Kinsey et al., 1953). The percentage having such experience has now increased to about 80 percent of single women by age 25. This is a much greater increase, than that which has occurred among men since 1900. Similar data for men born before 1900 indicates that the vast majority of them had experience with premarital sexual intercourse (Kinsey et al., 1948). Most of the premarital experience of men at that time, however, was with prostitutes. This has now become a relatively rare experience for unmarried young men (Hunt, 1974).

The conclusions that can be drawn from these comparisons of historical change is that it is women's premarital sexual behavior which largely accounts for the changes in premarital sexual intercourse. Therefore, to really understand why premarital sexual interaction has changed, we must first understand why the sexual behavior of women has changed.

premarital sexual intercourse: interpersonal aspects

The evidence of greatly increased incidence of premarital sexual intercourse does not carry with it any suggestion of young people having frequent sexual intercourse with many partners. Indeed, it is quite possible that three generations ago, men had more frequent premarital intercourse and with a wider variety of partners (largely prostitutes). Even more important than any change in the incidence of premarital intercourse is social change in the interpersonal context of that experience.

Premarital sexual activity among unmarried teenagers today remains much more limited in frequency and variety than is marital sexual activity. Premarital sexual intercourse is usually more infrequent and sporadic. The variety of sexual practices are much more limited. Even the number of partners with whom young people have sexual intercourse remains limited. If we can speak of a "sexual revolution" (whatever that may mean), the notion is more appropriate for sex in marriage than sex before marriage.

Frequency and number of partners. Accurate information about frequency of intercourse and the number of sexual partners among teenage women can be found in the national interview study of 15- to 19-year-olds previously mentioned (Zelnik and Kanter, 1977). Among the teenage women in the study 25 percent had sexual intercourse only one or two times; 12 percent experienced it three to five times; and only 15 percent had it six or more times. Clearly, these data reveal rather limited sexual experience. Concerning the number of male sexual partners, the data reveal that 50 percent of the sexually experienced women had only one partner. Among the other sexually experienced women, 31 percent had two or three partners; 9 percent had four or five partners; and 10 percent had six or more partners. What these data indicate is that most teenage women who have sexual intercourse, limit that experience to a very few sexual partners. It would appear that few teenage women are sexually promiscuous in the sense of having indiscriminate sexual intercourse. Most teenage women have sexual intercourse with one or two partners in a going-steady relationship.

If young people begin to have sexual intercourse during early adolescence and stay single for many years, they are likely to experience intercourse with many partners. Several research projects have found that married women who began to have sexual intercourse during early adolescence had many more premarital sexual partners than did women who began to have intercourse during late adolescence or their early 20s (Travis and Sadd, 1977). This relationship between early experience and number of partners is probably the same for men.

Among young people who remain unmarried into their 20s, the likelihood of experiencing sexual intercourse with more than one person increases. Yet, a national sex survey found that half of single women in their 20s had the experience with only one partner, usually their prospective husband (Hunt, 1974). Single men have experience with a greater number of partners than do single women. Yet, even among men in their 20s, less than half have had sexual intercourse with six or more partners (Hunt, 1974).

The frequency of premarital sexual intercourse among older youth, however, is much higher than it is among teenagers. Once a sexual affair begins among older singles, it is likely to be more persistent with sexual intercourse occurring every week. The difference is probably due to greater privacy in the living arrangements among singles in their 20s. They are less likely than are teenagers to live in their parents' home.

Level of intimate relatedness. During the 1920s, the sharp increase in premarital intercourse occurred for women mainly during engagement. In other words, female sexuality remained as it had always been, linked to an exclusive intimate relationship with one sexual partner. Most men, on the other hand, did not limit their sexual expression to an intimate relationship. In contrast, a majority of men had sexual experience with nonintimates, mainly prostitutes. This, of course, was the behavioral result of the double standard. Has there been any significant change in this pattern since the 1920s?

The available research on premarital sexual relationships indicates that past patterns are gradually changing. Men and women are becoming more alike in the kind of relationship in which they experience premarital intercourse. More and more men limit their sexual experience to an exclusive, intimate relationship. One national survey, for example, found that only 3 percent of young unmarried men now have sexual intercourse with prostitutes (Hunt, 1974). There are still a great many unmarried men who have sexual intercourse with nonintimates such as pickups and casual dates. However, the direction of change for men is toward the traditional female pattern. The change among women has been less marked. More women are having premarital sexual intercourse, but they still retain a preference for sex within an intimate relationship. In other words, male and female premarital sexual behavior is converging, but essentially in the direction of traditional female sexual patterns.

One major study of premarital sexual relationships among college students offers insight into the nature of that change (Lewis and Burr, 1975). The research used a sample of 2453 students selected from colleges in Minnesota, Oregon, California, Texas, and Georgia. It found that the vast majority of college women who had premarital sexual intercourse had that experience during engagement, or in a "going steady" relationship. Very few women had sexual intercourse with first dates or infrequent dates. However, many men did experience sexual intercourse with casual dates. Nevertheless, more men did experience sexual intercourse within intimate relationships than had ever experienced it in a casual dating relationship. Although male-female differences continue to exist, the implication of this research and others is that a gradually increasing proportion of unmmarried men are limiting sexual intercourse to an intimate relationship (Jedlicka, 1975).

Casual sex by mutual agreement occurs more often than it did three generations ago. However, it remains limited mostly to older singles who have gone through several love affairs and among certain counterculture youth groups (Hunt, 1974). Many older singles are quite willing to enjoy casual "one-night stands" after meeting in a singles bar. While this has always been true of many men, it is also true of an increasing number of older women singles. Indeed, some men now have the unhappy experience of being dropped after a "one-night stand." Some men, now, must worry about being sexually evaluated, by "liberated" women.

Exploitive game playing also continues to exist. While most young men prefer to have intercourse in a love relationship, many of them are not beyond the occasional use of manipulation and seduction. Many men still gain recognition from their circle of buddies through bragging about their sexual conquests. Many women still experience sexual coercion in casual dating when they feel forced into sexual acts out of fear (Kanin and Parcell, 1977). Anxieties about sexual game playing have not disappeared with the coming of the new morality.

Premarital intercourse: its personal meaning.   Few research projects have investigated the meaning of premarital intercourse to partners in a sexual relationship. One excellent research project, however, did study this matter in a sample of 231 college student dating couples over a period of two years (Peplau et al., 1977). The researchers divided their sample into three types of couples: (1) traditional couples who abstained from sexual intercourse; (2) romantic couples who waited to be sure of a love relationship before having sexual intercourse; and (3) erotically oriented couples who accepted sexual intercourse as a "recreational" activity, without sharing a previous love relationship. Sexual intercourse had a different personal meaning for the participants in these three different kinds of relationships.

Between the traditional couples, abstaining from sexual intercourse was taken as a symbol of their love and as a mark of respect for the woman. Although these couples engaged in heavy petting, for them, refraining from sexual intercourse meant that they shared a relationship which went deeper than physical attraction. Nevertheless, the men in these relationships typically reported that they personally would have preferred to have had intercourse. The women were significantly less interested in doing so. A majority of the men indicated that their girlfriend's desire to avoid intercourse was a major reason for the couple's abstinence. The abstaining students were significantly less permissive in their attitudes toward sexual activity than were the other students. They regarded a permanent commitment to marriage, and not simply a love relationship, to be a necessary justification for premarital intercourse. A great many of them also tended to regard premarital intercourse as being immoral.

The romantically oriented couples, in contrast, tended to subscribe to the standard of permissiveness with affection. For them, sexual intercourse was seen as an expression of their emotional closeness. They dated an average of six months before they felt that sexual intercourse was justified by their affection for each other. Although both partners shared a primary concern for their emotional intimacy, the men indicated a greater interest in sexual pleasure. After they had sexual intercourse, they were apt to regard it as adding a further dimension to their relationship. Nevertheless, they tended to have sexual intercourse less frequently than did the erotically oriented couples and were more likely to feel guilty about it.

The erotically oriented couples first had sexual intercourse after dating only an average of one month. Most of these men and women were sexually experienced when they began dating. These couples were capable of seeing sexual intercourse as an expression of emotional intimacy. Yet they also regarded recreational sex without love as being acceptable for them. They were more interested in sexual pleasure as a dating goal than were the other couples. In addition, they regarded sexual activity as having the potential for developing closer emotional intimacy. For these couples, love had the potential of growing out of a sexual relationship.

How satisfied and successful were the couples having these different kinds of relationships? Fortunately, the researchers were able to probe this question in their two year follow-up study (Peplau et al., 1977). The findings may be a bit surprising. The different couples reported no greater or less satisfaction with their relationships. In addition, there was no difference in the proportion of these couples who ultimately broke up, continued dating, or got married. Therefore, the researchers concluded that there is no evidence that either sexual abstinence, a gradual movement toward sexual intercourse, or an early beginning of sexual intercourse consistently increases, or decreases, the development of a lasting relationship, at least for young people of college age.

premarital cohabitation

In 1968, a Barnard College woman in New York City made the national news when she protested being expelled from college for living with her boyfriend without being married. It was certainly not the first time that had happened. However, during a period of intense criticism of established custom, a minor scandal became linked to a national controversy. If premarital intercourse is itself a controversial social issue, premarital cohabitation is even more so. The cohabitation of unmarried people is against the law in 20 states, with possible penalties for conviction ranging up to 3 years in jail (*Newsweek*, 1977). Premarital sexual intercourse is also illegal in 16 states under laws against fornication. Yet the Census Bureau estimates that at least 1.3 million American men and women are living together without being married.

After cohabitation became a matter of national attention, a considerable amount of research was focused upon cohabitation among college students. Yet, a recent national survey of men between the ages of 20 and 30 found that cohabitation is much more common in the noncollege population than among college students (Clayton and Voss, 1977). Indeed, unmarried cohabitation has traditionally been common among some groups of poor people. In addition, there are indications that cohabitation may be increasing among divorced people, and even among the elderly for economic reasons (*Newsweek,* 1977). The national survey of young men was part of a federally funded project and therefore was able to interview a representative sample of 2510 men across the country (Clayton and Voss, 1977). It found that 29 percent of black men and 16 percent of white men had cohabited for at least six months. It also found that 5 percent of the men were cohabiting with someone at the time of the survey. Although more men who led a generally unconventional lifestyle had cohabited, cohabiting men as a whole represented widely varied social backgrounds, educational levels, and lifestyles.

The research studies of premarital cohabitation among college students have found that cohabiting relationships take a variety of forms (Macklin, 1972; Lewis et al., 1977). Cohabitation may be: (1) a prelude to marriage; (2) a trial marriage; (3) a long-term alternative to marriage, (4) a going-steady and living together extension of courtship; or (5) an arrangement designed mainly for social, sexual, and economic convenience. Actually, a great many cohabitors gradually drift into the arrangement and do not hold well-defined expectations for the long-term future of their relationships.

It is quite likely that on college campuses at least, cohabitation begins primarily as a "going very steady" relationship without any clear commitment toward marriage (Macklin, 1972). Even if cohabitors do not definitely plan to get married, most of them are committed to an exclusive, intimate relationship. One study was able to compare 61 cohabiting college students with 61 engaged students and 61 married students (Lewis et al., 1977). It found, surprisingly, that the cohabiting students were just as committed to continuing an exclusive relationship as were the engaged couples.

There is little adequate research on the percentage of cohabiting relationships which eventually end with marriage. It is quite likely, however, that a large percentage of cohabitors do not eventually get married (Macklin, 1972; Clayton and Voss, 1977).

While it is clear that most adults disapprove of premarital cohabitation, there is widespread sympathy for it among college students. College students who approve of cohabitation offer a variety of reasons for doing so (Macklin, 1972). They offer such reasons as a desire to avoid loneliness and the dating game; a desire for a more emotionally intimate relationship; doubts about marriage and a desire to try out a living together arrangement; or simple convenience in continuing a prior sexual relationship.

One study investigated attitudes toward cohabitation in research carried out during 1970 with a sample of 539 students from one college in the midwest and one in the northeast (Silverman, 1977). Cohabitation was approved under a variety of conditions by 81 percent of the northeast students and 71 percent of the midwest students. Significantly fewer women approved of cohabitation under any circumstances or were personally unwilling to cohabit even if they approved of it for others. Religiosity, as measured by frequency of church attendance, also influenced attitudes toward cohabitation. Significantly fewer traditionally religious students approved of cohabitation under any circumstances.

Considering the wide approval of cohabitation among unmarried young people, it is likely to be a source of social controversy for some time to come. It is also likely to continue to increase regardless of any controversy.

THE ISSUE OF ABSTINENCE VERSUS CONTRACEPTION

There are two basic ways of avoiding unwanted pregnancies: (1) abstaining from sexual intercourse, and (2) practicing effective contraception. Until quite recently, almost all public authorities have urged unmarried people to abstain from sexual activity, as the only responsible way of avoiding the tragedy of unwanted premarital pregnancy. That public policy has not been effective, considering the extent of sexual activity among unmarried young people. A policy of preaching premarital abstinence, as regulated by moral ideals and guilt, might work today in certain subcultural enclaves, such as among the Amish or Hassidic Jews. Elsewhere, it is likely to contribute little at all, toward attempts to reduce the risk of premarital pregnancy.

It was not until the early 1970s that the emphasis of some public authorities shifted from encouraging abstinence, to programs for contraceptive education and distribution, directed toward unmarried young people. A growing number of privately and publicly sponsored medical clinics, now distribute birth control information and materials to unmarried young people, without any necessity of parental approval (Irwin, 1972). In addition, public opinion appears to have shifted towards a policy of promoting contraceptive education for teenagers (Blake, 1973). A 1977 Gallup survey found that 69 percent of American adults approved of birth control education in the high schools (Family Planning Perspectives, 1978). Finally, also, behavioral science research has shifted attention from the question of why unmarried people have sexual intercourse, to the question of why they do not practice effective contraception. A summary of that research is presented in Chapter 3.

premarital pregnancy

It is estimated that between one and a half million and two million pregnancies occur among unmarried women every year. Premarital pregnancies affect the lives of a very sizable proportion of unmarried women. According to a 1971 Bureau of the Census estimate, about 20 percent of first born children of all white women were premaritally conceived (Bureau of the Census, 1974). A more common outcome of premarital pregnancy is abortion, especially since its legalization. In 1975, about 740,000 legal abortions were performed on unmarried women, which constituted about three-fourths of all legal abortions for that year (Sullivan et al., 1977). In 1975, the number of illegitimate births was estimated to be at least 447,000 for the year (Baldwin, 1977).

The rate of illegitimate births among black women is relatively higher than it is among white women, in comparison to their representation in the population. This situation is a consequence of the fact that a much greater percentage of premarital pregnant white women get abortions or get married (Zelnik and

Kanter, 1978a). Premaritally pregnant black women are comparatively less likely to seek abortions or to marry. Therefore, the consequences of premarital intercourse and pregnancy are more easily visible among black women than among white women. This is so, even though in absolute numbers there are many more premarital pregnancies, among unmarried white women.

Premarital pregnancies are the source of many personal and social problems, whether the outcome is an undesired marriage, unwed motherhood, or abortion. Premarital pregnancy, leading to marriage, is a major cause of marital instability. One research project, for example, followed the marriages of 203 teenage women, who married after becoming premaritally pregnant (Furstenburg, 1976). It found that after four years of marriage, about half of the marriages had dissolved. Premarital pregnancies, which lead to unwed motherhood, severely constrict opportunities for marriage and economic independence, especially for teenagers. Unwed mothers and their children are the largest segment of welfare recipients. Finally, abortion as a solution to premarital pregnancy, is morally repugnant to many people, and continues to be a heated social controversy.

It seems clear that only public policies aimed at encouraging premarital contraception have any practical possibility of reducing the extent of premarital pregnancy. The scientific research and technology to deal with the problem is already available. However, solutions to social problems are more often a matter of politics, than science. Whether or not a political solution to the problem of premarital pregnancy will be found in the near future is an open question.

POSTMARITAL SEXUAL INTERACTION

sexual interaction among the divorced

A great many people who have nonmarital sexual relations do so after having been married and divorced. While much controversy and research is concerned with premarital sex, relatively little attention is paid to postmarital sex.

A sizable number of young couples get divorced. The Bureau of the Census currently projects that about one-third of all marriages of persons between the ages of 25 and 35 will end in divorce (Bureau of Census, 1976). In the year 1975, there were about 3.5 million men and about 6.3 million women who were divorced or separated and not yet remarried in the United States population (Bureau of Census, 1976). Divorced people are now a sizable portion of single adults.

Postmarital sexual interaction among divorced people differs considerably from premarital sexual interaction. Almost all divorced men and at least 75 percent of divorced women under the age of 40 have postmarital intercourse

(Gebhard, 1970; Hunt, 1974). Divorced men and women have sexual intercourse surprisingly frequently. Their rate of sexual intercourse is about as frequent as that of married people of the same age (Hunt, 1974). Divorced men and women also have sexual experience with significantly more partners than do never-married singles. Younger divorced men have sexual intercourse with an average of eight women over the period of a year (Hunt, 1974). Only about 20 percent of them have that experience with prostitutes. Among divorced women who are sexually active, the average number of partners is about four men over the period of a year (Hunt, 1974).

Divorced men and women also tend to practice greater variety in their sexual activity than do never-married singles. About 90 percent of divorced men and about 80 percent of divorced women, for example, engage in oral-genital sex (Hunt, 1974). This level of oral-genital activity is about as high as that among young married couples. It is much higher than that of singles. Divorced people are also much more likely than even young married couples to practice uncommon positions for sexual intercourse, such as a sitting position or the rear-entry position (Hunt, 1974). They are also considerably more likely to experience anal intercourse. In addition, one large-scale study found that 45 percent of divorced women combine marijuana and sexual activity and many of them often do so (Travis and Sadd, 1977). Their marijuana use is substantially higher than that of married women. In summary, the foregoing data indicate that the sexual activity of most divorced people is unconstrained by traditional expectations for sexual abstinence among the unmarried.

Divorced people regard their postmarital sexual activity to be as pleasurable as married couples regard marital sex. One national survey found that about 90 percent of divorced men and about 66 percent of divorced women reported that their postmarital sex life is very pleasurable (Hunt, 1974). Another research project carried out by the Institute for Sex Research investigated frequency of orgasm in a large sample of divorced women (Gebhard, 1970). It found that about 50 to 60 percent of divorced women achieve orgasm on nearly every occasion of sexual intercourse. This is a greater frequency of orgasm than among married women. The rather high frequency of orgasm of divorced women may be a consequence of their variety of sexual practices. It may also be due to their greater possibility than married women for engaging in sexual activity only when they are in the mood for it. Nevertheless, a great many divorced people also report that their sexual activity often lacks the emotional satisfactions found in an affectionate, intimate relationship (Hunt, 1974).

Although about 80 percent of divorced people begin sexual relations within a year after their divorce, most of them must face painful personal difficulties (Gebhard, 1970; Hunt, 1974). Divorce is an emotional shock for most people, even if their previous marital life was deeply disturbing to them. It can be a severe blow to a person's self-esteem, engendering a sense of failure. Some divorced men and women plunge into sexual affairs immediately after their divorce to buttress their lowered self-esteem (Hunt, 1966). Others find it difficult to be sexually responsive after an experience of acute sexual conflict during the last years of their marriage (Hunt, 1966). In their sexual affairs, divorced men and women are, at first, deeply ambivalent about seeking intimate relationships. They desire the emotional satisfactions of sex in an intimate relationship, but remain fearful of the familiar emotional pains of intimacy. Nevertheless, most divorced people are eventually drawn into sexual love affairs and remarry.

The vast majority of divorced men and women remarry (80 percent of men and 75 percent of women). The average interval before their remarriage is three years (Bureau of Census, 1976). Research on the remarriage of divorced people indicates that their second marriages are as satisfying on the average as are marriages in general (Bernard, 1968).

sexual interaction among the widowed

The average age of widows and widowers is considerably older than that of divorcees. Therefore, it is not surprising that they tend to be less sexually active. Yet, even on an age by age comparison, widowed men and women are less likely to engage in postmarital sexual relations than are divorcees (Gebhard, 1970). They may be constrained by affectionate memories of their deceased spouse, as well as the disapproval of their children. In addition, widowed people may be less motivated to seek remarriage than are divorcees. Significantly fewer of them do remarry. If they date less often, they have fewer opportunities than do divorcees to engage in sexual activity.

There is, however, a male-female difference in the sexual activity of widowed people. One study found that only 43 percent of widowed women ever experienced postmarital intercourse (Gebhard, 1970). However, the incidence is much higher among widowed men, with nearly 80 percent of them experiencing postmarital intercourse (Kinsey et al., 1948).

WHY IS PREMARITAL SEXUAL BEHAVIOR CHANGING?

It was previously noted that changes in nonmarital sexual behavior are primarily a reflection of social conditions which are changing the sexual behavior of unmarried persons, especially women. What are these social conditions? How do they personally affect young people?

In a historical perspective, it is obvious that the current change is only part of a long-range change in the nonmarital sexual behavior of unmarried persons. In addition, from cross-cultural research we know that the same change which is occurring in American society is also occurring in all other advanced industrial societies. The change has even gone further in Scandinavia, Germany, and

England (Luckey and Nass, 1969; Christensen and Gregg, 1970; Schmidt and Sigush, 1972; Schofield, 1973). In brief, the change is an outcome of increased desire and opportunity.

One obvious social condition which has given rise to increased sexual activity among unmarried women is the increased privacy of young people. The increased incidence of premarital intercourse is an inevitable result of the opportunity of unmarried men and women to associate with each other in a maximum of privacy. When young people live at home, their homes are often free of their parents' supervision for a large part of the day. The home of working parents is now the most common location for teenagers to have sexual intercourse (Zelnik and Kanter, 1977). When young people live away from home, their privacy is enhanced further. Automobiles and apartments in cities provide additional freedom from supervision.

Beyond the obvious historical changes in the privacy of young people there are more subtle changes in male-female power relations. Women are increasingly being socialized to expect equality with men in their freedom and advantages. As recently as the 1960s, for example, college women had more restrictive dormitory regulations imposed upon them than did college men. That inequality was swept away in most places by the social criticism of the late 1960s. Today, a great many colleges have coed dormitories and relaxed rules governing off-campus housing arrangements. The value of equality makes it wrong to impose restrictions upon the behavior of women which are not also imposed upon men.

The great emphasis upon the importance of finding love makes it an equalizer in male-female relations. Beliefs about romantic love impose restraints upon the freedom of men to pursue indiscriminate sexual affairs. Romantic love beliefs are destroying the justification for the double standard. However, romantic love beliefs also enable women to justify sexual freedom in pursuit of love. If it is desire which encourages women to have premarital intercourse, it is the desire for a loving relationship more than for sexual pleasure.

Most traditional religious groups have actively opposed change in premarital sexual attitudes. Fewer young people who are highly religious in the traditional sense have premarital intercourse than do those who consider themselves to be irreligious (Bell and Balter, 1973; Hunt, 1974). Nevertheless, change is occurring, even in traditional religions. Some of them, such as Unitarians and Quakers, are beginning to accept premarital sex within the context of a love relationship. It is easy for traditional religion to oppose the hedonistic pursuit of sexual pleasure. It is much more difficult for traditional religion to oppose the morality of love as a justification for premarital sexual expression. In the past, religious belief had a much greater impact upon the non-marital sexual behavior of women than of men (Kavolis, 1962).

The effects of the birth control pill upon premarital sexual behavior was not immediate. It was not until the 1970s that the pill became readily available to unmarried youth through medical clinics and private physicians (Zelnik and

Kanter, 1977). Many unmarried young people still do not employ effective contraceptive measures or any contraception at all. There is still a gap between the attraction of premarital intercourse and the avoidance of contraception which results in a great many unwanted pregnancies.

It is popularly believed that the increasing incidence of premarital sexual intercourse is a result of the "breakdown" of parental authority. That is not quite true. American parents have never been willing to chaperone their children. They have always encouraged a measure of independence in the thought and behavior of their children. In reality, there is little that parents can do to stop the changes in premarital sexual behavior.

In recent years, there has been a renewal of research interest in the family life-cycle. Placing the understanding of marital and sexual satisfaction within the perspective of an evolving relationship is very useful. Such a perspective enables insight into the situational influences upon sexual satisfaction within a marital relationship. Much research indicates that marital sexual interaction is more greatly affected by a couple's current marital situation than by their past childhood and adolescent sexual socialization.

Several research projects have investigated marital satisfaction over the life-cycle by means of questionnaire surveys and interviews with samples of married couples across the spectrum of ages (Rollins and Cannon, 1974; Spanier et al., 1975; Miller, 1976). Almost all researchers have found a gradual decline in marital satisfaction after initial cohabitation followed by a sharper decline after the first child is born. Then, during the extended child-rearing period marital satisfaction levels off. According to most studies, there is increasing marital satisfaction reported among couples after their children have left home. Reports of marital sexual satisfaction also follow this pattern of gradually declining satisfaction (Burr, 1970).

The decline of marital satisfaction over the life-cycle is a general finding for the population of married couples. The mutual biography of any particular couple may vary from this general pattern. The marriages of some couples experience a rapid termination. Some marriages undergo ups and downs of satisfactions at different stages. Still other couples experience growing levels of marital satisfaction.

13 marital sexual interaction

We need to know much more about the factors which cause declining marital satisfaction over the years. However, the available research already offers insight into some of the aggravating conditions. One of these conditions is the psychological stress caused by the push and pull of trying to accomplish diverse marital tasks: financial support, childrearing, and home care. The pressures of accomplishing these tasks during the expensive and exhausting child-rearing period are particularly likely to reduce possibilities for the pleasures of companionship and sexual activity (Miller, 1976). In addition, various life-cycle transitions create problems of changing circumstances. Some people are able to make the passage more easily than are others (Sheehy, 1974, 1976).

Research comparing the life satisfactions of married and single persons offers a case for balanced optimism about marital life (Glenn, 1975; Campbell et al., 1976). These research studies, which have all used large representative samples of Americans, indicate that married people are consistently more satisfied with their lives than are any category of unmarried people (including young singles, the divorced, the widowed, and the never-married). Even married couples during the stressful child-rearing period report higher levels of happiness with their life situations than do any category of unmarried persons.

In conclusion, it would appear that the satisfactions people find in marriage tends to gradually decline with time. However, single people are still unable to find alternative gratifications. This is perhaps why remarriage rates remain high among divorced people, even though Americans are experiencing the highest divorce rate in their history (Norton and Glick, 1976). There may be nowhere else to go to seek the rewards of intimacy.

marital and sexual satisfaction

The research on marital satisfaction indicates that a couple's level of sexual satisfaction and satisfaction with the marriage as a whole affect each other (Clark and Wallin, 1965; Dentler and Pineo, 1960). It is a rare marriage in which sexual dissatisfaction does not diminish marital satisfaction. It is also a rare marriage where marital dissatisfaction does not diminish sexual dissatisfaction. Some evidence for the close interrelationship of marital and sexual satisfaction can be found in a questionnaire survey of 100,000 women (Travis and Sadd, 1977). Among wives who reported on overall satisfying marital relationship, about 80 percent also reported similarly high satisfaction in their sexual relations. In comparison, among wives who reported a dissatisfying marital relationship, only 14 percent reported experiencing a good or very good sexual relationship.

Within every marriage there are really two marriages: his and hers (Bernard, 1972). The interrelationships of sexual and marital satisfaction is somewhat different for wives and husbands (Udry, 1968). Sexual dissatisfaction in marriage is more likely to reduce a husband's level of overall marital satisfaction than that of a wife. On the other hand, a wife's sexual responsiveness is much more dependent upon her overall marital satisfaction than is that of a husband. This distinction is a consequence of the different meanings which men and women attribute to sex and to marriage (Udry, 1968).

Men usually hold higher expectations for sexual pleasure in marriage than do women. Women, in turn, expect a satisfying sexual relationship to flow from an emotionally gratifying marital relationship. Sexual gratification is more closely associated with men's self-esteem than women's self-esteem. Therefore, the sexual responsiveness of a man's partner is likely to be taken by the man as a confirmation of his self-worth. Yet a woman's sexual responsiveness is more likely than that of a man to be depressed by marital dissatisfaction.

In summary, husbands and wives both desire sexual satisfaction within an enjoyable marital relationship. But, the direction of interrelationship tends to be different for the two sexes. The following diagram illustrates this distinction (from Udry, 1968). To understand sexual satisfaction in marriage it is necessary to understand what contributes to marital satisfaction.

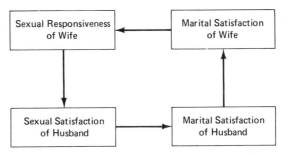

(The arrows indicate the direction of major effect.)

A couple's level of sexual satisfaction is often a sensitive indicator of their level of satisfaction with other, less obvious aspects of their relationship. Frequent arguments between spouses diminish their mutual desire for sexual intercourse. One study of 27 married couples, for example, found that the frequency of a couple's arguments was directly correlated with their frequency of intercourse (Howard and Dawes, 1967). Another research project investigated married people's reasons for abstaining from sexual intercourse in a sample of 144 men and 221 women who had been married an average of eleven years (Edwards and Booth, 1976b). The most common reason offered for abstaining from sexual intercourse was marital discord.

Marriage counselors report that sexual problems are one of the most troublesome areas in marital relations among the couples who seek their professional help (Gochros, 1972; DeBurger, 1975). Knowledge gained from scientific investigations of marital sexual interaction can be very helpful in counseling troubled married couples.

the transition to sexual cohabitation

Studies of sexual satisfaction over the life-cycle have found that most married couples report their highest level of sexual satisfaction during their early years together (Burr, 1970). Nevertheless, during the early years young couples also report more disagreement in the sexual area of marriage than any other area (Landis and Landis, 1973). The explanation of this curious paradox is unclear. Most probably, the novelty of a newly evolving sexual relationship intensifies enthusiasm for sexual activity before routine erodes that emotional satisfaction. Also, during the early years of marriage, couples have more companionship and privacy than after children arrive. Yet at the same time many young couples must deal with unanticipated sexual problems.

The beginning of sexual cohabitation requires an adaptation to sexual activity as an aspect of an intimate relationship. It is usually the interpersonal aspects of sexuality which are most troublesome for newlyweds. They may have difficulties in communicating about their sexual preferences or conflict over their sexual expectations of each other. They may have sexual anxieties which interfere with a mutually pleasurable pacing of their sexual activity. They may get caught up in the dilemmas of sexual bargaining. When their sexual interaction becomes more and more routine, they must then deal with the dilemma of balancing familiarity with new experience to avoid sexual boredom.

There have been few research investigations of the honeymoon period. One study investigated the honeymoon vacation experience of a small sample of recently married college students, few of whom had much previous sexual experience (Rapoport and Rapoport, 1964). The couples reported considerable anxiety about their ability to deal with sexual activity in an intimate relationship. The new husbands and wives both worried about their ability to satisfy their partners and to establish a mutually agreeable sexual relationship.

An study of the sexual behavior of young adults in England sheds some light on the particular sexual difficulties which are most commonly experienced during early marriage (Schofield, 1973). About 25 percent of the people studied said that they experienced some distinct kind of sexual problem in early marriage. The range of problems included: anxieties over sexual performance, feelings of having sexual intercourse too infrequently, a loss of interest in sexual activity, guilt about unfamiliar sexual practices, difficulties in finding mutually satisfying sexual preferences, fears about pregnancy, and difficulties finding a mutually acceptable contraceptive method.

Some couples make the transition to sexual cohabitation before getting married. One study of college students who were living in premarital cohabitation found that most of them reported experiencing some form of sexual difficulty in their relationship (Macklin, 1972). These included differences in sexual interest, lack of orgasm, fear of pregnancy, sexual inhibitions, and occasional impotence.

Premarital intercourse and marital satisfaction.   Any possible long-range effect of premarital sexual experience upon the marital relationship is quite controversial because of widespread social conflict over premarital sex in American society. It should not be surprising then that even the opinions of scholars who have studied the question are contradictory. Curiously, the social issue usually focuses upon women's premarital experience rather than men's. This is a reflection of the double standard which regards wide sexual experience to be taboo for women, but useful for men's sexual adjustment in marriage.

An important study of sexual adjustment during the first two weeks of marriage compared the experience of wives who had premarital intercourse with those who were virgins before their marriage (Kanin and Howard, 1958). The research questioned 177 wives of college students. The women who had premarital intercourse reported greater sexual satisfaction on their wedding night and the following two weeks than did the virginal brides. The sexual experience of the wedding night was found to be satisfying by about 71 percent of the premaritally experienced wives but only 47 percent of the virginal wives. Satisfaction with the sexual aspect of marriage during the first two weeks was reported by 92 percent of the premaritally experienced wives, but only 76 percent of those wives who did not have premarital intercourse. This research indicates that wives who begin having sexual intercourse with their husbands previous to marriage find it easier to cope with the transition to sexual cohabitation. Perhaps this is simply because sexually experienced persons have had more time to learn how to deal with the difficulties of sexual intimacy.

One research project studied couples who had been married twenty years (Ard, 1974). It found that the vast majority of both premaritally experienced and inexperienced spouses reported no unfavorable effect of their premarital sexual history. It appears that married people can easily justify their own premarital experience or virginity.

Research concerning the relationship between premarital virginity and marital satisfaction indicates that slightly more women (but not men) who were virgins at marriage report being satisfied with their marriage (Locke, 1951; Burgess and Wallin, 1953). Yet other research has found that fewer such women experience orgasm in their marital sexual activity (Kinsey et al., 1953; Kanin and Howard, 1958).

In balance, the available evidence appears to indicate that the timing of initial sexual intercourse, whether before or after marriage, has no general effect upon the evolution of marital and sexual adjustment. What may matter most for future marital and sexual satisfaction is the quality of a couple's interpersonal relationship and whether their sexual attitudes are mutually agreeable.

parenthood and sexual interaction

The transition to parenthood.   The initial cohabitation period with its intense companionship is very short for many couples. Just as they are in the process of adapting to one set of changes, they encounter another. According to census figures, the average length of time between a couple's wedding and the birth of their first child is currently only about one and one-half years (Glick, 1977). The early period of marriage is a matter of mere months, rather than years, for a great number of Americans. According to a Census Bureau study done in 1971, about 20 percent of white women and 58 percent of black women conceived their first child before they were maried, (Norton and Glick, 1976). Before they are able to work out solutions to many early interpersonal difficulties, a great many young couples must encounter the additional challenges of parenthood.

After the birth of the first child, marital and sexual difficulties are found to be most common among couples: (1) who previously had low marital satisfaction; and (2) who experience an unplanned pregnancy (Russell, 1974). The first child is often unplanned when there is lack of birth control or faulty contraception. This unanticipated event frequently causes wives to fear another unwanted pregnancy. Fear of an unwanted pregnancy usually inhibits a wife's desire for sexual intercourse and is found to contribute significantly to sexual dissatisfaction (Landis et al., 1950).

Contrary to traditional belief, the arrival of children does not change an unhappy marriage into a satisfying one. Instead, the satisfaction of raising children is often the only reason why unhappily married couples stay married (Luckey and Bain, 1970).

Wives experience significantly more difficulties and stress during the transition to parenthood than do husbands (Hobbs and Cole, 1976). Wives are likely to be very much concerned about possible changes in their physical attractiveness (Russell, 1974). The extra work in caring for the baby causes many wives to feel tired and irritable. A great many wives also complain about being neglected by their husbands, because of a sudden reduction in marital companionship activities (Ryder, 1973). Husbands and wives may both experience increased financial worries (Hobbs and Cole, 1976).

In the past, new parents lived near their own parents and relatives, who would help lighten their work load. Today, a couple is likely to be isolated from their relatives by distance. Employment may take one parent away from home leaving the other to care for preschool children alone. The situation causes many young parents, especially mothers, to feel exhausted, depressed, and in desperate need of emotinal support (Rossi, 1968).

Young parents with their first child report less marital satisfaction than do similar couples without children, according to a ten-year series of research projects (Feldman and Feldman, 1977). The main factor reducing a couple's level of marital satisfaction is the rapid reduction in companionship (Miller, 1976). One type of companionship activity which is likely to be reduced by the fatigue and distraction of infant care is marital sexual activity. Among couples with an infant, more husbands report being sexually dissatisfied and more wives report concerns about their sexual relationship than among couples who do not have children (Feldman and Feldman, 1977).

There are many gratifications, of course, that may be found in parenthood. These include an enjoyment in seeing the infant's development and play, a new pride in performing parental roles, and a new focus of conversation (Russell, 1974). The vast majority of married couples probably experience only slight to moderate difficulties during the transition to parenthood (Russell, 1974; Hobbs and Cole, 1976). However, most family life-cycle research does indicate that the difficulty and stress increase with the passing of time and the arrival of more children.

Children and marital sexual interaction.   There has been a tremendous amount of research about the effects of parents upon the behavior of their children. Curiously, however, there has been practically no research into the effects of children upon their parents' behavior. We still know very little about how children affect sexual interaction between their parents. However, a few available pieces of the puzzle offer at least part of the picture.

Many studies of marital satisfaction have found that satisfaction declines with the number of children present, at least for the average family (Figley, 1973; Miller, 1976; Feldman and Feldman, 1977). This may come as a surprise in the light of the popular belief that a happy marriage and children go together. Nevertheless, one study of 2480 couples from ages 20 to over 65 found clear evidence that couples without children report higher marital satisfaction than do couples who are raising children, at all durations of marriage (Renne, 1976). The sample included young couples who had not yet had children, older childless couples, older couples who were formerly parents, and couples who were currently raising children. Among couples without children, 45 percent of both spouses agreed that their marriage was happy, but only 24 percent of child-rearing couples reported a similar agreement.

Certain factors may help to explain the common decline in marital satisfaction with the arrival of children. Recreational companionship activities are a major source of marital satisfaction for middle class couples. The frequency of such activities declines with the presence of children because of the increased expense of babysitters and the scarcity of time (Miller, 1976). The presence of children may also have the effect of reducing intimate self-disclosure between husband and wife and refocusing communication upon the lives of their children. An increasing number of children may give rise to more arguments over child-rearing. One study of a large number of married couples found that child discipline was the second most common area of dispute after sex (Landis and Landis, 1973).

A decline in the frequency of marital sexual activity begins during the first pregnancy (Solberg et al., 1973). Even before a child is born, the continuity of its parents' sexual relationship is interrupted by pregnancy. It is common for couples to abstain from sexual activity over the period from the last weeks of pregnancy through the first weeks after birth. Some couples continue to enjoy noncoital sexual activities during that time via manual and oral caressing. However, a great many couples do not do so. This means that during the transition to parenthood a young couple may experience two or three months of sexual abstinence. Following a period of rather frequent sexual activity during the newlywed period, the transition to parenthood can give rise to unanticipated marital stress. Afterward, while they have an infant in the house, many couples find their sexual activity diminished by fatigue in the evening and a crying baby at night.

There have been few studies of marital sexual satisfaction in relation to the number of children in a family. One relevant study was done with a very large representative sample of American married couples (James, 1974). It found that the frequency of sexual intercourse declines with the number of children in a

family. This is surprising because it is popularly assumed that parents of large families have more sexual activity. (However, more children may be a consequence of less contraception.) In reality, couples who are childless have the highest frequency of sexual intercourse (James, 1974). Their higher rate of sexual activity probably results from their greater companionship. In addition, since they have more privacy, childless couples can be more spontaneous in their sexual encounters. Their sexual activity need not be limited to evenings in bedrooms. They can respond directly to their feelings of affection and to desires of the moment, rather than having them programmed by the necessities of household matters.

marital roles and sexual interaction

Marital roles and sexual satisfaction.   Child-rearing is one of the central concerns of most married couples. Yet there are a great many other tasks necessary to maintain a family, from budgeting income to cooking food. Spouses work out various kinds of arrangements to handle these tasks. In organizing the relationship, they develop expectations for each other's behavior which are technically termed *marital roles*. Two basic patterns of marital roles are: (1) the traditional pattern; and (2) the companionship pattern. In reality, most American families follow a mixture of both, some being more traditional and others being more companionship-oriented.

The traditional pattern of marital roles is characterized by considerable segregation in the activities of husbands and wives. Husbands and wives expect each other to make different and separate contributions to the maintenance of the family. They believe that there are distinctly different kinds of "men's work" and "women's work." The husband is primarily expected to be the "breadwinner." A wife may seek employment only if her husband is unable to provide sufficient income. This is, then, generally regarded as an unfortunate circumstance. Wives are expected to be primarily mothers and housekeepers. Husbands are not expected to share in housekeeping and parental responsibilities except those which are distinctly sex-typed as being masculine. These may include mowing the lawn, making household repairs, and playing baseball with sons. Even the recreational activities and amusements of spouses are sex-typed and engaged in separately. In social gatherings, husbands and wives usually separate themselves into men's and women's groups for conversation.

The companionship pattern emphasizes a much greater sharing of activities and interests. Few activities are sex-typed as being distinctly feminine or masculine. Husbands are expected to participate in housekeeping and parental tasks. Such a sharing of tasks does not necessarily mean that both spouses engage in the same activity together at the same time. Instead, they usually divide up tasks within various areas of concern (such as house-cleaning, household repairs, consumer purchasing, budgeting, child care). A wife may seek employment for various reasons, including: (1) to pursue a career; (2) to obtain extra income; or

(3) for self-development. Husbands and wives expect each other to share interests and to engage in recreational activities together. In social gatherings, the women and men join together in conversation rather than segregating into groups of men and women.

These patterns of marital roles exert a significant influence upon sexual interaction. One major study of family life investigated the relationship between marital roles and the sexual interaction of husbands and wives in a sample of 137 middle- and lower-class couples (Rainwater, 1965). This research project was particularly important because it employed long interviews, rather than questionnaires. The interviews revealed that the interrelationship of marital roles and sexual interaction is very complex with many exceptions to general principles. Nevertheless, certain general findings stand out. When marital roles are highly segregated, spouses are much more likely to regard sexual activity as being a simple matter of physical relief, rather than an expression of emtional intimacy. In traditional marital relationships, a majority of spouses believe that the husband normally enjoys sexual intercourse much more than does the wife. Many of the wives complain that their husband is inconsiderate of their wishes for less sexual activity. On the other hand, many husbands misperceive their wife as not being interested in sexual activity.

In contrast, when spouses maintain the companionship pattern, a much greater proportion of them report a mutual enjoyment of sexual activity (Rainwater, 1965). The husband is much more likely to report that he is concerned about his wife's sexual satisfaction. The wives confirm the importance of their husband's greater concern and they are much more likely to report finding considerable pleasure in sexual activity.

In conclusion, it would appear that greater companionship in marriage promotes a greater mutuality of sexual enjoyment.

Many behavioral scientists believe that women who hold more modern gender role attitudes are also more likely to have a higher interest in sexual pleasure than are women who accept the traditional role. Some confirmation for this hypothesis comes from a large-scale nationally representative study of women's frequency of sexual intercourse in marriage (Westoff, 1974). It found that wives who agree with modern attitudes toward the female gender role also report significantly higher frequencies of sexual intercourse than do traditional wives. The research also found that employed wives had higher frequencies of intercourse than did wives who were not employed (Westoff, 1974).

Recent research has turned attention to the husband's work role and its effects upon marital and sexual satisfaction. Some men invest much more time and energy in their work role than do others. Many blue-collar husbands, for example, do much overtime work or work at two jobs. Most professional husbands frequently must take home work on evenings and weekends. How does a husband's work load time affect a couple's marital and sexual satisfaction? One research project investigated this question in a random sample of 390 couples living in Seattle (Clark et al. 1978). The research found that the amount of time a husband spent in work activity did not affect his wife's reports of marital and sexual satisfaction. Key factors in the relative satisfaction of the wives were the level of their husband's income and their level of expectation for their husband's marital contributions in housekeeping, recreation, and self-disclosure. Wives with high expectations and with low income tended to report greatest marital dissatisfaction.

The "depressed housewife" syndrome.   It is undeniable that millions of American women find that being a full-time housewife and mother is deeply rewarding (Lopata, 1971). Housewives who have satisfying relationships with their husbands, as well as nearby family and friends, are those who are most satisfied with their situation (Ferree, 1976). Yet, it is equally undeniable that millions of full-time housewives find the situation to be depressing (Radloff, 1975).

In recent years there has been a flurry of speculation, as well as some research, about "the depressed housewife syndrome." A thorough review of the research on depression found that women in all industrial societies have higher rates of depression than do men (Weissman and Klerman, 1977). There has been much speculation about the influence of female hormone cycles in depression. Yet an exclusively biological explanation for gender differences in depression does not fit the data. When never-married, single men and women are compared, it is bachelors and not spinsters who have higher rates of depression (Radloff, 1975; Weissman and Klerman, 1977). In contrast, married women have particularly high rates of depression in comparison to married men.

Some behavioral scientists have suggested that certain aspects of the traditional female gender role may promote depression in many women (Bernard, 1972; Grove and Tudor, 1973). The findings of a large-scale research project conducted by the National Institute of Mental Health offers some support for this possibility (Radloff, 1975). It found that the incidence of depression is significantly higher among housewives than it is among employed wives. Yet even employed wives are more likely to experience depression than are husbands. The male-female difference in rates of depression continues to be found even when married women are employed.

Perhaps the meanings people learn to attribute to their situations are the crucial factors in depression. In this relation, a key finding may be that unemployed husbands are the only category of husbands who have higher rates of depression than do wives (Radloff, 1975). An adequate explanation has not yet been developed to account for these gender differences in depression. Perhaps unemployed men are similar to many housewives in having learned to react to their situation with feelings of undesired dependence and helplessness. They see themselves as having no meaningful future.

Depression not only mutes a person's emotional responsiveness but also his or her sexual responsiveness. Most depressed men and women have little sexual desire (Mead, 1974). One study compared the marital relations of a sample of depressed wives with a sample of nondepressed wives (Bullock et al., 1972). It found that depression had a definite impact upon sexual interaction. The depressed wives continued to have sexual intercourse in response to their husband's initiative, but at a substantially reduced frequency. Even more significant was the finding that they experienced a marked disinterest in sexual activity and an inability to experience orgasm. The depressed wives experienced little enjoyment in sexual activity. Yet they continued to comply with their husband's requests partly as a result of guilt feelings. Most of the depressed wives were unable to communicate their sexual disinterest or even disgust in any direct manner to their husband. The depressed wives' sexual activity was not an expression of a desire for sexual intimacy. Instead, it was an outcome of feelings of helplessness and submissiveness. Their continuation of sexual intercourse aggravated feelings of resentment toward their husband. They usually expressed this hostility toward their husband in an indirect manner, through constant nagging and criticism.

Depression in men, in contrast to women, is much more likely to impair their ability to continue sexual intercourse. In addition to a marked reduction in sexual desire, depressed men usually experience considerable difficulty in achieving erection (Proctor, 1973; Mead, 1974). The elimination of depression, usually restores sexual enthusiasm in both men and women, if they have a satisfying marital relationship.

The research on gender roles, depression, and marital sexuality illustrates the necessity of understanding marital sexual interaction within a broad social context. Current changes in gender role expectations are now causing stresses and conflicts which may have been less common three generations ago.

THE POST-PARENTAL PERIOD

the transition to post-parental marriage

It appears that the speculation about the difficulty of parents in making the transition to an "empty nest" family has been incorrect (Troll, 1971). Quite to the contrary, recent family life-cycle research shows that the average married couple reported increased marital satisfaction after the last child had left home (Rollins and Feldman, 1977).

One study, for example, investigated the psychological well-being of 318 middle class women whose last child had graduated from high school from high school from two and one-half years to six months prior to the research (Harkins, 1978). It found that no significant indications of psychological distress had been experienced by these mothers as they made the transition to an "empty nest" family.

The post-parental period of marriage is happiest for those couples who have had a previously high level of marital satisfaction (Stinnett et al., 1970). Some couples, in contrast, may have only remained married because of satisfactions they derived from parenthood (Luckey and Bain, 1970). They are the couples most likely to experience increased marital dissatisfaction during the post-parental period. For most couples, the post-parental period is almost as satisfying as the newlywed period (Troll, 1971). One study of the marital relationships of a sample of 408 couples over the age of 60 found that over half of them regarded that time as being the happiest period in their marriage (Stinnett et al., 1972). These elderly couples reported that their companionship and self-disclosure were the most satisfying aspects of their relationship.

Among the elderly couples, marital satisfaction strengthens their personal morale (Stinnett et al., 1970). Indeed, some research offers evidence that having an intimate confidant helps to ward off feelings of depression which are common among elderly people in American society (Lowenthal and Haven, 1968). In this regard, it is interesting to note that men are much more exclusively dependent upon their wife as a confidant. Elderly women tend to have more diverse confidants, including their friends and children, in addition to their husband. This may be the reason why widowers suffer higher rates of depression than do widows (Lowenthal and Haven, 1968).

It is also interesting to note that married people, both male and female, have substantially lower death rates than do unmarried people (Martin, 1975). This lower rate even includes death from disease. Perhaps intimacy has survival value for the human species.

aging and marital sexual interaction

Traditional belief holds that sexual interest declines and disappears along with the passing of years. Mature adults of middle age are expected to have become bored with sexual activity. The elderly are widely regarded as being simply devoid of any sexual appetite (LaTorre and Kear, 1977). Indeed, sexual activity between elderly men and women is often considered a bit indecent. These erroneous beliefs are probably a consequence of the traditional association of sexual activity with procreation, rather than with affection and playfulness. Yet we are now on the verge of another major historical change affecting sexual behavior: redefining the elderly as sexual beings. It is part of a broader social change which recognizes the inherent sexuality of people from birth until death and places a positive value upon it.

One measure of the difficulty that this social change will encounter comes from a study of the beliefs of a sample of 646 college students about the sexual practices of their parents (Pocs and Godow, 1977). One-fourth of the students believed that their parents had stopped having sexual intercourse, even though their parents' ages ranged from only 41 to 50. Half of the students thought that their parents had sexual intercourse once per month or less. These young people had probably greatly underestimated their parents' sexual activity—probably as much as their parents underestimated their children's sexual involvement.

Although there has been a reasonable amount of research about the sexual behavior of middle aged and older people, little of it has concerned itself with interpersonal interaction. Therefore, we have come to know more about individual sexual behavior in the later years than we do about sexual interaction within a marital relationship. There is a particular lack of knowledge about the interrelationship of intimacy and sexual activity among middle aged and older people.

The best data about the age-related decreasing frequency of sexual intercourse comes from a recent large-scale research project investigating sexual behavior in a nationally representative sample of over 2000 adults (Wilson, 1975). It found that the frequency of sexual intercourse gradually decreases among people in their 40s and 50s, and then rapidly decreases among people over the age of 60. In this large sample, only 3 percent of men and 13 percent of women between the ages of 30 and 59 reported never having sexual intercourse. In contrast, after the age of 60, 25 percent of men and 50 percent of women reported such abstinence. In terms of high frequencies of intercourse, 14 percent of the men and 12 percent of the women between the ages of 30 and 59 reported having sexual intercourse more than twice per week. After the age of 60, only 3 percent of men and 11 percent of women reported having intercourse more than twice per week. Many smaller-scale studies of middle age and elderly people have had similar findings (Pfeiffer et al., 1972; Martin, 1975).

It is interesting to note that after the age of 60, not all people experience a decrease in their frequency of sexual activity. One study of sexual behavior in a sample of people ages 60 to 94 actually found that about 15 percent of the people reported increasing levels of sexual activity over a period of several years (Pfeiffer, 1969). The important point is that the vast majority of middle aged people are sexually active, as well as a great many of the elderly who still have a sexual partner. Indeed, one new program of sex therapy for the elderly (over age 60) markedly revived sexual interests and activity (Sviland, 1975).

Physiological changes.   An exclusively biological explanation does not appear to be adequate, to account for decreasing sexual activity with age. Neither can it explain individual differences in the frequency of such activity. A popular belief holds that as aging proceeds, declining levels of sex hormones directly cause a reduction of sexual activity. However, an extensive review of the relation between hormones and sexual activity found no substantial evidence to support that belief (Schiavi and White, 1976). There may be little prospect of finding a chemical fountain of sexual youth.

However, certain aspects of biological aging are definitely associated with decreasing sexual activity when interrelated with personal attitudes and interpersonal experience. These biological changes involve specific alterations in male and female genital anatomy and physiology. The biological effects of aging, in turn, can cause a decreased desire for sexual activity. This is especially likely to occur if modifications are not made in more youthful patterns of marital sexual interaction.

The changes which occur in men include: (1) sexual arousal is slower and erection is less rapid; (2) more direct stimulation to the penis is needed to maintain a firm erection; (3) erection can be maintained for a longer time before ejaculation; (4) when erection diminishes during extended foreplay, it may be difficult to return to full erection; (5) a prolonged refractory period, measured in hours, exists before another erection can occur; (6) fewer genital spasms occur during orgasm resulting in a shorter, less intense orgasm; and (7) a more diffuse, less genitally-centered sensation of pleasure occurs during orgasm (Masters and Johnson, 1968; Kaplan, 1974; Berman and Lief, 1976). These changes are not necessarily disadvantageous for pleasurable sexual relations. However, they are quite contrary to men's youthful expectations for a rapid and firm erection and intense orgasmic response. Therefore, these biological changes can easily arouse anxiety and disappointment in aging men. Usually, these changes occur very gradually in men during their 30s and 40s, and then more rapidly when men are in their 50s and 60s.

There are fewer and less pronounced changes in women's sexual functioning, even after menopause. These changes include: (1) a reduction in the amount and rapidity of vaginal lubrication; (2) a decrease of muscular elasticity in the vaginal walls; (3) occasional easy irritation of vaginal tissues because of insufficient lubrication and elasticity; and (4) a reduction in the number of vaginal and uterine spasms during orgasm resulting in a shorter, less intense orgasm (Masters and Johnson, 1966; Kaplan, 1974; Berman and Lief, 1976). The ability of women to experience multiple orgasms, however, remains unchanged with age. Although these biological changes are less contrary to women's youthful expectations than those of men, they still necessitate some interpersonal adjustment. Aging women have greater need for more direct stimulation than that obtained from purely genital contact. Aging women may also need to use an artificial lubricant during sexual intercourse.

Personal attitudes toward sexual aging.   Personal attitudes have a great influence upon the evolution of sexual responsiveness. If sexual activity is regarded as being merely a release of genital tension, then sexual activity may decline rapidly. In contrast, if sexual activity is regarded as a positive enjoyment of intimate relatedness, it is likely to be pursued in one form or another as long as a couple maintains good health. Chronic illness and depression quickly reduce the desire for sexual activity. Among some aging men, fear of having a heart attack during sexual intercourse inhibits sexual activity. However, this fear is usually quite unnecessary even for cardiac patients (Scheingold and Wagner, 1974). Many aging people hold myths which discourage their sexual activity by regarding it as being "immature" or "indecent." The belief that sexual desire evaporates with age also provides an excuse for people to abstain from sexual activity who have not enjoyed it during their earlier years. In essence, misfortunes of health and habit can conspire to diminish sexual desire over the years.

Interpersonal aspects. The traditional erotic roles of men and women also promote decreasing sexual activity. Traditionally woman's sexual behavior over the years becomes increasingly dependent upon the sexual initiative of her partner (Pfeiffer et al., 1972). Wives usually report that their reason for terminating sexual intercourse was their husband's lack of interest or sexual impotence, and husbands are found to agree with them. The traditional erotic role of men is assertive, while that of women is passively receptive. Women's sexual expression is essentially reactive to male initiative. Consequently, when a man's sexual initiative begins to diminish over the years, so does the frequency of sexual activity in marriage.

Wives who have become accustomed to their husband's sexual initiative find it difficult to refocus their concern upon sexually stimulating their husband. Yet, as men become slower to respond to erection and develop a need for more direct stimulation, they become more dependent upon their wife's ability to be sexually assertive. If marital sexual interaction is to persist. It may be necessary for aging wives to gradually take a more assertive erotic role than that for which past tradition has prepared them (Cleveland, 1976). Yet that seems to be unlikely to occur. The average aging woman loses her interest in sexual activity earlier and more rapidly than does the average aging man (Pfeiffer et al., 1972).

Married couples who continue their sexual activity through the years are most likely to be those who enjoyed each other sexually during their earlier years together (Pfeiffer and Davis, 1972). Aside from good health, previous sexual enjoyment probably contributes more toward the persistence of marital sexual interaction than any other factor.

As persons age, they can adjust their sexual interaction to the physiological changes they experience if they are able to communicate easily about sexual matters. Aging transforms the nature of sexual interaction. Enjoyable marital sexual interaction becomes increasingly less dependent upon the experience of a powerful sexual orgasm. Instead, an adequate adjustment to the physiological changes of aging depends upon an ability to enjoy a broader tactile sensuality in a relationship of affection and care (Cleveland, 1976). Pleasurable sexual interaction among the elderly is more a matter of enjoying erotic playfulness, than the build-up and release of strong bodily tensions. Among the elderly, an expectation for orgasm on every occasion of sexual activity may actually inhibit a couple's enjoyment of each other (Cleveland, 1976). In a sense, it might be best to regard sexual aging as a transformation of a more youthful form of sexuality rather than a decline or end of sexual enjoyment.

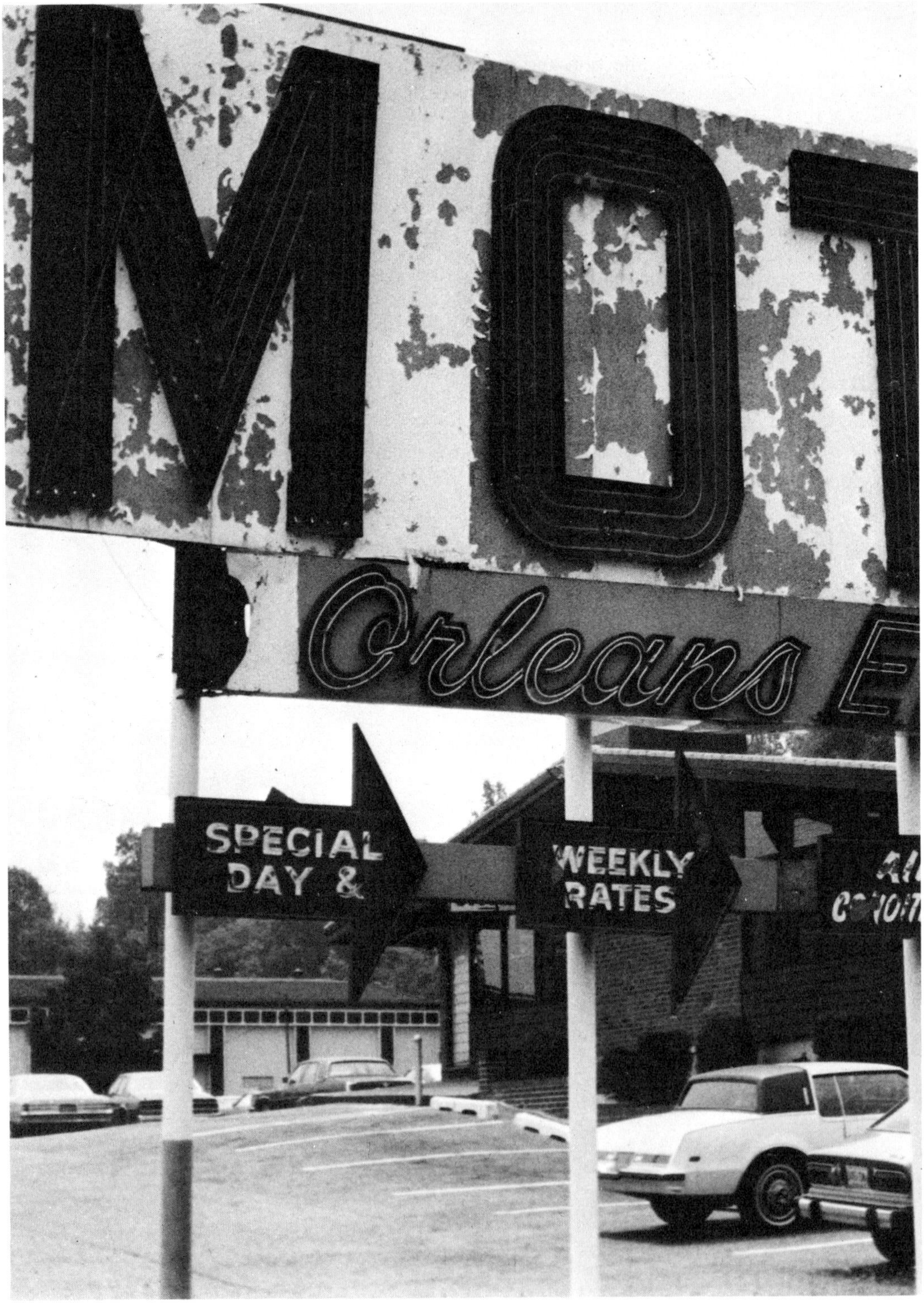
Orleans
SPECIAL DAY &
WEEKLY RATES

Extramarital sexual interaction involves sexual intercourse or other erotic activities between two people, at least one of whom is married to someone else. This particular aspect of human sexuality has been the subject of innumerable novels, films, theatre dramas, operas, and soap operas. There has probably been more speculation and less adequate research about extramarital sex than about any other facet of human sexuality.

Most of the serious writing about extramarital sex is either condemnatory moralizing or favorable radical argumentation. Such writings are filled with terms like "healthy-unhealthy," "normal-abnormal," and "mature-immature," all of which reveal approving or disapproving evaluations. They are employed equally adeptly by writers of all persuasions. This chapter will try to steer clear of such argumentation and simply explore the available research findings.

Two basic forms of extramarital sex may be distinguished: (1) secretive; and (2) consensual. In comparison, secretive extramarital sex is far more common. It may involve sexual activity with prostitutes, or in isolated sexual encounters, or in conventional love "affairs." Consensual extramarital sex, in contrast, involves some kind of agreement between spouses—either tacit or candid—permitting each other to engage in extramarital sexual involvement. It may involve an "open marriage" agreement, mate-swapping, or group marriage. In this chapter the more common type of extramarital sex, the secretive type, will be examined.

14 extramarital sexual interaction

ATTITUDES TOWARD EXTRAMARITAL SEX

A well-respected national survey conducted by the Institute for Sex Research of Indiana University investigated the public attitudes of Americans toward various forms of sexual behavior (Levitt and Klassen, 1973). It found that about 72 percent of Americans regard extramarital sex as being "always wrong" and another 14 percent regard it as "almost always wrong." Only about 11 percent of Americans regard it to be "wrong only sometimes." Yet it is a striking curiosity that many people who publicly condemn extramarital sex also experience it. There is a wide gap between public attitudes and private practice in this area.

The research into public attitudes toward extramarital sex really doesn't tell us much about personal attitudes. Several studies have asked samples of married couples whether or not they have ever had passing desires for sexual intercourse with someone other than their spouse (Locke, 1951; R. Johnson, 1970). These studies have found that about half of married men, but only 3 to 4 percent of married women admit to having sexual fantasies about extramarital sex. It is likely that women are more guilt ridden about adulterous sexual fantasies than are men. When asked if they believe that most (other) women have "desires" for sexual intercourse with someone other than their husband, the results are more revealing. The percentage of women who believe other women have such "desires" is much greater than the percentage who will admit to their own extramarital fantasies (R. Johnson, 1970).

personal reasons for avoiding extramarital sex

Whatever proportion of people have fleeting daydreams about sexual experience outside of marriage, relatively few people act them out. Why do people avoid extramarital sex in a society where there seems to be ample opportunity? One national survey asked its respondents why they had avoided involvement in extramarital sex (Hunt, 1974). The most common response was the feeling that it is wrong for religious or moral reasons. A closer examination of this expressed attitude suggests that the moral reservations were held as personal ethics, rather than as part of a formal religious code. Simply put, a great many people feel that extramarital sex is a betrayal of trust in a love relationship. The immediacy of an intimate relationship may be a much greater constraining force than religious morality, in most people's attitudes toward adultery. Many people in the study expressed concern about hurting their spouse, or damaging their marital relationship (Hunt, 1974).

Another study of 6000 men who were business executives found that only a small proportion said that lack of opportunity was a reason why they did not become involved in extramarital affairs (J. Johnson, 1974). Most of the respondents who avoided extramarital sexual involvement said that "moral scruples" or "no desire" was the reason. One other study investigated attitudes of people who did not become involved in extramarital sex (Sprey, 1972). Besides moral values and lack of opportunity, many people expressed the feeling that they had little to gain from such activity, considering the time, money, and attention it would require.

In summary, the personal attitudes of the majority of people who disapprove of extramarital sex are shaped by the contraints of ethical values concerned with intimate relations, as well as calculations of emotional costs. In American society, there may be ample opportunities for extramarital sex, yet relatively few people are willing to pursue them. Those who do pursue them believe that the possible emotional benefits outweigh the costs and they are able to find psychological justifications which allay guilt feelings.

personal reasons for seeking extramarital sex

There have been few careful and systematic research studies of the reasons people offer for their involvement in extramarital sex. Kinsey (1953) summarized the explanations offered by the women his staff interviewed, who had extramarital sexual experience. Their expressed motivations included: (1) curiosity, or the desire of new sexual and emotional experience; (2) the desire to make advantageous social contacts to improve their status; (3) the desire to retaliate for their husband's extramarital involvement or some other form of perceived mistreatment; (4) the desire to express a sense of independence from their husband; (5) the desire for affection; and (6) the desire to please their husband who had encouraged their extramarital sexual involvement.

In the previously mentioned study of business executives, the approximately 1000 men who admitted having affairs were questioned about their reasons for pursuing extramarital sex (H. Johnson, 1974). Their most common expressed motivations included: (1) the desire for new sexual experience; (2) the erotic attraction to a woman whom they previously had known socially; and (3) the desire for sexual and/or emotional satisfactions which they could not obtain from their wives.

The most important principle that can be drawn from the foregoing research is that people who get involved in extramarital sexual relationships do so in pursuit of widely differing goals. In other words, there is no single motive for extramarital sex. (Just as there exists no single motive for premarital or marital sex.) Individuals involved in extramarital sex seek multiple goals.

There may be very little rapport between the personal goals of extramarital sexual partners. Extramarital erotic role relations usually must be spontaneously fabricated. As a result, sexual partners may be quite unsure about what to expect from each other. They may as easily find affection or exploitation, tender concern or abusive treatment, appreciation or blackmail.

THE INCIDENCE OF EXTRAMARITAL SEX

male-female comparisons

Kinsey's research found that at least one experience of extramarital sexual intercourse was reported by 26 percent of women and by about 50 percent of men by the time they reached the age of 40 (Kinsey et al., 1953). A more recent national sex survey found that in the age group of 35 to 44, the incidence of extramarital sex was 18 percent for women and 47 percent for men (Hunt, 1974). However, one questionnaire survey of 100,000 women found that about 40 percent admitted having extramarital sex by age 40 (Travis and Sadd, 1977).

The major change since Kinsey's research has been an increase in extramarital sex among young women. Kinsey found that only about 8 percent of married women under 25 years of age had extramarital sex; but about 24 percent did so by that age in 1974 (Hunt, 1974). Other research also has found a similarly increased incidence of extramarital sex among young women (Bell et al., 1975; Travis and Sadd, 1977). So far, there is no evidence that the incidence of extramarital sex among men is increasing. It appears that the incidence of male and female extramarital sex is converging among the youngest generation of Americans. Many sociologists now predict that the incidence of male and female extramarital sex will become equal as younger American women reach middle age. It is likely that in a decade or two about half of all married people will have experienced extramarital sex.

The reported incidence of extramarital sexual intercourse does not indicate anything about the number of partners with whom people have such experience. The available research indicates that most people who have extramarital sexual experience limit that experience to a few sexual partners over their lifetime. Only a small proportion of married people have many extramarital sexual encounters with many partners.

Adequate data about the number of extramarital sexual partners is available only for women. Among women with extramarital experience, Kinsey's research found that 41 percent limited that experience to only one partner (Kinsey et al., 1953). Another 40 percent of the experienced women had extramarital sex with two to five partners, and the remainder had six or more partners. The *Redbook* magazine survey found that among wives who had extramarital sex, 50 percent of the women had only one partner and another 40 percent had two to five partners (Travis and Sadd, 1977). Other recent national research has had similar findings (Hunt, 1974; Bell and Peltz, 1974).

The number of partners with whom men have had extramarital sexual intercourse is probably somewhat greater because of the experience of some men with prostitutes. Kinsey found that between 8 percent and 15 percent of men's extramarital intercourse was with prostitutes (Kinsey et al., 1948).

There is not much adequate data about the frequency of extramarital intercourse, whether the activity involves transient sexual encounters or affairs which last over some period of time. One careful research study of 588 wives who had extramarital sexual experience found that their average frequency of intercourse with each extramarital partner was six times (Bell et al., 1975). One-third of the wives had extramarital intercourse more than ten times with a partner, while 16 percent limited themselves to only one occasion. The *Redbook* magazine survey had similar findings (Travis and Sadd, 1977). Thus, it appears that for women, short-term extramarital affairs are more common than are isolated sexual encounters. Comparable data for men is not yet available.

cross-cultural comparisons

Cross-cultural data about extramarital sexual relations offer us valuable insight into its social significance within American society. Unfortunately, few behavioral scientists in other nations have been able to carry out large-scale studies of sexual behavior mainly because of the problems of financing such research. One thing that the cross-cultural information makes clear is that the nature of extramarital sex differs depending upon the culture of a society.

France is a society which has produced a great many novels and motion pictures concerned with the theme of affairs. In America, it is widely believed that most Frenchmen have a mistress who happens to be someone else's wife. However, the available research indicates that extramarital sex is less common in France than it is in the United States.

A national sex survey was conducted in France by the French Institute of Public Opinion under the direction of a team of sociologists and medical doctors (Simon et al., 1972). It found that 10 percent of French women and 30 percent of French men admitted having extramarital sexual experience. (These incidence figures are probably somewhat low because of the under-reporting of extramarital sex caused by poor research methodology.) More important, the research found that an increasing proportion of younger French women admitted having extramarital sex. The increasing extramarital experience among young women converging with the incidence among men is similar to the situation occurring in the United States.

The culture of France is much more similar to American society than is that of Japan. Japan is a distinctly male-dominated society. It is also not influenced by the Christian moral ideal prohibiting extramarital sex. In the past, Japanese men maintained a right to have extramarital sex with different kinds of prostitutes without any necessity for secrecy (Iga, 1968; Asayama, 1975). In contrast, extramarital sex on the part of a wife was a crime and was socially regarded to be a grave moral offense. (In many ways, these Japanese sexual patterns are similar to those found in the Southern European societies of Spain, Italy, and Greece.) Contemporary research data from Japan indicate a persistence of these male-female differences in extramarital sex (Asayama, 1975). Among Japanese men, between 60 percent to 75 percent experience extramarital intercourse in contrast with an incidence of only 4 percent to 5 percent among Japanese women. When Japanese women do become involved in affairs they are much more likely than are American women to become involved in a very lengthy love affair (Maykovich, 1976).

These cross-cultural data suggest certain conclusions. Male dominance in a society results in the open, or tacit, acceptance of extramarital sex for men, but a strong moral condemnation of it for women. The increasing social equality of women will provide increased opportunities for women to experience extramarital sex and may lead to an increased incidence of female extramarital sexual experience.

SECRETIVE EXTRAMARITAL SEX

marital relations and extramarital sex

In a sense, every occasion of extramarital sex involves at least three people, and usually four. This perspective is simply a way of pointing out that an understanding of extramarital sex must encompass the marital relationship of individuals who have such experiences. The marital relationship both effects and is affected by extramarital sexual involvement. Rarely is it irrelevant.

Some research (Cuber and Harroff, 1965; Cuber, 1969) suggests that specific patterns of extramarital sexual interaction reflect specific patterns of marital interaction: (1) in conflict-ridden marriages, for example, extramarital sex is often an expression of hostility and resentment; (2) in marriages characterized by emotional apathy and indifference, extramarital sex is frequently a means of dealing with boredom and lack of affection; (3) in some marriages, sexual interaction may be rare or even absent although the overall marital relationship may be satisfying in other ways. (In such cases, one spouse may not desire any sexual activity or may be chronically ill; or one spouse may be constantly traveling for business reasons.) In sexually deficient, but otherwise satisfying marriages, extramarital sex may compliment the marital relationship, often with an explicit agreement about such an arrangement. It is likely to involve extramarital sex in the form of brief sexual encounters, rather than love affairs, on the part of one spouse; (4) in some rare marriages, couples may have a satisfying relationship, but consent to extramarital sexual involvement as an aspect of their relationship itself. These are very unconventional couples, who have an open marriage agreement or are involved in mate-swapping as a form of marital recreation. The basic point is that there is no one simple cause and effect relationship between marital relations and extramarital sex.

Marital dissatisfaction. A substantial amount of research evidence confirms the widespread belief that marital dissatisfaction is the most common factor in American society which promotes extramarital sexual involvement (Travis and Sadd, 1977; Bell et al., 1975; Edwards and Booth, 1976a). These research projects have found that people who report having had extramarital sex are much more likely to report being dissatisfied with their marriages than are people who report having had no extramarital sexual experience.

One study of 2262 married women, for example, found that 55 percent of the wives who rated their marriages as being "poor or very poor" had extramarital intercourse. This compared with only 20 percent of the wives who rated their marriages as being "very good" (Bell et al., 1975). A surprising exception to the general principle is that a sizable proportion of happily married women have extramarital sex. The *Redbook* magazine survey of 100,000 women also found that about 20 percent of wives who rated their marriages as being "very good" had extramarital sexual experience (Travis and Sadd, 1977). According to some research, happily married women who have extramarital sex tend to be less religious, and more sexually experimental, than are happily married women who do not have extramarital sex (Bell et al., 1976).

Some case studies of the positive contributions of extramarital sex to marital satisfaction have been reported by a few marriage counselors (Myers and Leggitt, 1975). In some cases, secretive extramarital sexual involvement may provide a source of affection or sexual pleasure for people who are unable to find these satisfactions with their spouse, yet do not want a divorce.

It is likely that much extramarital sex is a result of people's disillusionment with the affectional and sexual aspects of marriage. Many people find their marital relations less romantic and passionate than they have expected in their youth. Feelings of disappointment and boredom may lead them to test whether or not pastures are greener somewhere else.

Sexual dissatisfaction.   The available research indicates that dissatisfaction with marital sexual relations is a major factor promoting extramarital sexual involvement among husbands (R. Johnson, 1970; H. Johnson, 1974). In contrast, sexual dissatisfaction is less likely to promote extramarital sex among traditionalist women. Yet, among younger, modernist women who have a high interest in sexual pleasure, marital sexual dissatisfaction is associated with higher rates of extramarital sex (Bell et al., 1975).

Some research has also found that women who have premarital sexual intercourse are more likely to have extramarital intercourse, especially if they become sexually involved at an early age and have experience with many partners (Kinsey et al., 1953; Travis and Sadd, 1977). The cause and effect relationship is not clear. Perhaps, the wide premarital sexual experience of some women (and men) causes them to be less tolerant of minor sexual problems in marriage. They may make comparisons between their mate and others leading to a belief that the "grass is greener" somewhere else.

Marital conflict.   There is a two-way relationship between extramarital sex and marital conflict. Marital conflict can contribute to marital and sexual dissatisfaction, thereby promoting extramarital sexual involvement. On the other hand, extramarital sex can provoke and intensify marital conflict in a previously satisfying marriage, thereby creating marital dissatisfaction.

Frequent arguments between spouses diminish their mutual desire for sexual intercourse (Howard and Dawes, 1976). In turn, infrequent intercourse between spouses may increase their likelihood of having extramarital sex. One study of about 500 married men and women found that infrequent marital intercourse was associated with higher frequencies of extramarital sexual involvement (Edwards and Booth, 1976a).

There is little adequate research which has investigated extramarital sex as a special source of marital conflict. There is some research into the marital conflicts of couples seeking divorce, which has found adultery to be a commonly expressed issue of contention (Weiss, 1975). However, it is unclear whether extramarital sex is a mere catalyst for underlying conflict. In some states, adultery is still one of the few legal grounds for divorce. Therefore, the actual role of extramarital sex in divorce is not easily known. It is estimated that in 15 percent to 35 percent of divorce cases, extramarital sex is a major precipitating conflict (Levinger, 1976).

Divorced people are much more likely to have had extramarital sexual experience than are people who remain married. One study of several hundred divorced women found that 31 percent of them had extramarital sexual relations during their last year of marriage (Gebhard, 1970). A broader, national sex survey found that 52 percent of divorced women had extramarital intercourse, in contrast with only 17 percent of women who were married (Hunt, 1974). These data do not confirm the belief that extramarital sex is a major cause of disruptive marital conflict, but they do indicate that the proposition must be taken seriously.

Marriage counselors disagree sharply about the effects of extramarital sex upon marital relationships (Mead et al., 1975). They report that in some cases, the discovery that one spouse has been involved in extramarital sex doesn't produce marital conflict. However, feelings of distrust, jealousy, and guilt are probably more common. Single, isolated sexual encounters are less likely to be perceived as a threat to marriage than are prolonged extramarital love affairs. But, even in cases of isolated sexual encounters, some spouses feel that they have been deceived and their trust betrayed. Many husbands and wives feel that such incidents are a symbolic insult to their affectional and sexual adequacy as a mate.

In some cases, the revelation of adultery doesn't produce immediately expressed conflict. Instead, it becomes a lingering source of repressed conflict and anxiety. The spouse who has had extramarital experience may use the possibility of its repetition as an implied threat in marital negotiations, while the other spouse may use it as a reproach.

Personal values. Religious morality constrains many maritally dissatisfied people who might otherwise seek extramarital affairs. Some research has found that people who consider themselves to be religiously devout are much less likely to have any extramarital sexual experience than are the religiously inactive

(Kinsey et al., 1948, 1953; Travis, and Sadd, 1977). In addition, the interpersonal ethic of intimate trust may be a major constraining force in cases where there is only moderate marital dissatisfaction (Hunt, 1974).

There is not much adequate research concerning possible guilt feelings in response to extramarital involvement. One study of a large number of wealthy Americans who had extramarital sexual experience found that most of them expressed feelings of regret, but not guilt, about their involvements (Cuber, 1969). A national sex survey which interviewed many people about their extramarital experience found that feelings of guilt and fear of discovery were common initial reactions (Hunt, 1974). However, most people who continued their extramarital sexual activities soon developed rationalizations to justify their involvement and ease their guilt feelings. Fear of discovery and public shame may play a greater role than guilt in discouraging persistent adultery.

Opportunity. In relation to marriage, the structure of opportunities for extramarital sex is also an important consideration. Marital relationships usually take place within a routine schedule of activities. Secretive extramarital sex usually necessitates some deviation from the routine schedule of events by one spouse. This creates suspicions about unusual preoccupations on the part of the other spouse. Opportunities for extramarital sexual activity which do not cause deviations from marital routine are structured into the lifestyles of some people more than others. Traveling executives and salespeople, for example, have greater such opportunities than do people who work a regular schedule close to home. In some big business circles, prostitutes are commonly employed as a technique of sales promotion (Cuber and Harroff, 1965; H. Johnson, 1974). When there is social encouragement and easy opportunity, the temptation for transient sexual encounters may be indulged, even by happily married men and women.

Evidence for the important effects of differential opportunities for extramarital sex can be found in a comparison between full-time housewives and employed wives. One study of 100,000 women who answered a sex questionnaire for *Redbook* magazine found that almost half (47 percent) of the employed wives had extramarital intercourse, in comparison with 27 percent of full-time housewives in the age group of 35 to 39 years (Travis and Sadd, 1977). Thus, it interesting to note that the incidence of extramarital sex among employed women is about the same as it is among men (most of whom are employed).

extramarital relationships

Social interaction.   There are a great variety of social relationships which lead to extramarital sexual involvement. They vary from momentary sexual encounters with prostitutes to long lasting affairs between lovers. Other than prostitution, none of them has received much research attention.

Bars are common meeting places for obtaining transient extramarital sexual partners (Roebuck and Spray, 1967). These encounters usually involve married men with single or divorced women who frequent the bars. The sexual activity which takes place, usually at motels, is the essential expectation of such relationships. Usually, such sexual encounters do not develop into love affairs, primarily because the men involved desire sexual activity without emotional attachment.

Another location where such transient extramarital sex takes place is at conventions. The men and women involved in short sexual encounters usually do not have to fear discovery by acquaintances. In such cases, the people involved are usually both married and do not desire any lasting entanglements.

More long lasting affairs often develop out of the relationships between co-workers in factories and offices. In some work places, extramarital affairs are relatively common, while at other places they are cautiously avoided. The people having extramarital affairs usually work in close association, on factory work teams, or in the same office (Roy, 1974; H. Johnson, 1974). Their sexual activity is limited by their work and home schedules. It usually has to take place in a rush, after work hours, without overly delaying their arrival home. This form of extramarital involvement is often the subject of gossip at the work place, and it is rather easily detected by suspicious spouses. Coworker affairs are not easily terminated, on the other hand, because of the work association of those having an affair.

Long-lasting affairs outside of work relationships are probably most common among people of considerable wealth (Cuber, 1969). Such extramarital sex usually involves two married people who wish to avoid divorce. They may prefer such an arrangement to avoid the stigma of divorce, or to maintain their parental roles. Very often the spouses of those having a long-term affair realize what is happening. However, they avoid dispute about it because they may also be involved in affairs. In a sense, such couples have an implicit "open marriage" without any explicit agreement. The marriages may be empty-shell marriages, devoid of emotional attachment, or they may simply be comfortable alliances of convenience. The lovers' relationship may be centered upon sexual activity, but sometimes it involves a genuine love relationship.

Sexual interaction. There is some evidence that extramarital sex is usually quite inhibited by the circumstances in which it occurs. The available research indicates that on the average, extramarital sex is less varied and is experienced with less emotional satisfaction than is marital sexual interaction.

One national sex survey investigated the variety of sexual activities engaged in by people who have extramarital sexual experience (Hunt, 1974). Most unconventional sexual positions, such as the female-above and rear-entry positions were reported to be less commonly used in extramarital sex than in marital sex. In addition, women experience orgasm less frequently in extramarital sex than is the case in marital sex. In contrast with people's rating of their marital sex, fewer men and women report that their experience with extramarital sex had been "very pleasurable" (Hunt, 1974). The *Redbook* survey of 100,000 women had similar findings about extramarital sex (Travis and Sadd, 1977). Oral-genital sex, for example, was found to be much less common between extramarital partners than it was between husbands and wives.

The research seems to show that the secretiveness, fear of detection, frequent lack of adequate privacy, anxiety, and guilt feelings may serve to inhibit sexual responsiveness, especially in brief extramarital encounters. Consequently, most extramarital sex bears little resemblance to the passionate and romantic affairs often portrayed in Hollywood movies. It may also bear little resemblance to the sexual fantasies of people who might daydream about having an extramarital affair. Therefore, it should not be surprising that many men and women come away from an extramarital encounter with renewed feelings of appreciation for their marriage (Travis and Sadd, 1977).

part five

SEXUAL VARIANCE

the cultural relativity of deviant behavior

In every society, some patterns of sexual behavior are condemned as immoral, bizarre, unnatural, or dangerous. This is so, even though particular patterns of condemned sexual behavior differ from society to society. Behavior which is contrary to the dominant social rules in a society and is widely disapproved in that society is called *deviant behavior*. Sexual variance is only one form of deviant behavior. The examples which are given in this chapter deal with sexual behavior, but deviance may involve any rule breaking behavior from picking one's nose in public to murder. We will begin by exploring the basic concept of deviant behavior, and then focus upon sexual variance.

The concept of deviant behavior presented in this chapter was originally developed by sociologists (Clinard, 1974; Bell, 1976; Goode, 1978). Sociologists needed some way of understanding why certain behaviors are acceptable in one culture, whereas in other cultures the same behaviors are regarded as outrageously immoral. Why are some forms of behavior a matter of conformity in one society, while the same behavior is contrary to custom or the law in other societies? Mass murder is a good example. How could the mass murder of Jews be enforced in Nazi Germany; the mass murder of Armenians be approved in Turkey; or the slaughter of whole Indian tribes be accepted in the United States? The answer suggested by sociologists is that these mass murders were an expression of conformity, rather than rule breaking. Other, less shocking examples help to understand the sociological concept of deviance. Drinking alcoholic beverages

15 sexual variance

is conventional (conformist) behavior in many societies, yet in Saudi Arabia it would be severely punished according to the law of the land. Similarly, marijuana smoking is a conventional recreational practice in some societies, while in other societies it is severely condemned and punished. The sociological concept of deviance does not mean statistically unusual, perverted, or pathological.

The behavioral science perspective on deviant behavior recognizes the cultural relativity of rules for human behavior. This means that behavior which is seen as "deviant" differs over historical time, between societies, and even between groups within a large complex society such as our own. Whether or not any particular behavior is deviant is not a matter that any expert can decide. It is not a matter of expert judgment. Deviance is not a particular quality of behavior which may be discovered by an expert. Almost any behavior is deviant somewhere in the world. Even marital sexual intercourse can be deviant. The Shakers, according to their religious code, prohibited all sexual intercourse. Therefore, if one was a Shaker and had marital sex, one would be engaging in deviant sexual behavior.

This perspective on deviance is relative, rather than absolute. It recognizes that deviance cannot be defined in terms of any worldwide, unchanging qualities. Deviance and conformity can only be defined as a relationship between behavior and a group's reaction to it.

Early Americans would have certainly condemned sexual slavery, forced intercourse, and the breeding of people like cattle. They would have done so, that is, if the people involved were free white people, rather than enslaved black people. White slave owners did not define black people as people. Therefore, they tolerated or even encouraged sexual practices which they otherwise would have regarded as outrageously perverted.

Mate-swapping is strongly condemned in American society. Yet among mate-swappers, sexual behavior is simply conformity to group expectations, and people present at swinging sessions may experience subtle conformity pressures to participate. In a few tribal societies, wife lending is a hospitality custom, and a matter of conformity to rules for good manners toward male guests.

In many rural and tribal societies, sexual intercourse during menstruation is regarded as a dangerous offense against nature and the gods. People may be put to death for such an offense. In contrast, few Americans regard sexual intercourse during menstruation to be a grave, immoral perversion.

A common misunderstanding of the relative perspective on deviant behavior is to regard it as offering approval for behavior which is commonly regarded as bizarre and immoral. The previous illustrations of the relativism of deviance do not imply any approval or disapproval of sexual slavery, mate-swapping, or sexual intercourse during menstruation. The scientific understanding of deviant behavior does not offer a "do anything you desire" philosophy. It only attempts to study human sexual behavior without moral preconceptions, in the same way that biologists study the sexual behavior of other animals.

The goal of this chapter is to present accurate information and useful conceptions about sexual behavior in our society. It is not intended to approve, justify, or condemn.

deviance is rule-breaking behavior

Another aspect of this perspective on deviance needs clarification. Deviance is not a matter of numbers. It is not necessarily behavior which is unusual, or rare, or exhibited only by a minority. Deviance is a matter of rules and expectations. The establishment of rules and standardized expectations is ultimately a consequence of the power relations between groups within a society. Often the dominant rules in a society reflect the values of the majority of its members. Sometimes, however, the dominant rules reflect the values of particularly powerful special interest groups or cliques.

The definition of *deviant behavior* as behavior which is contrary to dominant social rules gives recognition to the fact that different groups in a complex society often hold different rules. Some informal norms and laws have greater effect upon the behavior of people in a society because they are supported by greater political power. That power sometimes derives from a cultural consensus and sometimes from the influence of vested interest alliances.

Some illustrations offer insight into the rule-related, rather than quantity-related, aspect of deviant behavior. The overwhelming majority of Americans practice masturbation sometime in their life. Yet the practice continues to be deviant behavior, because it is contrary to informal social expectations. Punishment for the behavior may have changed from harsh to mild disapproval. Nevertheless, the practice continues to be an object of social disapproval and subtle punishment. Extramarital sex is quite common in American society, at least as an incidental and transient experience. Yet it remains so strongly condemned that some people who publicly admit to it may find their lives ruined. In the recent past, people who performed abortions were severely punished by the law. The rules were changed by the political process. Now, hundreds of thousands of abortions are carried out by medical doctors without fear of punishment.

Deviant behavior is very often believed to be dangerous. The perceived harmfulness may be physical in the sense of causing bodily harm. The belief that some pattern of sexual behavior is dangerous, however, doesn't necessarily mean that it is actually dangerous. Masturbation, for example, was once believed to be gravely dangerous, even though there was no manifest evidence to support that belief. It was firmly believed by medical doctors that masturbation caused insanity, acne, impotence, and broken health (Neuman, 1975). Homosexual behavior is widely believed to be a danger to society, yet there is no evidence for that assumption.

It is rather common for deviant sexual behavior to be widely perceived as being dangerous in the absence of obvious and concrete evidence of its harmfulness. We must be careful not to ridicule tribal peoples who believe that sexual intercourse during menstruation is dangerous. Our own cultural perceptions of dangerousnous are also often grounded in simple superstition. Western cultures, in particular, have had a long history of exaggerated concern about the dangers of many forms of sexual behavior.

sexual variance as deviant behavior

A clear-cut departure from past thinking about sexual deviance is easier to understand if we consider the essential elements of any form of deviant behavior. Think about an isolated person, alone on a desert island. What would be necessary for him or her to exhibit deviant behavior? First, of course, it is necessary to have a person (an "actor") to have deviance. Second, it is necessary for that person to exhibit some behavior (an act). Past interpretations of deviance stopped at this point and ignored the most crucial element of deviance: that it is necessary to have other people react to the person's behavior and condemn it as contrary to their expectations. This third element may be termed other people, society, or simply an "audience" of reacting persons. Therefore, a model, or paradigm, for understanding deviant behavior must contain the following elements.

Deviant Behavior = Actor + Act + Audience

The study of deviant behavior begins where past interpretations of deviance end. It begins with the "audience" and asks the question: "Why do people condemn any act?" (Erikson, 1964). The isolated person on that desert island could not exhibit deviant behavior. Deviance is not in the actor, nor in the act. Instead, it is the reaction of an audience which makes certain acts and actors deviant (Shur, 1971). This approach does not assume that any personality (actor) or any behavior (act) is "abnormal" in itself.

In conclusion, there is nothing "in" any pattern of sexual behavior which automatically makes it deviant, no matter how offensive, revolting or dangerous is appears to our mind's eye. *Deviance* is a quality attributed to some patterns of sexual behavior by a society or a group within society as a reflection of that group's dominant social expectations and moral values.

In recent years, the term *sexual variance* has come into common use as a substitute for the term sexual deviance. There are various practical reasons for this substitution of terms: (1) the term *sexual deviance* is easily misunderstood to imply some kind of universal perversion; (2) the term *variance* connotes the idea of variety in behavior which is consistent with cultural relativism. Therefore, for the remainder of this chapter, the term *sexual variance* will be used to refer to patterns of sexual behavior which are contrary to the dominant social expectations in a society.

As a matter of practical convenience, sexual variance will be identified from the perspective of American society-at-large, rather than from the perspective of special subcultures or other societies. (See Chapter 8 for a detailed exploration of American sexual attitudes.)

Categories of sexual variance.   There are many ways of categorizing forms of sexual variance. Most schemes focus either upon the act or the actor. In contrast, the following categorizing scheme focuses upon the audience, or societal reaction, because that is what defines any pattern of sexual behavior as deviant.

Two objects of social disapproval can be identified: (1) sexual arousal by unusual stimuli; and (2) coercive sexual behavior. People who are aroused by unusual sexual stimuli are those who have learned to attribute very personal erotic meaning to people, objects, and situations which are not culturally attributed erotic meaning in American society. When a person learns to attribute erotic meaning to an unusual stimulus, it functions as a reinforcement (reward) which evokes sexual arousal for them and becomes a goal of their sexual behavior. The second category, coercive sexual behavior, involves the use of some kind of force or threat to obtain the participation of a partner. People who exhibit coercive sexual behavior may be sexually aroused by their hostile aggression, or they may simply rely upon some means of coercion to obtain sexual contact. In some cases, of course, the two categories are overlapping.

sexual variance as personal and social problems

A useful understanding of sexual variance must harness behavioral science insights from research about deviant behavior. It must also be able to generate techniques of helping people, who desire assistance in the solution of their sexual problems.

A good place to begin is with the meaning of "a problem" in human life. *A problem* is simply some situation which is contrary to someone's expectations. It is something, which "should not be." Problematic sexual behavior, therefore, is behavior which "should not be" according to someone's expectations. Someone wants the behavior changed or stopped. No sexual behavior is automatically a "problem" simply because it occurs.

Sexual problems may be personal and social. First, an individual's sexual behavior may be contrary to dominant social expectations in society. The problem for the audience is that they want the sexual behavior stopped. Second, an individual's sexual behavior may be contrary to his or her own personal self-expectations. When this happens, these individuals may react to their self with fear, anxiety, guilt, regret, or depression. Their personal sexual problem is that they want their own sexual behavior (or thoughts or emotions) changed to meet their own expectations. The two categories of problematic sexual behavior are obviously related. People whose sexual behavior is disapproved of by society can easily internalize that disapproval and learn to feel guilty about their own behavior.

Knowledge of the origins of a person's sexual behavior may be useful in changing it. However, no developmental source of sexual behavior automatically makes it a problem. People regard certain patterns of sexual behavior as unfortunate, or immoral, or criminal and impose these definitions upon themself or others. That is what makes the behavior "a problem"—not its developmental origins in the life of a person.

Some citizens seek laws to suppress or change sexual behavior which they believe "should not be." When a form of sexual behavior is made contrary to the law, that sexual behavior becomes a social problem. When people disagree with the law, they try to change the law through the political process. Professionals in the helping services usually try to avoid getting caught up in the enforcement of moral codes and law. Their primary responsibility is to help clients, who volunteer for assistance in changing sexual behavior the client feels is a personal problem.

SEXUAL VARIANCE IN AMERICAN SOCIETY

sexual arousal by unusual stimuli

Fetishism.   Some people learn to respond with sexual arousal to the sight or touch of inanimate objects. A great many men, for example, can be mildly sexually aroused by the sight of women's underclothes. Some adolescent boys even become sexually aroused when viewing brassieres and panties on clothes store dummies. Sometimes inanimate objects become an extremely important source of sexual arousal for a person. Such a sexual pattern is referred to as fetishism, and the inanimate object is a fetish.

A great variety of objects are pursued by fetishists, who may collect and cherish them like mystical objects. Sometimes fetish objects are directly associated with the nude body, such as underclothes or nylon stockings (Gebhard, 1976). Other fetish objects have no direct association with the body, such as articles of fur, leather, and rubber (Gebhard, 1976). Fetishists may use their objects in masturbation or may request that their sexual partners wear them during sexual activity. Sexual arousal by a fetish object is a matter of degree. In extreme cases, the fetishist cannot experience sexual arousal without the presence of the fetish object as a stimulus.

There have been no research investigations of fetishism. The available information comes from clinical case studies of people who seek counseling help. All that is really known about this form of sexual variance is that: (1) it seems to be limited to European and American societies; (2) it is rare in females; and (3) it usually begins to be exhibited during adolescence (Gebhard, 1976). It is likely that an object becomes a fetish when an adolescent male habitually uses it in his sexual fantasies and masturbation, thereby gradually attributing it potent erotic meaning. It is more difficult to understand the choice of fetish objects. Such choice is probably a result of the symbolic association of certain objects with female nudity or pleasant tactile sensations which are symbolically linked to sexual arousal. Fetishism is probably limited to Western societies because of the widespread inhibition of adolescent sexuality in the West—a social environment where indirect sexual symbolism is commonplace in advertising.

The sex industry caters to masturbation with fetish objects. Rubberized female dummies and genitals are often sold through ''adult'' book stores. In recent years, all sorts of vibrators have been sold for female masturbation, many of them shaped like penises. It is possible that these may become fetish objects for some women. In addition, some stores sell special women's underclothes for use during sexual activity.

Fetish behavior can become a personal sexual problem when it causes anxiety and guilt. It may also become a minor social problem when fetishists rely upon stealing to obtain their fetish objects.

Transvestism.   Transvestism is a pattern of behavior in which a person obtains erotic pleasure from wearing the clothes characteristic of the other sex. Transvestism is really a broad category for a wide range of behaviors. In some people, transvestism has the character of fetishism, as when wearing the underclothes of the other sex is necessary for sexual arousal to occur. More often, such ''cross-dressing'' is further elaborated to express a transvestite's dual masculine and feminine gender identity (Money and Ehrhardt, 1972). Most male transvestites, for example, assume a feminine self-concept and mannerisms when they periodically engage in cross-dressing. One study of 504 male transvestites found that 78 percent of them considered themselves to have ''a different personality'' when they dressed entirely as a woman (Prince and Bentler, 1972). In such cases, the male transvestite typically exhibits traditional, stereotypic masculine behavior when dressed as a male and traditional, stereotypic feminine behavior when dressed as a female (Feinbloom, 1976). It is questionable whether or not transvestism would exist in a culture where male and female behavior and clothing was very similar.

Today, almost all transvestites who come to official attention are men. However, the historical record offers many examples of female transvestites (Bullough, 1976). The reason may be that there are now few articles of clothing which are typical of men and not also commonly worn by women. Bras, panties, dresses, nylon stockings, and nightgowns, however, remain items of female clothing.

Some transvestites have organized associations which publish magazines for ''cross-dressers.'' Few transvestites ever seek the assistance of helping professionals (Prince and Bentler, 1972). In the past, information about transvestites was obtained only from limited psychiatric case studies. Recently, there have been several investigations of transvestites using large numbers of subjects drawn from members of transvestite organizations.

One survey of 504 male transvestites found that the vast majority (89 percent) were exclusively heterosexual in their sexual behavior (Prince and Bentler, 1972). A few cross-dressers were bisexuals (9 percent) or homosexuals (1 percent). A small minority (about 12 percent) of cross-dressers were male transexuals. Transexual men are men with a female self-concept and who feel trapped in the body of the "wrong" sex.

The personal meaning of cross-dressing is probably very different for heterosexual transvestites, effeminate homosexuals, and transexuals (Lester, 1975). In the vast majority of cases, desires for cross-dressing begin during childhood or adolescence (Prince and Bentler, 1972). It is likely that cross-dressing provides erotic stimulation only for heterosexual transvestites. Some men make an occupation as female impersonators in night club acts. One study found that almost all such men are effeminate homosexuals, rather than true transvestites (Newton, 1972). Their behavior, known as "drag," is usually an amusement for them, lacking erotic significance.

The previously mentioned study also found that the vast majority of transvestites were currently married, or had been married (Prince and Bentler, 1972). Transvestism was secretive behavior for 27 percent of the married men. However, in a majority of cases, the men's wives knew about their behavior. Such behavior frequently led to severe marital conflict and divorce. On the other hand, many wives cooperated with their husbands' cross-dressing desires by permitting sexual intercourse while their husbands were clothed in feminine articles of attire. Many transvestites seek prostitutes as sexual partners who will cooperate with their desire for cross-dressing during sexual activity. One study of over 1000 clients of call girls found 4 percent of the men engaged in some degree of cross-dressing (Stein, 1974).

The problematic aspects of transvestism are similar to those of fetishism. When it engenders anxiety and guilt, it becomes a personal sexual problem. Transvestism is a social problem in cases where it causes marital conflict. Cross-dressing is a crime in many states, and occasionally men are arrested for wearing women's clothes in public places (MacNamara and Sagarin, 1977).

Little is known about the development origins of transvestism. Information from psychiatric case studies may be misleading because such rare cases are probably unrepresentative of most transvestites (Prince and Bentler, 1972).

Voyeurism. *Voyeurism* refers to sexual arousal in response to viewing nudity or sexual activity. According to current research, both men and women are erotically responsive to the sight of nudity and sexual activity. A great variety of sex magazines, books, and films appeal to the common interest in voyeurism. Indeed, one of the principle themes of much advertising is designed to catch attention by appealing to voyeurism.

One study found organized voyeurism to be common among construction workers who make a sport of spying on women who are undressing or engaging in sexual activity (Feigelman, 1974). Many houses of prostitution have arrangements to meet desires for watching sexual activity. Such arrangements may consist of presenting "exhibitions" of sexual activity which usually consist of simulated lesbian behavior (Stein, 1974). Another arrangement for voyeurs is to maintain rooms with two-way mirrors through which the activities of prostitutes with unsuspecting clients may be viewed by other clients (Smith, 1976).

Voyeurism is also an aspect of group sex activity. One variation, called *triolism,* consists of one person watching two others engage in sexual activity after which that person may also participate. In swinger's magazines, there are many advertisements by married couples for male or female partners to join them in triolism (Bartell, 1971). In some cases, a husband may arrange for the seduction of his wife, in order to watch the sexual activity. When such activity is arranged by deception, it usually results in severe marital conflict.

Another form of voyeurism occurs when lone men expend considerable effort to spy into people's windows (Smith, 1976). Such acts involve invasions of privacy and are usually criminal offenses in most states (MacNamara and Sagarin, 1977). "Peeping Toms" are usually adolescents or young men. Most of them tend to be shy with women in the sense of being very fearful of sexual rejection (Gebhard et al., 1965). In traditional psychiatric literature, voyeurism is often equated with "peeping" because the men apprehended for such offenses are often sent for psychiatric treatment (Smith, 1976). Peepers rarely spy upon women whom they know (Gebhard et al., 1965). Instead, they seem to be sexually aroused by making forbidden intrusions into the privacy of strangers. Most peepers masturbate while engaging in voyeurism. Usually peepers are not dangerous. However, some habitual peepers do later become rapists (Gebhard et al., 1965).

Hypersexuality.   No category of sexual variance is more obviously reflective of traditional Western moral value judgment than is hypersexuality. Hypersexuality refers to sexual arousal in response to constant change in sexual partners. It involves erotic response to the novelty of unfamiliar sex partners. Many people's sex fantasies are fabricated out of the imagery of such novelty. However, few people expend much energy in pursuit of constant sexual variety.

In the past, few people—except those who were extremely powerful and wealthy—had the opportunity to pursue such a goal (Levitt, 1973). There are numerous historical examples of Roman emperors, medieval potentates, and Victorian philanderers who constantly sought new sexual partners. There are even records of rulers in polygamous societies who required a different bedmate every night, some of them preferring only virgins. Such behavior has been labeled as *promiscuity, nymphomania,* or *satyriasis.* These labels may be little more than condemnatory moral judgments (Levitt, 1973).

In contemporary American society, hypersexuality is illustrated in the behavior of unmarried and married swingers who constantly seek new sex partners. In some cases, call girl prostitutes actively enjoy the sexual variety in their work and are sexually aroused by most of their clients (Pomeroy, 1965). There are also some people whose premarital and extramarital sexual behavior is nearly as indiscriminate as that of swingers, without being as organized. Such people are objects of strong moral condemnation. When their behavior becomes a matter of public attention, they may be fired from their jobs or suffer other informal punishments. If they are juveniles, they are likely to be put under the control of legal authorities.

Hypersexual behavior may also result in the personal problems of guilt and loneliness. In some cases, inorgasmic women seek indiscriminate sexual partners to deal with their sexual problems and to affirm feelings of feminine attractiveness.

Homosexuality.   No other form of sexual variance is a source of such intense social controversy and political conflict as is homosexuality in American society today. Homosexual erotic responsiveness involves sexual arousal in response to same-sex stimuli. These stimuli may take the form of sex fantasies, viewing same-sex nudity, or bodily contact with people of the same sex.

Homosexuality is the topic of the next chapter. It is an important social issue, and is also at the cutting-edge of competing interpretations of sexual variance.

Sexual sadism and masochism.   The terms *sadism* and *masochism* are used widely in reference to emotional responses and behavior which are often completely unrelated to sexual activity. However, as forms of sexual variance, sadism, and masochism both refer to sexual arousal associated with pain. *Sexual sadism* may be defined as sexual arousal in response to viewing expressions of pain in other people. In contrast, *masochism* may be defined as sexual arousal in response to one's own feelings of pain. As forms of sexual variance, they are relatively rare, even though they have attracted the attention of much theorizing. Actually, there have been few adequate scientific investigations of these aspects of human sexuality (Lester, 1975). Most of the available information comes from a few case studies of dramatically bizarre individuals.

One recent national survey of sexual behavior found that mild forms of sadism and masochism are practiced by a very small minority of Americans (Hunt, 1974). The respondents were asked if they had obtained sexual pleasure in the past year from inflicting or receiving pain during sexual activity. Among males, 3.5 percent had experienced pleasure while inflicting pain and 1.6 percent had experienced pleasure from receiving pain. Among women, almost exactly reverse percentages were found. Among women, 1.3 percent had experienced pleasure while inflicting pain and 3.1 percent had experienced pleasure from receiving pain. Sado-masochistic practices were concentrated among younger, single people (under age 35), rather than among married couples. The behavior consisted of giving or receiving pain via hitting, punching, slapping, scratching, spanking, or pinching. Another sexual practice which has sado-masochistic overtones is called *bondage*. In this practice, one consenting partner is tied up, while the other applies gradual sexual stimulation (Gebhard, 1976). There is no data about how commonly this practice occurs.

Some clients of prostitutes also request these practices, although most prostitutes are only willing to inflict pain on masochistic clients (Stein, 1974). A considerable amount of pornography appeals to sadistic fantasies by showing, in words or pictures, men threatening, humiliating, or inflicting pain upon women. A much smaller portion of pornography puts the male in a masochistic role. One content analysis of sex magazines found that about 10 percent of them had distinctively sado-masochistic content (Gayford, 1978). Kinsey's research found that about 22 percent of men and 12 percent of women admitted to experiencing some degree of sexual arousal in response to sado-masochistic stories (Kinsey et al., 1953).

Some social psychological experiments have recently investigated responses to sado-masochistic fantasy stories (Malamuth et al., 1977; Feshback and Malamuth, 1978). This research is part of an effort to determine the nature of the link between aggression and sexuality. The research has found that many men and some women respond with sexual arousal to sado-masochistic stories, if the recipient of pain is believed to react voluntarily and with pleasure. In contrast, if the victim is seen to react involuntarily and with disgust, a response of sexual arousal tends to be inhibited. The element of voluntarism appears to relieve many people's potential guilt feelings and to disinhibit sexual arousal in response to cues of pain combined with those of sexual pleasure.

In a small proportion of men, and even fewer women, sado-masochism is a preferred form of sexual activity, sometimes being necessary for sexual arousal to occur. Such people are those who can be regarded as true sado-masochists. Few such people are exclusively sadists or masochists, the two patterns of response being mixed in the same person (Gebhard, 1976). *Sado-masochists* may actually be sexually inhibited people who experience anxieties about enjoying sexual pleasure (Gebhard, 1976). Sado-masochism is frequently combined with fetishism, especially that involving leather and tight-fitting clothes (Spengler, 1977).

A West German study gave detailed questionnaires to 245 sado-masochistic men who were members of sado-masochist organizations, or who had placed advertisements for partners in sex magazines (Spengler, 1977). The research found that 30 percent of the men were exclusively heterosexual, 31 percent were bisexual and 38 percent were exclusively homosexual. There is no way of knowing whether or not this distribution is representative of sado-masochists. However, the researchers reasoned that exclusively heterosexual male sado-masochists are less likely to find willing female partners, except among a few prostitutes.

Sadistic practices are coercive sexual behavior if the recipients of pain are not willing masochists. Sadistic sexual arousal may be an important element in many cases of rape. (See the section on sexual assault and rape in this chapter.)

Sado-masochism can also become a social problem when it results in marital conflict. It is quite unlikely to be mutually agreeable between sex partners, unless both partners are sexually aroused by mild sado-masochistic practices. Sado-masochism can also be a personal problem if an individual is unable to become sexually aroused without this kind of stimulation.

coercive sexual behavior

Sexual assault and rape. The most obvious form of coercive sexual behavior involves using violence, or threats of physical harm, to force another person to be a partner to sexual activity. Such behavior is now called *sexual assault.* The victim of a sexual assault may be forcefully used as an object for various forms of sexual contact.

Technical legal definitions of the term *rape* do not cover most forms of sexual assault. The exact legal meaning of *rape* varies from society to society and from state to state. In most of the United States, *rape* is very narrowly defined as the act of vaginal penetration by a man with a woman who is not his wife, in which the woman resists, and her resistance is overcome by force (Gammage and Hemphill, 1974). In the past, many behavioral scientists unfortunately relied upon this narrow legal definition. When they were guided by the legal definition, they neglected to investigate a wide variety of forms of sexual assault.

Recent behavioral research indicates that sexual assaults are quite common in American society. Violently forced sexual intercourse in marriage, for example, is probably much more common than is popularly imagined. The new research on family violence and wife-beating has finally turned attention to this much neglected issue (Gelles, 1977). It has found that a significant proportion of the wives who are beaten are also raped. A series of research projects has also found that sexual assault is very common in dating relationships (Kanin, 1970; Kanin and Parcell, 1977). The forms of sexual assault which women may experience from their dates include everything from forced breast and genital fondling to forced intercourse. One study of a sample of 282 college student women found that 32 percent of them reported having had sexual intercourse with a date who used some kind of offensive duress to obtain sexual contact with them (Kanin and Parcell, 1977). Since the sample was not representative, there is no way of knowing if coerced intercourse is that prevalent among college students. Sexual assault is also common in prisons, when men are forced to perform fellatio or to submit to anal intercourse, often after physical violence or threats are applied to make them submit (A. Davis, 1973). Most sexual assaults in prisons involve gang rapes of resistant victims.

Even rape, as legally defined, is quite common in the United States. The exact incidence of rape is unknown, simply because most rapes remain unreported to the police. A great many victims of rape are fearful of reporting the assaults because of the social and legal degradation which they can expect to experience. A federal government study estimated that four rapes actually occur for each one reported to the police (President's Commission, 1967). In 1977, there were 63,020 officially recorded rapes reported to the police, in the United States (FBI, 1977). If this number represents only one-fourth of all rapes, then the actual number of rapes was over 250,000 in that year. Although rape is relatively common, few rapists are convicted. In 1977, only 30 percent of the men arrested for rape were convicted for that offense (FBI, 1977). One estimate is that only 3 percent of all men who commit rape are ever sent to jail (Schram, 1978). Therefore, studies of rapists in prison may be quite unrepresentative of the men who commit such offenses, most of whom are never detected.

The circumstances of rape. However, the available research about rape—drawn from interviews with victims and rapists—does offer useful information about the circumstances of rape. Rape is rarely a spontaneous "crime of passion." Indeed, a majority of rapes are planned in advance (Amir, 1971; Schram, 1978). Some are planned well in advance, as the rapist identifies a specific victim or location, plans means of controlling his victim, and considers means of escape. In other cases, such planning takes place only shortly before the rape. The most common location for rape is in the victim's residence. In some cases, the victim is known to the rapist as an acquaintance, neighbor, girlfriend, or drinking associate (Amir, 1971). The vast majority of rape victims are relatively young. This indicates a deliberate selectivity on the part of rapists. Most rape victims are under the age of 30, and half are under 21 (Schram, 1978).

The image of most rapes as being brutally violent may be incorrect. Most commonly, it appears that rapists use verbal abuse, muscular strength, and threats with a weapon (Amir, 1971; Schram, 1978). Physical beating as a form of coercion is less common. Most victims fearfully submit during a sudden assault. Extreme physical violence is most common in cases where the victim strongly resists the assault or where the rapist is a sadist (Amir, 1971; Schram, 1978). Only about 20 percent of all victims manage to put up a strong fight, and such victims are those who are most likely to be brutally harmed (Amir, 1971). Ironically, when a victim strongly resists, there is also a greater likelihood that the rapist will flee the scene (Schram, 1978). This poses a very difficult choice for a woman who might be sexually assaulted. If she does strongly resist by screaming and fighting, the rapist might be as likely to flee as to do her severe physical harm.

The humiliation and sexual coercion of rape often goes beyond forced vaginal intercourse. Other forms of sexual contact are frequently demanded by rapists, including fellatio, cunnilingus, and anal intercourse (Holmstrom and Burgess, 1978). Many rapists are sexually dysfunctional during rape, and this may aggravate their violent aggressiveness. One study of 170 convicted rapists found that one-third of them experienced a sexual dysfunction during the rape (Groth and Burgess, 1977). About 16 percent of the rapists had difficulties maintaining an erection, and another 15 percent had difficulties ejaculating without very prolonged intercourse.

Group rapes are the circumstances in which a victim is most likely to experience deliberate and extensive attempts to degrade her, including repeated intercourse, nongenital sexual contacts, and forced acts of servitude (Amir, 1971). Rapes by two or more men account for at least 25 percent of all incidents of rape (Geis and Chappell, 1971). Group rapes by soldiers are particularly common in wars and are sometimes encouraged by military authorities as a means of terrorizing an enemy population (Brownmiller, 1975).

Most rapists are under the age of 30. The vast majority of rapists are young men between the ages of 18 and 25 (Schram, 1978). It should not be surprising then that a majority of rapists are not married (Amir, 1971). Most convicted rapists come from a lower socioeconomic background and reside in poor urban and rural areas (Amir, 1971). However, it is not known whether such a socioeconomic background is typical of undetected rapists. Convicted rapists also come disproportionately from impoverished ethnic groups (Curtis, 1976). Again, it is not known whether such background is typical of undetected rapists. It is known, however, that the vast majority of rapes occur between people of the same race (Amir, 1971). Young black women are the most common victims of rapists (Schram, 1978). It is probable that the degrading social forces of disorganized poverty promote the violent aggressiveness and callousness toward women which is learned by rapists (Curtis, 1976).

Learning sexual aggression. Rape behavior is a response to social learning partaking of both shared cultural experience and relatively uncommon personal experience. In the past, explanations of rape behavior focused almost exclusively upon the personal learnings of rapists. This gave rise to the incorrect notion of rapists as being psychologically "abnormal" and greatly different from most other men. However, in recent years attention has shifted to attempts to identify the sociocultural learnings which encourage rape behavior (Brownmiller, 1975; Russell, 1975). The importance of this dimension of learning is evident from the fact that sexual assaults do not occur in some societies, are uncommon in other societies, and are very common in still other societies (Chappell, Geis, and Geis, 1977).

Rape behavior is likely to be encouraged by cultural patterns which socialize men to link attitudes of hostile aggressiveness with the sexual dominance of women by men. Rape may be encouraged by cultures: (1) where physical violence is easily justified; (2) where sexual interaction is regarded as an expression of male power and dominance over women; (3) where male callousness and lack of empathy for women is tolerated; and (4) where there is considerable hostility between men and women in interpersonal relationships. This combination of cultural patterns is relatively common in many social groups within American society and helps to account for the prevalence of sexual assaults in our country.

Unfortunately, most psychological studies of convicted rapists are inadequate (Albin, 1977). They are unrepresentative of the vast majority of men who commit sexual assaults. In addition, few past psychological studies have ever employed comparison groups of nonrapists to check the descriptions of convicted rapists. Increasing numbers of behavioral scientists who have studied convicted rapists suggest that rapists exhibit rather diverse personality characteristics (Pacht, 1976; Albin, 1977). Any personality differences between men who rape and those who do not may be a matter of degree, rather than all-or-none distinctions. In a society such as ours which encourages many men to learn sexual aggression, rape behavior may simply be more likely to occur among men who have learned to over-conform to a masculine stereotype of sexual aggressiveness (Becker and Abel, 1978). In other words, rapists may be men who: (1) can more easily justify physical violence; (2) are more concerned about expressing dominance toward women; and (3) are more callous and hostile toward women as a category of people.

One important experimental research study found that the sexual response patterns of rapists could be distinguished from nonrapists (Abel et al., 1977). The research used a sample of 20 men who had committed rapes, only two of whom were arrested for the offense. (The men were referred for therapy by helping professionals, family members, or themselves.) The sexual response patterns of these rapists were investigated by exposing them to audio tape descriptions of: (1) mutually consenting, pleasurable intercourse; (2) aggressively forced sexual intercourse; and (3) physical aggression without sexual activity. Their degree of sexual arousal was measured by an instrument which gauged their erections. As a control, their sexual response patterns were compared with a sample of nonrapists who were given similar tests. The nonrapists were only mildly sexually aroused, if at all, by the descriptions of forced intercourse. In contrast, most of the rapists exhibited considerable sexual arousal to both the descriptions of forced intercourse as well as to those of mutually enjoyable intercourse. However, the rapists who had histories of sadistic behavior exhibited little sexual arousal to mutually enjoyable intercourse, but considerable arousal to descriptions of forced intercourse and even aggression without sex. In conclusion, it appears that rapists associate sexual pleasure with physical aggression much more than do nonrapists.

The foregoing research should not be taken as evidence that only rapists respond with sexual arousal to the imagery of sexual aggression. It is possible for men to deliberately inhibit their erectile responses (Henson and Rubin, 1971). A more recent experimental research study has shown that nonrapist college student males respond with sexual arousal to audio tapes of forced intercourse after they have (or even believe they have) consumed an alcoholic beverage (Briddell et al., 1978). The researchers concluded that the belief that alcohol disinhibits sexual arousal provides a socially acceptable excuse for people to engage in behavior which is otherwise unacceptable. It is noteworthy that many rapists use alcohol before a rape and many of them excuse their behavior as a reaction to their alcohol consumption (Amir, 1971; Rada, 1975).

sexual abuse of children

The category of the sexual abuse of children is a broad rubric for several forms of sexual variance, which involve coercive sexual behavior with children. *Sexual abuse of children* may be defined as the use of violence, threats, deception, or parental authority by an adult to encourage a child to be a partner in sexual activity. This designation includes: (1) incest between adult relatives and children; (2) the sexual molesting of children by adult strangers; and (3) the employment of children in pornography and prostitution.

The recent national concern about child abuse and the research investigations of it have generated a new concern about sexual child abuse (Walters, 1975). New state laws which mandate that helping professionals report cases of physical child abuse have resulted in the detection of many cases of sexual child abuse (Brant and Tisza, 1977). In the past, such cases would probably not have come to public attention. Just as in cases of rape, most cases of incest and child molestation remain "hidden" by a conspiracy of silence, designed to protect the child and family from further embarrassment (Gagnon, 1965; Herman and Hirschman, 1977).

There is no really adequate research on the incidence of coercive sexual contacts between children and adults. The Kinsey research offers some limited information (Kinsey et al., 1948, 1953). In data obtained from 4441 women, it was found that 24 percent of them could recall having experienced sexual advances by adult men (strangers and relatives) during their pre-adolescent years. The most common of these sexual advances involved exhibition of the male genitals, fondling without genital contact, or manipulation of the female genitals (Gagnon, 1965). Experiences of sexual intercourse were rare. About half of the adults involved were total strangers, but the other half consisted of adult acquaintances and relatives. The vast majority of these incidents were single, isolated encounters, rather than frequently repeated sexual involvements.

Repeated acts of sexual coercion are most likely to take place in incestuous relations between adult men and female children. Such relations are those most likely to evoke both lasting fears and guilt feelings (Herman and Hirschman,

1977). It appears that male children are very rarely the objects of sexual coercion by adult women. One study of over 200 cases of the sexual abuse of children which come to the attention of public agencies found only three cases of adult females reported for sexually abusing a male child (Walters, 1975). Most of the victims of sexual abuse were pre-adolescents and early adolescents, rather than younger children. Most of the adult aggressors were the natural fathers, step-fathers, or mother's boyfriend's, rather than adult strangers. Sexual abuse at home may be far from rare. One estimate, drawn from the reports of social work agencies, is that over 200,000 children are victimized by it every year (Mac-Farlane, 1978).

Father-daughter sexual abuse is most likely to result in lasting personal problems for the female victim (Herman and Hirschman, 1977). Common among these personal problems are intense guilt feelings, a strongly negative self-concept, and sexual unresponsiveness with men. There is some evidence that a disproportionate number of victims of father-daughter incest become runaway teenagers, drug addicts, and teenage prostitutes (James, 1977). A father's sexual advances toward his daughter can trap her into a continuing in-cestuous relationship by the threat of parental power and the reward of parental affection. Most girls blame themselves rather than their fathers for their vic-timization, unless they are beaten and physically abused (Herman and Hirschman, 1977). They may also be blamed by others and socially stigmatized if their fathers are respected members of the community.

Past studies of men imprisoned for incest may offer misleading conclu-sions. The vast majority of the men involved in the sexual abuse of children are never detected by social workers or prosecuted by legal authorities (Walters, 1975). One major study of the victims of incest and sexual child abuse found that men involved do not otherwise display any dramatically unusual behavior. They are not necessarily alcoholics, wife-beaters, or sadists. Most are respected mem-bers of their communities (Walters, 1975).

Sexual encounters between strangers and children are actually much less likely to result in any lasting personal problems for the child (Gagnon, 1965; Gagnon and Simon, 1970). Minimal difficulties are most likely if parents and authorities do not themselves act in such a way as to evoke anxiety, fear, and guilt in the child. Sexual child molestation usually does not involve violence or attempts at sexual intercourse (McCaghy, 1967). Most commonly, child molestors attempt to masturbate their victim or to get their victim to masturbate them. There is little reliable research about the personalities of child molestors. Attempts to make personality typologies encounter so many exceptions that they can be quite midleading (McCaghy, 1967).

While there is widespread public concern about the homosexual molesta-tion of male children, its incidence is actually low in comparison with heterosex-ual child abuse (Newton, 1978). A recent research study of a sample of 175 men convicted for sexual child abuse found that adult homosexuality and homosexual attraction to male children may be quite different (Groth and Birnbaum, 1978). None of the men who had molested boys were exclusively homosexual in their sexual relations with adults. They were either heterosexual or bisexual in relations with adults and reported being attracted to the "feminine" qualities of male children.

sexual offensiveness

Sexual offensiveness involves coercive sexual behavior in which a victim is forced to witness undesired sexual activity. The most common form of sexual offensiveness is sexual exhibitionism. *Sexual exhibitionism* may be defined as the deliberate exposure of one's nude body or genitals to another person without their consent and in a manner which is regarded as being offensive. Sexual exhibitionism is coercive behavior in the sense that it involves an unwanted intrusion into another person's privacy (Davis and Davis, 1976).

Such sexual offensiveness may only be possible in societies where public nudity and genital exposure are regarded as being obscene (Stephens, 1971). Sexual enhibitionism seems to be rare outside of Europe and the Americas (Rooth, 1973). Sexual offensiveness may provide sexual arousal for the exhibitionist, as well as a release of hostile feelings toward the other sex. However, it is first necessary for a witness to hold a definition of genital exposure as sexually obscene and offensive behavior. Therefore, it is most useful to define sexually offensive behavior in relation to the reactions of an "audience," rather than any presumed motives of the exhibitor.

The crucial role of the audience in the definition of sexual variance is particularly clear in cases of sexual exhibitionism. All forms of public bodily exposure cannot be classified as being sexually offensive. Strippers, for example, offer bodily exposure to a consenting audience in exchange for money. Nudists usually pursue their activity in locations where public nudity is a social expectation and where the wearing of clothes may be regarded as being offensive (Weinberg, 1970). Recently, some young people have attempted to turn certain beaches into locations for nude swimming. While they may be arrested for indecent exposure, their public nudity is not uniformly regarded as being obscene and sexually offensive (Douglas, Rasmussen, and Flanagan, 1977). Instead, beach nudity is the focus of community conflict over the social definition of public nudity. Similarly, bodily exposure in the college student fad of "streaking" is more often regarded as an amusement than an expression of sexual offensiveness. A lone streaker, on the other hand, may be regarded by a surprised audience as a sexual exhibitionist.

The classic sexual exhibitionist, or "flasher," is a lone man who exposes himself to an unsuspecting woman and then runs away. It is noteworthy that there are few records of women flashers. One reason for this male-female difference may be that men do not usually regard female nudity as being obscene and sexually offensive, even when they are a surprised audience. It is difficult for a woman to use her body insultingly toward men, although there are reports of women projecting their buttocks out of car windows (''mooning'') as an insulting gesture. Only in rare cases are women ever referred to psychiatrists to change sexually offensive exhibitionism (Hollender et al., 1977).

The behavior of sexual exhibitionism varies, but almost always relies upon the element of surprise. The exhibitionist may suddenly expose himself to a lone female in an isolated public place, or may use a car for quick exposure and escape (MacDonald, 1973). Most exhibitionists expose themselves to adult women, but some do so to children. The women to whom they expose themselves are almost always strangers, rather than intimates or acquaintances (McWhorter, 1977). Most exhibitionists do not touch their victims or pursue them, but instead flee the scene quickly after surprising their victims (Davis and Davis, 1976). Exhibitionists may masturbate immediately before, during, or following the incident of exposure, although some do not do so. Most victims of sexual offensiveness react with anxiety and fear to the unexpected encounter, but many victims also react with anger, embarrassment, or deliberate inattention (Davis and Davis, 1976).

Research on the personalities of arrested exhibitionists offers no conclusive information (Lester, 1975). Contrary to popular belief that most exhibitionists are elderly men, most of those who are arrested are under the age of 35 (McWhorter, 1977). The majority are teenagers and men in their early twenties. Clinical studies of exhibitionists who are psychiatric patients or prisoners suggest that these men lack adequate masculine self-esteem and assertiveness with women (McWhorter, 1977). Their exhibitionism may be a means of expressing sexual aggression in attempts to cope with anxiety-provoking experiences with female intimates (girlfriends, wives, mothers). However, there is no way of knowing if these characteristics also apply to the majority of men who engage in sexual offensiveness and are never arrested.

Another form of sexual offensiveness involves making obscene telephone calls. The obscene telephone caller exposes his surprised victim to sexually offensive language, rather than his body. Many obscene callers masturbate while talking to their victims. They may choose someone's name randomly from a telephone book, or may call some location where they expect a woman to answer the telephone. As far as is known, obscene callers are men. The little available evidence about it indicates that this form of sexual variance may be quite common (Lester, 1975).

sexual harassment

Another form of sexual coercion has recently received public attention partly as a result of the efforts of feminist journalists and others. *Sexual harassment* refers to the use of a position of authority and threats of economic retribution to force a person to be a partner to sexual activity. Most commonly it occurs when a male employer or executive uses his position to force a female employee to serve his sexual desires under the threat of being fired. It also occurs when a professional uses his authority to manipulate an unwilling female client into sexual activity with him.

As yet, very little research has attempted to investigate sexual harassment in industry and the professions (Evans, 1978; Farley, 1978). This form of behavior is undoubtedly considered to be contrary to normative expectations by most Americans. Some men may tolerate it, considering it to be merely "a fact of life"—except in cases where their wives or daughters are victimized. However, since sexual harassment involves subtle entrapment, is easily concealed, and does not come to the attention of law enforcement agencies, it has been all but ignored. There are few legal recourses for a victim of sexual harassment. Usually, a woman must either leave her job or comply with the sexual demands of her superiors (Farley, 1978).

In the helping professions, it has been traditionally considered unethical behavior for a professional to have sexual relations with a patient. In addition, it can be grounds for a malpractice suit. Several small, unrepresentative questionnaire surveys have investigated the extent of sexual contacts between physicians, psychiatrists, psychologists, and their patients (Kardener et al., 1973; Perry, 1976; Holroyd and Brodsky, 1977). In these studies, between 5 percent and 11 percent of the respondents admitted having had sexual intercourse with their patients. Almost all who did so were male professionals. Some journalistic attempts have also been made to investigate the incidence of sexual contacts between college professors and their students which—as in the case of helping professionals—is considered equally unethical (Munich, 1978). This concern reflects a stronger condemnation of sexual harassment in these fields, rather than any greater incidence compared with other occupations. Actually, sexual harassment is probably much more extensive in industrial bureaucracies and more difficult to identify (Farley, 1978).

THE MEDICAL INTERPRETATION OF SEXUAL VARIANCE

sin and sickness in sexual variance

Contemporary common sense concepts of sexual variance remain rooted in Judeo-Christian attitudes toward human sexuality (Kinsey et al., 1949). Basically, this tradition considers any form of sexual activity which does not have procreation within marriage as its purpose to be an expression of "sinfulness." Masturbation, oral-genital contact, and anal intercourse are regarded as being similar to rape, homosexual behavior, and incest as offenses against God's law. The wrongfulness of such behavior is regarded as absolute and universal, as much as God's law is absolute and universal.

In the Middle Ages, speculation about the nature of human sexuality was became more secular, it became necessary to buttress theological beliefs about human sexuality rested upon theological justifications. As Western societies become more secular, it became necessary to buttress theological beliefs about human sexuality with more earthly rationales. Consequently, sexual variance came to be seen as behavior contrary to the laws of Nature, as well as those of God. This viewpoint gave rise to the concept of "unnatural" sex acts. An unnatural sex act continued to be the same thing as a sinful sex act, one which did not have procreation as its purpose. The secular rationale was that Nature had assigned the purpose of procreation to sexual anatomy.

The attempt to understand sexual variance on the basis of "natural" biological law paved the way for medical explanations of sexual variance. No biological malfunction could be found in the bodies of sexual deviants to explain their "unnatural" sex acts. Since sinful temptation by the devil could not be accepted in medical circles, a more secular explanation had to be found. What medical doctors did was quite imaginative. They applied the concept of disease to the mind and regarded "the mind" as an entity which could malfunction. In that convenient maneuver, a belief in the sinful soul was replaced by a belief in the sick psyche.

People who were guilty of "unnatural" sex acts would, then, be seen as subject to change by medical therapy, rather than by punishment. The term "unnatural" was replaced by the medical term of "abnormal" (Kinsey et al., 1949). Medical therapy was regarded as a lot more compassionate than imprisonment or eternal damnation. It was for this reason that many people whose morality was more humanistic than traditionally Christian were drawn to the "mental illness" explanation of sexual variance. The authority for determining what was sexually "abnormal" shifted from religious officials to medical doctors—primarily psychiatrists. Psychiatry is that branch of medical practice which is concerned with the treatment of mental illness.

The medicalization of sexual variance was believed (by both advocates and antagonists) to eliminate moral value judgments from attempts to change people's sexual behavior. However, it did not. Instead, morality was concealed in concepts of mental health and illness, psychological normality and abnormality (Lazarus, 1975).

The concept of sexual variance as abnormal, "sick" sexual behavior may be the most common way of understanding it in American society today. Among people of little education, however, "sick" sex simply means sinful, criminal, and perverted. It is definitely used as a moral condemnation. In contrast, for people in the helping professions, "sick" sexual behavior is that which is symptomatic of a mental illness.

the psychiatric-medical model

Thinking about deviant behavior as an expression of some kind of sickness is a way of trying to understand its origin and nature. This model of thinking about deviant behavior is called the psychiatric-medical model. A model in any science consists of an analogy between something that is already well understood and something else which is inadequately understood. In this case, an analogy is made between the nature of physical illness and sexual variance.

The psychiatric-medical model for understanding serious forms of deviant behavior developed during the nineteenth century. It has been very broadly applied in social policies designed to deal with sexual variance, the illegal use of drugs, the heavy use of alcohol, persistent stealing, and even juvenile delinquency (Kittrie, 1971). Sometimes it is even used to characterize people who have unusual political beliefs, such as the student radicals of the 1960s, or American Nazis, or advocates of the Women's Liberation Movement. Whenever it is applied, the psychiatric-medical model of abnormality has the following basic components:

1. *Mental Malfunctions.* A mental illness is conceived to be a malfunction in the mind. In this way, the "mind" is regarded as a kind of entity with functioning parts like the body. The malfunction in mental illness, however, does not originate in physical, bodily sources. Instead, mental malfunctions are believed to originate in a person's life experiences. Certain experiences are believed to cause disturbances or disorders in the functioning of a person's mind. Following this line of reasoning, sexual variance is conceived as arising from a disturbed (diseased) way of thinking.

2. *Symptoms.* In bodily disease, observable physical problems are taken as indicators of an unseen malfunction in the body. These indicators are called *symptoms.* In mental disease, "abnormal" behavior is regarded to be a symptom of an underlying mental malfunction. Following this line of reasoning, abnormal sexual behavior is taken as a symptom, or indicator, of an underlying mental illness.

   Abnormal behavior can be recognized as that which has the following characteristics: (1) the behavior is bizarre, in the sense of being very unusual; (2) the behavior causes a person feelings of severe anxiety; (3) the behavior is inefficient, in the sense that it impedes a person's attempts to achieve his or her goals or to adjust to social expectations (Buss, 1966). Following this line of reasoning, abnormal sexual behavior is any sexual behavior which is bizarre, results in severe anxiety, and interferes with a person's attempts to have heterosexual intercourse in a loving relationship. These characteristics, are therefore, symptoms of mental illness.

3. *Therapy.* The treatment of sick people which is designed to cure their disease is called *medical therapy.* Effective medical therapy is designed to eliminate the underlying disease, not just suppress the symptoms. (Cold remedies, for example, may be considered ineffective, because they only suppress the symptoms of a cold, without eliminating the disease.) When medical therapy is applied to deviant behavior, the goal is to "cure" the underlying diseased mind, rather than merely suppress the bizarre behavior. Following this line of reasoning, medical therapy is aimed at changing a person's sick

way of thinking about sex, rather than merely eliminating their abnormal sexual behavior.

criticisms of the psychiatric-medical model

The psychiatric-medical model of deviant behavior appears to be a very reasonable explanation of bizarre behavior. It has certainly been convincing enough to have become a matter of common sense wisdom after only several generations. Yet, since the early 1960s, criticism of it has gradually been accumulating among behavioral scientists and even among leading psychiatrists (Szasz, 1960; 1970, 1974; Torrey, 1974; Clinard, 1974; Bullough, 1975; Mischel, 1977). The following section presents the most common criticisms of the psychiatric-medical model of sexual variance. (It should be kept in mind that none of the following criticisms are meant to justify any form of sexual variance.)

Diseases of the mind do not exist.   Opponents of the psychiatric-medical model believe mental diseases do not exist for three reasons. First, only living tissue in bodies can become diseased. In this sense, the brain may be affected by a disease, but not the mind. Brain tumors, syphilis, and senility cause malfunctions in the brain and affect a person's behavior. These are examples of illnesses of the brain. However, there is no such thing as a "mental" illness. There are no malfunctions of the mind because the mind is not an entity with life of its own. The term *mind* is merely a convenient way of referring to the brain's cognitive (thinking) processes.

Second, the judgment that a person's thinking is sick or abnormal is a moral judgment. It is as much a matter of moral evaluation to label as abnormal a person's way of thinking about sex, as it is to claim that their religious and political beliefs are abnormal.

The notion of mental illness presupposes the existence of a condition of "mental health" or "normality." Any such condition has been impossible to identify, because it can only be described in terms of ideals for human living (Lazarus, 1975). Some psychiatrists are aware of and explicit about their moral judgments. Others deeply believe in the "objectivity" of the medical explanation. Sexual abnormality continues to be defined as sexual behavior other than heterosexual coitus. This definition affirms an ancient value judgment in favor of procreative sex. Many psychiatrists persist in defining noncoital sexual behavior as being abnormal (Khan and Solomon, 1974). Humanistic values are sometimes now applied. These values stress the normality of sex as an expression of love and care. Therefore, some psychiatrists prefer to define abnormal sex as sex without love, or sex which causes harm to others (Khan and Solomon, 1974).

Unfortunately, it is impossible to separate any concept of sexual abnormality from social expectations and moral ideals (Marmor, 1971). Sexual abnormality is not an empirically measurable condition, but a value-laden concept (Tallent, 1977). The concept of sexual normality (and abnormality) can only be measured against personal and cultural ideals. Labeling any form of sexual behavior as "abnormal" is simply another way of condemning it. In brief, then, normal and abnormal patterns do not actually exist in sexual behavior. Normality exists only as a expectation and concept in the eye of the beholder.

Third, the existence of deviant behavior cannot be explained on the basis of "sick" motives. Personal motives are simply personal desires and goals, Knowledge of a person's desires and goals is useful in understanding specific individuals. However, people hold widely different goals for the same behavior.

There are no special "deviant" motives for deviant sexual behavior. This becomes clear when it is realized that sexual deviance is defined by societal reactions to behavior, rather than any particular quality in the behavior itself. Deviant sexual behavior is best explained in terms of the same principles of social learning, which are used to explain sexual behavior that conforms to dominant social expectations (Clinard, 1974).

A complex motivational analysis is rarely used to explain people's behavior when they conform to conventional social expectations. It is only when people do something regarded as unexpected or unusual that it seems necessary to resort to a search for peculiar motives (Scott and Lyman, 1968). The incorrect logic seems to be that unusual behavior is a result of unusual motives. People who seek sexual intercourse with their marriage partners rarely have their motives questioned by others, or rarely even question their own motives. In contrast, husbands and wives who avoid sexual intercourse with one another are now subject to motivational analysis. Similarly, during the Victorian past, women who had premarital sexual intercourse evoked questions about their peculiar motives. Ultimately, the whole notion of motives has come to be questioned by behavioral scientists. The meaning of a motive is very unclear. What are the observable referents to which the term refers? If it is something in a person's thinking which they themselves may not recognize, how can any scientist "see" it to know it better? Motivational explanations for behavior may be a scientific dead end.

Behavior is not a symptom.   Critics of the psychiatric-medical model state that behavior is not a symptom. First, if no organic malfunction exists, then behavior is not a symptom of disease or health. Instead, behavior is a product of past learning plus situational rewards and punishments.

The judgment that a person's behavior is a symptom of "wrong" thinking is ultimately a moral judgment. This is evident in psychiatric disputes over just what is, or is not, a "symptom" of mental illness. The basis for judging what is a symptom has shifted with the tides of change in popular morality and psychiatric fashion.

Frequent masturbation was identified as a symptom (and cause) of insanity during the Victorian era. Until recently, a desire for frequent oral-genital sex, particularly to the point of orgasm, was commonly considered to be a "symptom" of "sick" motives. Homosexual behavior was an official mental illness, until its status was changed by a vote of the American Psychiatric Association in

1974 (Spector, 1977). Psychiatric opinion has followed changes in popular moral opinion much more closely than it has followed the findings of behavioral science research, especially in matters of sexual behavior.

Several research studies have found groups of psychiatrists to be in wide disagreement over the question of which behavior, in specific individuals, can be taken as symptomatic of abnormality (Clinard, 1974; Torrey, 1974). In one important research study, a group of researchers got themselves admitted to a mental hospital simply by telling the admitting psychiatrist that they heard voices (Rosenhan, 1973). Once they were admitted, they did nothing unusual. Nevertheless, all were diagnosed as being mentally ill. The staff even collected observations to support that "expert" diagnosis. Such research demonstrates that the labels of "abnormal" or "mentally ill" are rather easily attached to people on the basis of medical authority, rather than on the basis of any standard measure. The issue here is not a question of competence versus incompetence, but one of differences in the basic concepts used to understand human behavior.

In the end, psychiatric disputes over the symptom diagnosis of sexual behavior are moral and political disputes. Like religious disputes, they cannot be settled by reference to empirical data.

Therapy is not a cure. Critics of the psychiatric-medical model also emphasize that therapy is not a cure. First, psychotherapy is basically re-education. It essentially involves techniques aimed at changing a person's behavior and way of thinking. As such, the techniques of psychotherapy more closely resemble ideological conversion and re-education, than they resemble medical treatment of the body. Psychotherapy does not cure any illness.

Some people desperately want counseling and professional assistance in changing their sexual behavior. Some people exhibit dangerous sexual behavior which society wants to change. There are many good reasons for changing people's behavior. However, the decision to change behavior poses unavoidable moral and political choices. Professionals, whose business it is to change their clients' behavior, must be self-conscious and honest about the values they employ. It is deceptive to consider re-education (therapy) as being always like a helpful medicine.

Forced psychotherapy has been used by both the Soviet and American governments to change behavior deemed socially undesirable (Szasz, 1963; Torrey, 1974). It is always done in the name of helping people.

In the past, the social control of sexual variance was accomplished through religious codes of conduct and criminal law. Medical practice now may have a great potential for becoming an extension of police power (Zola, 1972). Increasingly effective chemical and psychological techniques are being developed for regulating sexual behavior. These techniques can be equally useful in attempts to enforce conformity of sexual preferences and in efforts to offer genuine help to people who want assistance. The practice of psychiatric medicine may get entangled in the network of social control (Steadman, 1972). When medical profes-

Table 15-1 Models of Sexual Variance

	The Psychiatric-Medical Model	The Social-Learning Model
1. The question of normal-abnormal, psychological health-illness in behavior	1. Sexual behavior is either normal or abnormal, healthy or sick.	1. All judgments of normality and healthiness in sexual behavior are ultimately moral judgments.
2. The basic nature of sexual variance	2. Sexual behavior is abnormal and sick if it exhibits the following characteristics: (a) Bizarreness—very unusual; (b) Discomfort—it results in severe anxiety; (c) Inefficiency—does not have heterosexual intercourse as its primary goal	2. All judgments of abnormality are moralistic. However, any sexual behavior can be a problem: (a) if it is socially defined as a problem by society; or, (b) if a person regards his or her own behavior as a problem for himself or herself.
3. The basic origin of sexual variance	3. Sexual abnormality is a symptom of a mental disorder reflecting psychological conflicts and anxieties about normal sexual behavior.	3. Sexual variance is socially condemned sexual behavior, but is learned through the same learning processes as is more conventional sexual behavior. The learning usually results from personal erotic meanings, rather than culturally accepted ones.
4. Treatment of sexual variance	4. A person whose sexual behavior is abnormal needs intensive psychotherapy to help relieve the underlying mental illness. It is the obligation of the therapist to cure a sick person.	4. (a) If behavior is illegal, it is a matter for the criminal justice system. (b) If a person regards his or her behavior as a problem he or she can be helped to change it. (c) If a person does not regard his or her behavior as a problem, a therapist has no obligation to change it.

sionals use the psychiatric-medical model of sexual variance, they may become agents of social control, enforcing religious and legal codes of sexual conduct.

Second, psychotherapy sometimes administers punishment in the guise of help. When people's behavior is stigmatized by being labeled "abnormal" (or "immature," or "emotionally disturbed"), they are, in effect, being condemned (Halleck, 1971). The process of psychiatric stigmatization has created a considerable amount of human misery. Such labeling promotes a climate of fear, guilt, and suspicion. Some people even suspect their own sanity and fear that they are going crazy.

Most people no longer worry about whether or not their sexual practices are morally virtuous. Instead, they worry about whether or not they are sexually "normal." Some people sometimes read psychiatric literature in which the sexual practices that they enjoy are labeled "abnormal." Many outdated books remain on library shelves. Some persons may not read widely enough to realize that there are great differences in psychiatric opinion. The authority of medical experts and medical language may impress and scare them. Consequently, they suffer from guilt and anxiety which necessitates their consultation with a psychiatrist who thereupon "cures" them of their emotional disturbance.

a comparison of models of sexual variance

It is difficult to compare the social psychological and medical interpretations of sexual variance. They employ different vocabularies and they have entirely different ways of conceptualizing the nature of sexual behavior.

Table 15–1 offers a simplified way of understanding the differences between the psychiatric-medical model and the social learning model of sexual variance.

the meaning of homosexuality

Among behavioral scientists, there is no common agreement about the meanings of the terms *homosexuality* and a *homosexual* . All attempts at such definition encounter major difficulties (Marmor, 1976). To get to the heart of the matter, it is useful to make a distinction between homosexual acts—behavior—and homosexual persons.

Homosexual behavior may be defined as behavior between members of the same sex which results in sexual arousal. The sexual actions do not necessarily have to result in orgasm to be defined as homosexual. However, this definition excludes any same sex contact which does not result in sexual arousal. In many societies, kissing, hugging, and caressing occur between members of the same sex as a culturally accepted custom carrying no erotic significance and causing no sexual arousal. Whether or not any act is homosexual is a matter which can be objectively verified by determining if sexual arousal occurs.

While it is possible to verify homosexual behavior objectively, a homosexual person and homosexuality are more difficult to describe in an objective manner. What criterion is most useful for scientific analysis: homosexual behavior, or homosexual feelings, or a self-concept as a homosexual? The following definitions will certainly not satisfy everyone, but they have proven to be quite useful in behavioral research.

Homosexual is a distinction made by an "audience" or by the person's self. The term *homosexual* is primarily an identity label which a person may (or may

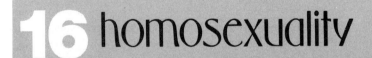

16 homosexuality

not) apply to his or her self-concept as a description of his or her self. Therefore, in this chapter, a *homosexual* is defined as a person who labels himself or herself a homosexual. In other words, a homosexual is a person who holds a homosexual self-concept or personal identity. Whether or not a person is a homosexual is a subjective matter which only the person himself or herself can determine. A person is a homosexual who affirms: ''I am a homosexual'' to the self and to others. The term *gay* is now used by many homosexual persons to refer to themselves. Many prefer this term because they feel that it neutralizes the traditional derogatory connotations of *homosexual.* In this chapter, however, the technical term will be retained without any derogation intended.

The term *homosexuality* is used in this book to refer to a primary or exclusive erotic responsiveness toward members of the same sex (Whitam, 1977a). In contrast, the term *heterosexuality* is used to refer to a primary or exclusive erotic responsiveness toward members of the other sex. *Erotic responsiveness* is indicated by the stimuli which evoke sexual arousal in daydream sex fantasies, night dreams, visual stimulation, as well as in direct tactile stimulation. In heterosexuality, the contents are primarily other-sex stimuli, while in homosexuality, the contents are primarily same-sex stimuli. When a person's erotic responsiveness is more or less evenly distributed between other-sex and same-sex stimuli, they exhibit *bisexuality.*

If homosexuality is an erotic orientation, what is the meaning of *latent homosexuality*? The concept of latent homosexuality derives from psychoanalytic theory. It is no longer widely accepted among behavioral scientists (Marmor, 1976). The concept of latent homosexuality suggests that some people have an ''unconscious'' predisposition toward homosexual behavior which may be expressed in the form of femininity in men and masculinity in women. Popularly, the term *latent homosexual* has become part of the vocabulary of *homophobia,* the fear or hatred of homosexuals. It is used as a derogatory remark to ridicule people who do not conform to traditional gender-role stereotypes.

Some heterosexual adults are deeply troubled by occasional homosexual fantasies, especially when they worry about being a ''latent homosexual.'' They may even panic with fear that they may be carried away by ''unconscious'' forces, into the ''sickness'' of homosexuality. Many past psychiatric writings about latent homosexuality may have aggravated these unnecessary anxieties (Schimel, 1972).

The spectrum of sexualities.   Kinsey and his coworkers developed a rating scale to identify variations in sexuality between exclusive heterosexuality and exclusive homosexuality (Kinsey et al., 1948, 1953). The scale has seven locations with ''0'' representing the exclusive heterosexual pole and ''6'' representing the exclusive homosexual pole. The scale locations are designed to reflect a person's erotic responsiveness as well as behavior. The rating can be used to reflect a particular time period in a person's life, or the whole life history. At the heterosexual pole are people who have experienced erotic responsiveness only to members of the other sex and whose sexual behavior has only been with the other sex. At the homosexual pole are people whose erotic responsiveness and behavior has been exclusively with members of the same sex. In the middle of the scale, at location "3," are people whose erotic responsiveness and behavior has been more or less equally bisexual.

This rating scale is very useful because it enables researchers to avoid the oversimplification of dividing people's sexuality into only two, sharply distinct categories: heterosexual and homosexual. In 1948, the Kinsey research, for example, found that among men at age 45, about 89 percent had a "0" rating of exclusive heterosexuality (Kinsey et al., 1948). The remainder of men at that age had ratings distributed across the spectrum, with only about 2 percent of men being at the exclusive homosexual pole.

Recently, Kinsey's Institute for Sex Research completed a research project which studied the largest sample of homosexual persons ever investigated (Bell and Weinberg, 1978). The research involved careful, lengthy interviews with 686 male homosexuals and 293 female homosexuals recruited from the area around San Francisco. The Kinsey rating scale was used with each subject. The results reveal the diversity of sexualities, even among people who consider themselves to be homosexuals. Most of the subjects in the study rated their behavior as "5" or "6" along the scale indicating that their sexual behavior was mainly or exclusively with members of the same sex. Yet a significant minority of the subjects had experienced heterosexual intercourse during the year previous to the study. And a majority had experienced it at least once in their life. On the level of sexual "feelings," the subjects were even more diverse. About half of the subjects rated themselves as less than "6," indicating some heterosexual erotic responsiveness. Their heterosexual erotic responsiveness was manifested in masturbatory fantasies, night dreams, and sexual arousal in response to members of the other sex.

In conclusion, there are many self-identified homosexuals of both sexes who have had pleasurable heterosexual activity and remain aware of having a potential for sexual arousal by members of the other sex. On the other hand, there are some self-identified homosexuals who have never experienced sexual arousal in response to the other sex (Bell and Weinberg, 1978). Further, there are many self-identified heterosexuals of both sexes who have had pleasurable homosexual activity. There are a majority of others who have never experienced homosexual activity.

bisexuality

Much research has revealed that some people who regard themselves as heterosexuals or bisexuals also sometimes engage in homosexual behavior (Blumstein and Schwartz, 1976a,b). The particular social contexts of bisexuality vary considerably. Sometimes homosexual activity is highly situational and occurs when opportunities for heterosexual activity are blocked or absent. Sometimes it occurs as a result of exploratory sexual adventurism. In some cases, people who have an emerging homosexual identity engage in both homosexual and heterosexual activity. In other cases, people regard themselves as being bisexual and enjoy both heterosexual and homosexual contacts without having a distinct preference. Some people are simply *ambisexual* and are rather unconcerned about the sources of their orgasms.

Situational homosexual activity is prevalent in both men's and women's prisons (Ward and Kassebaum, 1964; Kirkham, 1971; Davis, 1973). The sexual behavior of most prison inmates is usually exclusively heterosexual before and after imprisonment. Even though they may engage in frequent homosexual acts while in prison, they do not regard themselves as being homosexuals. They maintain a heterosexual self-concept and regard their homosexual acts to be a result of the absence of heterosexual outlets.

One study found that a great many women in the occupation of strip-teasing engage in sexual activity with other women with whom they work (McCaghy and Skipper, 1969). Most of these women do not consider themselves lesbians. They regard their sexual involvement with women to be a consequence of their difficulty in establishing affectionate relationships with men.

In group sex, a great many women engage in sexual activity with other women, yet almost all of them do not regard themselves as homosexuals (Bartell, 1971). Most of these women have a bisexual self-concept and affirm an erotic preference for heterosexual activity. Curiously, in group sex very few men become involved in homosexual activity.

One research project investigated the homosexual behavior of men having impersonal oral-genital sex in public toilets (Humphreys, 1970, 1971). Surprisingly, it found that a great many such men did not consider themselves to be homosexuals. A majority (54 percent) of these men were married but did not have sexual intercourse as frequently as they desired because of the sexual disinterest of their wives. Many of the men regarded impersonal homosexual sex as a preferable alternative to masturbation or the pursuit of extramarital affairs.

Another research project investigated lower class boys who were homosexual street prostitutes (Reiss, 1961). It found that almost all of them maintained a heterosexual self-concept, even though they allowed themselves to be fellated by adult homosexual men in exchange for money. The boys are able to neutralize the homosexual implications of their sexual activity by regarding their motivation as the desire for money, rather than for sexual pleasure.

A recent research project investigated the sexual behavior of male athletes at four universities and found homosexual behavior to be common among them (Garner and Smith, 1977). In a sample of 82 athletes who filled out a detailed questionnaire, the researchers found that about 40 percent of the men had engaged in at least two homosexual acts to orgasm during the previous two years. Almost all of these athletes also engaged in sexual activity with women during the same two year period. Only 8 percent of these athletes were exclusively homosexual in their behavior. The close body contact in all-male groups may encourage a certain amount of sexual experimentation.

In recent years, the idea of bisexual experimentation has become fashionable in some (but not all) circles of radical feminists (Margold, 1974). Some radical feminist beliefs encourage the possibility of sexual intimacy between women who are close friends as an affirmation of their strong emotional bonds (Hite, 1976). Sexual "affairs" between women may also be encouraged by the belief that heterosexual relations involve the dominance of women by men, but homosexual relations involve truly empathetic equals (Kelly, 1972). Some research has found that these beliefs do motivate some women to become involved in homosexual activity while maintaining a heterosexual or bisexual identity (Bode, 1976; Blumstein and Schwartz, 1976a). However, some clinical case studies indicate that when such sexual experimentation occurs during adolescence, it may cause some young women painful confusion over their sexual identity (Defries, 1976).

the incidence of homosexual behavior

The only two sources of national survey data indicating the incidence of homosexual behavior among adult Americans are found in the research of Kinsey (1948, 1953) and Hunt (1974). However, both research projects had major methodological inadequacies in their collection of data relevant to homosexual behavior.

Some general conclusions about homosexual behavior are still possible, even if the national incidence data are not very adequate. Most people who experience some homosexual contact do so during the teenage years, between puberty and age 16 (Gebhard, 1972). After the age of 16, the incidence of homosexual behavior rapidly declines. Married people have a lower incidence of homosexual behavior during adulthood than do unmarried people (Gebhard, 1972). Few people first experience a homosexual contact after being married. Among unmarried people, on the other hand, the incidence of people who first experience a homosexual contact gradually increases over the years when people remain unmarried. Probably about half of men who are still unmarried by age 40 have had some homosexual contact (Gebhard, 1972).

Several research projects have investigated the incidence of homosexual experience in samples of pre-adolescents and adolescents, rather than from the sometimes faulty memories of adults (Ramsey, 1943; Elias and Gebhard, 1969; Sorenson, 1973). The results vary greatly because of the differing ways in which homosexual experience is defined. Some researchers, for example, include cases of mutual genital exhibition without bodily contact between same-sex children as being homosexual experiences. However, the inclusion of such cases as incidents of homosexual behavior is highly questionable, especially if sexual arousal does not occur. The incidence of adolescent homosexual behavior in these studies varies between 11 percent and 50 percent among boys, between 6 percent and 35 percent among girls. Most adolescent homosexual behavior is a consequence of same-sex exploratory play during early adolescence when heterosexual social life is minimal. It is a result of curiosity, rather than erotic attraction, and usually occurs only a few times with one or two partners (Gagnon and Simon, 1973; Hunt, 1974).

Disagreement about the incidence of homosexual behavior focuses upon the issue of what percentage of adult men and women have any homosexual contact. There is less dispute about the percentage of adults whose sexual behavior is mainly to exclusively homosexual. At this point, only crude estimates can be made from past research efforts.

A survey of research done for the National Institute of Mental Health estimated that between 25 percent and 33 percent of American males have at least one homosexual contact, but most of that behavior is confined to the teenage years (Gebhard, 1972). About 4 percent of adult men (mostly unmarried) are estimated to be mainly to exclusively homosexual in their behavior. The incidence of female homosexual behavior is somewhat less concentrated during the teenage years and is believed to be lower than that among males. It is estimated that between 10 percent and 12 percent of American females have at least one homosexual contact (Gebhard, 1972). About 1 or 2 percent of adult women (mostly unmarried) are estimated to be mainly to exclusively homosexual in their behavior. These estimates lean heavily upon Kinsey's research data which probably exaggerate the incidence of male homosexual behavior and under-represent the incidence of female homosexual behavior because of problems in sample selection (Hunt, 1974).

In summary, what these data suggest is that the percentage of males who have had homosexual contact is about two to three times the percentage of women who have had such contact. Similarly, the percentage of men who are homosexuals (who have a homosexual self-concept) is about twice the percentage of homosexual women.

In the decade of the seventies, self-identified homosexuals have become more visible publicly, at least in the news and on television. Homosexuality has become a controversial social and political issue. The question arises whether homosexual behavior is becoming increasingly common. The available research, done since the time of Kinsey's work, indicates no increase in the proportion of Americans who have had homosexual experience (Hunt, 1974; Levin, 1975).

THE ORIGINS OF HOMOSEXUALITY

social learning theory

As yet, there is no fully adequate explanation for the origins of homosexuality. This should not be surprising, since there is not yet any fully adequate explanation for the origins of heterosexuality. However, a great many behavioral scientists today regard the social learning perspective to offer the most useful understanding of homosexual behavior and homosexual persons (Acosta, 1975).

Social learning theory emphasizes the effects of reinforcements (rewards and punishments) in the learning of homosexual erotic response and homosexual behavior. It also emphasizes the crucial role of symbolic processes in the transformation of a person's self-concept (Churchill, 1967; Dank, 1971; Gagnon and Simon, 1973; Blumstein and Schwartz, 1974; Plummer, 1975).

Attempts to understand homosexuality are ultimately rooted in attempts to comprehend the basic nature of human sexuality itself. One possible basic assumption is that some kind of predisposition for heterosexual behavior is biologically inborn in humans and that a homosexual predisposition may accidentally be inborn in a few people. An alternative is to assume that all people are born bisexual, with equal predisposition for heterosexual and homosexual behavior and that society suppresses people's homosexual inclinations. Social learning theories accept neither assumption. They begin quite differently by assuming that people are born with none of these predispositions. Instead, they regard infants as born simply as sexual beings in the sense of having the capacity for physiological sexual arousal. They find no evidence that any particular stimuli "naturally" activates sexual arousal. Instead, humans learn to associate various stimuli with sexual arousal. Socially structured reinforcements in our society channel most people's learning toward heterosexual stimuli. A few people, however, learn to develop homosexual behavior as a result of their personal experiences. According to this point of view, humans are not born heterosexual or even bisexual, but simply sexual.

There is a growing consensus among behavioral scientists that homosexual behavior has many different origins (Bell, 1974; Marmor, 1976). Past attempts of researchers to find the single underlying "cause" of homosexuality may have been futile. Homosexuality, just like heterosexuality, probably has multiple origins.

Initial homosexual contact most commonly occurs at the time when adolescents also begin to have heterosexual erotic experience. Social learning theory suggests that a person's initial homosexual behavior is expressed in response to anticipated rewards for such behavior. Rewards (pleasures) are usually more effective in eliciting behavior than is punishment. Yet, punishment may still play an important role in shaping homosexual behavior. People may have emotionally painful heterosexual experiences, which make homosexual involvement more likely. Whether or not experiences are found to be emotionally pleasurable or painful depends largely upon the personal meanings which people attribute to their experience (Gross, 1978).

Some possible rewards for homosexual interaction may be: (1) a same-sex love relationship; (2) same-sex play leading to genital stimulation; or (3) the anticipation of sexual pleasure in response to homosexual erotic fantasies. Some possible painful experiences which may become associated with heterosexual behavior include: (1) sex guilt about early heterosexual activity; (2) blocked opportunities for heterosexual activity; and (3) humiliating sexual experiences with the other sex.

Social learning theory regards homosexuality as primarily a matter of learning an erotic response to members of one's own sex. An alternative, psychoanalytic viewpoint emphasizes that homosexuality is primarily a matter of learning a confused gender identity. The hypothesis is that if a young person becomes confused about his or her "proper" gender identity, he or she is likely to become an adult homosexual. This idea has already become a part of conventional wisdom about the "cause" of homosexuality. However, social learning theory reverses this direction of cause and effect. Instead, it suggests that if a young person becomes involved in homosexual behavior, the experience may cause the person to become anxious and confused about his or her gender identity. This is particularly likely to occur in cultures where male and female gender roles are very rigidly stereotyped as opposites (Hooker, 1965; Carrier, 1977).

The social learning theory assumption that homosexuality has multiple and varied origins runs counter to the assumption that adult homosexuality has its origin in a person's childhood experience with his or her parents. The notion that the parent-child relationship "causes" adult homosexuality has also become conventional wisdom. Yet, there is little persuasive evidence for such a conclusion, and much recent research evidence indicates that childhood experience is not necessarily crucial to the development of adult homosexuality. One large-scale study, for example, compared the childhood experience of 307 male homosexuals with that of 138 male heterosexuals (Siegelman, 1974). The research found no substantial difference between the two groups in their childhood experiences with their parents. The only exception was the finding that significantly more of the homosexual men described both of their parents as more rejecting and less loving and reported that they were less close to their fathers than was reported by the heterosexual men. Yet these findings cannot be taken to indicate that unloving parents predispose their children toward homosexuality. That may be only one factor in a total mix of factors.

Other factors in childhood experience may also play a role in the eventual development of adult homosexuality. These include early sex-guilt training by parents and a child's development of idealized anti-erotic images of the other sex. There is some evidence that boys in our culture who develop effeminate interests and mannerisms are more likely to become adult homosexuals than boys who do not (Whitam, 1977b). Such boys may easily be labeled "sissies" by their peers and experience blocked opportunities for heterosexual activity in dating. Yet this does not mean that all effeminate boys inevitably become adult homosexuals. Other research indicates that a girl's childhood experience of sexual molestation and rape by an adult male can lead her to develop aversive attitudes toward all heterosexual activity (Gundlach, 1977). Some women who have had such childhood experience may find a homosexual relationship to be more emotionally pleasurable. Again, such a relationship depends largely upon the personal meanings which a girl attributes to her experience.

It does not appear to be the case that children of homosexual parents become adult homosexuals. One study investigated 37 children who were raised by a homosexual or transexual mother (Green, 1978). All of the children who had reached adolescence were exclusively heterosexual in their erotic fantasies and sexual behavior.

the search for biological factors

There has been a long research tradition seeking the origin of homosexuality in some biological abnormality. Since homosexual behavior was at one time culturally regarded as an "abnormality," the logic of such a search was quite enticing. The origin of homosexual behavior has been sought in body morphology, in chromosomes, and in hormones. So far, there is no evidence of any special biological factors relevant to homosexual behavior in humans.

Since techniques have been developed for measuring levels of sex hormones from urine and blood samples, attempts have been made to find differences in hormone levels between heterosexuals and homosexuals. The results have been largely inconclusive because of many contradictory findings (Meyer-Bahlburg, 1977). Such research is complicated by the fact that an individual's sex hormone level fluctuates considerably. In addition, environmental stresses and the use of many drugs can also cause hormonal changes. Presently, there is no conclusive evidence that the sex hormone levels of adult heterosexuals and homosexuals differ uniformly in any substantial way (Meyer-Bahlburg, 1977).

In recent years, an entirely new line of hormonal theorizing has taken shape. The new possibility is that sex hormone abnormalities which occur during fetal development can cause an adult predisposition for homosexual behavior, at least in some cases. Research with rats and monkeys has produced female sexual behavior in male animals and male sexual behavior in female animals (Dorner et al., 1975; Goy and Goldfoot, 1975). This is done by inducing abnormalities in the sex hormone levels of the animals during a critical period of their prenatal development or shortly after birth. The suggestion is that the infant animals' brains have been chemically changed so that they exhibit opposite-sex behavior in maturity. However, the fetal hormone manipulations also masculinize the bodies of the female animals, so that they are partially hermaphrodites in genital structure.

Following the findings of animal research, the suggestion is that hormonal abnormalities during a critical period of fetal brain development can cause a predisposition for homosexual behavior at puberty. Currently, there is no evidence from human research to support such speculation.

Although this animal research is fascinating, its relevance to human sexual behavior is unclear (Meyer-Bahlburg, 1977). It is a great leap of speculation to suggest close similarities between the sexual behavior of rats and monkeys and that of human beings. In humans, for example, there are no instinctive patterns of sexual behavior. In the animal research, the behavior of mounting the rear of another animal is regarded as being instinctively male. Instinctive female sexual behavior in animals involves presenting the posterior and genitals for mounting.

There is no really comparable male and female sexual behavior in humans. There are no sexual positions among humans which can seriously be taken to correspond to instinctual female "presenting" and male "mounting." In addition, no differences have been found in the genital anatomy of female homosexuals and heterosexuals.

Even though they are animals, humans are a rather unique species, with species-specific patterns of behavior. The nature of human homosexual behavior is unlike that found in lower order animals. A pattern of exclusive homosexual behavior, for example, is not found in subhuman mammals, even though occasional homosexual contacts are quite commonly observed (Meyer-Bahlburg, 1977).

In conclusion, biological explanations of homosexuality must be regarded with considerable caution, especially when they reflect popular superstitions and oversimplifications.

initial homosexual behavior in girls

The first homosexual activity of girls who eventually become adult homosexuals usually takes place as part of a same sex romantic love relationship (Gagnon and Simon, 1973; Cronin, 1974). Initial female homosexual activity is less commonly a consequence of adolescent sexual exploration and sex play. The first homosexual encounter takes place before the age of 20 for the vast majority of women who have any such experience (Hedblom, 1973; Saghir and Robins, 1973). Another adolescent girl, rather than an adult woman, is much more likely to be the first homosexual partner. First homosexual encounters are about as often self-initiated, as they are a result of another girl's initiative (Hedblom, 1973).

An initial homosexual encounter between adolescent girls usually does not include any direct genital manipulation, although that does occur for a substantial minority (Gagnon and Simon, 1973; Saghir and Robins, 1973). Usually, initial female homosexual interaction begins with kissing, hugging, and body contact as an expression of affection. With more experience over time, it moves toward genital contact. In all these ways, initial female homosexual involvement is similar to the evolution of female heterosexual involvement. The essential difference is that other females are the objects of affection, erotic response, and sex fantasy.

In a vast majority of cases, recurrent homosexual fantasies precede any overt homosexual behavior (Hedblom, 1973; Saghir and Robins, 1973). These homosexual fantasies are essentially romantic daydreams about love affairs with members of the same sex. They sometimes first occur during the pre-adolescent years, but almost always before the end of adolescence (Hedblom, 1973; Saghir and Robins, 1973). Therefore, most adolescent girls who experience any homosexual involvement have an emotional readiness for affectional homosexual encounters, long before they actually occur (Hedblom, 1973). Many of these girls previously experience occasions of homosexual erotic response during casual bodily contact with other girls, for example, during play, hand holding, sleeping with a friend overnight, or when practicing kissing with a friend (Saghir and Robins, 1973).

The role of female romantic fantasies in the evolution of female homosexual behavior is obviously crucial. Unfortunately, there is yet little understanding of how sexual daydreams become linked with affectional attraction toward members of the same sex. One possibility may be that romantic same-sex daydreams may be reinforced by masturbation (McGuire et al., 1965; Marquis, 1970). There is some evidence that girls with homosexual experience begin masturbation earlier in adolescence and are more likely to masturbate than are girls with only heterosexual experience (Saghir and Robins, 1973; Goode and Haber, 1977). There is also some evidence that such girls are also more likely to be heterosexually active in petting and sexual intercourse at an earlier age than are girls without any homosexual experience (Saghir and Robins, 1973; Goode and Haber, 1977). Recurrent adolescent homosexual fantasies may be a result of displeasurable reactions to particularly early heterosexual relationships.

Almost all adolescent girls who become involved in homosexual activity also have some experience with heterosexual petting or intercourse (Gagnon and Simon, 1973; Saghir and Robins, 1973). A majority of such girls also experience heterosexual erotic response and sexual arousal. Most girls who continue their homosexual relationships in later life do so not because they find heterosexual activity displeasurable, but because they find homosexual activity as pleasurable or even more so (Saghir and Robins, 1973). The emotional and symbolic rewards of homosexual relationships for them outweigh those of their heterosexual relationship.

initial homosexual behavior in boys

The pre-adolescent period (ages 10 to 13) is the period when same-sex contacts leading to sexual arousal are most commonly experienced by boys (Kinsey et al., 1948). Those boys who continue homosexual behavior into adulthood are particularly likely to experience, at a very early age, sexual activity with males leading to orgasm previous to any sexual activity with girls (Manosevitz, 1970; Saghir and Robins, 1973). Pre-adolescent homosexual activity occurs at a time when boys usually have little to do with girls and seek only other boys as companions.

Male homosexual behavior during pre-adolescence is usually a result of exploratory sex play (Gagnon and Simon, 1973). It is much less often an expression of a close affectionate comradeship, although this is sometimes the case. Initial male homosexual experience almost always occurs with boys of similar age, rather than with adult males (Saghir and Robins, 1973).

Initial male homosexual behavior most commonly involves mutual genital masturbation (Kinsey, 1948; Saghir and Robins, 1973). Some boys make a game of such activity during pre-adolescence and early adolescence without attributing it adult homosexual meaning at the time (Kinsey, 1948; Martinson, 1976). It is less common for initial homosexual contacts to involve fellatio. Although for those boys who continue homosexual interaction through later adolescence, fellatio becomes the predominate sexual activity (Saghir and Robins, 1973). In addition, initial homosexual interaction among boys as compared with girls is much less likely to involve any affectionate kissing and caressing (Saghir and Robins, 1973).

Most boys who have any homosexual experience have it only once or several times and discontinue further homosexual activity. Some boys, however, find it sufficiently rewarding to continue. Boy who eventually become homosexuals are particularly likely to incorporate homosexual activity into their daydream sex fantasies during masturbation (Saghir and Robins, 1973). This cognitive rehearsal of homosexual activity associated with orgasm during masturbation reinforces homosexual erotic response, so these boys increasingly experience sexual arousal in response to males (McGuire et al., 1965; Marquis, 1970).

Some boys who eventually become homosexuals never have sexual fantasies about females and never experience erotic response to females. However, a majority of boys who become homosexuals do experience heterosexual fantasies, erotic response, and even sexual intercourse (Manosevitz, 1970; Saghir and Robins, 1973). Their persistent homosexual involvement through adolescence may function to diminish their heterosexual responsiveness. Gradually their sexuality becomes channeled toward a predominant homosexual erotic orientation. Ultimately, they may be unable to attain erection during heterosexual activity. Even if they do, they may obtain less emotional satisfaction from heterosexual intercourse than from homosexual activity.

THE DEVELOPMENT OF HOMOSEXUALITY

the development of homosexual identity

In this chapter, a distinction has been made between homosexual acts and homosexual persons. People who engage in homosexual behavior do not automatically regard themselves as being homosexuals. Social learning theory suggests that the creation of a homosexual identity is a product of a person's attempt to give meaning to undefined, ambiguous, and confusing sexual experience (Plummer, 1975).

As people gradually come to regard themselves as being homosexuals, they must cognitively redefine the negative meaning of homosexuality and establish a positive emotional response to it (Dank, 1971). Generally, people define their identity through their relationships with other people. A person in the process of becoming a homosexual painfully struggles to find an acceptable identity within the context of their homosexual relationships. They are as influenced, as is anyone else, by negative cultural stereotypes of homosexuals.

The process of developing a homosexual identity involves the transformation of a person's self-concept and precipitates an identity crisis. The homosexual identity crisis is termed *coming out* (Dank, 1971). During the period of coming out, an emerging homosexual confronts himself or herself with the questions: Who am I? What am I becoming? An answer, in the form of the label "a homosexual," is both terrifying and satisfying. It is terrifying because of the social stigma, condemnation, and possible persecution. Yet it is also satisfying simply because any concrete identity is better than constantly unanswered questions. It should not be surprising, then, that a great many homosexuals report that their final acceptance of a homosexual identity was felt as an emotional relief (Dank, 1971; Schafer, 1976).

Female homosexual identity. There are very few studies of the development of homosexual identity in women who are not psychiatric clients. Those which are available indicate that most women establish a homosexual self-concept within the context of a love relationship with another woman (Gagnon and Simon, 1973; Cronin, 1974; Cunningham, 1977). They are likely to regard their sexual attraction toward other women simply as an expression of affection. The ability to love and be loved is a traditional feminine self-ideal, and sexual contact is an accepted part of a love relationship. Therefore, most lesbians are able to accept their homosexual attraction as a natural expression of an affectionate preference for women, rather than for men. Indeed, many lesbians regard themselves as having made a conscious choice to love women, who they believe are more loving than are men (Cunningham, 1977).

Nevertheless, accepting the self-label of homosexual is usually painfully difficult, especially at first. Some women resist an acknowledgement of a homosexual identity for many years, even while involved in a homosexual love relationship (Cunningham, 1977). They often find little rapport between their own feminine self-image and the public stereotype of lesbians as masculine "dykes." In addition, accepting themselves as homosexuals may mean sacrificing the traditional feminine goals of marriage, motherhood, and family life.

Many homosexual women do get married, although the exact percentage remains unknown. In a major research project on homosexuality carried out recently by the Institute for Sex Research, it was found that 35 percent of white homosexual women and 47 percent of black homosexual women had been married (Bell and Weinberg, 1978). A majority of these women considered their marriages to be unhappy, and their marriages lasted—on the average—only a few years. Relatively few of the women considered themselves to be homosexual prior to their marriage. Most of those who did consider themselves to be homosexual did not tell their husbands. A majority of the women said that their homosexuality was a precipitating factor in the break-up of their marriage. They had sexual intercourse much less frequently in their marriages than did a comparison group of heterosexual women. Yet about half of the homosexual women had given birth to children. A large number of their marriages ended when they became involved with another woman.

Most homosexual women desire to establish an exclusive partnership with another woman. They are much less interested, than are male homosexuals, in constantly finding new partners for sexual activity (Cotton, 1975). Lesbian relationships tend to last longer, and lesbians have many fewer partners in their lifetimes than do male homosexuals (Bell and Weinberg, 1978). It is for these reasons that lesbians are much less publicly visible in homosexual bars and clubs than are male homosexuals. Much like other women sexually, they do not tend to actively seek out partners in public places.

In lesbian partnerships, some women role play traditional masculine and feminine gender roles (Jensen, 1974). The "butch" role imitates traditionally masculine manners and activities, while the "femme" role follows a pattern of exaggerated femininity. However, such gender role playing in lesbian partnerships is now becoming rare, as both heterosexuals and homosexuals are coming to reject rigid stereotypes of masculinity and femininity (Cronin, 1974; Cunningham, 1977). One study of a large number of lesbians, for example, found that 75 percent of them never role played either a "butch" or "femme" role in their homosexual relationships (Ponse, 1976b).

The lesbian community is much more secretive and less public than is the male homosexual community (Ponse, 1976a). Therefore, it is easy to underestimate the number of female homosexuals in a community. The lesbian community largely consists of networks of close friends who visit each other socially at home. These friendship networks offer group support for a woman's positive affirmation of a homosexual identity (Ponse, 1976a). However, they also discourage any desires for affectionate and sexual relationships with men (Blumstein and Schwartz, 1974).

Male homosexuality identity. The establishment of a homosexual identity is preceded by many years during which young men attempt to come to terms with the meanings of their recurrent homosexual fantasies, erotic responses, and desires. By the end of their teenage years, most males who eventually become homosexuals have already recognized that their attraction to men is sexual in nature (Dank, 1971; Whitam, 1977). One large-scale study of 386 self-identified homosexuals found that it took an average of six years for these men to come out and define themselves as homosexuals (Dank, 1971). The average age at which they finally established a homosexual identity was 21 (Dank, 1974). This means that for most emerging homosexual men, the homosexual identity crisis parallels and is part of their more general adolescent identity crisis. However, there is great variation. The period of coming out may extend over twenty years for some homosexual men, especially among those who marry (Dank, 1974).

Unlike female homosexuals, only a minority of male homosexuals come to adopt a homosexual identity in the context of a same-sex love relationship (Dank, 1971). Nevertheless, social relationships usually do play a crucial role in the establishment of male homosexual identity. Most commonly, men finally establish a homosexual identity through casual associations with men already involved in the homosexual community (Dank, 1971). Many male homosexuals ultimately come out while associating with self-identified homosexuals in same-sex contexts, such as in the military, school dormitories, or prisons. Finally, some male homosexuals adopt a homosexual identity simply after reading about homosexuality and concluding that the descriptions fit their sexual experience (Dank, 1971).

The exact percentage of homosexual men who get married is unknown. The study of homosexuality done by the Institute for Sex Research found that 20 percent of white homosexual men and 13 percent of black homosexual men had been married (Bell and Weinberg, 1978). Homosexual men are much less likely to ever marry than are homosexual women. The married homosexual men had sexual intercourse with their wives—on the average—less often than did a comparison group of heterosexual men. A majority of them had occasional to frequent sex fantasies about men while having sexual intercourse with their wife. The marriages of homosexual men tended to last longer than did the marriages of homosexual women. Some, however, broke up because the men became involved in affairs with other men or because their wife would not tolerate their extramarital homosexual behavior. Less than a third had told their wife about their homosexuality prior to their marriage. A majority of the men fathered children while they were married. Homosexual men often marry out of a desire for social acceptance and a family life (Ross, 1971). Many also marry before establishing a firm homosexual identity, or in an attempt to "cure" their homosexual preferences (Dank, 1972).

Some homosexual men maintain their marriages for decades while engaging in secretive impersonal sex (Dank, 1974). In the homosexual community, such men are known as "closet queens." These men often try to protect themselves from suspicion by creating a public image of conspicuous morality, including the expression of strongly anti-homosexual attitudes (Dank, 1974). However, many of them are plagued by constant paranoid fears of detection or blackmail (Scott and Lyman, 1968).

Contrary to popular belief, not all homosexual males behave in an effeminate manner (Hooker, 1965). Many male homosexuals attempt to present a "macho" masculine image of themselves. Indeed, among many groups of homosexual men, effeminacy is regarded with contempt (Dank, 1974). Role playing feminine behavior is most commonly exhibited by young homosexuals during their identity crisis, when they are searching to give meaning to their erotic orientation (Gagnon and Simon, 1973). The emergent homosexual may imitate the effeminate stereotype at that time, in an attempt to confirm in his eyes—and those of a homosexual reference group—that he is indeed one of them. Some male homosexuals continue to role play effeminate behavior for many years, but most do not (Hooker, 1965).

Role playing distinctive gender roles is a cultural and personal expectation, but it is not a necessary component of homosexual identity. In cultures where people expect rigid distinctions between male and female behavior, homosexual men are likely to link their identity to either feminine or exaggerated masculine mannerisms (Carrier, 1977). In American society, gender role playing is most common among male homosexuals from lower class backgrounds (Farrell and Morrione, 1974). In contrast, middle class male homosexuals are similar to middle class heterosexuals, in holding more flexible gender role expectations.

The emergent homosexual male suffers intense feelings of "being different." These painful feelings encourage him to seek others with whom he finds a shared sense of similarity (Sawchuk, 1974). Association with members of the homosexual community is experienced as an emotional relief. This positive feeling functions to reinforce a homosexual identity. He may learn to regard bisexual behavior as only a passing stage in the process of coming out (Warren, 1974). He may also learn from the homosexual community beliefs which help him to neutralize guilt feelings about homosexual behavior (Hooker, 1967). Even more important is his realization that homosexuals are not effeminate, dangerous perverts. This experience makes it easier for the emergent homosexual to accept a homosexual identity and value himself as a person (Warren, 1974).

The male homosexual community is composed of both public and secretive associations. The visible, public aspect of the homosexual community consists of gay bars, gay organizations, newspapers, and bookstores. It also consists of certain places where contacts for impersonal sex are arranged such as steam baths, gyms, and public toilets (Leznoff and Westley, 1956; Hooker, 1967). Homosexual men in high status occupations, however, tend to avoid involvement in these public agencies. Instead, they arrange their social relationships through friendship networks or cliques (Leznoff and Westley, 1956).

homosexual erotic response

The social learning of homosexual behavior involves learning positive cognitive-emotional meanings to attribute to homosexual interaction. In other words, it involves learning a homosexual erotic response. The two basic dimensions of homosexual erotic response are: (1) positive, affirming beliefs; and (2) pleasurable emotional evaluations of homosexual interaction.

As the following research indicates, homosexual erotic response is basically similar to heterosexual erotic response, except for the gender of preferred partners. It is basically consistent with the erotic socialization which homosexuals experience as males or females. In addition, research evidence indicates that sexual pleasure is no more and no less an important life concern of homosexuals than it is for heterosexuals (Bell and Weinberg, 1978).

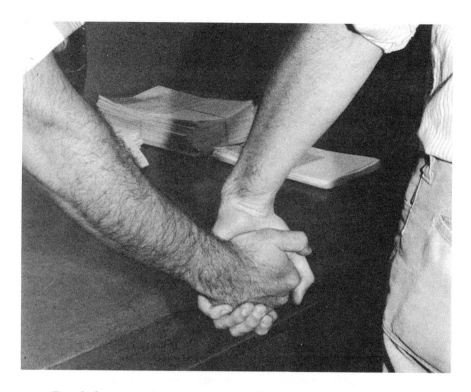

Female homosexual erotic response.   The cognitive dimensions of female homosexual erotic response are reflected in beliefs which affirm the superiority of love between women. Some lesbians claim, for example, that women in love are more emotionally sensitive, caring, and gentle with their partners than are men (Kelly, 1972). This difference is often explained on the basis of special attributes, such as women's intuition and responsiveness to nonverbal communication. It may also be explained on the basis of the desire of women for relationships of equality, rather than that of control and dominance which is said to be typical of men (Kelly, 1972).

The superiority of sexual interaction between women may be affirmed by the belief that sex for women, unlike men, is an expression of an overall love relationship. There is nothing particularly unusual about these beliefs (Kelly, 1972). They are widely held by heterosexual women, also. Even the belief that women are more attractive than are men reflects widely held cultural assumptions which may be used to affirm homosexual attraction (Blumstein and Schwartz, 1974).

These beliefs are linked with emotional evaluations of homosexual relations. One study, for example, asked a sample of homosexual women who recently had heterosexual intercourse to evaluate the differences they perceived between their homosexual and heterosexual experience (Schafer, 1976). Homosexual activity was evaluated as being more tender, intimate, sympathetic, and considerate by most of the women. In contrast, a majority of the same women regarded heterosexual intercourse as being more "aggressive." Homosexual women may be more conscious, than are many men, of female desires for verbal and nonverbal interplay and feedback during sexual activity. In addition, sexual interaction between homosexual women may be more relaxed and emotionally expressive and less oriented toward the achievement of orgasm than is sexual interaction guided by male erotic expectations (Bode, 1976; Hite, 1976).

Kinsey was perhaps the first researcher to point out that homosexual women use those techniques of sexual arousal which are most likely to be particularly pleasurable for women (Kinsey et al., 1953). Homosexual women are sensitive to their partner's desire for slow, general body stimulation which only gradually moves toward genital stimulation. They may be more aware than are many men of female desires for clitoral stimulation (Hite, 1976). They may also be more capable of offering each other multiple orgasms during periods of lengthy sexual play.

The technique of sexual arousal used by female homosexuals most commonly is masturbation to orgasm (Kinsey et al., 1953; Saghir and Robins, 1973; Hunt, 1974). Oral-genital stimulation is the next most commonly employed technique, even though receiving cunnilingus is the most commonly favored sexual experience reported by female homosexuals (Bell and Weinberg, 1978). A less commonly used technique involves one partner rubbing her genital area against the other's body while they embrace. Contrary to popular belief, few homosexual women ever use penis substitutes (dildoes) during sexual activity.

Male homosexual erotic response. It is quite likely that male homosexual erotic response is an extention of early male erotic socialization linked to male stimuli instead of female stimuli. One large-scale research project asked homosexual men about the particular sexual stimuli which they found most arousing (Bell and Weinberg, 1978). Their responses emphasized a masculine appearance and male body parts, rather than personality traits (as emphasized by lesbians). A great many were especially interested in the size of their partner's genitals. It seems that male homosexual erotic response is centered upon body-oriented sexual stimuli. Male homosexual erotic response may be an extension of early male fascination with male genitals elaborated to the male body (Tripp, 1975).

An emphasis upon genital pleasure may be a key aspect of the emotional dimension of male homosexual erotic response, as compared with that of female homosexuals. The first homosexual experience of the vast majority of boys who eventually became adult homosexuals involves genital manipulation to orgasm, while this is not the case for most female homosexuals.

Homosexual practices among males include mutual masturbation, fellatio, anal intercourse, and body rubbing to orgasm. Mutual masturbation is the most common form of homosexual activity experienced during early adolescence

(Saghir and Robins, 1973). However, among adult homosexuals, fellatio is the most common sexual practice and receiving fellatio is the most commonly preferred sexual experience (Saghir and Robins, 1973; Bell and Weinberg, 1978). Anal intercourse is also a common practice, but less so than is oral-genital sex (Bell and Weinberg, 1978). Finally, full body contact simulating movements of intercourse is less frequently practiced.

Male homosexual partnerships tend to be short and unstable. Nevertheless, most homosexual men voice a desire to establish a permanent, loving intimate relationship (Hooker, 1967; Sonenschein, 1968). Some homosexual men maintain long monogamous partnerships, while others have practically no sexual contact at all. However, promiscuous involvement in relatively impersonal sex is common (Sonenschein, 1968; Cotton, 1975; Bell and Weinberg, 1978). A rather indiscriminate choice of sexual partners appears to be more common among male homosexuals than it is among single male heterosexuals. A substantial majority have some sexual contacts with partners whom they never met before (Bell and Weinberg, 1978).

The promiscuity of many male homosexuals appears to be a result of several social forces which conspire to produce instability in their sexual relationships. First, their adolescent erotic socialization as males, as compared with females, emphasizes the separation of sexual pleasure from emotional involvement (Hooker, 1967). Consequently, the sexual patterns of male homosexuals are an exaggeration of early male socialization. Their desire for sexual variety is unrestrained by the influence of female companionship (Schafer, 1977). It is probably for this reason, also, that male homosexual partnerships as compared with those of females are characterized by more jealousy and less loyalty (Cotton, 1975). Second, the difficulties of male homosexuals in a homophobic society encourage impersonal sex. It is much more difficult for aging men than aging women to share an apartment and engage in social activities together without provoking suspicions of being homosexuals. Two women living together are easily accepted as spinsters, while two men are seen as an "odd couple." Consequently, many male homosexuals prefer to live alone (Cotton, 1975). In the hope of avoiding social entanglements which might lead to detection, many male homosexuals seek secretive and impersonal sex (Leznoff and Westley, 1956).

HOMOSEXUALITY AND PERSONAL PROBLEMS

diverse homosexual lifestyles

The role that homosexuality has in the lives of homosexual men and women varies considerably. Just as there are many ways in which heterosexuals express their sexuality, so too there are diverse homosexual lifestyles. It is a gross oversimplification to think of homosexuals as all being alike in the way they lead their lives. The recent research of Kinsey's Institute for Sex Research, which interviewed 686 homosexual men and 293 homosexual women, was able to make useful distinctions between various homosexual lifestyles (Bell and Weinberg, 1978). The distinctions made are as follows:

1. *Close-coupled* homosexuals resemble happily married heterosexuals. They maintain a close relationship with another person and seek their sexual and emotional satisfaction primarily in that relationship. They have the fewest sexual problems and are the least likely to seek outside sexual partners. Although they do not have the highest level of sexual activity, they are the most likely to report being satisfied with their sexual lives. They are also very unlikely to regret being homosexual.

2. *Open-coupled* homosexuals also live with a special sexual partner. However, they are less monogamous and more likely to seek other sexual partners outside their relationship. Many of them seek sexual encounters without the knowledge of their special partner. They do more "cruising" (partner seeking in public places) and are more sexually active than the average respondent. In the study, this lifestyle was the one most common among the males, while it was relatively rare among the women. The women were more likely to be "close-coupled."

3. *Functional* homosexuals resemble swinging singles in their lifestyle. They are not particularly interested in finding a special partner with whom to establish an exclusive relationship. They are more interested in sexual pleasure, have more frequent sexual activity, and more numerous partners than any other group of homosexuals. Functional homosexuals spend a great deal of time with many friends, cruise bars frequently for sexual partners, and are active participants in the gay subculture. They are the most likely homosexuals to ever have been arrested for an offense related to their homosexual behavior. Yet, functional homosexuals are less likely to regret being homosexual than any other group.

4. *Dysfunctional* homosexuals suffer from more regret about their homosexuality than does any other group. They also report having more problems in sexual functioning (difficulties such as attaining erection or orgasm) than does any other group. They tend to consider themselves as being sexually unattractive, report more difficulties in finding agreeable sexual partners, and worry more about being able to maintain affection for a partner. Nevertheless, the males reported frequently cruising for sexual encounters. Many aspects of their lives, in addition to the sexual aspect, are beset with frustration.

5. *Asexual* homosexuals are withdrawn and socially isolated individuals. They score lowest on their sexual interest and activity and rate their sexual attractiveness as being very low. They tend to spend their leisure time alone and have infrequent contact with friends. They do less cruising than any other group except close-coupled homosexuals. Asexual homosexuals are not very much interested in establishing a relationship with a special partner. Finally, asexual homosexuals rate themselves as being less exclusively homosexual and more bisexual than the other groups.

the psychological adjustment of homosexuals

It cannot automatically be assumed that homosexuals have more personal problems than do heterosexuals. This is a question for research—and one which has stirred quite a bit of controversy.

Traditionally, the Western cultural heritage regarded homosexuality as a "perversion." The medical model of sexual variance incorporated this perspective into its definition of homosexuality as a form of mental illness. Homsexuality was officially defined as a form of mental illness by the American Psychiatric Association until 1974. It was always assumed to be a personal problem. Case studies of homosexual patients, done by helping professionals, seemed to confirm a picture of homosexuals as psychologically tormented individuals. However, these studies of patients are unrepresentative of all homosexuals. They offer a poor basis for a judgment of the psychological well-being of all homosexuals. Such a picture of homosexuals is now rejected by most helping professionals.

Only recently have behavioral scientists carried out carefully controlled research studies comparing large samples of nonpatient homosexuals with heterosexuals from similar social backgrounds. A thorough review of these research projects found little evidence to conclude that homosexuals have more personal problems than do heterosexuals (Hart et al., 1978).

The recent research project of the Institute for Sex Research was the most extensive effort to compare the psychological well being of nonpatient homosexuals with heterosexuals (Bell and Weinberg, 1978). The researchers gave a large number of psychological tests to both their sample of homosexuals and a comparative sample of heterosexuals. The research measured such factors as their general state of health, psychosomatic symptoms, self-reported happiness, exhuberance, self-acceptance, loneliness, worry, depression, tension, paranoia, and suicidal feelings. The research found that the psychological well-being of homosexuals is related to their particular lifestyle. In general, dysfunctional and asexual homosexuals were found to have lower psychological well-being than heterosexuals. On the other hand, close-coupled and functional homosexuals are similar to heterosexuals in their psychological well-being. The findings are as follows:

1. Close-coupled homosexuals seem to benefit greatly from their intimate partnership. They are less tense and paranoid and more exhuberant about life than average. They are more happy, more self-accepting, less lonely, and less depressed than other homosexuals.

2. Open-coupled homosexuals worry more about their homosexual behavior, especially when cruising for partners. They also worry more about their relationship with their special partner than do close-coupled homosexuals. Open-coupled lesbians tend to experience more feelings of loneliness and less self-acceptance than do open-coupled male homosexuals.

3. Functional homosexuals tend to be energetic, self-reliant, cheerful, and optimistic individuals. Their psychological well-being does not differ very much from heterosexuals, except that they are somewhat more likely to have feelings of loneliness.

4. Dysfunctional homosexuals are those who have the most personal problems. They are more lonely, worrisome, paranoid, depressed, tense, and unhappy than other homosexuals, especially the males. Dysfunctional and asexual homosexuals indicate much lower self-acceptance than do heterosexuals.

Both of these groups are the ones most likely to seek professional assistance for emotional problems.

5. Asexual homosexuals have similarly low psychological well-being as dysfunctional homosexuals. They differ from dysfunctionals primarily in being much more socially isolated and withdrawn. Asexual lesbians have the highest incidence of suicidal feelings.

professional services for homosexuals

Today, the ethics of trying to eliminate homosexuality is widely questioned by helping professionals (Davidson, 1977). Many helping professionals now refuse to try to terminate homosexual behavior unless a client is deeply troubled by his or her behavior and is strongly motivated (without ambivalence) to change it. These helping professionals do not regard homosexual behavior as a disease and refuse to play the role of society's police agents (Bancroft, 1974; Davidson, 1977). Some helping professionals now offer counseling designed to enable homosexuals clients to accept their homosexuality without anxiety and guilt (Bianco, 1976).

In a sense, then, there are two alternative treatments available to homosexuals who wish to use the services of helping professionals: (1) conversion therapies aimed at changing a client's homosexuality to heterosexuality; (2) adjustment therapies aimed at helping a client live a fulfilling life as a homosexual. The latter therapies are similar to the helping services provided to heterosexuals. Counseling may be offered to build self-acceptance, to cope with anxiety-provoking situations, or to manage depression. Relationship counseling, similar to marital counseling, may be offered to homosexual partners who experience distressed relationships. Sex therapy is even being offered to help homosexuals overcome sexual dysfunctions which are suffered by some homosexuals, just as they are by some heterosexuals. Since the late 1960s, these two forms of assistance have been offered to homosexuals by Masters and Johnson's foundation in St. Louis with considerable success (Masters and Johnson, 1979).

There are a wide variety of conversion therapies, including behavior modification techniques and psychoanalysis (Acosta, 1975). As yet, there is no evidence that any specific conversion therapy is more effective in achieving that goal than any other. The most effective techniques appear to produce lasting conversion to heterosexuality in about one-third of clients (Bancroft, 1974). In general, conversion therapy has been most effective with homosexuals: (1) who are young, usually below 35 years of age; (2) who had their first homosexual encounter after the age of 16; (3) who have had some enjoyable heterosexual activity, and are more bisexual in their erotic response; and (4) who do not also experience gender identity confusion (Marmor and Green, 1977). In actual practice, few exclusive homosexuals seek conversion therapy.

In American society, there are three basic viewpoints about social policy toward homosexuals: (1) homosexuals are sinners and criminals who sould be punished; (2) homosexuals should be tolerated as sick people who can be cured; and (3) homosexuals are a persecuted minority group whose human rights need to be protected. Conflict over social policy between people holding these contrasting viewpoints has made homosexuality a political issue.

the law and law enforcement

Homosexual acts are criminal offenses under state laws against sodomy. These same sodomy laws also criminalize certain sexual acts between husbands and wives. Sodomy is a legal term, rather than a behavioral one. It means an "unnatural sex act." The specific sex acts were considered so disgusting when the laws were originally conceived that the behavior could not be written explicitly into legal codes. The sex acts were simply referred to as: "abominable crimes against nature, not fit to be named among Christians."

Homosexual acts were first criminalized in Europe, when Christianity became the state religion of the Roman Empire (Churchill, 1967). A sentence of death was usually imposed, most commonly, by burning at the stake. Homosexuality was thereafter considered a form of religious heresy (Szasz, 1970). The Inquisition in Spain, for example, sought out homosexuals as fervently as it did Jews, Protestants, and other heretics. After the French Revolution, however, the Code Napoleon eliminated all laws regulating private sexual acts between consenting adults, whether heterosexual or homosexual. Since that time, most European nations have followed suit, and eliminated all special sex laws based upon religious tradition. This has not been the case, however, in the United States, which has more laws regulating sexual behavior than does any nation in the world.

In the forty-two states that still have sodomy laws, the law usually makes fellatio, cunnilingus, and anal intercourse criminal sex acts. Although these laws apply to both heterosexual and homosexual relations, they are only rarely used to prosecute sex acts between men and women (*Iowa Law Review,* 1976). Instead, sodomy laws are now almost exclusively aimed at the suppression of homosexual acts between males. Homosexual acts between females seems almost never to have been a concern of the American criminal justice system (Kinsey et al., 1953). Sodomy laws carry punishments ranging from fines to life imprisonment, although the most common sentence is 10 to 15 years in jail.

In actual practice, few homosexuals are ever prosecuted and imprisoned under the sodomy laws. It is difficult to apprehend either heterosexuals or homosexuals for the commission of "sex crimes" that are carried out in privacy between consenting adults (*Iowa Law Review,* 1976). There is always a problem in obtaining the testimony of witnesses. Occasionally, police use decoys to entrap male homosexuals by posing as homosexuals, in attempts to obtain homosexual solicitations (Weinberg and Williams, 1974). Most police attempts to regulate homosexual conduct are aimed at the public social life of homosexuals. Arrests are usually made under laws governing disorderly conduct, vagrancy, or liquor licenses (Weinberg and Williams, 1974). However, some arrests for sodomy are made using concealed observation in public toilets, frequented by men seeking impersonal homosexual contacts.

Some research has found that police, as an occupational group, are particularly homophobic (Niederhoffer, 1967). They rank homosexuals as one of the two most disliked groups, with whom they must deal (the other being "cop-fighters"). Their homophobia is probably a consequence of their poor education. Police training manuals often portray homosexuals as dangerous perverts (Dank, 1974). Relations between the police and the homosexual community are often highly antagonistic, and sometimes violent.

the homosexual civil rights movement

In recent years, an increasing number of states have repealed their laws against sodomy (*Iowa Law Review,* 1976). This change has generally been a response to a growing desire to modernize and simplify state laws. Some social groups want to go further and institute laws prohibiting discrimination against homosexuals in employment and housing. Some cities have already passed anti-discrimination laws. In one major city, Miami, such a law was passed, only to become the center of national controversy in 1977. The anti-discrimination law was repealed in a referendum vote of Miami citizens. The matter came to national attention, after Anita Bryant organized efforts to repeal the law. The effort to repeal the law was characterized by appeals to fear and hostility, employing conventional stereotypes of homosexuals as sex maniacs and child molestors. Much of it carried the tone of a fanatical crusade for traditional religious morality.

In the past, religious groups almost uniformly regarded homosexual acts as an abominable sin. However, uniformity among religious groups no longer exists. In 1970, the national assembly of the Unitarian Church passed a resolution in favor of anti-discrimination legislation, and called upon its members to work for the civil liberties of homosexuals, as a moral responsibility. In 1975, the United Church of Christ (formerly the Congregationalist Church) took a similar position. Also in 1975, the National Council of Churches passed a resolution in support of anti-discrimination legislation. Some other denominations have also modified their traditional view of homosexuals. Several denominations have even organized special programs that offer assistance to their homosexual members.

Gay organizations are groups of homosexuals organized to pursue a variety of goals. The early gay organizations of the 1950s, such as the Mattachine Society and the Daughters of Bilitis, were primarily secretive organizations that offered group support to socially isolated homosexuals. In relation to the surrounding community, they sometimes attempted programs of education about homosexuality (Weinberg and Williams, 1974). During the late 1960s, a shift in focus to political activism occurred among many younger members of gay organizations. Their goal came to be called "gay liberation," and involved attempts to deal directly with stigmatization and discrimination by engaging in political action.

At this point, the lobby in favor of anti-discrimination legislation includes some professional groups, civil liberties groups, feminist groups, and liberal church groups, as well as gay organizations.

The future is likely to see intensified conflict over the issue of social policy toward homosexuals. The social conflict is largely between heterosexuals over differences in moral judgment, and the power to enforce moral judgment through the law. At this point in American history, the weight of popular opinion continues to support the past tradition of homophobia.

bibliography

ABEL, GENE G., DAVID H. BARLOW, EDWARD B. BLANCHARD, and DONALD GUILD, "The Components of Rapists' Sexual Arousal," *Archives of General Psychiatry,* 34, no. 8 (Aug. 1977), 895–903.

ABEL, THEODORA and NATALIE F. JOFFE, "Cultural Backgrounds of Female Puberty," *American Journal of Psychotherapy* (1950), 4, 90–113.

"Abortion Deaths in Sharp Decline," *New York Times,* (May 28, 1975), 9.

"Abortion Foes Gain Support As They Intensify Campaign," *New York Times,* (Oct. 23, 1977), 1, 24.

ABRAMSON, PAUL R. and DONALD L. MOSHER, "Development of a Measure of Negative Attitudes Toward Masturbation," *Journal of Consulting and Clinical Psychology,* 43, no. 4 (August 1975), 485–90.

ABRAMSON, PAUL R., "The Relationship of the Frequency of Masturbation to Several Aspects of Personality and Behavior," *Journal of Sex Research,* 9, no. 3 (May 1973), 132–42.

ACOSTA, FRANK X., "Etiology and Treatment of Homosexuality: A Review," *Archives of Sexual Behavior,* 4, no. 1 (Jan. 1975), 9–29.

AHLSTROM, SYDNEY E., *A Religious History of the American People.* New Haven, Conn.: Yale University Press, 1972.

ALBIN, ROCHELL SEMMEL, "Psychological Studies of Rape," *Signs: A Journal of Women in Culture and Society,* 3, no. 2 (Winter 1977), 423–35.

ALLGEIER, ELIZABETH R. and ARTHUR F. FOGEL, "Coital Position and Sex Roles: Responses to Cross-Sex Behavior in Bed," *Journal of Consulting and Clinical Psychology,* 46, no. 3 (June 1978), 588–89.

AMES, ROBERT, "Physical Maturing of Boys as Related to Adult Social Behavior," *California Journal of Educational Research,* 8, (1957), 69–75.

AMIR, MENACHEM, *Patterns in Forcible Rape.* Chicago: University of Chicago Press, 1971.

APFELBAUM, BERNARD, "A Critique and Reformulation of Some Basic Assumptions in Sex Therapy: The Relation Between Sexual Arousal and Sexual Performance." Paper presented at the International Congress of Sexology, 1976 Montreal.

ARAFAT, IBTIHAJ S. and WAYNE L. COTTON, "Masturbation Practices of Males and Females," *Journal of Sex Research,* 10, no. 4 (Nov. 1974), 293–307.

ARD, BEN N. JR., "Premarital Sexual Experience: A Longitudinal Study," *Journal of Sex Research,* 10, no. 1 (Feb. 1974), 32–39.

———, "Sex in Lasting Marriages: A Longitudinal Study," *Journal of Sex Research,* 13, no. 4 (Nov. 1977), 274–85.

ARKIN, WILLIAM, "Military Socialization and Masculinity," *Journal of Social Issues,* 34, no. 1 (Winter 1978), 151–68.

ARNOLD, MAGDA B., *Emotion and Personality,* vol. I and II, New York: Columbia University Press, 1960.

ASAYAMA, SHIN' ICHI, "Adolescent Sex Development and Adult Sex Behavior in Japan," *Journal of Sex Research,* 11, no. 2 (May 1975), 91–112.

ASCHER, L. MICHAEL and RUTH E. CLIFFORD, "Behavioral Considerations in the Treatment of Sexual Dysfunction, *Progress in Behavior Modification,* vol. 3, pp. 241–91. Edited by Michel Hersen, Richard M. Eisler, and Peter M. Miller. New York: Academic Press, 1976.

BACH, GEORGE R. AND PETER WYDEN, *The Intimate Enemy: How to Fight Fair in Love and Marriage.* New York: Avon Books, 1968.

BALDWIN, WENDY H., "Adolescent Pregnancy and Childbearing — Growing Concerns for Americans," *Population Bulletin,* 31, no. 2, Washington, D.C. Population Reference Bureau, Inc., May 1977.

BALSWICK, JACK O. and CHARLES PEEK, "The Inexpressive Male: A Tragedy of American Society," *Family Coordinator,* 20, (Oct. 1971), 363–68).

BALSWICK, JACK O. and CHRISTINE P. AVERTT, "Differences in Expressiveness: Gender, Interpersonal Orientation, and Perceived Parental Expressiveness as Contributing Factors," *Journal of Marriage and the Family,* 39, no. 1 (Feb. 1977), 121–27.

BANCROFT, JOHN, *Deviant Sexual Behavior: Modification and Assessment.* London: Oxford University Press, 1974.

BANDURA, ALBERT and RICHARD H. WALTERS, *Adolescent Aggression.* New York: Ronald Press, 1959.

BANDURA, ALBERT and RICHARD H. WALTERS, *Social Learning and Personality Development.* New York: Holt, Rinehart and Winston, 1963.

BARBACH, LONNIE GARFIELD, *For Yourself: The Fulfillment of Female Sexuality.* New York: New American Library, 1975.

BARBER, BERNARD, *Science and the Social Order.* New York: Free Press, 1952.

BARCLAY, ANDREW M., "Sexual Fantasies in Men and Women," *Medical Aspects of Human Sexuality,* 7, no. 5 (May 1973), 205, 209–12, 216.

BARDIS, PANOS D., "Family Forms and Variations Historically Considered," *Handbook of Marriage and the Family,* pp. 403–61. Edited by Harold T. Christensen. Skokie, Ill.: Rand McNally, 1964.

BARDWICK, JUDITH M., *Psychology of Women.* New York: Harper & Row, Pub., 1971.

BARKER-BENFIELD, BENJAMIN, *Horrors of the Half-Known Life.* New York: Harper and Row, Pub., 1976.

BARRY, WILLIAM A., "Marriage Research and Conflict: An Integrative Review," *Psychological Bulletin,* 73, no. 1 (Jan. 1970), 41–54.

BARTELL, GILBERT D., *Group Sex.* New York: NAL, 1971.

BARTLETT, RICHARD A., *The New Country: A Social History of the American Frontier, 1776–1890.* New York: Oxford University Press, 1974.

BAUMAN, KARL E. AND ROBERT R. WILSON, "Sexual Behavior of Unmarried University Students in 1968 and 1972," *Journal of Sex Research,* 10, no. 4 (Nov. 1974), 327–33.

BAYER, ALAN E., "Sexual Permissiveness and Correlates as Determined Through Interaction Analysis," *Journal of Marriage and the Family,* 39, no. 1 (Feb. 1977), 29–40.

BAYLEY, NANCY, "Individual Patterns of Development," *Child Development* (1956), 27, no. 1, 45–74.

BEACH, FRANK A., "It's All in Your Mind," *Psychology Today,* (July 1969), 33–35 & 60.

BEACH, FRANK A. and H. FOWLER, "Effects of 'Situational Anxiety' on Sexual Behavior in Male Rats," *Journal of Comparative Physiological Psychology,* 52, (1959), 245.

BECKER, HOWARD S., "Becoming a Marijuana User," *American Journal of Sociology,* 49, (Nov. 1953), 235–42.

BECKER, JUDITH V. and GENE G. ABEL, "Men and the Victimization of Women," *Victimization of Women,* pp. 29–52. Edited by Jane R. Chapman and Margaret Gages. Beverly Hills, Calif.: Sage Publications, Inc., 1978.

BELL, ALAN P., "Attitudes Towards Nudity by Social Class," *Medical Aspects of Human Sexuality,* 3, no. 9 (Sept. 1969), 101–10.

——, "Homosexualities: Their Range and Character," *Nebraska Symposium on Motivation, 1973,* pp. 1–26. Edited by James K. Cole and Richard Diensthier. Lincoln, Neb.: University of Nebraska Press, 1974.

BELL, ALAN P. and MARTIN S. WEINBERG, *Homosexualties: A Study of Diversity Among Men and Women.* New York: Simon and Schuster, 1978.

BELL, ROBERT R., "Sex as a Weapon and Changing Social Roles," *Medical Aspects of Human Sexuality,* 4, no. 6 (June 1970), 99, 102–05, 110–11.

——, *Social Deviance: A Substantive Analysis* (2nd ed.). (Homewood, Ill.: Dorsey), 1976.

——, "Changing Aspects of Marital Sexuality," *Sexuality Today and Tomorrow,* pp. 213–18. Edited by Sol Gordon and Roger W. Libbey. Belmont, Calif.: Wadsworth, 1976.

BELL, ROBERT R. and BLUMBERG, "Courtship Stages and Intimacy Attitudes," *The Family Coordinator,* (March 1960), 61–63.

BELL, ROBERT R., STANLEY TURNER, and LAWRENCE ROSEN, "A Multivariate Analysis of Female Extramarital Coitus," *Journal of Marriage and the Family,* 37, no. 2 (May 1975), 375–83.

BELL, RUTH DAVIDSON et al., "Preparation for Childbirth," *Our Bodies, Ourselves,* pp. 267–96. New York: Simon and Schuster, 1976.

BELSEY, MARK A., YVONNE RUSSELL, and KAY KINNEAR, "Cardiovascular Disease and Oral Contraceptives: A Reappraisal of Vital Statistics Data," *Family Planning Perspectives* (March/April, 1979), 11, 84–89.

BERG, D. H., "Sexual Subcultures and Contemporary Heterosexual Interaction Patterns Among Adolescents," *Adolescence,* 10, no. 4 (Winter 1975), 543–48.

BERMAN, ELLEN M. and HAROLD I. LIEF, "Sex and the Aging Process," *Sex and the Life Cycle,* pp. 125–34. Edited by Wilbur Oaks, Gerald Mechiode, and Ilda Ficher. New York: Grune and Stratton, 1976.

BERMAN, JOHN AND DON OSBORN, "Specific Self-Esteem and Sexual Permissiveness," *Psychological Reports* (1975), 36, 323–326.

BERNARD, JESSIE, "Sex in Remarriage," *Medical Aspects of Human Sexuality,* 2, (Oct. 1968), 54–61.

——, *The Future of Marriage.* New York: World, 1972.

BERNSTEIN, ANNE C. and PHILIP A. COWAN, "Children's Concepts of How People Get Babies," *Child Development,* 46, (March 1975), 77–91.

BERSCHEID, ELLEN and ELAINE WALSTER, *Interpersonal Attraction.* Reading, Mass.: Addison-Wesley, 1969.

——, "Beauty and the Best," *Psychology Today,* (May 1972), 189–193.

——, "A Little Bit About Love," *Foundations of Interpersonal Attraction,* pp. 355–81. Edited by Ted L. Huston. New York: Academic Press, 1974.

——, "Physical Attractiveness," *Advances in Experimental Social Psychology, vol. 7,* pp. 157–215. Edited by Leonard Berkowitz. New York: Academic Press, 1974.

BIANCO, FERNANDO J., "Homosexuality: Fundamental Therapeutic Program." Paper presented at the International Congress of Sexology, 1976, Montreal.

BIDDULPH, LOWELL G., "Athletic Achievement and the Personal and Social Adjustment of High School Boys," *Research Quarterly of the American Association of Health, Physical Education and Recreation* (1954), 25, 1–7.

BLAKE, JUDITH, "The Teenage Birth Control Dilemma and Public Opinion," *Science,* (May 11, 1973), 180, 708–712.

BLOOD, ROBERT O., JR. and DONALD M. WOLFE, *Husbands and Wives.* New York: Free Press, 1960.

BLUMSTEIN, PHILIP W. and PEPPER SCHWARTZ, "Lesbianism and Bisexuality," *Sexual Deviance and Sexual Deviants,* pp. 278–95. Edited by Erich Goode and Richard Troiden. New York: Morrow, 1974.

———, "Bisexuality in Women," *Archives of Sexual Behavior* (1976a), 5, no. 2, 171–81.

———, "Bisexuality in Men," *Urban Life,* 5, no. 3 (Oct. 1976b), 339–58.

BODE, JANET, *View From Another Closet.* New York: Hawthorne, 1976.

BORLAND, DOLORES M., "An Alternative Model of the Wheel Theory," *The Family Coordinator,* 24, (July 1975), 289–92.

Boston Women's Health Book Collective, *Our Bodies, Ourselves.* New York: Simon and Schuster, 1976.

BRACK, DATHA CLAPPER, "Social Forces, Feminism, and Breastfeeding," *Nursing Outlook,* 23, no. 9 (Sept. 1975), 556–61.

BRAGONIER, J. ROBERT, "Influence of Oral Contraception on Sexual Response," *Medical Aspects of Human Sexuality,* (Oct. 1976), 130–43.

BRANT, RENEE S. T. and VERONICA B. TISZA, "The Sexually Misused Child," *American Journal of Orthopsychiatry,* 47, no. 1 (Jan. 1977), 80–90.

BRIDDELL, DAN W. and G. TERRENCE WILSON, "Effects of Alcohol and Expectancy Set on Male Sexual Arousal," *Journal of Abnormal Psychology,* 85, no. 2 (April 1976), 225–34.

BRIDDELL, DAN W., et al., "Effects of Alcohol and Cognitive Set on Sexual Arousal to Deviant Stimuli," *Journal of Abnormal Psychology,* 87, no. 4 (Aug. 1978), 418–30.

BRIGGS, JEAN L., "Eskimo Women: Makers of Men." *Many Sisters: Women in Cross Cultural Perspective,* pp. 261–304. Edited by Carolyn J. Matthiasson. New York: Free Press, 1974.

BRODERICK, CARLFRED B. and STANLEY E. FOWLER, "New Patterns of Relationships Between the Sexes Among Preadolescents," *Marriage and Family Living* (1961), 23, no. 1, 27–30.

BRODERICK, CARLFRED B., "Sexual Behavior Among Preadolescents," *Journal of Social Issues,* 22, no. 2 (April 1966), 6–21.

BROWN, J. K., "Adolescent Initiation Rites Among Preliterate Peoples," *Studies in Adolescence,* pp. 59–68. Edited by Robert E. Grinder. New York: Macmillan, 1969.

BROWN, SARA S., E. JAMES LIEBERMAN, and WARREN B. MILLER, "Young Adults as Partners and Planners." Paper presented to the Public Health Association, Nov. 1975.

BROWN, WALTER ARMIN, PETER M. MONTI, and DONALD P. CORRIVEAU, "Serum Testosterone and Sexual Activity and Interest in Men," *Archives of Sexual Behavior,* 7, no. 2 (March 1978), 97–103.

BROWNMILLER, SUSAN, *Against Our Will.* New York: Simon and Schuster, 1975.

BRYSON, JEFF B., "The Nature of Sexual Jealousy: An Exploratory Study." Paper presented to the American Psychological Association. Sept. 1976.

———, "Situational Determinants of the Expression of Jealousy." Paper presented to the American Psychological Association Aug. 1977.

BUCK, CAROL and KATHLEEN STAVRAKY, "The Relationship Between Age of Menarche and Age at Marriage Among Childbearing Women," *Human Biology* (1967), 39, 93–102.

BUCK, ROSS W., "Nonverbal Communication of Affect in Children," Report 73-8, 1973. Presented at American Psychology Association Meeting, Sept. 1973. Pittsburgh, Pa.: Department of Psychology, Carnegie-Mellon University, 1973.

BUCK, ROSS W., ROBERT E. MILLER, and WILLIAM F. CAUL, "Sex, Personality and Physiological Variables in the Communication of Affect Via Facial Expression," *Journal of Personality and Social Psychology* (1974), 30, no. 4, 587–96.

BULLOCK, RUTH C., RISE SIEGEL, MYRNA WEISSMAN, and E. S. PAYKEL, "The Weeping Wife: Marital Relations of Depressed Women," *Journal of Marriage and the Family,* 34, no. 3 (Aug. 1972), 488–95.

BULLOUGH, VERN L., "Sex and the Medical Model," *Journal of Sex Research,* 11, no. 4 (Nov. 1975), 291–303.

——, *Sexual Variance in Society and History.* New York: John Wiley, 1976.

BULLOUGH, VERN and BONNIE BULLOUGH, *Sin, Sickness, and Sanity.* New York: NAL, 1977.

Bureau of the Census, *U.S. Fertility Histories and Birth Expectations of American Women: June, 1971.* Washington, D.C.: U.S. Government Printing Office, 1974.

——, *Number Timing and Duration of Marriages and Divorces in the United States: June, 1975.* Washington, D.C.: U.S. Government Printing Office, 1976.

BURGESS, ERNEST W. and PAUL WALLIN, *Engagement and Marriage.* Philadelphia: Lippincott, 1953.

BURKE, RONALD J., TAMARA WEIR, and DENISE HARRISON, "Disclosure of Problems and Tensions Experienced by Marital Partners," *Psychological Reports,* 38, (April, 1976), 531–42.

BURR, WESLEY R., "Satisfaction with Various Aspects of Marriage Over the Life Cycle: A Random Middle Class Sample," *Journal of Marriage and the Family.* 32, no. 1 (Feb. 1970), 29–37.

BURSTEIN, BONNIE, "Life History and Current Values as Predictors of Sexual Behaviors and Satisfaction in College Women." Paper presented to the Western Psychological Association, April 1975.

BUSS, ARNOLD, *Psychology.* New York: John Wiley, 1966.

BUTLER, CAROL A., "New Data About Female Sexual Response," *Journal of Sex and Marital Therapy,* 2, no. 1 (Spring 1976), 40–46.

BYRNE, DONN, "A Pregnant Pause in the Sexual Revolution," *Psychology Today,* 11, no. 2 (July, 1977), 67–68. New York: Academic Press, 1971.

CALDEN, GEORGE, RICHARD M. LUNDY, and RICHARD J. SCHLAFER, "Sex Differences in Body Concepts," *Journal of Consulting Psychology* (1959), 23, no. 4, 378.

CALHOUN, ARTHUR W., *A Social History of the American Family, vol. I.* New York: Barnes and Noble, 1917. Reprinted 1960.

CAMPBELL, ANGUS, PHILIP E. CONVERSE, and WILLARD L. RODGERS, *The Quality of American Life: Perceptions, Evaluations and Satisfactions.* New York: Russell Sage Foundation, 1976.

CAREY, JAMES, "Changing Courtship Patterns in the Popular Song," *American Journal of Sociology,* 74 (May 1969), 720–31.

CARLSON, JOHN, "The Sexual Role,". *Structure and Analysis of the Family,* pp. 101–110. Edited by F. Ivan Nye. Beverly Hills, Calif.: Sage Publications, Inc., 1976.

CARNS, DONALD E., "Talking About Sex: Notes on First Coitus and the Double Sexual Standard," *Journal of Marriage and the Family,* 35, no. 4 (Nov. 1973), 677–688.

CARRIER, JOSEPH M., " 'Sex-Role Preference' as an Explanatory Variable in Homosexual Behavior," *Archives of Sexual Behavior,* 6, no. 1 (Jan. 1977), 53–65.

CAVANAGH, JOHN R., "Rhythm of Sexual Desire in Women," *Medical Aspects of Human Sexuality,* (Feb. 1969), 29–39.

CHAPPELL, DUNCAN, ROBLEY GEIS, and GILBERT GEIS, ed. *Forcible Rape: The Crime, the Victim and the Offender.* New York: Columbia University Press, 1977.

CHRISTENSEN, HAROLD T. and CHRISTINA F. GREGG, "Changing Sex Norms in America and Scandinavia," *Journal of Marriage and the Family,* 32, (Nov. 1970), 616–27.

CHURCHILL, WAINWRIGHT, *Homosexual Behavior Among Males: A Cross-Cultural and Cross-Species Investigation.* Englewood Cliffs, N.J.: Prentice-Hall, 1967.

CLANTON, GORDON and LYNN G. SMITH, ed. *Jealousy.* Englewood Cliffs, N.J.: Prentice-Hall, 1977.

CLARK, ANN L. and RALPH W. HALE, "Sex During and After Pregnancy," *American Journal of Nursing,* 74, (Aug. 1974), 1430–31.

CLARK, ALEXANDER L. and PAUL WALLIN, "Women's Sexual Responsiveness and the Duration and Quality of Their Marriages," *American Journal of Sociology* (1965), 71, 187–96.

CLARK, ROBERT A., IVAN F. NYE, and VIKTOR GECAS, "Husbands' Work Involvement and Marital Role Performance," *Journal of Marriage and the Family,* 40, no. 1 (Feb. 1978), 9–21.

CLAYTON, RICHARD R. and HARWIN L. VOSS, "Shacking Up: Cohabitation in the 1970's," *Journal of Marriage and the Family,* 39, no. 2 (May 1977), 273–83.

CLEVELAND, MARTHA, "Sex in Marriage: At 40 and Beyond," *Family Coordinator* (July, 1976), 25, 233–40.

CLINARD, MARSHALL B., *Sociology of Deviant Behavior.* New York: Holt, Rinehart and Winston, 1974.

COLEMAN, JAMES S., "Athletics in High School," *The Annals of the American Academy of Political and Social Science,* 338, (Nov. 1961).

CONGER, JOHN JANEWAY, *Adolescence and Youth.* New York: Harper and Row, Pub., 1973.

"Is Breast-Feeding Best for Babies." *Consumer Reports.* 42, no. 3 (March, 1977), 152–57.

COOMBS, ROBERT H., "Value Consensus and Partner Satisfaction Among Dating Couples," *Journal of Marriage and the Family,* 28, (May 1966), 166–173.

COOPER, ALAN J., "Factors in Male Sexual Inadequacy: A Review," *Journal of Nervous and Mental Disease,* 149, no. 4, (1969a), 337–59.

———, "Clinical and Therapeutic Studies in Premature Ejaculation," *Comparative Psychiatry,* 10, (1969b), 285–95.

———, "Some Personality Factors in Frigidity," *Journal of Psychosomatic Research,* 13, (1969c), 149–55.

COSER, LEWIS, *The Functions of Social Conflict.* New York: Free Press, 1956.

COTTON, WAYNE L., "Social and Sexual Relationships of Lesbians," *Journal of Sex Research,* 11, no. 2 (May 1975), 139–48.

CRAIN, STEVEN AND SUSAN ROTH, "Interactional and Interpretive Processes in Sexual Initiative in Married Couples." Paper presented to the American Psychological Association, August 1977.

CRONIN, DENISE, "Coming Out Among Lesbians," *Sexual Deviance and Sexual Deviants,* pp. 268–77. Edited by Erich Goode and Richard Troiden. New York: Morrow, 1974.

CUBER, JOHN F. AND PEGGY B. HARROFF, *The Significant Americans: A Study of the Sexual* Gerhard Neubeck. Englewood Cliffs, N.J.: Prentice-Hall, 1969.

CUBER, JOHN F., and PEGGY B. HARROFF, *The Significant Americans: A Study of the Sexual Behavior of the Affluent.* New York: Appleton-Century–Crofts, 1965.

CUNNINGHAM, NANCY E., "Lesbian Socialization and Identity," *People as Partners, Second Edition,* pp. 386–406. Edited by Jacqueline A. Wiseman. New York: Harper & Row, Pub., 1977.

CURRAN, JAMES P., "Convergence Toward a Single Sexual Standard," *Exploring Human Sexuality*, pp. 194–200. Edited by Donn Byrne and Lois A. Byrne. New York: Thomas Y. Crowell, 1977.

CURTIS, LYNN A., "Rape, Race and Culture: Some Speculations in Search of a Theory," *Sexual Assault*, pp. 117–34. Edited by Marcia J. Walker and Stanley L. Brodsky. Lexington, Mass: Heath, 1976.

CVETKOVICH, GEORGE, BARBARA GROTE, ANN BJORSETH, and JULIA SARKISSIAN, "On the Psychology of Adolescents' Use of Contraceptives," *Journal of Sex Research* 11, no. 3 (Aug. 1975), 256–70.

DALTON, KATHARINA, *The Menstrual Cycle*. New York: Pantheon, 1969.

DANK, BARRY M., "Coming Out in the Gay World," *Psychiatry* 34, (1971), 180–97.

———, "Why Homosexuals Marry Women," *Medical Aspects of Human Sexuality*, 6, (Aug. 1972), 14–23.

———, "The Homosexual," *Sexual Deviance and Sexual Deviants*, pp. 174–210. Edited by Erich Goode and Richard Troiden. New York: Morrow, 1974.

DAVID, DEBORAH S. and ROBERT BANNON, Eds. *The Forty-Nine Percent Majority: The Male Sex Role*. Reading, Mass: Addison-Wesley, 1976.

DAVIDSON, GERALD C., "Homosexuality and the Ethics of Behavioral Intervention," *Journal of Homosexuality*, 2, no. 3 (Spring 1977), 195–204.

DAVIDSON, VIRGINIA, "Psychiatry's Problem With No Name: Therapist-Patient Sex," *American Journal of Psychoanalysis*, 37, no. 1 (Spring 1977), 43–50.

DAVIS, ALAN J., "Sexual Assaults in the Philadelphia Prison System," *The Sexual Scene*, pp. 219–36. Edited by John H. Gagnon and William Simon. New Brunswick, N.J.: Transaction Books, 1973.

DAVIS, KEITH E., "Sex on Campus: Is There a Revolution?" *Medical Aspects of Human Sexuality*, (Jan. 1971), 128–42.

DAVIS, MURRAY S., *Intimate Relations*. New York: Free Press, 1973.

DAVIS, PETER, "Contextual Sex-Saliency and Sexual Activity: The Relative Effects of Family and Peer Group in the Sexual Socialization Process," *Journal of Marriage and the Family*, 36, no. 11 (Feb. 1974), 196–201.

DAVIS, SHARON K. and PHILIP W. DAVIS, "Meanings and Process in Erotic Offensiveness," *Urban Life and Culture*, 5, (Oct. 1976), 377–96.

DEBURGER, JAMES, "Sex in Troubled Marriages," *Sexual Issues in Marriage*, pp. 65–74. Edited by Leonard Gross. Jamaica, N.Y.: Spectrum Publ., 1975.

DEFRIES, ZIRA, "Pseudohomosexuality in Feminist Students," *American Journal of Psychiatry*, 133, no. 4 (April 1976), 400–04.

DEGLER, CARL N., "What Ought To Be and What Was: Women's Sexuality in the Nineteenth Century," *American Historical Review*, 79, no. 5 (Dec. 1974), 1467–90.

DEMENT, WILLIAM C., *Some Must Watch, While Some Must Sleep*. New York: W. H. Freeman and Company Publishers, 1972, 1974.

DEMOS, JOHN, *A Little Commonwealth*. New York: Oxford University Press, 1970.

DENTLER, ROBERT A. and PETER PINEO, "Sexual Adjustment, Marital Adjustment and Personal Growth of Husbands: A Panel Analysis," *Marriage and Family Living*, 22, no. 1 (Feb. 1960), 45–48.

DERLEGA, VALERIAN J. and ALAN L. CHAIKIN, *Sharing Intimacy: What We Reveal to Others and Why*. Englewood Cliffs, N.J.: Prentice-Hall, 1975.

DIERS, CAROL JEAN, "Historical Trends in the Age at Menarche and Menopause," *Psychological Reports* 34, (1974), 931–37.

DINGWALL, ERIC J., *The American Woman*. New York: Holt, Rinehart & Winston, 1956.

DOERING, CHARLES H., KEITH BRODIE, HELENA C. KRAEMER, RUDOLP H. MOOS, HEATHER B. BECKER, and DAVID A. HAMBURG, "Negative Affect and Plasma Testosterone: A Longitudinal Human Study," *Psychosomatic Medicine,* 37, no. 6 (Nov. 1975), 484–91.

DOERING, CHARLES H., C. KRAEMER, H. KEITH BRODIE, and DAVID A. HAMBURG, "A Cycle of Plasma Testosterone in the Human Male," *Journal of Clinical Endocrinology and Metabolism* 40, (1975), 492–500.

DORNER, GUNTER, WOLFGANG ROHDE, FRITZ STAHL, LOTHAR KRELL, and WOLF-GUNTHER MASIUS, "A Neuroendocrine Predisposition for Homosexuality in Men," *Archives of Sexual Behavior,* 4, no. 1 (Jan. 1975), 1–8.

DOUGLAS, JACK D., PAUL K. RASMUSSEN, and CAROL ANN FLANAGAN, *The Nude Beach.* Beverly Hills, Calif.: Sage Publications, Inc., 1977.

EASTMAN, WILLIAM F., "First Intercourse," *Sexual Behavior* 2, (March 1972), 22–27.

EDWARDS, JOHN N. and ALAN BOOTH, "Sexual Behavior In and Out of Marriage: An Assessment of Correlates," *Journal of Marriage and the Family,* 38, no. 1 (Feb. 1967a), 73–81.

———, "The Cessation of Marital Intercourse," *American Journal of Psychiatry,* 133, no. 11, (Nov. 1976b), 1333–36.

EHRMANN, WINSTON, *Premarital Dating Behavior.* New York: Holt, Rinehart & Winston, 1959.

ELIAS, JAMES and PAUL GEBHARD, "Sexuality and Sexual Learning in Childhood," *Phi Delta Kappan,* 50, no. 7, (March 1969), 401–05.

ELIAS, JAMES, "Exposure of Adolescents to Erotic Materials," *Technical Report of the Commission on Obscenity and Pornography, vol. IX,* pp. 273–312 Washington, D.C.: U.S. Government Printing Office, 1971.

ELIAS, MARILYN, "Stand-In For Eros," *Human Behavior,* (March 1977), 17–23.

EKMAN, PAUL, "Face Muscles Talk Every Language," *Psychology Today,* (Sept. 1975), 35–39.

EMERSON, JOAN, "Behavior in Private Places: Definitions of Reality in Gynecological Examination," *Recent Sociology No. 2,* pp. 73–100. Edited by Hans Peter Dreitzel. New York: MacMillan, 1970.

ERIKSON, KAI, "Notes on the Sociology of Deviance," *The Other Side,* pp. 9–23. Edited by Howard S. Becker. New York: Free Press, 1964.

ERIKSON, KAI T., *Wayward Puritans.* New York: John Wiley, 1966.

EVANS, LAURA J., "Sexual Harassment: Women's Hidden Occupational Hazard," *Victimization of Women,* pp. 203–223. Edited by Jane R. Chapman and Margaret Gates. Beverly Hills, Calif.: Sage, 1978.

FARADAY, ANN, *Dream Power.* New York: Berkeley Publishing Co. 1972.

———, *The Dream Game.* New York: Harper & Row, Pub., 1974.

FARLEY, LIN, *Sexual Shake-Down: The Sexual Harassment of Women on the Job.* New York: McGraw-Hill, 1978.

FARRELL, RONALD A. and THOMAS J. MORRIONE, "Social Interaction and Stereotypic Responses of Homosexuals", *Archives of Sexual Behavior* (Sept. 1974), 3, 425–42.

FEDERAL BUREAU OF INVESTIGATION, *Uniform Crime Reports, 1977.* Washington, D.C.: Government Printing Office, 1977.

FEIGEN, GERALD M., "Injuries from Anal Coitus," *Medical Aspects of Human Sexuality,* p. 136. Edited by Harold J. Lief. Baltimore, Md.: Williams and Wilkins, 1975.

FEIGELMAN, WILLIAM, "Peeping: The Pattern of Voyeurism Among Construction Workers," *Urban Life and Culture,* 3, no. 1 (April 1974), 25–49.

FEINBLOOM, DEBORAH HILLER, *Transvestites and Transsexuals.* New York: Dell Pub. Co., Inc., 1976.

FELDMAN, HAROLD and MARGARET FELDMAN, "Effect of Parenthood on Three Points in Marriage." Unpublished Research Report at Cornell University: Dept. of Human Development and Family Studies, 1977.

FERREE, MYRA MARX, "Working-Class Jobs: Housework and Paid Work as Sources of Satisfaction," *Social Problems,* 23, no. 4 (April 1976), 431–41.

FERRELL, MARY Z., WILLIAM L. TOLONE, and ROBERT H. WALSH, "Maturational and Societal Changes in the Sexual Double Standard: A Panel Analysis (1967–1971; 1970–1974)," *Journal of Marriage and the Family,* 39, no. 2 (May 1977), 255–71.

FESHBACH, SEYMOUR and NEIL MALAMUTH, "Sex and Aggression: Proving the Link," *Psychology Today,* (Nov. 1978), 111–17.

FIGLEY, CHARLES R., "Child Density and the Marital Relationship," *Journal of Marriage and the Family,* 35, no. 2 (May 1973), 272–82.

FINK, PAUL J., "Causes and Effects of Nonorgasmic Coitus in Women," *Sexual Behavior: Current Issues,* pp. 241–47. Edited by Leonard Gross. Jamaica, N.Y.: Spectrum Publ., 1974.

FINKLE, MADELON LUBIN and DAVID J. FINKLE, "Sexual and Contraceptive Knowledge, Attitudes and Behavior of Male Adolescents," *Family Planning Perspectives,* 7, no. 6 (Nov./Dec. 1975), 256–60.

FRANK, ELLEN, CAROL ANDERSON, and DEBRA RUBINSTEIN, "Frequency of Sexual Dysfunction in 'Normal' Couples," *New England Journal of Medicine* (July 20, 1978), 299, 111–15.

FRISCH, ROSE E. and ROGER REVELLE, "Height and Weight at Menarche and a Hypothesis of Critical Body Weights and Adolescent Events," *Science,* 169, (July 1970), 397–98.

FISHER, CHARLES, "Psychological Significance of the Dream-Sleep Cycle," *Experimental Studies of Dreaming,* pp. 76–127. Edited by Jerman Witkin and Helen B. Lewis. New York: Random House, 1967.

FISHER, SEYMOUR, *Understanding the Female Orgasm.* New York: Bantam, 1973a.

———, *The Female Orgasm.* New York: Basic Books, 1973b.

———, *Body Consciousness.* Englewood Cliffs, N.J.: Prentice-Hall, 1973c.

FISHER, WILLIAM A. and DONN BYRNE, "Sex Differences in Response to Erotica? Love or Lust." *Journal of Personality and Social Psychology,* 36, no. 2 (Feb. 1978), 117–25.

FOOTE, NELSON N., "Sex as Play," *Social Problems.* (1954), no. 1, 159–63.

FORD, CLELLAN S. and FRANK A. BEACH, *Patterns of Sexual Behavior.* New York: Harper and Row, Pub., 1951.

FORD, KATHLEEN, "Contraceptive Use in the United States, 1973–1976," *Family Planning Perspectives* (Sept./Oct., 1978), 10, no. 5, 264–69.

FOX, CYRIL A., "Some Aspects and Implications of Coital Physiology," *Journal of Sex and Marital Therapy,* 2, no. 3 (Fall 1976), 205–13.

FOX, GREER LITTON, "Sex-Role Attitudes as Predictors of Contraceptive Use Among Unmarried University Students," *Sex Roles,* (1977), 3, no. 3, 265–283.

FREUD, SIGMUND, *Three Essays on Sexuality,* vol. 7, Standard Edition, London: Hogarth Press, 1953. (First German Edition, 1905).

FREYBERG, JOAN T., "Hold High the Cardboard Sword," *Psychology Today,* (Feb. 1975), 63–64.

FRIJDA, NICO H., "Emotion and the Recognition of Emotion," *Feelings and Emotions,* pp. 241–250. Edited by Magda B. Arnold. New York: Academic Press, 1970.

FRUMKIN, ROBERT M., "Early English and American Sex Customs," *The Encyclopedia of Sexual Behavior, vol. I,* pp. 350–365. Edited by Albert Ellis and Albert Abarbanel. New York: Hawthorne, 1961.

FURSTENBURG, FRANK F., JR., "Premarital Pregnancy and Marital Instability," *Journal of Social Issues,* 32, no. 1 (1976), 67–86.

FURSTENBERG, FRANK, JR., LEON GORDIS, and MILTON MARKOWITZ, "Birth Control Knowledge and Attitudes Among Unmarried Pregnant Adolescents: A Preliminary Report," *Journal of Marriage and the Family,* 31, (Feb. 1969), 34–42.

GAGNON, JOHN H., "Female Child Victims of Sex Offenses," *Social Problems* (1965), 13, no. 2, 176–92.

GAGNON, JOHN H., "Physical Strength, Once of Significance," *The Impact of Science on Society,* 21, no. 1 (1971), UNESCO.

GAGNON, JOHN H. and WILLIAM SIMON, *Sexual Conduct: The Social Sources of Human Sexuality.* Chicago: Aldine, 1973.

GAGNON, JOHN H. and WILLIAM SIMON, *Sexual Encounters Between Adults and Children* New York: SIECUS, 1970.

GAGNON, JOHN H., WILLIAM SIMON, and ALAN J. BERGER, "Some Aspects of Sexual Adjustment in Early and Later Adolescence," *The Psychology of Adolescence,* pp. 275–298. Edited by Joseph Zubin and Alfred Freedman. New York: Grune and Stratton, 1970.

GALLUP, GEORGE, "Pre-Marital Sex is No Sin to Most Teens," (Associated Press), 1978.

GAMMAGE, ALLEN J. and CHARLES F. HEMPHILL, JR., *Basic Criminal Law.* New York: McGraw-Hill, 1974.

GARNER, BRIAN, and RICHARD W. SMITH, "Are There Really Any Gay Male Athletes? An Empirical Survey," *Journal of Sex Research,* 13, no. 1 (Feb. 1977), 22–34.

GARRIS, LORIE, ALLAN STECKLER, and JOHN R. MCINTIRE, "The Relationship Between Oral Contraceptives and Adolescent Sexual Behavior," *Journal of Sex Research,* 12, no. 2 (May 1976), 135–46.

GAYFORD, J. J., "Sex Magazines," *Medical Science and the Law,* 18, no. 1 (Jan. 1978), 44–51.

GAYLIN, JODY, "Those Sexy Victorians," *Psychology Today,* 10, no. 7 (Dec. 1976), 137–39 & 143.

GEBHARD, PAUL H., "The Acquisition of Basic Sex Information," *Journal of Sex Research,* 13, no. 3 (Aug. 1977), 148–69.

———, "Factors in Marital Orgasm, *Journal of Social Issues,* 22, no. 2 (April 1966), 88–95.

———, "Fetishism and Sadomasochism," *Sex Research: Studies from the Kinsey Institute,* pp. 156–166. Edited by Martin S. Weinberg. New York: Oxford University Press, 1976.

———, "Human Sexual Behavior: A Summary Statement," *Human Sexual Behavior: Variations in the Ethnographic Spectrum,* pp. 206–217. Edited by Donald S. Marshall and Robert C. Suggs. Englewood Cliffs, N.J.: Prentice-Hall, 1971.

———, "Incidence of Overt Homosexuality in the United States and Western Europe," *National Institute of Mental Health Task Force on Homosexuality: Final Report and Background Papers,* pp. 22–29. Edited by John Livengood. Washington, D.C.: U.S. Government Printing Office, 1972.

———, "Postmarital Coitus Among Widows and Divorcees," *After Divorce,* pp. 89–106. Edited by Paul Bohannan. New York: Doubleday, 1970.

———, "Sex Differences in Sexual Response," *Archives of Sexual Behavior,* 2, no. 3 (June 1973), 201–03.

GEBHARD, PAUL H., JOHN H. GAGNON, WARDELL B. POMEROY, and CORNELIA V. CHRISTENSON, *Sex Offenders: An Analysis of Types.* New York: Harper and Row, Pub., 1965.

GEBHARD, PAUL H., JAN ROBACH, and HANS GIESE, *The Sexuality of Women.* Briarcliff Manor, N.Y.: Stein and Day, 1970.

GECAS, VIKTOR and ROGER LIBBEY, "Sexual Behavior as Symbolic Interaction," *Journal of Sex Research,* 12, no. 1 (Feb. 1976), 33-49.

GEER, JAMES H. and ROBERT FUHR, "Cognitive Factors in Sexual Arousal: The Role of Distraction," *Journal of Consulting and Clinical Psychology,* 44, no. 2 (April 1976), 238-43.

GEIS, GILBERT and DUNCAN CHAPPELL, "Forcible Rape by Multiple Offenders," *Abstracts of Criminology,* 4, (1971), 431-36.

GELLES, RICHARD, J., "Power, Sex and Violence: The Case of Marital Rape," *The Family Coordinator,* 26, no. 4 (Oct. 1977), 339-47.

GIAMBRA, LEONARD M., "Daydreams: The Backburner of the Mind," *Psychology Today,* (Dec. 1974a), 66-68.

———, "Daydreaming Across the Life Span: Late Adolescent to Senior Citizen," *International Journal of Aging and Human Development,* 5, no. 2 (1974b), 115-40.

GIAMBRA, LEONARD M. and CLYDE E. MARTIN, "Sexual Daydreams and Quantitative Aspects of Sexual Activity: Some Relations for Males Across Adulthood," *Archives of Sexual Behavior,* 6, no. 6 (Nov. 1977), 497-505.

GILBERT, SHIRLEY J., "Self-Disclosure, Intimacy and Communication in Families," *The Family Coordinator,* 25, no. 3 (July 1976), 221-30.

GLENN, NORVAL D., "The Contribution of Marriage to the Psychological Well-Being of Males and Females," *Journal of Marriage and the Family,* 37, no. 3 (Aug. 1975), 594-601.

GLICK, IRA D. and SUSAN E. BENNETT, "Psychiatric Effects of Progesterone and Oral Contraceptives," *Psychiatric Complications of Medical Drugs,* 295-331. Edited by Richard I. Shader. New York: Raven Press, 1972.

GLICK, PAUL C., "Updating the Life Cycle of the Family," *Journal of Marriage and the Family,* 39, no. 1 (Feb. 1977), 5-13.

GOCHROS, HARVEY L., ed., "Treatment of Common Marital Sex Problems," *Human Sexuality and Social Work.* New York: Association Press, 1974.

GOFFMAN, ERVING, *Stigma.* Englewood Cliffs, N.J.: Prentice-Hall, 1963.

GOLDSTEIN, BERNARD, *Human Sexuality.* New York: McGraw-Hill, 1976.

GOLDSTEIN, MICHAEL, HAROLD S. KANT, and JOHN J. HARTMAN, *Pornography and Social Deviance.* Berkeley, Calif.: University of California Press, 1973.

GOODE, ERICH, *Deviant Behavior: An Interactionist Approach* (Englewood Cliffs, N.J.: Prentice-Hall), 1978.

———, "Sex and Marijuana," *Sexual Behavior: Current Issues,* pp. 155-164. Edited by Leonard Gross. Jamaica, N.Y.: Spectrum Publ., 1974.

GOODE, ERICH and LYNN HABER, "Sexual Correlates of Homosexual Experience: An Exploratory Study of College Women," *Journal of Sex Research,* 13, no. 1 (Feb. 1977), 12-21.

GORDON, MICHAEL, "From Unfortunate Necessity to a Cult of Mutual Orgasm: Sex in American Education Literature, 1930-1940." *Studies in the Sociology of Sex,* ed. James M. Henslin. New York: Appleton-Century-Crofts, 1971.

GOULDNER, ALVIN W., "The Norm of Reciprocity: A Preliminary Statement," *American Sociological Review,* 25, (1960), 161-79.

GOY, ROBERT W. and DAVID A. GOLDFOOT, "Neuroendocrinology: Animal Models and Problems of Human Sexuality," *Archives of Sexual Behavior,* 4, no. 4 (July 1975), 405-20.

GRATZ, ROBERTA BRANDES, "Never Again! Never Again?" *Ms.* (July 1977), 54-55.

GREEN, RICHARD, "Sexual Identity of 37 Children Raised by Homosexual or Transexual Parents," *American Journal of Psychiatry,* 135, no. 6 (June 1978), 692-97.

GREENBANK, R. K., "Are Medical Students Learning Psychiatry? *Pennsylvania Medical Journal,* 64, (1961), 989-92.

GREENBERG, JERROLD S. and FRANCIS X. ARCHAMBAULT, "Masturbation, Self-Esteem, and other Variables," *Journal of Sex Research,* 9, no. 1 (Feb. 1973), 41-51.

GRIFFITH, MAC and C. EUGENE WALKER, "Menstrual Cycle Phases and Personality Variables as Related to Response to Erotic Stimuli," *Archives of Sexual Behavior,* 4, no. 6 (Nov. 1975), 599-603.

GRIFFITT, WILLIAM, "Attitude Similarity and Attraction," *Foundations of Interpersonal Attraction,* pp. 285-308. Edited by Ted L. Huston. New York: Academic Press, 1974.

———, "Sexual Experience and Sexual Responsiveness: Sex Differences," *Archives of Sexual Behavior,* 4, no. 5 (Sept. 1975), 529-40.

GROSS, EDWARD, "Toward a Symbolic Interactionist Theory of Learning: A Rapproachment with Behaviorism," *Studies in Symbolic Interaction,* pp. 129-146. Edited by Norman K. Denzin. Greenwich, Conn.: J.A.I. Press.

GROTH, A. NICHOLAS and ANN WOLBERT BURGESS, "Sexual Dysfunction During Rape," *New England Journal of Medicine,* 297 (Oct. 6, 1977), 764-66.

GROTH, A. NICHOLAS and H. JEAN BIRNBAUM, "Adult Sexual Orientation and Attraction to Underage Persons," *Archives of Sexual Behavior,* 7, no. 3 (1978), 175-81.

GROVE, WALTER R. and JEANNETTE F. TUDOR, "Adult Sex Roles and Mental Illness," *American Journal of Sociology,* 78, no. 4 (Jan. 1973), 812-35.

GUNDLACH, RALPH H., "Sexual Molestation and Rape Reported by Homosexual and Heterosexual Women," *Journal of Homosexuality,* 2, no. 4 (Summer 1977), 367-84.

GUTTMACHER, ALAN F., *Pregnancy, Birth and Family Planning.* New York: Viking Press, 1973.

HALIKAS, JAMES A., DONALD W. GOODWIN, SAMUEL B. GUZE, "Marijuana Effects: A Survey of Regular Users," *Journal of the American Medical Association,* 217, (1971), 692-94.

HALLECK, SEYMOUR L., *The Politics of Therapy.* New York: Science House, 1971.

HAMBURG, DAVID A. and DONALD T. LUNDE, "Sex Hormones in the Development of Sex Differences in Human Behavior," *The Development of Sex Differences,* pp. 1-24. Edited by Eleanor E. Maccoby. Stanford, Calif.: Stanford University Press, 1966.

HANLEY, CHARLES, "Physique and Reputation of Junior High School Boys," *Child Development,* 22, no. 4 (1951), 247-60.

HARDY, KENNETH R., "An Appetitional Theory of Sexual Motivation," *Psychological Review,* 71, no. 1 (Jan. 1964), 1-18.

HARKINS, ELIZABETH BATES, "Effects of Empty Nest Transition on Self-Report of Psychological and Physical Well-Being," *Journal of Marriage and the Family,* 40, no. 3 (Aug. 1978), 549-56.

HARPER, ROBERT A., "Petting," *Encyclopedia of Sexual Behavior,* pp. 812-818. Edited by Albert Ellis and Albert Abarbanel. New York: Hawthorne, 1961.

HARITON, E. BARBARA and JEROME L. SINGER, "Women's Fantasies During Sexual Intercourse," *Journal of Consulting and Clinical Psychology,* 42, no. 3 (June 1974), 313-22.

HART, GAVIN, *Sexual Maladjustment and Disease: An Introduction to Modern Venereology.* Chicago: Nelson-Hall, 1977.

HART, MAUREEN, *et al.,* "Psychological Adjustment of Nonpatient Homosexuals: Critical Review of the Research Literature," *Journal of Clincial Psychiatry,* 39, no. 7 (July 1978), 604–09.

HARTMANN, ERNEST L., *The Functions of Sleep.* New Haven: Conn.: Yale University Press, 1973.

HASKELL, MOLLY, "Rape Fantasy," *Ms.,* 5, no. 5 (Nov. 1976), 85-86, 93-98.

HEDBLOM, JACK H., "Dimensions of Lesbian Sexual Experience," *Archives of Sexual Behavior,* 2, no. 4 (Dec. 1973), 329-41.

HEIMAN, JULIA R., "Woman's Sexual Arousal," *Psychology Today,* (April, 1975), 91-94.

——, "Responses to Erotica: An Exploration of Human Sexual Arousal." Unpublished Doctoral Dissertation, State University of New York at Stony Brook, April, 1975.

HEIMAN, JULIA, LESLIE LOPICCOLO, and JOSEPH LOPICCOLO, *Becoming Orgasmic: A Sexual Growth Program for Women.* Englewood Cliffs, N.J.: Prentice-Hall, 1976.

HENSON, DONALD E. and H. B. RUBIN, "Voluntary Control of Eroticism," *Journal of Applied Behavior Analysis,* 4, no. 1 (Spring 1971), 37-44.

HERMAN, JUDITH and LISA HIRSCHMAN, "Father-Daughter Incest," *Signs: Journal of Women in Culture and Society,* 2, no. 4 (Summer 1977), 735-56.

HERRELL, JAMES M., "Sex Differences in Emotional Responses to 'Erotic Literature'," *Journal of Consulting and Clinical Psychology,* 43, no. 6 (Dec. 1975), 921.

HILL, MICHAEL K. and HARRY A. LANDO, "Physical Attractiveness and Sex-Role Stereotypes in Impression Formation," *Perceptual and Motor Skills,* 43, (1976), 1251-55.

HILL, WINFRED F., "Social Learning and the Acquisition of Values," *Psychological Review,* 67, no. 5 (1960), 317-31.

HIRSCHMAN, CHARLES and JAMES A. SWEET, "Social Background and Breastfeeding Among American Mothers," *Social Biology,* 21, no. 1 (1974), 34-57.

HITE, SHERE. *The Hite Report.* New York: Macmillan, 1976.

HOBBS, DANIEL F., JR. and SUE P. COLE, "TRANSITION TO PARENTHOOD: A DECADE REPLICATION," *Journal of Marriage and the Family,* 38, no. 4, (Nov. 1976), 723-31.

HOFFMAN, MARTIN L., "Empathy, Role Taking, Guilt and Development of Altruistic Motives," *Moral Development and Behavior,* pp. 124-143. Edited by Thomas Lickona. New York: Holt, Rinehart and Winston, 1976.

HOLLENDER, MARC H., WINSTON BROWN, and HOWARD B. ROBACK, "Genital Exhibitionism in Women," *American Journal of Psychiatry,* vol. 134, no. 4 (April 1977), 436-38.

HOLMSTROM, LYNDA LYTLE and ANN WOLBERT BURGESS, "Sexual Behavior of Assailant and Victim During Rape." Paper presented to the American Sociological Association. Sept. 1978.

HOLROYD, JEAN COREY and ANNETTE M. BRODSKY, "Psychologists' Attitudes and Practices Regarding Erotic and Nonerotic Physical Contact with Patients," *American Psychologist,* 32, no. 10 (Oct. 1977), 843-49.

HOOKER, EVELYN, "An Empirical Study of Some Relations Between Sexual Partners and Gender Identity in Male Homosexuals," *Sex Research: New Developments,* pp. 24-52. Edited by John Money. New York: Holt, Rinehart and Winston, 1965.

——, "The Homosexual Community," *Sexual Deviance,* 167-183. Edited by John H. Gagnon and William Simon. New York: Harper and Row, Pub., 1967.

HOTCHKISS, SANDY, "After Mastectomy," *Human Behavior,* (July 1976), 40-41.

HOWARD, JOHN W. and ROBYN M. DAWES, "Linear Prediction of Marital Happiness," *Personality and Social Psychology Bulletin,* 2, (Fall 1976), 478-80.

HOVLAND, CARL I., "Computer Simulation of Thinking," *American Psychologist,* 15, (1960), 687-93.

HSU, FRANCIS L. K., "Suppression Versus Repression: A Limited Psychological Interpretation of Four Cultures," *Psychiatry,* 12, no. 3 (1949), 223-42.

HUMPHREYS, LAUD, *Tearoom Trade: Impersonal Sex in Public Places.* Chicago: Aldine, 1970, 1975.

———, "Impersonal Sex and Perceived Satisfaction," *Studies in the Sociology of Sex,* pp. 351-74. Edited by James M. Henslin (New York: Appleton-Century-Crofts), 1971.

HUNT, MORTON, *The World of the Formerly Married.* New York: McGraw-Hill, 1966.

———, *Sexual Behavior in the 1970's.* New York: Dell, 1974.

HUROWITZ, LAURIE and EUGENE L. GAIER, "Adolescent Erotica and Female Self-Concept Development," *Adolescence,* 11, no. 44, (Winter 1976), 497-508.

HUSTON, TED L. Ed., *Foundations of Interpersonal Attraction.* New York: Academic Press, 1974.

IGA, MAMORU, "Sociocultural Factors in Japanese Prostitution and the 'Prostitution Prevention Law'," *Journal of Sex Research,* 4, no. 2 (May 1968), 127-46.

Iowa Law Review, "Constitutional Protection of Private Sexual Conduct Among Consenting Adults: Another Look at Sodomy Statutes," (Dec., 1976), 62, no. 2, 568-90.

IRWIN, PATRICK, "Acceptance of the Rights of Homosexuals: A Social Profile," *Journal of Homosexuality,* 3, no. 2 (Winter 1977), 107-21.

IRWIN, THEODORE, "Birth Control for Teenagers," *Sexual Behavior,* 2, (Feb. 1972), 41-46.

IVEY, MELVILLE E. and JUDITH M. BARDWICK, "Patterns of Affective Fluctuation in the Menstrual Cycle," *Psychosomatic Medicine,* 30, (1968), 336-45.

JACOBS, LARRY, ELLEN BERSCHEID, and ELAINE WALSTER, "Self-Esteem and Attraction," *Journal of Personality and Social Psychology,* 17, no. 1 (Jan. 1971), 84-91.

JAMES, JENNIFER and JANE MEYERDING, "Early Sexual Experiences as a Factor in Prostitution," *Archives of Sexual Behavior,* 7, no. 1 (1977), 31-42.

JAMES, WILLIAM H., "Marital Coital Rates, Spouses' Ages, Family Size and Social Class," *Journal of Sex Research,* 10, no. 3 (Aug. 1974), 205-18.

JARVIK, MURRAY E. and EDWARD M. BRECHER, "Drugs and Sex: Inhibition and Enhancement Effects," *Handbook of Sexology,* 1095-1106. Edited by John Money and Herman Musaph. New York: Elsevier-North Holland, 1977.

JEDLICKA, DAVOR, "Sequential Analysis of Perceived Commitment to Partners in Premarital Coitus," *Journal of Marriage and the Family,* 37, no. 2 (May 1975), 385-90.

JENSEN, MEHRI SAMANDARI, "Role Differentiation in Female Homosexual Quasi-Marital Unions," *Journal of Marriage and the Family,* 36, no. 2 (May 1974), 360-67.

JERRICK, STEPHEN J., "Federal Efforts to Control Sexually Transmitted Diseases," *Journal of School Health,* 48, no. 7 (Sept. 1978), 428-32.

JESSER, CLINTON J., "Reflections on Breast Attention," *Journal of Sex Research,* 7, no. 1 (February 1971), 13-25.

———, "Male Responses to Direct Verbal Sexual Initiatives of Females," *Journal of Sex Research,* 14, no. 2 (May 1978), 118-28.

JOE, VICTOR C., COKE R. BROWN, and ROB. JONES, "Conservatism as a Determinant of Sexual Experiences," *Journal of Personality Assessment,* 40, no. 5 (Oct. 1976), 516-21.

JOHNSON, HARRY J., *Executive Life-Styles.* New York: Thomas Y. Crowell, 1974.

JOHNSON, RALPH E., "Some Correlates of Extramarital Coitus," *Journal of Marriage and the Family*, 32, (Aug. 1970), 449-56.

JOURARD, SIDNEY M., *The Transparent Self*. New York: D. VanNostrand, 1971.

JOURARD, SIDNEY M., and PAUL F. SECORD, "Body-Cathexis and the Ideal Female Figure," *Journal of Abnormal and Social Psychology*, 50, (1955) 243-46.

JURICH, ANTHONY P., and JULIA A. JURICH, "The Effect of Cognitive Moral Development Upon the Selection of Premarital Sexual Standards," *Journal of Marriage and the Family*, 36, no. 4 (Nov. 1974), 736-41.

KAATS, GILBERT R., and KEITH E. DAVIS, "Effects of Volunteer Biases in Studies of Sexual Behavior and Attitudes," *Journal of Sex Research*, 7, no. 1 (Feb. 1971), 26-34.

———, "The Dynamics of Sexual Behavior of College Students," *Journal of Marriage and the Family*, 32, (Aug. 1970), 390-99.

KANE, FRANCIS J., MORRIS A. LIPTON, and JOHN A. EWING, "Hormonal Influences in Female Sexual Response," *Archives of General Psychiatry*, 20, (Feb. 1969), 202-09.

KANIN, EUGENE J., "Selected Dyadic Aspects of Male Sex Aggression," *Journal of Sex Research*, 5, no. 1 (Feb. 1969), 12-28.

———, "Sex Agression by College Men," *Medical Aspects of Human Sexuality*, (Sept. 1970), 28-40.

KANNIN, EUGENE J. and DAVID H. HOWARD, "Postmarital Consequences of Premarital Sex Adjustments," *American Sociological Review*, 23, (1958), 556-62.

KANIN, EUGENE J. and STANLEY R. PARCELL, "Sexual Agression: A Second Look at the Offended Female," *Archives of Sexual Behavior*, 6 no. 1 (Jan. 1977), 67-76.

KANTER, JOHN F. and MELVIN ZELNIK, "Contraception and Pregnancy: Experience of Young Unmarried Women in the United States," *Family Planning Perspectives*. 5, no. 1 (Winter 1973), 21-35.

KAPLAN, HELEN S., *The New Sex Therapy*. New York: Quadrangle, The N.Y. Times, 1974.

KARDENER, SHELDON H., MARIELLE FULLER, and IVAN N. MENSH, "A Survey of Physicians' Attitudes and Practices Regarding Erotic and Nonerotic Contact with Patients," *American Journal of Psychiatry*, 130, (1973), 1077-81.

KAVOLIS, VYTAUTAS, "Church Involvement and Marital Status as Restraints on Nonconforming Sexual Behavior," *Journal of Human Relations*, 11, no. 1 (Autumn 1962), 132-39.

KEGEL, A., "Sexual Functions of the Pubococcygeus Muscle," *Journal of Obstetrics and Gynecology*, 60, (1952), 521-24.

KELLER, JAMES F., EDWARD EAKES, DENNIS HINKLE, and GEORGE A. HUGHSTON, "Sexual Behavior and Guilt Among Women: A Cross-Generational Comparison," *Journal of Sex and Marital Therapy* (Winter, 1978), 4, no. 4, 259-65.

KELLY, JANIS, "Sister Love: An Exploration of the Need for Homosexual Experience," *The Family Coordinator*, vol. 21, (Oct. 1972).

KENNY, JAMES A., "Sexuality of Pregnant and Breastfeeding Women," *Archives of Sexual Behavior*, 2, no. 3 (1973), 215-29.

KHAN, NASIR A., and PHILIP SOLOMON, ed. "Normal and Abnormal Sexual Behavior," *Handbook of Psychiatry, Third Edition*. Los Altos, Calif.: Lange Medical Publications, 1974.

KIESLER, CHARLES A., "The Training of Psychiatrists and Psychologists," *American Psychologist*, 32, no. 2 (Feb. 1977), 107-08.

KIESLER, SARA B. and ROBERTA L. BARAL, "The Search for a Romantic Partner: The Effects of Self-Esteem and Physical Attractiveness on Romantic Behavior," *Personality and Social Behavior,* pp. 155–65. Edited by Kenneth J. Gergen and David Marlowe. Reading, Mass.: Addison-Wesley, 1970.

KINSEY, ALFRED C., WARDELL B. POMEROY, and CLYDE E. MARTIN, *Sexual Behavior in the Human Male.* Philadelphia, Penn.: Saunders, 1948.

KINSEY, ALFRED C., WARDELL B. POMEROY, CLYDE E. MARTIN, and PAUL H. GEBHARD, "Concepts of Normality and Abnormality in Sexual Behavior," *Psychosexual Development in Health and Disease,* pp. 11–32. New York: Grune and Stratton, 1949.

———, *Sexual Behavior in the Human Female,* Philadelphia, Penn.: Saunders, 1953.

KIRKHAM, GEORGE L., "Homosexuality in Prison," *Studies in the Sociology of Sex,* pp. 325–49. Edited by James M. Henslin. New York: Appleton-Century-Crofts, 1971.

KITTRIE, NICHOLAS N., *The Right to Be Different: Deviance and Enforced Therapy.* Baltimore, Md.: Johns Hopkins University Press, 1971.

KLINGER, ERIC, *Structure and Functions of Fantasy.* New York: John Wiley, 1971.

KLEINMAN, SHERRYL, "Female Premarital Sexual Careers," *Center for Youth Development and Research, Quarterly Focus,* (Winter, 1978).

KOCH, PATRICIA B., "A Comparison of the Sex Education of Primary-Aged Children as Expressed in Art in Sweden and the United States." Paper presented to The Society for the Scientific Study of Sex, Eastern Regional Meeting, April, 1978.

KOFF, WAYNE C., "Marijuana and Sexual Activity," *Journal of Sex Research,* 10, no. 3 (Aug. 1974), 194–204.

KOHLBERG, LAWRENCE, "Stage and Sequence: The Cognitive-Developmental Approach to Socialization," *Handbook of Socialization Theory and Research,* pp. 347–480. Edited by David A. Goslin. Skokie, Ill: Rand McNally, 1969.

KOHLENBERG, ROBERT J., "Directed Masturbation and the Treatment of Primary Orgasmic Dysfunction," *Archives of Sexual Behavior,* 3, no. 4 (July 1974), 349–56.

KOMAROVSKY, MIRRA, *Blue-Collar Marriage.* New York: Random House, 1964.

KONOPKA, GISELA, *Young Girls: A Portrait of Adolescence.* Englewood Cliffs, N.J.: Prentice-Hall, 1976.

KOPKIND, ANDREW, "Middle America Takes Its Clothes Off," *New Times,* 7, no. 4 (August 20, 1976), 32, 34, 40.

KREBS, DENNIS L., "Altruism — An Examination of the Concept and a Review of the Literature," *Psychological Bulletin,* 73, (1970), 258–302.

KUHLEN, RAYMOND G. and NANCY BRYANT HOULIHAN, "Adolescent Heterosexual Interest in 1942 and 1963," *Child Development,* 36, (1965), 1049–52.

KUHN, THOMAS S., *The Structure of Scientific Revolutions.* Chicago: University of Chicago Press, 1962, 1970.

KURTH, SUZANNE B., "Friendships and Friendly Relations," *Social Relationships.* Edited by Geo. McCall, et al. Chicago: Aldine, 1970, 136–70.

KUTNER, S. JEROME, "Sex Guilt and the Sexual Behavior Sequence," *The Journal of Sex Research,* 7, no. 2 (May 1971), 107–15.

KUTNER, NANCY G. and DONNA BROGAN, "An Investigation of Sex-Related Slang Vocabulary and Sex-Role Orientation Among Male and Female University Students," *Journal of Marriage and the Family,* 36, no. 3 (Aug. 1974), 474–83.

LaBARRE, WESTON, "The Cultural Basis of Emotions and Gestures," *Journal of Personality,* 16, (1947), 49–68.

LANDIS, JUDSON T. and MARY G. LANDIS, *Building a Successful Marriage.* Englewood Cliffs, N.J.: Prentice-Hall, 1973.

LANDIS, JUDSON T. and THOMAS POFFENBERGER, "The Marital and Sexual Adjustment of 330 Couples Who Chose Vasectomy As a Form of Birth Control," *Journal of Marriage and the Family,* 27, no. 1 (Feb. 1965), 57–58.

LANDIS, JUDSON T., THOMAS POFFENBERGER, and SHIRLEY POFFENBERGER, "The Effects of First Pregnancy Upon the Sexual Adjustment of 212 Couples," *American Sociological Review,* 15, (Dec. 1950), 766–72.

"Large Majority of Americans Favor Legal Abortion, Sex Education and Contraceptive Services for Teens," *Family Planning Perspectives,* 10, no. 3 (May/June 1978), 159–60.

LARSEN, VIRGINIA L., "Sources of Menstrual Information: A Comparison of Age Groups," *Family Life Coordinator,* 10, (1961), 41–43.

LASCHET, URSULA, "Antiandrogen in the Treatment of Sex Offenders: Mode of Action and Therapeutic Outcome," *Contemporary Sexual Behavior,* pp. 311–320. Edited by Joseph Zubin and John Money. Baltimore, Md.: Johns Hopkins University Press, 1973.

LATORRE, RONALD A. and KAREN KEAR, "Attitudes Toward Sex in The Aged," *Archives of Sexual Behavior,* 6, no. 3 (May 1977), 203–13.

LAZARUS, ARNOLD A., "Psychological Causes of Impotence," *Sexual Behavior Current Issues,* pp. 227–239. Edited by Leonard Gross. Jamaica, N.Y.: Spectrum Publ., 1974.

LAZARUS, RICHARD S., "The Healthy Personality—A Review of Conceptualizations and Research," *Society, Stress and Disease, Vol. II,* pp. 6–35. Edited by Lennart Levi. London: Oxford University Press, 1975.

LEHNE, GREGORY K., "Homophobia Among Men," *The Forty-Nine Percent Majority: The Male Sex Role,* pp. 66–88. Edited by Deborah S. David and Robert Brannon. Reading, Mass.: Addison-Wesley, 1976.

LEMERE, F. and J. SMITH, "Alcohol-Induced Sexual Impotence," *Americans Journal of Psychiatry,* 30, (1973), 212–13.

LEMERT, EDWIN M., "Paranoia and the Dynamics of Exclusion," *Sociometry,* 25, (1962), 2–20.

LESTER, DAVID, *Unusual Sexual Behavior.* Springfield, Ill.: Charles C. Thomas, 1975.

LEVIN, ROBERT J., "The End of the Double Standard," *Redbook Magazine,* (Oct. 1975), 38–44, 190–191.

LEVIN, R. J., "Thorarche — A Seasonal Influence But No Secular Trend," *Journal of Sex Research,* 12, no. 3 (Aug. 1976), 173–79.

LEVINGER, GEORGE, "Systematic Distortion in Spouses' Reports of Preferred and Actual Sexual Behavior," *Sociometry,* 29, no. 3 (1966), 291–99.

LEVINGER, GEORGE, "A Social Psychological Perspective on Marital Dissolution," *Journal of Social Issues,* 32, no. 1 (1976), 21–41.

LEVINGER, GEORGE and DAVID J. SENN, "Disclosure of Feelings in Marriage," *Merrill-Palmer Quarterly,* 13, (July 1967), 237–49.

LEVITT, EUGENE E., "Nymphomania," *Sexual Behavior,* (March 1973), 13–17.

LEVITT, EUGENE E. and ALBERT D. KLASSEN, JR., "Public Attitudes Toward Sexual Behaviors: The Latest Investigation of the Institute for Sex Research." Mimeographed paper available from the Institute for Sex Research. Bloomington, Ind.: Indiana University, 1973.

LEVITT, EUGENE E. and ALBERT D. KLASSEN, JR., "Public Attitudes Toward Homosexuality: Part of the 1970 National Survey by the Institute for Sex Research," *Journal of Homosexuality,* vol. 1, no. 1 (1974), 29–43.

LEWIS, LIONEL S. and DENNIS BRISSETT, "Sex as Work: A Study of Avocational Counseling," *Social Problems,* 15, no. 1 (1967), 8–17.

LEWIS, ROBERT A., "Parents and Peers: Socialization Agents in the Coital Behavior of Young Adults," *Journal of Sex Research,* 9, no. 2 (May 1973), 156–70.

LEWIS, ROBERT A. and WESLEY R. BURR, "Premarital Coitus and Commitment Among College Students," *Archives of Sexual Behavior,* 4, no. 1 (Jan. 1975), 73–79.

LEWIS, ROBERT A., GRAHAM B. SPANIER, VIRGINIA L. STORM, and CHARLOTTE F. LeHECKA, "Commitment in Married and Unmarried Cohabitation," *Sociological Focus,* 10, no. 4 (Oct. 1977), 367–74.

LEZNOFF, MAURICE and WILLIAM A. WESTLEY, "The Homosexual Community," *Social Problems,* 3, no. 4 (April 1956), 257–63.

LIBBY, ROGER and GILBERT D. NASS, "Parental Views on Teenage Sexual Behavior," *Journal of Sex Research,* 7, no. 3 (Aug. 1971), 226–36.

LINDEMANN, CONSTANCE, *Birth Control and Unmarried Young Women.* New York: Springer-Verlag, N.Y., 1974.

LINDESMITH, ALFRED R., ANSELM L. STRAUSS, and NORMAN K. DENZIN, *Social Psychology, Fourth Edition.* Hinsdale, Ill.: Dryden Press, 1975.

LINCOLN, RICHARD, BRIGITTE DORING-BRADLEY, BARBARA L. LINDHEIM, and MAUREEN A. COTTERILL, "The Court, the Congress and the President: Turning Back the Clock on the Pregnant Poor," *Family Planning Perspectives,* 9, no. 5 (Sept./Oct. 1977), 207–14.

LINNER, BRIGITTA, *Sex and Society in Sweden.* New York: Harper and Row, Pub., 1972.

"Living Together," *Newsweek,* (Aug. 1, 1977), 46–50.

LOCKE, HARVEY J., *Predicting Adjustment in Marriage: A Comparison of a Divorced and Happily Married Group.* New York: Holt, Rinehart and Winston, 1951.

LOGAN, FRANK A. and ALLAN R. WAGNER, *Punishment and Reward.* Boston: Allyn and Bacon, 1965.

LOPATA, HELENA Z., *Occupation: Housewife.* New York: Free Press, 1971.

LoPICCOLO, JOSEPH, "Mothers and Daughters: Perceived and Real Differences in Sexual Values," *Journal of Sex Research,* 9, no. 2 (May 1973), 171–77.

———, "Direct Treatment of Sexual Dysfunction in the Couple," *Handbook of Sexology,* pp. 1227–44. Edited by John Money and Herman Musaph. New York: Elsevier-North-Holland, 1977a.

———, "From Psychotherapy to Sex Therapy," *Society,* 14, no. 5 (July/Aug. 1977b), 60–68.

LoPICCOLO, JOSEPH, and W. CHARLES LOBITZ, "The Role of Masturbation in the Treatment of Orgasmic Dysfunction," *Archives of Sexual Behavior,* 2, no. 2 (Dec. 1972), 163–71.

LOWENTHAL, MARJORIE F. and CLAYTON HAVEN, "Interaction and Adaptation: Intimacy as a Critical Variable," *American Sociological Review,* 33, no. 1 (Feb. 1968), 20–30.

LOWRY, THEA SNYDER and THOMAS P. LOWRY, "Ethical Considerations in Sex Therapy," *Journal of Marriage and Family Counseling,* 1, no. 3 (July 1975), 229–36.

LUCE, GAY GAER, *Body Time.* New York: Random House, 1971.

LUCKEY, ELEANORE B. and GILBERT D. NASS, "A Comparison of Sexual Attitudes and Behavior in an International Sample," *Journal of Marriage and the Family,* 31, no. 2 (May 1969), 364–79.

LUCKEY, ELEANORE B. and JOYCE K. BAIN, "Children: A Factor in Marital Satisfaction," *Journal of Marriage and the Family,* 32, no. 1 (Feb. 1970), 43–44.

LUSCHEN, MARY E. and David M. Pierce, "Effect of the Menstrual Cycle on Mood and Sexual Arousability," *Journal of Sex Research*, 8, no. 1 (Feb. 1972), 41-47.

LUTTGE, WILLIAM G., "The Role of Gonadel Hormones in the Sexual Behavior of Rhesus Monkey and Human: A Literature Review," *Archives of Sexual Behavior*, 1, no. 1 (1971), 61-88.

LYNESS, JUDITH L., MILTON E. LIPETZ, and KEITH DAVIS, "Living Together: An Alternative to Marriage," *Journal of Marriage and the Family*, 34, (May 1972), 305-11.

MACCOBY, ELEANOR E. and CAROL N. JACKLIN, *The Psychology of Sex Differences*. Stanford, Calif.: Stanford University Press, 1974.

MACE, DAVID R., "Marital Intimacy and the Deadly Love-Anger Cycle," *Journal of Marriage and Family Counseling*, 2, (April 1976), 131-37.

MACDONALD, JOHN M., *Indecent Exposure*. Springfield, Ill.: Charles C. Thomas, 1973.

MACFARLANE, KEE, "Sexual Abuse of Children," *Victimization of Women*, pp. 81-109. Edited by Jane A. Chapman and Margaret Gates. Beverly Hills, Calif.: Sage Publications, Inc., 1978.

MACKLIN, ELEANOR D., "Heterosexual Cohabitation Among Unmarried College Students," *The Family Coordinator*, 21, (Oct. 1972), 463-72.

MACNAMARA, DONALD E. J. and EDWARD SAGARIN, *Sex, Crime and the Law*. New York: Free Press, 1977.

MAGUIRE, PETER, "The Psychological and Social Consequences of Breast Cancer," *Nursing Mirror*, 140, (April 3, 1975), 54-57.

MAHONEY, MICHAEL J., "Reflections on the Cognitive-Learning Trend in Psychotherapy," *American Psychologist*, 32, no. 1 (Jan. 1977), 5-13.

MALAMUTH, NEIL M., SEYMOUR FESHBACH, and YORAM JAFFE, "Sexual Arousal and Aggression: Recent Experiments and Theoretical Issues," *Journal of Social Issues*, 33, no. 2 (1977), 110-33.

MANCINI, JAY A. and DENNIS K. ORTHNER, "Recreational Sexuality Preferences Among Middle-Class Husbands and Wives," *Journal of Sex Research*, 14, no. 2 (May 1978), 96-106.

MANOSEVITZ, MARTIN, "Early Sexual Behavior in Adult Homosexual and Heterosexual Males," *Journal of Abnormal Psychology*, 76, no. 3 (1970), 396-402.

MARGOLD, JANE, "Bisexuality: The Newest Sex Style," *Cosmopolitan*, 176, (June 1974), 189-92.

MARMOR, JUDD, "'Normal' and 'Deviant' Sexual Behavior," *The Journal of the American Medical Association*, vol. 217, (July 12, 1971).

——, "Impotence and Ejaculatory Disturbances," The Sexual Experience, 403-411. Edited by Benjamin J. Sadock, Harold I. Kaplan and Alfred M. Freedman. Baltimore, Md.: Williams & Wilkens, 1976.

——, "Homosexuality and Sexual Orientation Disturbances," *The Sexual Experience*, pp. 374-91. Edited by Benjamin J. Sadock, Harold I. Kaplan, and Alfred M. Freeman. Baltimore, Md.: Williams and Wilkins, 1976.

MARMOR, JUDD, and RICHARD GREEN, "Homosexual Behavior," *Handbook of Sexology*, pp. 1051-1068. Edited by John Money and Herman Musaph. New York: Elsevier North-Holland, 1977.

MARQUIS, JOHN N., "Orgasmic Reconditioning: Changing Sexual Object Choice Through Controlling Masturbation Fantasies," *Journal of Behavior Therapy and Experimental Psychiatry*, 1, (1970), 263-71.

MARSHALL, DONALD S., "Sexual Behavior on Mangaia," *Human Sexual Behavior,* pp. 103–62. Edited by Donald S. Marshall, and Robert C. Suggs. Englewood Cliffs, N.J.: Prentice-Hall, 1971.

MARTIN, CLYDE E., in a personal communication, 1976.

——, "Marital and Sexual Factors in Relation to Age, Disease and Longevity," *Life History Research in Psychopathology,* vol. 4, pp. 326–47. Edited by R. D. Wirt, G. Winokur, and M. Roff. Minneapolis, Minn.: U. of Minnesota Press, 1975.

MARTIN, CY, *Whiskey and Wild Women.* New York: Hart Publishing Co., 1974.

MARTINSON, FLOYD M., *Infant and Child Sexuality: A Sociological Perspective,* (St. Peter, Minn.: Gustavus Adolphus College), 1973.

MARTINSON, FLOYD M., "Eroticism in Infancy and Childhood," *Journal of Sex Research,* 12, no. 4 (Nov. 1976), 251–62.

MASCHHOFF, T. A., W. E. FANSHIER, and D. J. HANSEN, "Vasectomy: Its Effect Upon Marital Stability," *Journal of Sex Research,* 12, no. 4 (Nov. 1976), 295–314.

MASTERS, WILLIAM H., "Ethics in Sex Research and Sex Therapy." Paper presented at the International Congress of Sexology, 1976, Montreal.

MASTERS, WILLIAM H. and VIRGINIA E. JOHNSON, *Human Sexual Response.* Boston: Little, Brown, 1966.

——, *Human Sexual Inadequacy.* Boston: Little, Brown, 1970.

——, "The Role of Religion in Sexual Dysfunction," *Sexuality and Human Values.* Edited by Mary S. Calderone. New York: Associated Press, 1974.

——, *Homosexuality in Perspective.* Boston: Little, Brown, 1979.

MAXWELL, JOSEPH W., ALAN R. SACK, ROBERT B. FRARY, and JAMES F. KELLER, "Factors Influencing Contraceptive Behavior of Single College Students," *Journal of Sex and Marital Therapy,* 3, no. 4 (Winter 1977), 265–73.

MAY, ROLLO, E. ANGEL, and H. F. ELLENBERGER, *Existence: A New Dimension In Psychology.* New York: Basic Books, 1958.

MAYKOVICH, MINAKO K., "Attitudes Versus Behavior in Extramarital Sexual Relations," *Journal of Marriage and the Family,* 38, no. 4 (Nov. 1976), 693–99.

McCAGHY, CHARLES H., "Child Molesters: A Study of Their Careers as Deviants," *Criminal Behavior Systems,* pp. 75–88. Edited by Marshall B. Clinard. New York: Holt, Rinehart and Winston, 1967.

McCAGHY, CHARLES H. and JAMES K. SKIPPER, JR., "LESBIAN BEHAVIORS AS AN ADAPTAtion to the Occupation of Stripping," *Social Problems,* 17, (Fall 1969), 262–70.

McGUIRE, R. J., J. M. CARLISLE, and B. G. YOUNG, "Sexual Deviations as Conditioned Behavior: A Hypothesis," *Behavior Research and Therapy,* 2, (1965), 185–90.

McINTOSH, MARY, "The Homosexual Role," *Social Problems,* 16, (Fall 1968), 182–92.

McNEILL, DAVID and NORMAN LIVSON, "Maturation Rate and Body Build in Women," *Child Development,* 34, (March 1963), 25–32.

McWHORTER, WILLIAM L., "Flashing and Dashing: Notes and Comments on the Etiology of Exhibitionism," *Sexual Deviancy in Social Context,* 101–10. Edited by Clifton D. Bryant. New York: New Viewpoints, 1977.

MEAD, BEVERLY T., WILLIAM W. ZELLER, O. SPURGEON ENGLISH, JOHN M. SUAREZ, and JOHN F. CUBER, "Viewpoints: What Impact Does Adultery Generally Have on a Marriage?" *Medical Aspects of Human Sexuality,* (Oct. 1975), 122–42.

MEAD, BEVERLY T., "Depression and Sex," *Sexual Behavior: Current Issues,* pp. 279–88. Edited by Leonard Gross. Jamaica, N.Y.: Spectrum Publ., 1974.

MESSENGER, JOHN C., "Sex and Repression in an Irish Folk Community," *Human Sexual Behavior,* pp. 3-37. Edited by Donald S. Marshall, and Robert C. Suggs. Englewood Cliffs, N.J.: Prentice-Hall, 1971.

MEYER-BAHLBURG, and F. L. HEINO, "Sex Hormones and Male Homosexuality in Comparative Perspective," *Archives of Sexual Behavior,* 6, no. 4 (1977), 297-325.

MILLER, BRENT C., "A Multivariate Developmental Model of Marital Satisfaction," *Journal of Marriage and the Family,* 38, no. 4 (Nov. 1976), 643-57.

MILLER PATRICIA Y. and WILLIAM SIMON, "Adolescent Sexual Behavior: Context and Change," *Social Problems,* 22, no. 1 (Oct. 1974), 58-75.

MILLS, C. WRIGHT, "Situated Actions and Vocabularies of Motive," *American Sociological Review,* 5, (Dec. 1940), 904-13.

MISCHEL, THEODORE, "The Concept of Mental Health and Disease: An Analysis of the Controversy Between Behavioral and Psychodynamic Approaches," *Journal of Medicine and Philosophy,* 2, no. 3 (Sept. 1977), 197-219.

MISCHEL, WALTER, "Toward a Cognitive Social Learning Reconceptualization of Personality," *Psychological Review,* 80, no. 4 (1973), 252-83.

MOLLER, HERBERT, "Sex Composition and Correlated Culture Patterns of Colonial America," *The William and Mary Quarterly,* 2, (Oct. 1945), 113-53.

MONEY, JOHN, "Sex Hormones and Other Variables in Human Eroticism," *Sex and Internal Secretions,* pp. 1383-1400. Edited by W. C. Young. Baltimore, Md.: Williams and Wilkins, 1961.

————, "Adolescent Psychohormonal Development," *Southwestern Medicine,* 48, (1967), 182-86.

MONEY, JOHN and ANKE A. EHRHARDT, *Man and Woman, Boy and Girl.* (Baltimore, Md.: Johns Hopkins University Press), 1972.

MOORE, JAMES E. and DIANE G. KENDALL, "Children's Concepts of Reproduction," JOURNAL OF SEX RESEARCH, 7, no. 1 (Feb. 1971), 42-61.

"More Abortion Patients Are Young, Unmarried, Nonwhite," *Family Planning Perspectives,* 9, no. 3, (May/June 1977), 130-31.

MORGAN, EDMUND S., "The Puritans and Sex," *New England Quarterly* (December 1942), pp. 591-607. Reprinted in Michael Gordon, Ed., *The American Family in Socio-Historical Perspective.* New York: St. Martin's Press, 1973.

MORRIS, NAOMI, "The Frequency of Sexual Intercourse During Pregnancy," *Archives of Sexual Behavior,* 4, no. 5 (Sept. 1975), 501-07.

MORRIS, NAOMI M. and J. RICHARD UDRY, "Periodicity in Sexual Behavior in Women," *Medical Aspects of Human Sexuality,* (April 1971), 140-51.

MORRISON, DENTON E. and CARLIN PAIGE HOLDEN, "The Burning Bra: The American Breast Fetish and Women's Liberation," *Sociology for Pleasure,* pp. 345-62. Edited by Marcello Truzzi. Englewood Cliffs, N.J.:Prentice-Hall, 1974.

MORTON, R. S., "Venereal Diseases," *Handbook of Sexology,* pp. 1009-22. Edited by John Money and Herman Musaph. New York: Elsevier North-Holland, 1977.

MOSHER, DONALD L., "Sex Guilt and Premarital Sexual Experience of College Students," *Journal of Consulting and Clinical Psychology,* 36, no. 1 (1971), 27-32.

————, "Sex Differences, Sex Experience, Sex Guilt and Explicitly Sexual Films," *Journal of Social Issues,* 29, no. 3 (1973), 95-112.

MOSHER, DONALD L. and IRENE GREENBERG, "Females' Affective Responses to Reading Erotic Literature," *Journal of Consulting and Clinical Psychology,* 33, no. 4 (1969), 472-77.

MUNICH, ADRIENNE, "Seduction in Academe," *Psychology Today*, 11, no. 9 (Feb. 1978), 82–84, 108.

MUNJACK, DENNIS J. and FRED R. STAPLES, "Psychological Characteristics of Women with Sexual Inhibition (Frigidity) in Sex Clinics," *The Journal of Nervous and Mental Disease*, 163, no. 2 (Aug. 1976), 117–23.

MURDOCK, GEORGE PETER, *Social Structure*. New York: Free Press, 1949.

MURSTEIN, BERNARD I., "Physical Attractiveness and Marital Choice," *Journal of Personality and Social Psychology*, 22, no. 1 (1972), 8–12.

MUSSEN, PAUL H. and MARY C. JONES, "Self-Conceptions, Motivations, and Interpersonal Relationships of Late- and Early-Maturing Boys," *Child Development*, 28, (1957), 243–56.

———, "The Behavior-Inferred Motivations of Late- and Early-Maturing Boys," *Child Development*, 28, (1958), 61–67.

MYERS, LONNY and HUNTER LEGGITT, "A New View of Adultery," *Sexual Issues in Marriage*. Edited by Leonard Gross. Jamaica, N.Y.: Spectrum Publ., 1975.

NATHAN, PETER E. and SANDRA L. HARRIS, *Psychopathology and Society*. New York: McGraw-Hill, 1975.

NATHANSON, I. T., L. E. TOWN, and J. C. AUB, "Normal Excretion of Sex Hormones in Childhood," *Endrocrinology*, 28, (1941), 851–65.

NIEDERHOFFER, ARTHUR, *Behind the Shield: The Police in Urban Society* (Garden City, N.Y.: Doubleday), 1967.

NEUBARDT, SELIG, "Anal Coitus," *Medical Aspects of Human Sexuality*, pp. 198–99. Edited by Harold J. Lief, Baltimore, Md.: Williams & Wilkins, 1975.

NEUMAN, R. P., "Masturbation, Madness and Modern Concepts of Childhood and Adolescence," *Journal of Social History*, 3, (Spring 1975), 1–27.

NEWCOMB, THEODORE M., *The Acquaintance Process*. New York: Holt, Rinehart and Winston, 1961.

NEWMAN, GUSTAVE, and CLAUDE R. NICHOLS, "Sexual Activities and Attitudes in Older Persons," *Journal of the American Medical Association*, 173, no. 1 (1960), 33–35.

NEWTON, ESTER, *Mother Camp: Female Impersonators in America*. Englewood Cliffs, N.J.: Prentice-Hall, 1972.

NEWTON, DAVID E., "Homosexual Behavior and Child Molestation: A Review of the Evidence," *Adolescence*, 13, no. 49 (Spring 1978), 29–43.

NEWTON, NILES, "Interrelationships between Sexual Responsiveness, Birth and Breast-Feeding," *Contemporary Sexual Behavior*, pp. 77–98. Edited by Joseph Zubin and John Money. Baltimore, Md.: Johns Hopkins University Press, 1973.

———, "Birth Rituals in Cross-Cultural Perspective: Some Practical Applications," *Being Female: Reproduction, Power, Change*, pp. 37–41. Edited by Dana Raphael. The Hague: Mouton, 1975.

NORTON, ARTHUR J. and PAUL C. GLICK, "Marital Instability: Past, Present and Future," *Journal of Social Issues*, 32, no. 1 (1976), 5–20.

NYBERG, KENNETH L. and JON P. ALSTON, "Analysis of Public Attitudes Toward Homosexual Behavior," *Journal of Homosexuality*, 2, no. 2 (Winter 1976–77), 99–107.

OBERHOLZER, EMIL, JR., *Delinquent Saints*. New York: Columbia University Press, 1956.

OBLER, MARTIN, "Systematic Desensitization in Sexual Disorders," *Journal of Behavior Therapy and Experimental Psychiatry,* 4, (1973), 93–101.

OLIVEN, JOHN F., *Clinical Sexuality*. Philadelphia, Penn.: Lippincott, 1974.

ORNSTEIN, ROBERT E., *The Psychology of Consciousness.* San Francisco, Calif.: W. H. Freeman and Company Publishers, 1972.

OPLER, MARVIN K., "Cross-Cultural Aspects of Kissing," *Medical Aspects of Human Sexuality,* 3, (Feb. 1969), 11-21.

PACHT, ASHER R., "The Rapist in Treatment: Professional Myths and Psychological Realities," *Sexual Assault: The Victim and the Rapist,* pp. 91-98. Edited by Marcia J. Walker and Stanley L. Brodsky. Lexington, Mass.: Heath, 1976.

PACKARD, VANCE, *The Sexual Wilderness.* New York: McKay, 1968.

PAIGE, KAREN E., "Effects of Oral Contraceptives on Affective Fluctuations Associated with the Menstrual Cycle," *Psychosomatic Medicine,* 33, no. 6 (Nov.-Dec. 1971), 515-37.

———, "Women Learn to Sing the Menstrual Blues," *Psychology Today,* (Sept. 1973), 41-46.

PARLEE, MARY BROWN, "The Premenstrual Syndrome," *Psychological Bulletin,* 80, (1973), 454-65.

PATAI, RAPHAEL, *The Arab Mind.* New York: Scribner's, 1973.

PEPLAU, LETITIA ANNE, ZICK RUBIN, and CHARLES T. HILL, "Sexual Intimacy in Dating Relationships," *Journal of Social Issues,* 33, no. 2 (Spring 1977), 86-109.

"Perils of Painless Childbirth," *Human Behavior,* (Oct. 1978), 543-544.

PERLMUTTER, JOHANNA F., MAJ-BRITT ROSENBAUM, MARGUERITE R. SHEARER, HELEN H. GLASER, and JULIA HEIMAN, "Do Women Always Know When They Have Had An Orgasm?" *Medical Aspects of Human Sexuality,* (Dec. 1975), 32-44.

PERRY, JUDITH ADAMS, "Physicians' Erotic and Nonerotic Physical Involvement with Patients," *American Journal of Psychiatry,* 133, no. 7 (July 1976), 838-40.

PETITTI, DIANA B., and WILLARD CATES, JR., "Restricting Medicaid Funds for Abortions: Projections of Excess Mortality for Women of Childbearing Age," *American Journal of Public Health,* 67, no. 9 (Sept. 1977), 860-62.

PFEIFFER, ERIC, "Geriatric Sex Behavior," *Medical Aspects of Human Sexuality,* 9, (July 1969), 19-28.

PFEIFFER, ERIC and GLENN C. DAVIS, "Determinants of Sexual Behavior in Middle and Old Age," *Journal of the American Geriatric Society,* 20, no. 4 (April 1972), 151-58.

PFEIFFER, ERIC, ADRIAAN VERWOERDT, and GLENN C. DAVIS, Sexual Behavior in Middle Life," *American Journal of Psychiatry,* 128, no. 10 (April 1972), 82-87.

PINCUS, JANE KATES, et al., "Pregnancy," *Our Bodies, Ourselves.* Edited by Boston Women's Health Book Collective. New York: Simon and Schuster, 1976, 251-66.

PINEO, PETER C., "Disenchantment in the Later Years," *Marriage and Family Living,* 23, no. 1 (Feb. 1961), 3-11.

Planned Parenthood of New York City, Inc. *Abortion: A Woman's Guide.* New York: Adelard-Schuman, 1973.

PLUMMER, KENNETH, *Sexual Stigma: An Interactionist Approach.* London: Routledge and Kegan Paul, Ltd., 1975.

PLUTCHIK, ROBERT, *The Emotions: Facts, Theories and a New Model.* New York: Random House, 1962.

POCS, OLLIE and ANNETTE G. GODOW, "Can Students View Parents As Sexual Beings?" *The Family Coordinator,* 26, no. 1 (Jan. 1977), 31-36.

POMEROY, WARDELL B., "Some Aspects of Prostitution," *Journal of Sex Research,* 1, no. 3 (Nov. 1965), 177-87.

———, *Boys and Sex.* New York: Dell Pub. Co., Inc., 1968.

———, *Girls and Sex.* New York: Dell Pub. Co., Inc., 1969.

PONSE, BARBARA, "Secrecy in the Lesbian World," *Urban Life,* 5, no. 3 (Oct. 1976a), 313–38.

———, "Role-Playing Among Lesbians." Paper presented to the American Sociological Association, 1976b.

President's Commission on Law Enforcement and the Administration of Justice, *The Challenge of Crime in a Free Society.* Washington, D.C.: U.S. Government Printing Office, 1967.

PRINCE, VIRGINIA and P. M. BENTLER, "Survey of 504 Cases of Transvestism," *Psychological Reports,* 31, (1972), 903–17.

PROCTER, R. C., "Impotence as a Symptom of Depression," *North Carolina Medical Journal,* 34, (1973), 876–78.

PULASKI, MARY ANN S., "The Rich Rewards of Make Believe," *Psychology Today,* 7, no. 8 (Jan. 1974), 68–74.

QUEEN, STUART A. and ROBERT W. HABENSTEIN, *The Family in Various Cultures.* Philadelphia, Penn.: Lippincott, 1974.

RABOCH, JAN and L. STARKA, "Reported Coital Activity for Men and Levels of Plasma Testosterone," *Archives of Sexual Behavior,* 2, no. 4 (Dec. 1973), 309–15.

RADA, R., "Alcoholism and Forcible Rape," *American Journal of Psychiatry,* 132, (1975), 444–46.

RADLOFF, LENORE, "Sex Differences in Depression: Effects of Occupation and Marital Status," *Sex Roles,* 1, no. 3 (1975), 249–65.

RAINWATER, LEE, *Family Design: Marital Sexuality, Family Size and Contraception.* Chicago: Aldine, 1965.

———, "Some Aspects of Lower Class Sexual Behavior," *Journal of Social Issues,* 22, no. 2 (April 1966), 96–108.

RAMEY, ESTELLE, "Men's Cycles (They Have Them Too, You Know)," *Ms.,* (Spring 1972), 8–14.

RAMSEY, GLENN V., "The Sexual Development of Boys," *American Journal of Psychology,* 56, (April 1943a), 217–34.

———, "The Sex Information of Younger Boys," *American Journal of Orthopsychiatry,* 13, (April 1943b), 347–52.

RAPOPORT, RHONA and ROBERT N. RAPOPORT, "New Light on the Honeymoon," *Human Relations,* 17, no. 1 (1964), 33–56.

REICHELT, PAUL A., "Changes in Sexual Behavior Among Unmarried Teenage Women Utilizing Oral Contraception," *Journal of Population,* 1, no. 1 (Spring 1978), 57–68.

REICHERT, JOHN L., "Competitive Athletics for Pre-Teenage Children," *Journal of the American Medical Association,* 166, no. 4 (1958), 1701–07.

REISS, ALBERT J., JR., "The Social Integration of Queers and Peers," *Social Problems,* 9, no. 3 (Fall 1961), 102–20.

REISS, IRA L., "Toward a Sociology of the Heterosexual Love Relationship," *Marriage and Family Living,* 22, no. 1 (May 1960), 139–45.

———, *Premarital Sexual Standards in America.* New York: Free Press, 1960.

———, *The Social Context of Premarital Sexual Permissiveness.* New York: Holt, Rinehart and Winston, 1967.

REISS, IRA L., ALBERT BANWART, and HARRY FOREMAN, "Premarital Contraceptive Usage: A Study and Some Theoretical Explorations," *Journal of Marriage and the Family,* (Aug. 1975), 619-30.

RENNE, KAREN S., "Childlessness, Health and Marital Satisfaction," *Social Biology,* 23, no. 3 (Autum 1976), 183-97.

REYNER, F. C., "The Venereal Factor in Cervical Cancer," *Medical Aspects of Human Sexuality,* (Aug. 1975), 77.

RICKEY, DON, JR., *Forty Miles a Day on Beans and Hay,* Norman, Oklahoma: University of Oklahoma Press, 1963.

ROBBINS, MINA B. and GORDON D. JENSEN, "Multiple Orgasm in Males," *Progress in Sexology,* pp. 323-28. Edited by Robert Gemme and Connie Wheeler, New York: Plenum, 1977.

ROBERTS, ELIZABETH J., DAVID KLINE, and JOHN GAGNON, *Family Life and Sexual Learning* (Cambridge, Mass.: Population Education Inc.), 1978.

ROBINSON, IRA E., KARL KING, and JACK O. BALSWICK, "The Premarital Sexual Revolution Among College Females," *The Family Coordinator,* 21, no. 2 (April 1972), 189-94.

ROBOCH, JAN and L. STARKA, "Reported Coital Activity of Men and Levels of Plasma Testosterone," *Archives of Sexual Behavior,* 2, no. 4 (1973), 309-15.

ROEBUCK, JULIAN and S. LEE SPRAY, "The Cocktail Lounge: A Study of Heterosexual Relations in a Public Organization," *American Journal of Sociology,* 72, (1967), 388-95.

ROLLINS, BOYD and KENNETH CANNON, "Marital Satisfaction Over the Family Life Cycle: A Reevaluation," *Journal of Marriage and the Family,* 36, no. 2 (May 1974), 271-82.

ROME, ESTER R., FRAN ANSLEY, and ABBY SCHWARZ, "Venereal Disease," *Our Bodies, Ourselves,* pp. 167-80. Edited by Boston Women's Health Book Cooperative. New York: Simon and Schuster, 1976.

ROOK, KAREN, and CONSTANCE L. HAMMEN, "A Cognitive Perspective on the Experience of Sexual Arousal," *Journal of Social Issues,* 33, no. 3 (Spring 1977), 7-29.

ROOT, A. W., "Endocrinology of Puberty: 1. Normal Sexual Maturation," *Journal of Pediatrics,* 83, (1973), 1-19.

ROOTH, GRAHAM, "Exhibitionism Outside Europe and America," *Archives of Sexual Behavior,* 2, no. 4 (Dec. 1973), 351-63.

ROPER ORGANIZATION, INC., *The Virginia Slims American Women's Opinion Poll, Volume III.* The Roper Organization, Inc.: Williamstown, Mass., 1974.

ROSE, ROBERT M., "The Psychological Effects of Androgens and Estrogens— A Review," *Psychiatric Complications of Medical Drugs,* pp. 251-93. Edited by Richard I. Shader. New York: Raven Press, 1972.

ROSENHAN, D. L., "On Being Sane in Insane Places," *Science,* 179, (Jan. 19, 1973), 250-58.

ROSS, H. LAURENCE, "Modes of Adjustment of Married Homosexuals," *Social Problems,* 18, (1971), 385-93.

ROSSI, ALICE, "Transition to Parenthood," *Journal of Marriage and the Family,* 30, (1968), 26-39.

ROY, DONALD, "Sex in the Factory: Informal Heterosexual Relations between Supervisors and Work Groups," *Deviant Behavior: Occupational and Organizational Bases,* pp. 44-66. Edited by Clifton D. Bryant. Skokie, Ill.: Rand McNally, 1974.

RUBENSTEIN, JUDITH S., FLETCHER G. WATSON, MARGARET E. DROLETTE, and HOWARD S. RUBENSTEIN, "Young Adolescents' Sexual Interests,' *Adolescence,* 9, no. 44 (Winter 1976), 487–96.

RUBIN, LILLIAM BRESLOW, *Worlds of Pain: Life in the Working-Class Family.* New York: Basic Books, 1976.

RUGOFF, MILTON, *Prudery and Passion.* New York: Putnam's, 1971.

RUSSELL, DIANA E. H., *The Politics of Rape.* Briarcliff Manor, N.Y.: Stein and Day, 1975.

RUSSELL, CANDYCE S., "Transition to Parenthood: Problems and Gratifications," *Journal of Marriage and the Family,* 36, no. 2 (May 1974), 294–301.

RYDER, ROBERT G., "Longitudinal Data Relating Marriage Satisfaction and Having a Child," *Journal of Marriage and the Family,* 35, no. 4 (Nov. 1973), 604–06.

RUTTER, MICHAEL, "Normal Psychosexual Development," *Journal of Child Psychology and Psychiatry,* 11, (1971), 259–83.

SAGARIN, EDWARD, "Autoeroticism: A Sociological Approach," *Sexual Self-Stimulation.* Edited by R. E. L. Masters. (Los Angeles, Calif.: Sherborne Press), 1968.

SAGHIR, MARCEL T. and ELI ROBINS, *Male and Female Homosexuality: A comprehensive Investigation.* Baltimore, Md.: Williams and Wilkins, 1973.

SALMON, UDALL J., and SAMUEL H. GEIST, "Effect of Androgen Upon Libido in Women," *Journal of Clinical Endocrinology,* 3, (1943), 235–38.

SANFORD, WENDY COPPEDGE, and BARBARA BRIDGEMAN PERKINS, et al., "Birth Control," *Our Bodies, Ourselves,* pp. 181–215. Edited by Boston Women's Health Book Collective. New York: Simon & Schuster, 1976.

SANFORD, WENDY COPPEDGE, et al., "Abortion," *Our Bodies, Ourselves,* 216–38. Edited by Boston Women's Health Book Collective. New York: Simon and Schuster, 1976.

SARTY, MERRILL E., "The 'Pretty Girl' as a Sexual and Reproductive Stereotype." Unpublished paper presented to the Western Psychological Association, April 1976, Sacramento, California.

SAWCHUK, PETER, "Becoming a Homosexual," *Decency and Deviance,* pp. 233–45. Edited by Jack Haas and Bill Shaffer. New York: McClelland & Stewart, 1974.

SCANZONI, JOHN, *Sexual Bargaining: Power Politics in the American Marriage.* Englewood Cliffs, N.J.: Prentice-Hall, 1972.

SCHACHTER, STANLEY, "The Interaction of Cognitive and Physiological Determinants of Emotional State," *Advances in Experimental Social Psychology,* pp. 49–80. Edited by Leonard Berkowitz.

SCHAFER, SIEGRID, "Sexual and Social Problems of Lesbians," *Journal of Sex Research,* 12, no. 1 (Feb. 1976), 50–69.

SCHAFER, SIEGRID, "Sociosexual Behavior in Male and Female Homosexuals: A Study of Sex Differences," *Archives of Sexual Behavior,* 6, no. 4 (Sept. 1977), 355–64.

SCHEINGOLD, LEE D. and NATHANIEL N. WAGNER, *Sex and the Aging Heart.* New York: Human Sciences Press, 1974.

SCHIAVI, RAUL and DANIEL WHITE, "Androgens and Male Sexual Function: A Review of Human Studies," *Journal of Sex and Marital Therapy,* 2, no. 3 (Fall 1976), 214–28.

SCHIMEL, JOHN L., "Homosexual Fantasies in Heterosexual Males," *Medical Aspects of Human Sexuality,* 6, (Feb. 1972), 138–51.

SCHIMEL, JOHN L., "Self-Esteem and Sex," *Sexual Behavior,* pp. 249–59. Edited by Leonard Gross. Jamaica, N.Y.: Spectrum Publ., 1974.

SCHMIDT, GUNTER, "Male-Female Differences in Sexual Arousal and Behavior During and After Exposure to Sexually Explicit Stimuli," *Archives of Sexual Behavior,* 4, no. 4 (July 1975), 353-65.

SCHMIDT, GUNTER and VOLKMAR SIGUSCH, "Sex Differences in Response to Psychosexual Stimulation by Films and Slides," *Journal of Sex Research,* 6, no. 4 (Nov. 1970), 268-83.

———, "Changes in Sexual Behavior Among Young Males and Females Between 1960-1970," *Archives of Sexual Behavior,* 2, no. 1 (1972), 27-45.

———, "Women's Sexual Arousal," *Contemporary Sexual Behavior,* pp. 117-44. Edited by Joseph Zubin and John Money. Baltimore, Md.: Johns Hopkins University Press, 1973.

SCHMIDT, GUNTER, VOLKMAR SIGUSCH, and SIEGRID SCHAFER, Responses to Reading Erotic Stories: Male-Female Differences," *Archives of Sexual Behavior,* 2, no. 3 (June 1973), 181-99.

SCHOFIELD, MICHAEL, *The Sexual Behavior of Young Adults.* Boston: Little, Brown, 1973.

SCHONFELD, W. A., "The Body and Body-Image in Adolescents," *Adolescence: Psychosocial Perspectives,* pp. 27-53. Edited by G. Caplan and S. Lebovici. New York: Basic Books, 1969.

SCHRAM, DONNA D., "Rape," *Victimization of Women.* Edited by Jane R. Chapman and Margaret Gages, Beverly Hills, Calif.: Sage, 1978, pp. 53-79.

SCHUMACHER, SALLIE, "Effectiveness of Sex Therapy." Paper presented at the International Congress of Sexology, 1976, Montreal.

SCOTT, MARVIN B. and STANFORD M. LYMAN, "Accounts," *American Sociological Review,* 33, no. 1 (Feb. 1968), 46-62.

———, "Paranoia, Homosexuality and Game Theory," *Journal of Health and Social Behavior,* 9, (Sept. 1968), 179-87.

SEARS, ROBERT R., ELEANOR E. MACCOBY, and HARRY LEVIN, *Patterns of Childbearing.* New York: Harper-Row, Pub., 1957.

"Sees Increase in Breast-Feeding," *Pediatric News,* (Feb. 1976), 1, 65.

SEMANS, J., "Premature Ejaculation: A New Approach," *Southern Medical Journal,* 49, (April 1956), 353-57.

SHAINESS, NATALIE, "A Re-evaluation of Some Aspects of Femininity through a Study of Menstruation: A Preliminary Report," *Comprehensive Psychiatry,* 2, (1961), 20-26.

SHAPIRO, HOWARD I., *The Birth Control Book.* New York: St. Martin's Press, 1977.

SHEEHY, GAIL, *Passages: Predictable Crises of Adult Life.* New York: Dutton, 1974, 1976.

SHERMAN, JULIA A., *On the Psychology of Women.* Springfield, Illinois: Chs. C Thomas, 1971.

———, "Shifts in Public Opinion Toward Abortion," *Intellect,* 104, (Jan. 1976), 280-81.

SHUR, EDWIN M., *Labeling Deviant Behavior.* New York: Harper-Row, Pub., 1971.

SHUSTERMAN, LISA ROSEMAN, "The Treatment of Impotence by Behavior Modification Techniques," *Journal of Sex Research,* 9, no. 3 (Aug. 1973), 226-40.

SHUTTLEWORTH, FRANK K., "A Biosocial and Developmental Theory of Male and Female Sexuality," *Marriage and Family Living,* 21, (May 1959), 163-70.

SIEGELMAN, MARVIN, "Parental Background of Male Homosexuals and Heterosexuals," *Archives of Sexual Behavior,* 3, no. 1 (Jan. 1974), 3-18.

SIGUSCH, VOLKMAR, GUNTER SCHMIDT, ANTJE REINFELD, and INGEBORG WEIDEMANN-SUTOR, "Psychosexual Stimulation: Sex Differences," *Journal of Sex Research,* 6, no. 1 (Feb. 1970), 10-24.

SILKA, LINDA and SARA KIESLER, "Couples Who Choose to Remain Childless," *Family Planning Perspectives,* 9, no. 1 (Jan/Feb. 1977), 16–25.

SILVERMAN, IRA J., "A Survey of Cohabitation on Two College Campuses," *Archives of Sexual Behavior,* 6, no. 1 (Jan. 1977), 11–20.

SIMMEL, GEORGE, "Friendship, Love and Secrecy," translated by Albion Small. *American Journal of Sociology,* 11, (1906), 457–64.

——, *Conflict and the Web of Group Affiliations.* Translated by Kurt H. Wolff and Reinhard Bendix. New York: Free Press, 1955.

SIMON, PIERRE, JEAN GONDONNEAU, LUCIEN MIRONER, and ANNE-MARIE DOURLEN-ROLLIER, *Le Comportement Sexuel des Français.* Paris: Editions Pierre Charron et Rene-Julliard, 1972.

SIMON, WILLIAM and JOHN H. GAGNON, "On Psychosexual Development," *Handbook of Socialization Theory and Research,* pp. 733–52. Edited by David A. Goslin. Skokie, Ill.: Rand McNally, 1969.

SINGER, JEROME L., *The Inner World of Daydreaming.* New York: Harper and Row, Pub., 1975.

SINGER, JOSEPHINE and IRVING SINGER, "Types of Female Orgasm," *Journal of Sex Research,* 8, no. 4 (Nov. 1972), 255–67.

SMITH, DANIEL SCOTT, "The Dating of the American Sexual Revolution: Evidence and Interpretation," *The American Family in Social-Historical Perspective,* pp. 321–35. Edited by Michael Gordon. New York: St. Martin's Press, 1973.

SMITH, DANIEL SCOTT and MICHAEL S. HINDUS, "Premarital Pregnancy in America 1640–1971: An Overview and Interpretation," *Journal of Interdisciplinary History,* 5, no. 4 (Spring 1975), 537–70.

SMITH, DON, "The Social Content of Pornography," *Journal of Communication,* 26, no. 1 (1976), 16–24.

SMITH, E., "A Follow-Up Study of Women Who Request Abortion," *American Journal of Orthopsychiatry,* 43, (1973), 574–85.

SMITH, R. SPENCER, "Voyeurism: A Review of the Literature," *Archives of Sexual Behavior,* 5, no. 6 (Nov. 1976), 585–602.

SOLBERG, DON A., JULIUS BUTLER, and NATHANIEL N. WAGNER, "Sexual Behavior in Pregnancy," *New England Journal of Medicine,* 288, no. 21 (May 24, 1973), 1098–1103.

SONENSCHEIN, DAVID, "The Ethnography of Male Homosexual Relationships," *Journal of Sex Research,* 4, no. 2 (May 1968), 69–83.

SORENSON, ROBERT C., *Adolescent Sexuality in Contemporary America.* New York: World Publishing Co., 1972, 1973.

SOTILE, WAYNE M. and PETER R. KILMAN, "Treatments of Psychogenic Female Sexual Dysfunctions," *Psychological Bulletin,* 84, no. 4 (July 1977), 619–33.

SPANIER, GRAHAM B., "Sources of Sex Information and Premarital Sexual Behavior," *Journal of Sex Research,* 13, no. 2 (May 1977), 73–88.

SPANIER, GRAHAM B., ROBERT A. LEWIS, and CHARLES L. COLE, "Marital Adjustment Over the Family Life Cycle: The Issue of Curvilinearity." *Journal of Marriage and the Family,* 37, no. 2 (May 1975), 263–75.

SPECTOR, MALCOLM, "Legitimizing Homosexuality," *Society,* 14, no. 5 (July/Aug. 1977), 52–56.

SPENGLER, ANDREAS, "Manifest Sadomasochism of Males: Results of an Empirical Study," *Archives of Sexual Behavior,* 6, no. 6 (Nov. 1977), 441–56.

SPITZ, CATHY J., ALICE R. GOLD, and DAVID B. ADAMS, "Cognitive and Hormonal Factors Affecting Coital Frequency," *Archives of Sexual Behavior,* 4, no. 3 (May 1975), 249-63.

SPREY, JETSE, "Extramarital Relationships," *Sexual Behavior,* 2, no. 8 (Aug., 1972), 34-40.

STEADMAN, HENRY J., "The Psychiatrist as a Conservative Agent of Social Control," *Social Problems,* 20, no. 3 (1972), 263-71.

STEELE, DANIEL G. and C. EUGENE WALKER, "Female Responsiveness to Erotic Films and the 'Ideal' Erotic Film From a Feminine Perspective," *Journal of Nervous and Mental Disease,* 162, no. 4 (April 1976), 266-73.

STEIN, MARTHA L., *Friends, Lovers, Slaves.* New York: Berkeley Medallion Books, 1974.

STEPHENS, WILLIAM N., "A Cross-Cultural Study of Modesty and Obscenity," *Technical Report of the Commission on Obscenity and Pornography, vol. IX,* 405-51. Washington, D.C.: U.S. Government Printing Office, 1971.

STEWART, R. L. and GLENN M. VERNON, "Four Correlates of Empathy in the Dating Situation," *Sociology and Social Research,* 43, (1959), 279-85.

STINNETT, NICK, JANET COLLINS, and JAMES E. MONTGOMERY, "Marital Need Satisfaction of Older Husbands and Wives," *Journal of Marriage and the Family,* 32, no. 3 (August 1970), 428-34.

STINNETT, NICK, LINDA M. CARTER, and JAMES E. MONTGOMERY, "Older Person's Perceptions of Their Marriages," *Journal of Marriage and the Family,* 34, no. 4 (Nov. 1972), 665-70.

STROEBE, WOLFGANG, CHESTER A. INSKO, VAIDA D. THOMPSON, and BRUCE D. LAYTON, "Effects of Physical Attractiveness, Attitude Similarity and Sex on Various Aspects of Interpersonal Attraction," *Journal of Personality and Social Psychology,* 18, no. 1 (1971), 79-81.

SULLIVAN, ELLEN, CHRISTOPHER TIETZE, and JOY G. DRYFOOS, "Legal Abortion in the United States, 1975-1976," *Family Planning Perspectives,* 9, no. 3, (May/June 1977), 116-29.

SULLEROT, EVELYNE, *Women, Change and Society.* New York: McGraw-Hill, 1973.

SVILAND, MARY ANN P., "Helping Elderly Couples Become Sexually Liberated: Psycho-Social Issues," *The Counseling Psychologist,* 5, no. 1 (1975), 67-72.

SWEET, WILLIAM WARREN, *Religion in the Development of American Culture, 1765-1840.* New York: Scribner's, 1952.

SYKES, GRESHAM M. and DAVID MATZA, "Techniques of Neutralization: A Theory of Delinquency," *The American Sociological Review,* 22, (Dec. 1957), 664-70.

SZAZ, THOMAS S., *Law, Liberty and Psychiatry.* New York: Macmillan, 1963.

——, *Ideology and Insanity.* New York: Doubleday, 1970.

——, *The Myth of Mental Illness.* Revised Edition. New York: Harper and Row, Pub., 1974.

TANNER, J. M., "Earlier Maturation in Man," *Scientific American,* 218, no. 1 (Jan. 1968), 21-27.

——, "Physical Growth," *Carmichael's Manual of Child Psychology,* pp. 77-156. Edited by Paul Mussen. New York: John Wiley, 1970.

TALLENT, NORMAN, "Sexual Deviation as a Diagnostic Entity: A Confused and Sinister Concept," *Bulletin of the Menninger Clinic,* 41, no. 1 (1977), 40-60.

TART, CHARLES T., "Marijuana Intoxication: Common Experiences," *Nature,* 226, (1970), 701-04.

TEEVAN, JAMES J., JR., "Reference Groups and Premarital Sexual Behavior," *Journal of Marriage and the Family,* (May 1972), 283–291.

THOMAS, WILLIAM I. and FLORIAN ZNANIECKI, *The Polish Peasant in Europe and America, vol. I.* New York: Knopf, 1927.

THORNBURG, HERSHEL D., "Age and First Sources of Sex Information as Reported by 88 College Women," *Journal of School Health,* 40, (1970), 156–58.

TIETZE, CHRISTOPHER, "The Pill and Mortality from Cardiovascular Disease: Another Look," *Family Planning Perspectives,* (March/April, 1979), 11 no. 2, 80–84.

———, "Induced Abortion," *Handbook of Sexology,* pp. 605–20. Edited by John Money and Herman Musaph. New York: Elsevier North-Holland, 1977b.

———, "New Estimates of Mortality Associated with Fertility Control," *Family Planning Perspectives,* 9, no. 2 (March/April 1977c), 74–76.

TIETZE, CHRISTOPHER and *Sarah Lewitt,* "Legal Abortion," *Scientific American,* 236, no. 1 (Jan. 1977), 21–27.

TIMONEN, SAKARI and *Berndt-Johan Procopem* "Premenstrual Syndrome and Physical Exercise," *Acta Obstetrica Gynecologica Scandinavica,* 50, (1971), 333.

TOLOR, ALEXANDER and PAUL V. DI GRAZIA, "Sexual Attitudes and Behavior Patterns During and Following Pregnancy," *Archives of Sexual Behavior,* 5, no. 6 (Nov. 1976), 539–51.

TORREY, E. FULLER, *The Death of Psychiatry.* Radnor, Pa.: Chilton, 1974.

TRAVIS, CAROL, "Good News About Sex," *New York,* 9, no. 49 (Dec. 6, 1976), 51–57.

———, "40,000 Men Tell About Their Sexual Behavior, Their Fantasies, Their Ideal Women and Their Wives," *Redbook Magazine,* 150, no. 4 (Feb. 1978a), 111–13, 176–81.

———, "The Sex Lives of Happy Men," *Redbook Magazine,* 150, no. 5 (March, 1978b), 109, 193–99.

TRAVIS, CAROL and SUSAN SADD, *The Redbook Report on Female Sexuality,* New York: Delacorte, 1975, 1977.

TRIPP, C. A., *The Homosexual Matrix.* New York: NAL, 1975.

TROLL, LILLIAN, "The Family of Later Life: A Decade Review," *Journal of Marriage and the Family,* 33, no. 2 (May 1971), 263–90.

UDRY, J. RICHARD, "Sex and Family Life," *The Annals of the American Academy of Political and Social Science,* 376, (March 1968), 25–35.

———, *The Social Context of Marriage.* Philadelphia, Pa.: Lippincott, 1974.

UDRY, J. RICHARD and NAOMI M. MORRIS, "Distribution of Coitus in the Menstrual Cycle," *Nature,* 220, (Nov. 9, 1968), 593–96.

UDRY, J. RICHARD, KARL E. BOUMAN, and NAOMI M. MORRIS, "Changes in Premarital Coital Experience of Recent Decade of Birth Cohorts of Urban American Women," *Journal of Marriage and the Family,* (Nov. 1975), 783–87.

UNITED STATES PUBLIC HEALTH SERVICE, *Age at Menarche.* Washington, D.C.: Department of Health, Education and Welfare, 1973.

VALINS, STUART, "Cognitive Effects of False Heart Rate Feedback," *Journal of Personality and Social Psychology,* 4, no. 4 (1966), 400–08.

VANCE, ELLEN BELLE and NATHANIEL N. WAGNER, "Written Descriptions of Orgasm: A Study of Sex Differences," *Archives of Sexual Behavior,* 5, (1976), 87–98.

VAN DE CASTLE, ROBERT L., *The Psychology of Dreaming.* Morristown, N.J.: General Learning Press, 1971.

———, "Sexual Dreams," *Sexual Behavior: Current Issues,* pp. 101–14. Edited by Leonard Gross. Jamaica, N.Y. Spectrum Publ., 1974.

VENER, ARTHUR M. and CYRUS S. STEWART, "Adolescent Sexual Behavior in Middle America Revisited: 1970-1973," *Journal of Marriage and the Family,* 36, no. 4 (Nov. 1974), 728-36.

VICTOR, JEFFREY S., Individualism in France: An Empirical Study of a National Characteristic. Unpublished Doctoral Dissertation at the State University of New York at Buffalo, June 1974.

——, "Privacy, Shame and Intimacy in a French Village," *Secrecy: A Cross-Cultural perspective.* Edited by Stanton Tefft. New York: Human Sciences Press, 1980.

——, "The Social Psychology of Sexual Arousal: A Symbolic Interactionist Interpretation." In: Denzin, Norman K., Editor. *Studies in Symbolic Interaction, vol. 1.* (Greenwich, Conn.: JAI Press), 1978, 147-180.

WABREK, ALAN J. and CAROLYN J. WABREK, "A Primer on Impotence," *Medical Aspects of Human Sexuality,* (Nov. 1976), 102-14.

WAKE, FRANK R., "Attitudes of Parents Towards the Premarital Sex Behavior of Their Children and Themselves," *Journal of Sex Research,* 5, no. 3 (Aug. 1969), 170-77.

WALLIN, PAUL, "A Study of Orgasm as a Condition of Women's Enjoyment of Intercourse," *Journal of Social Psychology,* 51, (1960), 191-98.

WALTERS, DAVID R., *Physical and Sexual Abuse of Children.* Bloomington, Ind.: Indiana University Press, 1975.

WALSTER, ELAINE, "Passionate Love," *Theories of Attraction and Love,* pp. 85-99. Edited by Bernard I. Murstein. New York: Springer-Verlag, N.Y., 1971.

WARD, DAVID A. and GENE G. KASSEBAUM, "Homosexuality: A Mode of Adaptation in a Prison for Women," *Social Problems,* 12, no. 2 (1964), 159-76.

WARREN, CAROL A. B., *Identity and Community in the Gay World.* New York: John Wiley, 1974.

WATERMAN, CAROLINE K. and JEFFREY S. NEVID, "Sex Differences in the Resolution of the Identity Crisis," *Journal of Youth and Adolescence,* 6, no. 4 (Dec. 1977), 337-42.

WAXENBERG, SHELDON E., MARVIN G. DRELLICH, and ARTHUR M. SUTHERLAND, "The Role of Hormones in Human Behavior: Changes in Female Sexuality After Adrenalectomy," *Journal of Clinical Endocrinology,* 19, (1959), 193-202.

WEATHERBY, DONALD, "Self-Perceived Rate of Physical Maturation and Personality in Late Adolescence," *Child Development,* 35, (1964), 1197-1210.

WEIL, ANDREW T., NORMAN ZINBERG, and JUDITH M. NELSEN, "Clinical and Psychological Effects of Marijuana in Man," *Science,* 162, (Dec. 13, 1968), 1234-42.

WEINBERG, MARTIN S., "Sexual Modesty, Social Meaning and the Nudist Camp," *Social Problems,* 7, (1965), 311-18.

——, "The Nudist Management of Respectability Strategy for, and Consequences of the Construction of Situated Morality," *Deviance and Respectability,* pp. 375-404. Edited by Jack D. Douglas. New York: Basic Books, 1970.

WEINBERG, MARTIN S. and COLIN J. WILLIAMS, *Male Homosexuals: The Problems and Adaptations.* New York: Oxford University Press, 1974.

WEISS, ROBERT S., *Marital Separation.* New York: Basic Books, 1975.

WEISSMAN, MYRNA M. and GERALD L. KLERMAN, "Sex Differences and the Epidemiology of Depression," *Archives of General Psychiatry,* 34, no. 1 (Jan. 1977), 98-110.

WEITMAN, SASHA R., "Intimacies: Notes Toward a Theory of Social Inclusion and Exclusion," *Archives Européennes de Sociologie,* 11, (1970), 348-67.

WELTER, BARBARA, "The Cult of True Womanhood: 1820-1860," *American Quarterly,* 18, no. 2 (1966), 151-74. Reprinted in *The American Family in Socio-Historical Perspective,* Michael Gordon, ed. New York: St. Martin's Press, 1973.

WESTIN, ALAN F., *Privacy and Freedom.* New York: Atheneum, 1967.

WESTOFF, CHARLES F., "Coital Frequency and Contraception," *Family Planning Perspectives,* 6, no. 3 (Summer 1974), 136-41.

WESTOFF, CHARLES F. and Elise F. Jones, "Contraception and Sterilization in the United States, 1965-1975," *Family Planning Perspectives,* 9, no. 4 (July/Aug. 1977a), 153-57.

——, "The Secularization of U.S. Catholic Birth Control Practices," *Family Planning Perspectives,* 9, no. 5 (Sept./Oct. 1977), 203-07.

WHITAM, FREDERICK L., "The Homosexual Role: A Reconsideration," *Journal of Sex Research,* 13, no. 1 (Feb. 1977), 1-11.

——, "Childhood Indicators of Male Homosexuality," *Archives of Sexual Behavior,* 6, no. 2 (March 1977), 89-96.

WHITLEY, MARILYN P., and SUSAN B. PAULSEN, "Assertiveness and Sexual Satisfaction in Employed Professional Women," *Journal of Marriage and the Family,* (Aug. 1975), 573-81.

WILSON, G. TERRENCE, "Alcohol and Human Sexual Behavior," *Behavior Research and Therapy,* 15, no. 4 (1977), 239-52.

WILSON, G. TERENCE and DAVID M. LAWSON, "Expectancies, Alcohol and Sexual Arousal in Male Social Drinkers," *Journal of Abnormal Psychology,* 85, no. 6 (Dec. 1976b), 587-94.

——, "Expectancies, Alcohol and Sexual Arousal in Women," *Journal of Abnormal Psychology,* 87, no. 3 (June 1978), 358-67.

WILSON, W. CODY, "The Distribution of Selected Sexual Attitudes and Behaviors Among the Adult Population of the United States," *Journal of Sex Research,* 11, no. 1 (Feb. 1975), 46-64.

WOLFENSTEIN, MARTHA, "Fun Morality: An Analysis of Recent American Child-Training Literature," *Journal of Social Issues,* 7, no. 1 (1951), 15-25.

WOLPE, JOSEPH, *Psychotherapy By Reciprocal Inhibition.* Palo Alto, Calif.: Stanford University Press, 1958.

——, *The Practice of Behavior Therapy, Second Edition.* Elmsford, N.Y.: Pergamon Press, 1973.

WOODS, NANCY FUGATE, *Human Sexuality in Health and Illness.* Saint Louis, Mo.: C. V. Mosby, 1975.

——, "Influences on Sexual Adaptation to Mastectomy," *Journal of Obstetric, Gynecologic and Neonatal Nursing,* 4, (May-June 1975), 33-37.

WRIGHT, MARY RUTH and J. L. McCARY, "Positive Effects of Sex Information on Emotional Patterns of Behavior," *Journal of Sex Research,* 5, no. 3 (August 1969), 162-69.

YANKELOVICH, DANIEL, *The New Morality: A Profile of American Youth in the 70's.* New York: McGraw-Hill, 1974.

ZELNICK, MELVIN and JOHN F. KANTER, "Sexual and Contraceptive Experience of Young Unmarried Women in the United States, 1976 and 1971," *Family Planning Perspectives,* 9, no. 3 (March-April 1977), 55-71.

——, "First Pregnancies to Women Aged 15-19: 1976 and 1971," *Family Planning Perspectives,* 10, no. 1 (Jan.-Feb. 1978a), 11-20.

——, "Contraceptive Patterns and Premarital Pregnancy Among Women Aged 15-19 in 1976," *Family Planning Perspectives,* 10, no. 3 (May-June, 1978b), 135-42.

ZOLA, IRVING KENNETH, "Medicine as an Institution of Social Control," *Sociological Review,* 20, (Nov. 1972), 487–504.

ZUCKERMAN, MARVIN, "The Sensation Seeking Motive," *Progress In Experimental Personality Research, vol. 7,* pp. 79–148. Edited by B. Maher. New York: Academic Press, 1974.

index